PULSE 2

Teacher's Book

Tim Bowen

Macmillan Education
4 Crinan Street, London N1 9XW, UK
A division of Macmillan Publishers Limited
Companies and representatives throughout the world

ISBN 978-0-230-43933-7

Text © Macmillan Publishers Limited 2014
Design and illustration © Macmillan Publishers Limited 2014
Written by Tim Bowen
The author has asserted his rights to be identified as the author of this work in accordance with the Copyright, Design and Patents Act 1988.

First published 2014

All rights reserved; no part of this publication may be reproduced, stored in a retrieval system, transmitted in any form, or by any means, electronic, mechanical, photocopying, recording or otherwise, without the prior written permission of the publishers.

Designed by James Osborne and Amanda Easter
Cover design by Andrew Oliver

Student's Book acknowledgements:
Original design by Andrew Oliver
Designed by emc design ltd
Illustrated by Beach: pp5, 63, 64, 88, 99; Mark Draisey pp 65; Peter Harper pp 24, 34, 46, 55, 66, 72, 78, 88, 98; Bob Lea pp 53, 54; Rory Walker (Beehive Illustration) pp 32, 47, 57, 87
Cover design by Andrew Oliver
Picture research by Julie-anne Wilce
The author would like to thank the team at Macmillan for their support and encouragement, and her daughter Evie for providing light relief when needed.
The publishers would like to thank the following teachers for their contribution to the project: Anna Martín Rauret, Col.legi Isabel de Villena, Esplugues de Llobregat, Barcelona; Beatriz Sayalero Martín, IES Gran Capitán, Madrid; Covadonga Gaitero Suárez, IES Josefina Aldecoa, Alcorcón, Madrid; Cristina Dopico Rey, IES Gregorio Marañón, Madrid; Eva Mª López del Valle, Institut Vinyet, Sitges, Barcelona; Gloria González Lupiañez, Col.legi Cor de Maria, Blanes, Girona; Julio César Fernández García, IES Galileo Galilei, Navia, Asturias; Mª Ángeles Jiménez Fernández, Institut CAR, Sant Cugat del Vallés, Barcelona; Susana Serrano Cano, Colegio Franciscanas de Montpelier, Valle de Trapaga, Vizcaya; Yolanda Iborra Bernabéu, Colegio Calasancio, Alicante.
Front cover images by: Macmillan, Getty, Photodisc/Getty Images, Bananastock, Photodisc, Corbis
Back cover images by: Nature Publishing Group, Studio 8, Thinkstock.
The author and publishers would like to thank the following for permission to reproduce their photographs:
Adrenaline Quarry p14(br); **Alamy**/ableimages p95(tr), Alamy/ ACE STOCK LIMITED p10(shopping), Alamy/allotment boy 1 p48(blind), Alamy/ Sergio Azenha p68(shoes), Alamy/Peter Barritt p15(br), Alamy/Steffen Binke p42(diver), Alamy/Blend Images p33(hurricane), Alamy/blickwinkel p39,72,104(br),(br),(beach), Alamy/James Boardman p80(football), Alamy/Victor Paul Borg p74(bike), Alamy/Jonathan Borzicchi p4(b), Alamy/ Stephen Bryant p36(a), Alamy/BSIP SA p97(itching), Alamy/Kristian Buus p30(London), Alamy/Roy Conchie p80(museum), Alamy/Cultura RM p90(m), Alamy/Design Pics Inc p11(skateboarding), Alamy/Discovod p68(polish), Alamy/Dorling Kindersley p89(bl), Alamy/Dreampictures p90(mr), Alamy/DWD-Media p58(cd), Alamy/epa european pressphoto agency b.v p30,33(Madrid),(2), Alamy/Foto Grebler p10(br), Alamy/David R. Frazier Photolibrary, Inc p66(car boot), Alamy/Ewing Galloway p79(ford), Alamy/GL Archive p25(br), Alamy/Paul Glendell p44(umbrella), Alamy/Paul Gordon p43(tr), Alamy/ David J. Green lifestyle themes p96(br), Alamy/David Gregs p58(family), Alamy/Anthony Grote p45(4), Alamy/Arina Habich p112(br), Alamy/Russell Hart p80(Arndale), Alamy/ Anthony Hatley p77(pushing), Alamy/John Henshall p42(grand canyon), Alamy/D. Hurst p31(cl), Alamy/incamerastock p58(menu), Alamy/Trevor Hunter p43(c), Alamy/Image Asset Management Ltd p35(cr), Alamy/imagebroker p79(farthing), Alamy/IML Image Group Ltd p42(blue cave), Almay/incamerastock page100(t), Alamy/INTERFOTO p35(br), Alamy/PANAGIOTIS KARAPANAGIOTIS p74(boat), Alamy/Christina Kennedy p94(tr), Alamy/Kuttig-People p13(2), Alamy/John Lund p33(10), Alamy/David Lyons p14,24(tram)(centre), Alamy/Dmitry Matrosov p13(1), Alamy/MBI p61,p97,115(bl),(boy),(mr), Alamy/Fausto Molinas p30(Athens), Alamy/David L. Moore – Lifestyle p64 (cl), Alamy/Jeff Morgan 16 p33(4), Alamy/keith morris p58(newspaper), Alamy/National Geographic Image Collection p88(c), Alamy/Newscast p74(tube), Alamy/ONOKY – Photononstop p94(mr), Alamy/ALAN OLIVER p10(crowd), Alamy/ Onsite p22(cr), Alamy/Ozimages p30(Sydney), Alamy/PhotoAlto sas p21,70(tr),(tl), Alamy/PHOVOIR p18(cr), Alamy/PictureNet Corporation p13(6), Alamy/Picture Partners p97(sneeze), Alamy/Radius Images p13(5), Alamy/Ed Rhodes p80(arts), Alamy/Robert Harding Picture Library p88(d), Alamy/Alistair Scott p98(sign), Alamy/Alex Segre p66(charity), Alamy/Uwe Skrzypczak p45(7), Alamy/David Smith p78(c), Alamy/Paula Solloway p4(a), Alamy/Nigel Spiers p33(6), Alamy/StockbrokerXtra p102(tr), Alamy/ StockShot p33(1), Alamy/Stocktrek Images, Inc p40(bl), Alamy/Jeremy Sutton-Hibbert p24(cr), Alamy/Ferenc Szelepcsenyi p13(3), Alamy/Pat Thielen p14(shark), Alamy/Pete Titmuss p110(3), Alamy/travelbild.com p 80(Chinatown), Alamy/Travelscape Images p11(parkour), Alamy/Mason Trullinger p90(ml), Alamy/Ken Welsh p104(flag), Alamy/Jim Wileman p122(mr), Alamy/YAY Media AS p117(boy), Alamy/ZUMA Press, Inc p33,p110(3),(2); **Bloomsbury Publishing Plc** p20(jobs); **Corbis** p57(tr), Corbis/Ricardo Azoury p77(traffic), Corbis/Jack Hollingsworth/Blend Images p118(br), Corbis/Edward Bock p16(cl), Corbis/Chris Collins p30(new york), Corbis/Laura Doss p106(br), Corbis/ FRANCK ROBICHON/epa p121(bl), Corbis/Randy Faris p114(b), Corbis/Charles Gullung p103(bl), Corbis/Judith Haeusler/cultura p4(d), Corbis/Hulton-Deutsch Collection p23(dancer), Corbis/NASA/Roger Ressmeyer p115(ml), Corbis/Colin McPherson p23(JK Rowling), Corbis/Christopher Morris p121(br), Corbis/Ocean p42,p83(amazon),(br), Corbis/Lilian Perez p12(br), Corbis/Fred Prouser/Reuters p40(cr), Corbis/FABIAN BIMMER/Reuters p48(zebra), Corbis/Alain Nogues/Sygma p52(space), Corbis/Onne van der Wal p16(tr); **Getty Images** p23,85,(Picasso),(Obama),(tr), Getty Images/altrendo images p13(4), Getty Images/Artzooks/Design Pics p38(tr), Getty Images/Auscape / UIG p45(6), Getty Images/Blend Images p51(br), Getty Images/Anders Blomqvist p107(mr), Getty Images/Bloomberg via Getty Images p23(Zuckerberg), Getty Images/Charles Bowman p79(train), Getty Images/Brand X Pictures p84(basketball), Getty Images/John Bryant p45(10), Getty Images/Anna Bryukhanova p93(b), Getty Images/John Cancalosi p72(bl), Getty Images/CountryStyle Photography p62(cr), Getty Images/Peter Dazeley p73(bl), Getty Images/Danita Delimont p74(Hamish), Getty Images/Martin Dimitrov p36(b), Getty Images/Michael Dunning p77(ayers), Getty Images/Krzysztof Dydynski p74(tram), Getty Images/Echo p38(tr), Getty Images/Eco/UIG p47(c), Getty Images/Lori Epstein p45(9), Getty Images/Craig Ferguson p68(sweets), Getty Images/filo p45(1), Getty Images/Tim Flach p56(c), Getty Images/Floortje p104(bl), Getty Images/fstop123 p62(bl), Getty Images/Fuse p54(bl), Getty Images/GARDEL Bertrand p82(tr), Getty Images/GlobalStock p117(woman), Getty Images/Rick Gomez p28(tl), Getty Images/ Chris Gramly p71(br), Getty Images/Charles Gullung p7(boring), Getty Images/Erika Gutierrez p63(tl), Getty Images/Izabela Habur p113(mr), Getty Images/Martin Harvey p46,98(rhino),(safari),(m), Getty Images/Jack Hollingsworth p119(mr), Getty Images/ Image Source p14,110,114,118(tr),(mb),(a),(bl), Getty Images/Bob Ingelhart p63(cl), Getty Images/Inti St Clair p108(mb), Getty Images/JGI/Jamie Grill p97(headache), Getty Images/KidStock p92(tr), Getty Images/paul kline p66(swap), Getty Images/Terry Lawrence p104(Alhambra), Getty Images/Ron Levine p34(tl), Getty Images/LWA/Dann Tardif p84(chess), Getty Images/Don Mason p116(bl), Getty Images/Monkey Business Images p111(mr), Getty Images/moodboard p84(football), Getty Images/MorePixels p97(doctor), Getty Images/omg p4(c), Getty Images/Max Oppenheim p47(1), Getty Images/Orchidpoet p42(Niagara), Getty Images/Panoramic Images p45(2), Getty Images/Nigel Pavitt p46(elephant), Getty Images/Photodisc p6(bl), Getty Images/ JACQUES Pierre/hemis.fr p110(1), Getty Images/PonyWang p33(8), Getty Images/ Popperfoto p23(farah), Getty Images/Toon Possemiers p50(tr), Getty Images/RagnaK p63(tr), Getty Images/Reniw-Imagery p33(7), Getty Images/Robert Harding World Imagery p42(Dead sea), Getty Images/rtyree1 p52(crops), Getty Images/Nicolas Russell p109(mb), Getty Images/Sami Sarkis p42(mountain), Getty Images/Christine Schneider p116(br), Getty Images/Science Photo Library/PASIEKA p52(dna), Getty Images/ Sebastián Crespo Photography p33(5), Getty Imags/Kristian Sekulic p94(br), Getty Images/Frank Siteman p113(br),Getty Images/Bob Smith p45(3), Getty Images/ STOCK4B-RF p106(bl), Getty Images/Stockbyte p10,112(computer),(bl), Getty Images/ Stocktrek Images p56(br), Getty Images/Andy Stothert p48(beach), Getty Images/Riitta Supperi p62(cl), Getty Images/SusanGaryPhotography p48(butterflies), Getty Images/ Tetra Images p114(br), Getty Images/Tetra Images-FBP p36(c), Getty Images/Maria Toutoudaki p58,67(coins),(cr), Getty Images/traveler1116 p104(cordoba), Getty Images/ uchar p123(bl), Getty Images/UIG via Getty Images p74(family), Getty Images/ULTRA.F p77(mountain), Getty Images/Frank van den Bergh p74(balloon), Getty Images/Visage p4(c), Getty images/VisitBritain/Britain on View p82(girl), Getty Images/Doug Waters p12(br), Getty Images/Brad Wilson p67(cl), Getty Images/Win Initiative p77(boat), Getty Images/WireImage p22(br), Getty Images/Forest Woodward p84(tennis), Getty Images/ Colin Varndell p57(cr), Getty Images/Ernst Vikne p89(tr), Getty Images/Vladimir Zakharov p30(Tokyo), Getty Images/Yellow Dog Productions p84(run), Getty Images/ Zero Creatives (cr); **HarperCollins** p20(beckham); **Alistair Heap** p76(r); **Jehoshua Kilen** p20(ryanis); **King Arthur's Labyrinth** p26(tl); **Murdo Macleod** p75(tr); **Macmillan Publishers Ltd**/Corbis p45(5), Macmillan Publishers Ltd/Creatas p45(8), Macmillan Publishers Ltd/Digital Stock p7(Whitehouse), Macmillan Publishers Ltd/Getty p57(br), Macmillan Publishers Ltd/ImageSource p12(b), Macmillan Publishers Ltd/Macmillan New Zealand p52(turbine), Macmillan Publishers Ltd/PhotoDisc/Getty Images p60(t), Macmillan Publishers Ltd/Stockbyte/PunchStock p52(lab), Macmillan Publishers Ltd/ Superstock p47(2); **John Mclellan** p31(ml); **Kai Michaels** p20(life,love,texting); **Kinect Sports**/Microsoft p68(game); **Penguin** p20(Jackson); **Reproduced with permission from Lonely Planet Europe Essentials** © 2011 Lonely Planet p20(Europe); Superstock/age fotostock p29(br), Superstock/ImageSource p12(bl), Superstock/ Kablonk p107(ml), Superstock/Ton Koene /age footstock p33(9), Superstock/Colin Monteath/age footstock p34(br); **Guim Valls Teruel** p77(solar); **The Sherlock Holmes Museum 221b Baker Street, London,** England www.sherlock-holmes.co.uk p28(tr); **Transport for Greater Manchester** p80(map).Commissioned photos by Studio8 pp5, 8, 9, 16, 17, 26, 27, 36, 37, 48, 49, 58, 59, 68, 69, 80, 81, 86, 90, 91, 100, 101
The authors and publishers are grateful for permission to reprint the following copyright material:
Material from article 'Paradise or prison? A remote Scottish island is looking for a new family. But there's no pub, no privacy and no electricity in the afternoon!' by Victoria Moore, copyright © Victoria Moore 2010, first published in The Daily Mail 14.07.10, reprinted by permission of the publisher; Material from article 'Saved by my iPod: Girl survived lightning strike after wire diverts 300,000 volts' first published in The Daily Mail 19.06.09, reprinted by permission of the publisher; Material about Thula Thula Wildlife Reserve, taken from www.thulathula.com, used with approval; Material about Lindsey Jacobellis, taken from www.lindseyjacobellis.com, used with approval.
These materials may contain links for third party websites. We have no control over, and are not responsible for, the contents of such third party websites. Please use care when accessing them.

Material curricular para la Educación Secundaria Obligatoria del área de Lengua Extranjera, Inglés, que corresponde al proyecto presentado para su supervisión y/o aprobación / homologación / registro en las Entidades de Educación de las Comunidades Autónomas.

Pulse conforms to the objectives set by the Common European Framework of Reference and its recommendations for the evaluation of language competence.
Printed and bound in Spain by Grafoprint

2018 2017 2016 2015 2014
10 9 8 7 6 5 4 3 2 1

CONTENTS

INTRODUCING PULSE

Pulse is a four-level ESO course which contains a wide range of up-to-date, real-world material of genuine interest to teenagers. With its fast-paced approach and use of authentic texts, topics and language, *Pulse* maximizes students' interest and provides sufficient challenge for twenty-first century learners.

The main aims of *Pulse* are to ensure your students fully develop their language competence, to teach tools and strategies for lifelong learning inside and outside the classroom, and to train students in exam skills, which will be valuable for ESO and beyond.

To achieve this, *Pulse* offers:

Linguistic content
Vocabulary and grammar in context
Pulse takes an inductive approach to vocabulary, ensuring that new lexis is introduced gradually and practised thoroughly. To ensure a challenging and meaningful learning experience, *Pulse* uses a variety of methods to present and practise vocabulary, including contextual presentations. Vocabulary sets are recorded on the Class Audio CD so that students can practise pronunciation.

Grammar structures are presented in a range of authentic-style texts that provide the context essential for understanding meaning. Clear grammar tables provide students with easy-to-navigate reference.

Integrated skills
With its integrated approach to skills, *Pulse* encourages students to develop their receptive and productive skills in parallel. Each unit of the *Student's Book* features an innovative **Integrated skills** spread which presents fully-integrated practice of reading, listening, writing and speaking to improve students' communication skills in a real-world context. Receptive skills are developed through an authentic reading text, followed by an engaging listening activity. The topical link continues with the coverage of productive skills: a videoed speaking model provides the basis for carefully-structured written and spoken production.

Reading
Pulse contains a rich variety of reading texts of interest to teenage learners. A range of text types introduce students to different types of reading material in an appropriately graded, structured way.

Writing: Interaction and production
Pulse takes a highly structured approach to writing. Students first interact with model compositions, before following step-by-step tasks which emphasize that good writing requires planning, drafting and rewriting.

Listening
Listening can be one of the most difficult skills to develop, so *Pulse* provides learners with the support they need before and during listening to aid comprehension and improve confidence.

Speaking: Interaction and production
Pulse gets students talking through **Express yourself** activities, which provide frequent opportunities to interact and exchange opinions.

The **Integrated skills** spread provides a fully-interactive speaking model in the *Digital Course*, which allows students to watch video clips of British people interacting in everyday situations. Through a series of step-by-step tasks, students are supported through production and practice of their own dialogues.

Lifelong learning skills
Self-study and self-evaluation
Pulse promotes learner autonomy by encouraging students to take an active role in their own learning.

To this end, *Pulse* provides self-study reference and practice material in both the *Student's Book* and the *Workbook*. The **Self-study bank** in the *Workbook* contains a wealth of extension and consolidation activities to reinforce and expand upon what students learn in class, plus **Word lists, Speaking reference** and **Pronunciation reference**.

Students are encouraged to evaluate their own learning through the **Self-evaluation** charts at the end of each *Workbook* unit. *Pulse* also promotes group evaluation of the **Collaborative projects** in the *Student's Book*.

Learning strategies
Pulse places high importance on developing learning strategies. The **Learning to Learn tips** provide useful learning ideas, while the **Analyse** boxes encourage students to reflect on the differences between their own language and English. In levels 3 and 4, *Pulse* also teaches critical thinking.

Socio-cultural and life skills

Pulse aims to equip students with the socio-cultural awareness and skills they need to become more informed global citizens. Using a carefully-developed approach, the focus moves from cultural awareness (levels 1 and 2) to social awareness (level 3) to life skills (level 4). The *Digital Course* includes video clips of cultural and social footage designed to supplement the corresponding pages in the Student's Book. These videos provide a window into the culture and society of many English-speaking countries, and are accompanied by worksheets in the *Teacher's Resource File*.

Cross-curricular contents

In levels 1 and 2 the **Grammar in context** activities in the *Student's Book* have a CLIL focus, each related to a different school subject. In addition, the *Teacher's Book* highlights links to other subjects on the school curriculum. In levels 3 and 4, the focus changes to literature. Each activity is based on a different graded Macmillan Reader, with extra information in the *Teacher's Book* for those who wish to use the Reader in class or as homework. Teachers can also find useful extra resources and information on how to exploit these and other Readers in class at www.macmillanreaders.com.

Digital competence

Pulse promotes digital competence in numerous ways. These include searching the internet to complete **Web quests**, and using software packages and online tools for productive tasks in the **Collaborative projects**. Students will expand their knowledge of web tools through the **Digital competence worksheets** in the *Teacher's Resource File*. The *Student Website* gives access to additional online practice activities and students also have access to **interactive digital material**, which trains them to use digital learning tools independently.

Evaluation material for teachers

Pulse provides teachers with all the necessary resources for continuous evaluation of linguistic skills and for evaluation of all the key competences. Learning outcomes can be evaluated using the Tests and Exams Multi-ROM, the CEFR Skills Exam Generator and the **External exam trainer** section of the Student's Book and Workbook.

Pulse aims to equip students with the skills they need for exam success by training them how to approach a wide range of exam tasks covering all four skills. The External exam trainer provides model answers and breaks down exam tasks in a step-by-step way in order to build students' confidence in exam situations.

Council of Europe and key competences

Pulse has been developed following the legal guidelines set out by the Council of Europe, whose curricular objective is not just teaching a language itself, but teaching how to communicate through it. Following the Council of Europe's Common European Framework of Reference for Languages (CEFR), students must be able to carry out progressive communication tasks in order to gradually develop their communicative competence in a foreign language.

The course contents of *Pulse* have been designed not only to fulfil the linguistic and communicative competences identified below, but also to develop skills in all key competences.

CLC   Competence in linguistic communication
CMST Competence in mathematics, science and technology
DC   Digital competence
SCC   Social and civic competences
CAE   Cultural awareness and expression
L2L   Learning to learn
SIE   Sense of initiative and entrepreneurship

Support and solutions for teachers

Pulse has a full range of components to support teachers and offer solutions for classroom challenges. These include:

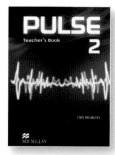  

Teacher's Book

Teacher's Resource File with Audio CD

Teacher's Resource File Multi-ROM

Digital Course

Class Audio CDs

Tests and Exams Pack

OVERVIEW OF COMPONENTS

Pulse Student's Book 2

The *Student's Book* includes:
- A six-page starter unit
- Nine ten-page units
- Three Collaborative projects
- An External exam trainer focusing on listening and speaking tasks

The Teacher's *Digital Course* features a fully-interactive version of the *Student's Book*, which is compatible with all devices including interactive whiteboards.

Vocabulary and Speaking

The **Think about it** activity engages students and encourages vocabulary recall.

The first vocabulary set is presented using a variety of techniques including photos and authentic contexts. They are recorded on the *Class Audio CD* for pronunciation practice.

The **Express yourself** discussion feature gets students talking and using topic vocabulary.

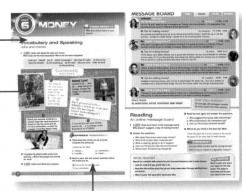

Reading

Reading texts present language in context and cover many real-world topics. *Pulse* uses a variety of text types, from web articles to magazine interviews. Reading texts are recorded on the *Class Audio CD*.

Grammar

Grammar is presented through clear grammar tables at the start of the page. Graded exercises help students practise what they learn.

The **Analyse** feature encourages students to reflect on the differences between grammar in English and their own language.

Each grammar section is linked to pronunciation tasks in the **Pronunciation lab** at the back of the book.

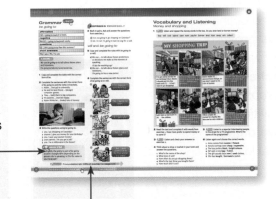

Vocabulary and Listening

The second vocabulary set is presented and practised.

An extended listening text develops listening skills while recycling target language in context.

Cultural awareness

The Cultural awareness reading text highlights an aspect of life in different English-speaking countries.

Each Cultural awareness page is linked to a **culture video** with footage of real life in the English-speaking world. The videos are accompanied by worksheets.

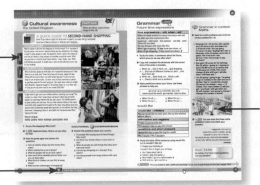

Grammar

The second grammar page presents and practises the new language.

All grammar presented in the unit is practised through the extended **Grammar in context** activity. Each exercise has a **CLIL** focus, covering different subjects from the school curriculum.

Integrated skills

A short real-world **reading** text engages students with the topic and practises comprehension.

Students **listen** to an authentic functional situation and test their understanding.

Students then watch a **videoed dialogue** of an everyday situation such as asking for directions.

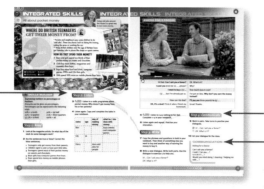

After listening to or watching the dialogue, students **write** their own dialogue.

Working in pairs, students practise **speaking** by acting out their new dialogue.

The **Communication kit** provides functional language for easy reference.

Writing

The **Writing** page provides a model for different text types.

A specific language point is highlighted in the **Writing focus** box and practised.

The **Writing task** guides students through the preparation and production of their own text.

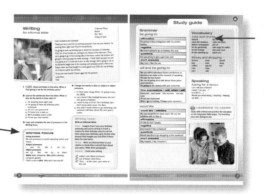

Study guide

The **Study guide** is a useful reference of all language presented in the unit.

It also encourages learner autonomy through the **Learning to Learn** tips.

Collaborative projects

These provide an opportunity for students to work collaboratively and develop their **digital competence** by creating a project using software packages or web tools.

The **Digital literacy** feature gives students tips on improving their digital skills.

External exam trainer

On the **Your exam preparation** page, students are presented with a typical exam task and prepare to answer it.

The **Model exam** gives students a clear example of a model question and answer.

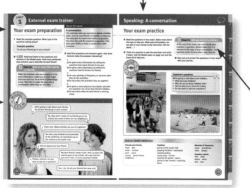

On the **Your exam practice** page students get the opportunity to put their exam strategies into action.

Exam tips give students advice and techniques to help them answer exam questions successfully.

Pulse Workbook 2

The *Workbook* includes:

- Practice activities testing all language presented in the Student's Book
- A full-colour Self-study bank including further practice, extension activities and reference material.
- Online audio

The **Workbook** is available in three editions: English, Castilian and Catalan. The Teacher's *Digital Course* features a fully-interactive version of the *Workbook*, which is compatible with all devices including interactive whiteboards.

Vocabulary 1

A variety of activities and tasks ensure successful revision of the vocabulary sets from the *Student's Book*.

The activities are graded from one star * to three stars *₊*. One star indicates an easier activity type.

Express yourself activities provide students with personalization opportunities.

Vocabulary 2

The second vocabulary set is practised with a range of activities and tasks.

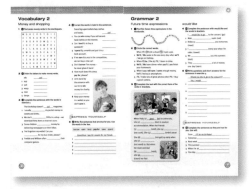

Grammar 1

Clear, easy-to-follow exercises provide students with extensive practice of all the grammar taught in *Pulse*.

Grammar 2

The Grammar 2 page offers thorough practice of the second grammar point presented in the *Student's Book* unit.

Reading

A wide variety of texts on theme-related topics and thorough practice of all question types.

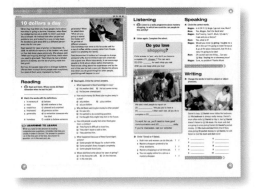

Communication skills

A broad range of **listening** texts and tasks link thematically to the units.

Speaking activities test students' recall of the functional language presented in the *Student's Book*.

Progress check

The Progress check provides an in-depth test of all vocabulary and grammar covered in the unit.

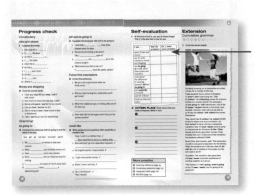

Self-evaluation and Extension

Students use the **chart** to evaluate their progress before creating an **action plan** for improvement.

The **extension** text provides **cumulative** practice of grammar covered throughout the book.

The *Self-study bank* includes:

- Grammar reference and practice
- Vocabulary extension
- Integrated skills
- Writing reference and practice

- External exam trainer
- Speaking reference
- Pronunciation reference
- Wordlist
- Irregular verb list

Grammar reference

The **Grammar reference** section provides extended grammar tables and explanations of all grammar covered in level 2 of *Pulse*. It is available in three language versions: English, Castilian and Catalan.

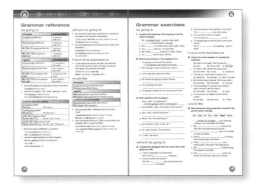

Grammar practice exercises are provided directly opposite the relevant Grammar reference pages.

Vocabulary extension

Vocabulary extension pages use visuals to present a new lexical set related to the topic of each unit. The vocabulary is recorded so that students can listen and then practise their pronunciation.

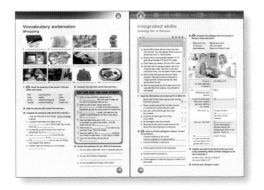

Integrated skills

The **Integrated skills** pages feature reading, listening, writing and speaking exercises that build on the Integrated skills section in the *Student's Book* through at-home practice.

Writing reference

An **annotated model text** linked to the unit topic shows students what they need to include in their own written work.

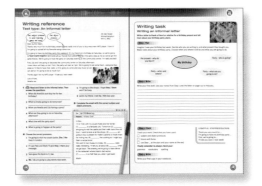

Writing tasks are broken down into steps to help students plan, prepare and produce their own writing texts at home.

External exam trainer

The **External exam trainer** section covers Reading and Writing exam tasks typical of external exams.

The **Model exam** gives students a clear example of a model question and answer.

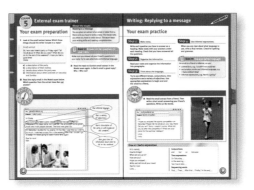

On the **Your exam practice** page students get the opportunity to put their exam strategies into action.

Exam tips give students advice and techniques to help them answer exam questions successfully.

Pulse Live! Digital Course

The *Pulse Live! Digital Course* is available in both teacher and student versions, providing tailored digital solutions which suit the technology available in all teaching environments. The *Pulse Live! Digital Course* is compatible with all devices including interactive whiteboards.

The Teacher's *Pulse Live! Digital Course* is a complete resource which groups digital versions of all *Pulse* teaching materials in one place for ease.

The course contains:
- Fully-interactive digital version of the **Student's Book** with integrated audio and video. Includes **answers** to help correction in class
- Fully-interactive digital version of the **Workbook** with integrated audio includes answers to help correction in class
- **Markbook** to keep track of students' marks and progress throughout the year

- **Interactive video** versions of the *Student's Book* **model dialogues** from the Integrated skills pages, which allow students to see and hear real-life functional speaking situations
- **Culture videos and worksheets** to accompany each unit of the *Student's Book*
- **Vocabulary trainer** to help students learn and practise core vocabulary from the **Student's Book**
- *Teacher's Resource File* materials
- *Tests & Exams Pack* materials
- Teacher's Notes
- Audioscripts for all components

Digital student versions of both the *Student's Book* and *Workbook* are also available. All students using the print *Workbook* also have access to **interactive digital materials**.

All of the *Digital Courses* link to the teacher's markbook to make correction and evaluation easier.

Additional resources for students
Macmillan Secondary Student's Website
The *Secondary Student's Website* provides learners with hundreds of additional activities to practise the language presented in the *Student's Book*. These exercises cover grammar, vocabulary, reading, writing and listening. Students can work at home or at school, and their results will always be recorded in the teacher's markbook. The website allows both students and teachers to monitor online work. **www.macmillansecondary.com**

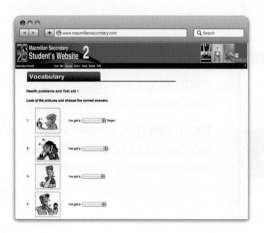

Macmillan Dictionary Online

www.macmillandictionary.com

The Macmillan Dictionary Online is a free dictionary and thesaurus. The website presents users with clear definitions, word sets and useful synonym boxes in addition to grammar information, example sentences, common phrases and recorded British and American pronunciations.

The Macmillan Dictionary Online also offers innovative tools and resources for teachers to use in class, including e-lessons and language games.

Students can also use the website for self-study to become more confident users of English. The website features interactive language games to practise irregular verbs and phrasal verbs which can be used to complement classroom learning.

www.macmillandictionary.com

Pulse resources for teachers

Teacher's Book

The *Teacher's Book* contains everything you need to successfully work with *Pulse* in class.

Each unit features a clear overview of the contents and objectives with full teaching notes, answer keys and audioscripts. There are clear lesson objectives, language and culture notes, and extra activities for fast finishers. The *Teacher's Book* also includes all *Student's Book* reference materials and the *Workbook* answer key.

Teacher's Resource File

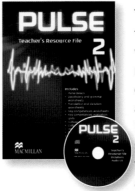

The *Teacher's Resource File* features a wealth of photocopiable worksheets and resources to recycle and practise language, develop skills and evaluate and assess your students. These include classroom diversity solutions, materials which link to other areas of the curriculum and worksheets to help students develop digital competence.

Teacher's Resource File Multi-ROM

The Multi-ROM includes all the *Teacher's Resource File* materials in editable Word format. It also includes the accompanying audio recordings.

Class Audio CDs

All the audio recordings from the *Student's Book* are included on three audio CDs, which come with complete track listings.

Tests and Exams Pack

Tests and Exams Multi-ROM
The Tests and Exams Multi-ROM is available on disk in editable Word format as well as PDFs. The material includes:

- A Key competences diagnostic test which can be used to assess the language level of students
- Tests available at three levels: basic, standard and extra. Each level has:
  - one placement test
  - nine progress tests
  - three end-of-term tests
  - one end-of-year test
- Answer keys, audio and audioscripts for all the tests and exams.

CEFR Skills Exam Generator Multi-ROM
The *Pulse Tests and Exams Pack* includes the *CEFR Skills Exam Generator Multi-ROM,* which gives teachers the opportunity to generate their own skills-based exams. Covering CEFR levels A1+/A2, A2+ and B1/B1+, the exams include a range of reading, writing and speaking tasks typical of external exams.

Teacher's Book

The *Teacher's Book* contains a variety of different features and tasks to help teachers make the best use of all *Pulse* materials.

Each unit of the *Teacher's Book* begins with an extensive double-page **Overview** of the unit. The overview covers the following categories: Unit objectives and Key competences, Linguistic contents, Skills, Lifelong learning skills, Evaluation, External exam trainer, Digital material, Digital competence, Reinforcement material, Extension material and Teacher's Resource File.

Clear **Lesson objectives** are included at the start of each lesson. These provide a useful summary of the new language that will be presented in class and tasks that students will perform.

Optional **Warmer** tasks are short and practical, helping to prepare students for the lesson ahead.

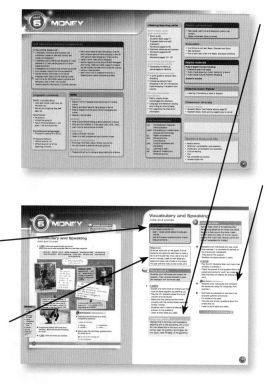

Language notes provide extra information about pronunciation, vocabulary or grammar for teachers. They may include a definition or the phonetic script of a difficult word or phrase, provide a more detailed grammar explanation or explain idiomatic use of English.

The **Culture note** feature provides additional cultural context for teachers. The boxes aim to give teachers useful information to answer questions that students might have about the people, places or events mentioned in the *Student's Book*.

The **Extra activity** boxes provide extra tasks for students who finish the *Student's Book* activities before their classmates. As such, this feature helps with classroom diversity.

Teacher's Resource File

With 290 pages of photocopiable material, complete answer keys and audioscripts, the *Teacher's Resource File* provides all the worksheets and extra materials you need to ensure your students have a meaningful and thorough learning experience with *Pulse*.

In addition, all materials are included on the *Teacher's Resource Multi-ROM* in editable Word format, so that you can tailor them to the needs of your class.

The *Teacher's Resource File* is divided into different sections to ensure easy navigation. The relevant answer key is located after the worksheets at the end of the section.

Pulse Basics

A 66-page photocopiable workbook tailored to lower-level students – an ideal solution for classroom diversity. It includes revision of key vocabulary and grammar in the *Student's Book*, reading and writing skills work, a language reference section and an answer key.

Vocabulary and Grammar Consolidation and Extension

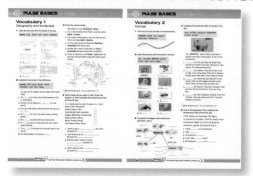

Each unit has two **Consolidation** worksheets and two **Extension** worksheets. These provide revision and extended practice of all vocabulary and grammar covered in the *Student's Book*.

Translation and Dictation

Translation and **dictation** exercises are linked to each unit.
Dictation exercises are recorded on the **Dictations Audio CD.**

Key competences worksheets

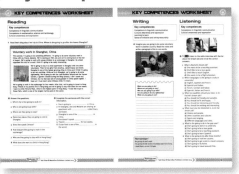

The **Key competences worksheets** provide further work on skills with reading, writing, listening and speaking pairwork activities. Relevant competences are clearly indicated on each worksheet.

Culture video worksheets

Each Cultural awareness page in the *Student's Book* is linked to a related **culture video** with engaging footage of real life in English-speaking countries. The videos are accompanied by **worksheets** which test students' comprehension during and after watching the videos, and **Teacher's notes** which explain how to make the most of the worksheets in class.

Evaluation rubrics

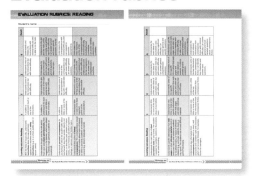

The **Evaluation rubrics** can be used to assess students' skills work and their progress throughout the year. Covering reading, writing, listening and speaking, the rubrics focus on specific learning outcomes covered during the course, such as writing a formal letter or giving a presentation. They include criteria for evaluation which show what students are achieving successfully.

Culture and CLIL worksheets

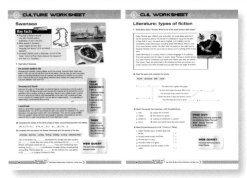

There is one Culture and one CLIL worksheet per unit. **Culture** worksheets are each about a different city in the English-speaking world, with activities focused on historical and cultural information. **CLIL** worksheets link cultural topics with other areas of the curriculum. **Teacher's notes** provide ideas for using the material in class.

Digital competence worksheets

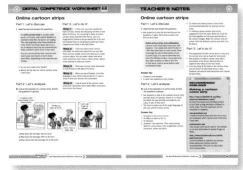

Students can develop their digital competence while learning English through the **Digital competence worksheets**, which teach them how to use free web tools to create projects such as avatars, podcasts and online biographies. Each worksheet comes with **Teacher's notes** which provide more information about the web tools and explain how to carry out the tasks successfully in class.

Vocabulary
Celebrations

1 🔊 1.02 Match the words in the box with the pictures. Then listen and repeat. Which celebrations can't you see?

> birthday Christmas Easter wedding
> New Year carnival

2 🔊 1.03 Listen and write the four celebrations in your notebook.

3 What other important celebrations are there in your country? Write two in your notebook.

Question words

What do you eat on Christmas Day?
How do you celebrate Easter?
When do the school holidays start?
Where do you go on New Year's Eve?
Which day don't you like?

Grammar Digital
Dates

4 Copy the dates into your notebook. Then say them.

02/05/08
2nd May 2008
💬 *The second of May, two thousand and eight.*

1 16/09/96   **3** 01/05/11
2 28/02/00   **4** 03/01/05

5 Work in pairs. Tell each other the dates.

💬 *Halloween's on the thirty-first of October.*

1 Christmas Day   **4** April Fool's Day
2 New Year's Day   **5** Valentine's Day
3 Christmas Eve

6 Copy and complete the questions with question words.

1 ... month do you like best?
2 ... is your birthday?
3 ... do you do on your birthday?
4 ... do you celebrate New Year?
5 ... would you like to go on holiday?

👆 EXPRESS YOURSELF

7 Work in pairs. Ask and answer the questions from exercise 6.

💬 *Which month do you like best?*
💬 *I like July best.*

Vocabulary
Celebrations

Lesson objectives

In this lesson students will:
- learn / revise words for different celebrations
- revise dates

Warmer

Write the letter *J* on the board. Tell students that three months begin with this letter. Invite students to come to the board to write the correct spelling of the three months (*January, June, July*). Do the same with *A* (*April, August*) and *M* (*March, May*). Elicit the remaining months and write them on the board.

1 **1.02**
- Students match the words in the word pool with the pictures.
- They compare answers in pairs.
- Play the CD. Students listen and repeat the words chorally and individually.
- Check answers as a class. Make sure students pronounce *Christmas* /ˈkrɪsməs/ correctly with a silent *t*.

2 **1.03**
- Tell students they will hear short extracts from four celebrations.
- Play the CD. Students listen and write the four celebrations in their notebooks.
- They compare answers in pairs.
- Check answers as a class. Point out that we say *Many happy returns* to congratulate someone who has a birthday.

3 • Explain the task.
- Students write two more celebrations from their country in their notebooks.
- They compare answers in pairs.
- Listen to their ideas as a class.

Grammar
Dates

4 • Write today's date on the board in numbers, eg 14/10/14. Ask students how to say the date. Elicit that it is *The fourteenth of October, twenty fourteen*.
- Students copy the dates into their notebooks.

- They work in pairs and practise the dates.
- Check answers as a class.
- Highlight the fact that we use *the* before the ordinal number (eg *the fourteenth*) and we use *of* before the month (eg *of October*).
- Point out that for years in the first decade of the 21st century we say *two thousand and one, two thousand and two*, etc. From 2010 onwards, we say *twenty ten, twenty eleven*, etc.

5 • Explain the task. Read the example sentence aloud to the class.
- Students work in pairs and tell each other the dates.
- Check answers as a class.

Culture note

UK newspapers often have stories or adverts on Aprils Fool's Day that are hoaxes. A hoax is a trick in which someone says that something is true when it is not.

Question words

6 • Make sure students understand all the question words in the box.
- They choose one of the question words to complete each sentence and copy the questions into their notebooks.
- They compare answers in pairs.
- Check answers as a class.

EXPRESS YOURSELF

7 • Nominate two students to read aloud the example question and answer to the class.
- Put students into pairs. They ask and answer the questions from exercise 6.
- Listen to some pairs as a class.

Digital course: Interactive grammar table

1.03 Audioscript, exercise 2

1 Woman: Congratulations! I hope you'll be very happy together!
2 Girl 1: Many happy returns!
Boy 1: Thanks! What's that?
Girl 1: Open it and see!
3 Party people: 10 … 9 … 8 … 7 … 6 … 5 … 4 … 3 … 2 … 1 … Happy New Year!
4 Boy 2: I like your costume!
Girl 2: Sorry?
Boy 2: I said I like your costume!
Girl 2: Oh thanks!

Vocabulary
Clothes

Warmer

Play a game to revise colours and clothes. Call out a colour, eg *red*. Those students wearing something red should stand up. If they are wearing something red and they don't stand up, they are out of the game. Continue the game with other colours and then with some basic clothes words, eg *jeans, shoes, trainers*.

1 1.04
- Explain the task. Students write the numbers 1–3 in their notebooks.
- Play the CD. Students listen and follow the text in their books.
- They write the correct names next to the numbers.
- They compare answers in pairs.
- Check answers as a class.

2
- Explain that the question *What are you wearing?* refers to now/at the moment/today.
- Students work individually and write the words for their clothes, using the words in blue from the text in exercise 1.
- Check answers as a class.

3
- Make sure students understand the task.
- Set a time limit of one minute.
- Listen to students' ideas as a class. Make a list of words on the board, eg *shoes, trousers, coat, shorts, skirt, socks, hat*.

Grammar
Possessive adjectives

4
- Fill in the first gap with the whole class as an example (*my*).
- Students work individually. They copy the table into their notebooks and write in the missing possessive adjectives.
- Check answers as a class.

5
- Explain the task.
- Students work individually and complete the sentences using possessive adjectives from the table in exercise 4.
- They compare answers in pairs.
- Check answers as a class.

6
- Students read the rules in the table for possessive *'s*.
- Highlight the example sentences in the table and the position of the apostrophe after plurals.
- Explain the task and show how the apostrophe is used to indicate possession in the example sentence in exercise 6. Point out that we say *Mr Bean's face* and never *The face of Mr Bean*.
- Students work individually and complete the exercise.
- Check answers as a class.

Finished?

Students write two more sentences like sentences 1 and 2 in exercise 5 about their classmates, using a name plus *'s* and a possessive adjective, eg *Michelle's T-shirt is yellow and her jeans are white*.

Digital course: Interactive grammar table

Vocabulary
Clothes

1 1.04 Listen and read. Then write the names of the people in your notebook.

Lucy

Chris

Nina

OUR FAVOURITE
CLOTHES

1 My favourite clothes are my **jeans**!
I wear them with a **T-shirt** in summer
and with a **jumper** in winter. I always
wear **trainers**.
Who am I?

2 I love my new **jacket**. It looks great
with my **scarf** and my brown **boots**!
Who am I?

3 This is my favourite **dress**. It looks
nice with these **sandals**.
I sometimes wear a **jacket** with it if
it's cold.
Who am I?

2 What are you wearing? Name your clothes with the words in blue.

3 Can you think of any more clothes words? Write as many as you can in one minute. ⏱

Grammar *Digital*
Possessive adjectives

4 Copy and complete the table.

subject pronoun	possessive adjective
I	(1) …
you	your
he / she / it	(2) … / her / (3) …
we	(4) …
you	your
they	(5) …

5 Complete the sentences with possessive adjectives.

1 Lucy's dress is brown and … sandals are brown.
2 Chris's jeans are blue and … jumper is grey.
3 Lucy, Chris and Nina are happy. They like … clothes!
4 I'm wearing a new jacket with … jeans.
5 Do you like fashion? What are … favourite clothes?

Possessive 's

We use **'s** or **'** to show possession.
We can use **'s** for *has*.
We can use **'s** for *is*.
Stella**'s** hair is blond. = *Her* hair is blond.
The boys**'** hats are new. = *Their* hats are new.
He**'s** got brown eyes. = He *has* got brown eyes.
Adam**'s** Scottish. = Adam *is* Scottish.

6 Write **'** in the correct place in the sentences.

Mr Beans face is funny.

Mr Bean's face is funny.

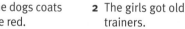

1 The dogs coats are red.

2 The girls got old trainers.

3 Janes happy.

4 The boys T-shirts are big.

Vocabulary
Languages around the world

1 In which of the countries in the box is English the
first language of most people? In which one isn't
English the main language?

> Australia   the USA   Scotland   India
> New Zealand   Ireland   Wales

2 Look at the countries. Copy and complete the table
with the languages they speak there.

> the Netherlands   Spain   Russia   China   France
> Italy   Poland   Japan   Germany

-ish	-an	-ese	-ch
			Dutch

3 Do the quiz in pairs. How much do you know about
English and other languages?

> **LOOK!**
>
> The United Kingdom is a country that includes
> England, Scotland, Wales and Northern Ireland.
> Three of those regions (England, Scotland and
> Wales) are in Great Britain.

The Language Quiz!

① How many
languages are there
in the world?

a) 600   b) 6,500   c) 16,000

② How many people
speak English as
their first language?

a) 50 million   b) 120 million   c) 400 million

③ Which language
is spoken by more
people than English?

a) Spanish   b) Russian   c) Chinese

④ What percentage
of the world's emails
are in English?

a) 40%   b) 50%   c) 65%

⑤ Which of these
English words is used
the most?

a) OK   b) yes   c) hello

Vocabulary
Languages around the world

Warmer

Play a game to introduce the topic. Write the letter *A* on the board. Ask students to give you the name of a country beginning with that letter, eg *Argentina, Angola, Armenia*. Continue with other letters of the alphabet, eg *B* (*Brazil*), *C* (*Chile*), *D* (*Denmark*), etc.

1
- Check students understand the task.
- Students compare answers in pairs.
- Check answers as a class.

Culture note

In Scotland, the number of speakers of Scots Gaelic is just 60,000 (1.2% of the population). In Ireland around 130,000 speak Irish Gaelic (about 2% of the population). In Wales, 560,000 (around 20% of the population) speak Welsh, a Celtic language completely different from English.

2
- Explain the task. Students copy the table into their notebooks.
- Students work individually and complete the table with the words for the language of each country. They compare answers in pairs.
- Check answers as a class.

Language note

Words ending in -*ese* are stressed on the final syllable, eg *Chinese, Japanese, Vietnamese. Portuguese.*

3
- Students work individually and choose the correct answer to each question.
- They compare answers in pairs.
- Check answers as a class.

Culture note

The ten most widely used words in English in order from one to ten are: *the, be, to, of, and, a, in, that, have, I.*

Look!

Students read the information in the Look! box. Great Britain is the largest island in the British Isles and contains most of England, Scotland and Wales (with the exception of islands like Anglesey, the Isle of Wight and the Hebrides).

Grammar
can / can't

Digital

Lesson objectives

In this lesson students will:
- revise *can / can't*
- revise the affirmative, negative, question forms and short answers of *be*
- say what they like and don't like doing

Warmer

Write the phrase *free time* on the board. Students work in pairs and discuss what they do in their free time. Listen to their ideas as a class and make a list on the board, eg *watch TV, listen to music, play computer games,* etc.

1 • Students read the information in the table about *can / can't*.
- Remind students that we never use *to* after *can / can't*.
- Students work individually and complete the sentences with *can* or *can't* so that they are true for them.
- They compare answers in pairs.
- Listen to their answers as a class.

Language note

In affirmative sentences with *can*, *can* is not stressed, eg *I can* /kən/ *swim*. In negative sentences with *can't*, *can't* is stressed, eg *I can't* /kɑːnt/ *swim*.

Look!

Highlight the example sentences and the use of the *-ing* form after *like, love* and *hate*.

2 • Write *I like ...* and *I don't like ...* on the board. Complete the sentences with activities that are true for you, eg *I like watching TV. I don't like cleaning the house.*
- Explain the task and remind students to change the verb to the *-ing* form after *I like* and *I don't like*.
- Students work individually and write sentences that are true for them.
- Students compare answers in pairs.
- Listen to students' answers as a class. Make sure they are grammatically correct.

be

3 • Write on the board *He is English*. Ask students to contract the verb. Elicit and write on the board *He's English*.
- Students copy the table into their notebooks. They then write the short forms of each verb.
- Students compare answers in pairs.
- Check answers as a class. Highlight that the contractions *aren't* and *isn't* are used in this course. Point out that *are not* can also be contracted by *'re not* and and *is not* by *'s not*.

4 • Explain the task. Read the example sentence and correction to the class.
- Students work individually and decide which statements are true. They rewrite the false ones.
- They compare answers in pairs.
- Check answers as a class.

Culture note

London is the biggest city in the UK. The second biggest is Birmingham. Manchester, Leeds and Liverpool are also big cities in the UK.

5 • Students read the questions and short answers in the table.
- Explain the task.
- Students work individually and write true short answers to the questions.
- Check answers as a class.

Look!

Highlight the example sentences. Remind students that we use *there's / there isn't* for singular nouns and *there are / there aren't* for plural nouns.

6 • Students work individually and write sentences using *There's / There are* in the affirmative (✓) and negative (✗).
- Check answers as a class. Point out that we use *some* after *There are* and *any* after *There aren't*.

Digital course: Interactive grammar table »»

Grammar

can / can't

can / can't + verb

We use *can / can't* to show ability / lack of ability. After *can / can't*, we use the infinitive without *to*.
I **can speak** English.
He **can't speak** Japanese.

Exercise 1

students' own answers

1 Complete the sentences about you with *can* or *can't*.

I can't speak Chinese.

1 I ... play a musical instrument.
2 I ... count to 100 in English.
3 I ... swim.
4 I ... drive a car.
5 I ... make a cup of coffee.

LOOK!

like / love / hate + verb + *-ing*
I like playing computer games.
Lisa loves eating chocolate!
They hate getting up early!

Exercise 2

students' own answers

2 What activities do you like doing in English? What don't you like doing? Write sentences.

I like reading books.
I don't like learning grammar.

1 learn new words
2 do grammar exercises
3 watch DVDs
4 read magazine articles
5 listen to music
6 write essays

be

Exercise 3

affirmative
I'm 15 years old.
He / She / It's from Spain.
You / We / They're Chinese.
negative
I'm not from Italy.
He / She / It isn't my best friend.
You / We / They aren't in London.

affirmative

I **am** 15 years old.
He / She / It **is** from Spain.
We / You / They **are** Chinese.

negative

I **am not** from Italy.
He / She / It **is not** my best friend.
We / You / They **are not** in London.

3 Copy the table into your notebook. Rewrite the sentences using the short form of *be*.

I'm 15 years old.

4 Are the sentences true or false? Correct the false sentences. Use short forms of *be*.

Edinburgh is the capital of England.
Edinburgh isn't the capital of England. It's the capital of Scotland.

1 Great Britain is an island.
2 Juan and Pilar are English names.
3 London and Manchester are small cities.
4 British people's favourite drink is tea.

questions and short answers

Am I a teenager?
Yes, I **am**. / No, I'm **not**.
Are we / you / they friends?
Yes, we / you **are**. / No, we / you **aren't**.
Is he / she your teacher?
Yes, he / she **is**. / No, he / she **isn't**.

Exercise 4

1 **True**
2 **False**
   Juan and Pilar aren't English names. They're Spanish names.
3 **False**
   London and Manchester aren't small cities. They're big cities.
4 **True**

5 Answer the questions for you. Use short answers.

Is this your notebook?   No, it isn't.

1 Is this your first English lesson?
2 Are your friends in your English class?
3 Are you on page 15 of this book?
4 Is English your favourite subject?

LOOK!

there's / there are
There's a famous bridge in Sydney.
There isn't a royal family in the USA.
There are some American programmes on TV.
There aren't any beaches in Madrid.

Exercise 5

1 Yes, it is. / No, it isn't.
2 Yes, they are. / No, they aren't.
3 No, I'm not.
4 Yes, it is. / No, it isn't.

6 Write affirmative (✔) and negative (✗) sentences with *There is* and *There are*.

lakes in Scotland. ✔
There are some lakes in Scotland.

1 a White House in London. ✗
2 famous actors from Wales. ✔
3 kangaroos in the UK. ✗
4 a town called Boring in the USA. ✔

Exercise 6

1 There isn't a White House in London.
2 There are some famous actors from Wales.
3 There aren't any kangaroos in the UK.
4 There's a town called Boring in the USA.

School lessons

My favourite subject is French. I love languages! What's your favourite subject?

Exercise 1

1 poster
2 board
3 pencil case
4 schoolbag
5 pencil
6 pen
7 laptop
8 rubber
9 notebook

1 Match 1–9 with words in the box. Use a dictionary to help you with the words you don't know.

> laptop notebook board poster
> schoolbag pen pencil rubber pencil case

2 Which things in exercise 1 do you have in class today?

3 🔊1.05 Look at the keyboard. Can you say the letters of the alphabet in English in alphabetical order? Listen and repeat.

q w e r t y u i o p
a s d f g h j k l
z x c v b n m

4 Work in pairs. Ask and answer questions about the spellings of words from exercise 1.

● *How do you spell 'rubber'?*
○ *R–u–b–e–r?*
● *No, that's wrong. Try again.*
○ *R–u–b–b–e–r?*
● *Yes, that's right.*

5 🔊1.06 Match the questions with the answers. Listen and check your answers.

1 What does 'poster' mean?
2 How do you say '*lápiz*' in English?
3 Can you write it on the board, please?
4 Sorry, I don't understand.
5 What page are we on?

a) OK, I'll repeat it.
b) Page 18.
c) '*Cartel*'.
d) Pencil.
e) Yes, of course.

Exercise 5

1 c
2 d
3 e
4 a
5 b

6 Translate the instructions into your language. Who usually says these things in class?

1 Sit down.
2 Turn to page 32.
3 Close your books.
4 Work in pairs.
5 Look the words up in a dictionary.

Exercise 6

students' own answers

The teacher usually says these things in class.

Integrated skills
School lessons

Warmer

Ask students to read the information about Lucy in the speech bubble. Then write the question *What's your favourite subject?* on the board. Students answer the question in pairs. Listen to answers as a class.

1
- Students match the words in the word pool with items 1–9 in the pictures.
- Students compare answers in pairs.
- They use a dictionary to look up the words they don't know.
- Check answers as a class.

2
- Explain the task.
- Students look at the words again and say which of the items they have in class today.

Extra activity

Play a game of *I spy*. Start with *I spy something beginning with t*. The student who guesses the correct answer (*table*) continues the game. Continue until many of the basic classroom words have been covered (*chair, door, window, light,* etc).

3 🔊 1.05
- Check students understand the task.
- Put students into pairs. Students take turns to say the letters in English in the correct alphabetical order.
- Play the CD. Students listen and repeat the letters of the alphabet in alphabetical order chorally and individually.

4
- Nominate two students to read aloud the model dialogue to the class.
- Put students into pairs. They ask and answer questions about the spellings of the words in the word pool in exercise 1.
- Listen to some pairs as a class.

5 🔊 1.06
- Explain the task. Students match the questions and the answers.
- Students compare answers in pairs.
- Play the CD. Students listen and check their answers.
- Check answers as a class.

6
- Students work individually and translate the instructions into their language.
- They compare their translations in pairs.
- Check answers as a class. Elicit who usually gives these instructions (*the teacher*).

🔊 1.05 Audioscript, exercise 3

A, B, C, D, E, F, G
H, I, J, K, L, M, N, O, P
Q, R, S, T, U, V
W, X, Y, Z

Integrated skills – continued
Getting to know people

7 **1.07**
- Ask students to look at the picture. Elicit where the children are (*outside school*).
- Play the CD. Students listen and fill gaps 1–3.
- Students compare answers in pairs.
- Check answers as a class.

8
- Play the CD again. Students listen and repeat each line of Chris and Lucy's dialogue.
- Note the main stress and falling intonation in *What's your name?*, *What year are you in?* and *Where do you live?*

9
- Students copy the questions in bold from Chris and Lucy's dialogue into their notebooks.
- Students write answers that are true for them.

Skills builder

Speaking: *Me too* and *Me neither*
Ask students to read the Skills builder box. Highlight the example dialogue. To practise, say *I like ice cream* and elicit *Me too!* from the class. Then say, *I don't like Mondays* and elicit *Me neither!* from the class.

10
- Ask students to look at the Communication kit: Getting to know people. Encourage them to use these questions and the response *Nice to meet you* in their dialogue.
- Students work individually and write their dialogue, using the dialogue in the book as a model.
- Monitor while they are writing and give help if necessary.

11
- Students practise their dialogues in pairs.
- For extra practice, they swap roles in both dialogues.
- Choose some pairs to act out their dialogue for the class.

GETTING TO KNOW PEOPLE

Watch!

So, **what's your name**?	My name's Lucy. What about you?
I'm Chris.	Nice to meet you, Chris. **What year are you in**?
(1)	Me too! I'm in Mr Brown's class.
Cool. **Where do you live**?	On (2) ... .
Oh, I live near there. Shall we (3) ... together?	OK, Let's go!

Exercise 7

1 Year 9
2 Ash Road
3 walk home

7 1.07 Listen to Chris and Lucy talking. Copy and complete 1–3.

8 Listen again and repeat. Practise your intonation.

9 Copy the questions in bold into your notebook. Then write answers that are true for you.

SKILLS BUILDER

Speaking: *Me too* and *Me neither*
Use *Me too* and *Me neither* to show that something is also true for you. After affirmative statements use *Me too*, and after negative statements use *Me neither*.

🔵 *I'm 14.*
🔘 *Me too!*
🔵 *I'm not from the UK.*
🔘 *Me neither!*

10 Write a new dialogue. Use the dialogue in exercise 7 to help you.

11 Work in pairs. Take turns to practise your dialogues.

🔵 *So, what's your name?*
🔘 *My name's …*

COMMUNICATION KIT

Getting to know people

What's your name?
Nice to meet you.
How old are you?
Where are you from?
What year are you in?
Whose class are you in?
Where do you live?

UNIT 1 — WHAT DO YOU LIKE?

Unit objectives and key competences

In this unit the student will learn ...

- understand, memorize and correctly use vocabulary related to free time activities and skills and abilities **CLC SCC CAE**
- understand and correctly use the present simple and the present continuous and know when to use which, draw parallels to **L1** and produce them in a short speaking activity **CLC L2L**
- understand and correctly use the present simple or present continuous with time words **CLC L2L**
- about tourist attractions in the United Kingdom and compare with tourist attractions in their country **CLC CAE SCC**
- about museums and galleries by watching a short video **CLC DC CAE**

In this unit the student will learn how to ...

- identify specific information in a magazine article about urban sports **CLC SCC CAE**
- look online for information about an urban sport and share the information with a partner **CLC DC SCC CAE SIE**
- identify specific information in a presentation about a TV talent show **CLC SCC CAE**
- read an advert about an activity camp, listen to a phone conversation about an activity camp and learn how to ask for personal information **CLC SCC CAE**
- write a personal profile **CLC SIE L2L**
- prepare for and do a conversation activity exam **CLC SIE L2L**

Linguistic contents

Main vocabulary

- Free time activities: *play computer games, go for a run, watch a DVD,* etc
- Words that go with time expressions: *on Monday morning, at the weekend,* etc
- Skills and abilities: *act, tell jokes, paint,* etc

Grammar

- Present simple
- Present continuous
- When to use the present simple and the present continuous

Functional language

- Phrases for asking for personal information
- Phrases for having a conversation about a familiar topic
- Phrases for asking questions

Pronunciation

- Third person verb endings
- Intonation in questions

Skills

Reading

- Read a magazine interview about urban sports
- Read a text about tourist attractions in the United Kingdom
- Read an advert about an activity camp
- Read a personal profile

Writing: Interaction and production

- Write a personalized dialogue giving personal information
- Write a personal profile in three steps: plan, write, check
- Learn how to use the present simple, present continuous and *because* and *so*

Listening

- Listen to part of a TV talent show
- Listen to a phone conversation about an activity camp

Spoken interaction

- Exchange information about weekend activities
- Ask and answer questions using the present continuous
- Ask and answer questions about your skills and abilities

Spoken production

- Prepare and act out a dialogue about asking for and giving personal information
- Prepare and do a speaking conversation exam

Lifelong learning skills

Self-study and self-evaluation

- Study guide:
  Student's book page 19
- Progress check and self-evaluation:
  Workbook pages 14–15
- Grammar reference and practice:
  Workbook pages 84–85
- Wordlist:
  Workbook pages 151–157

Learning strategies and thinking skills

- Giving your email address and phone number

Cultural awareness

- Tourist attractions in the UK
- Comparing tourist attractions in the UK with tourist attractions in students' own countries and regions

Cross-curricular contents

- Art: a TV talent show: skills and abilities
- Language and literature: reading and compiling a personal profile
- ICT: searching the internet for information

Key competences

CLC	Competence in linguistic communication
CMST	Competence in mathematics, science and technology
DC	Digital competence
SCC	Social and civic competences
CAE	Cultural awareness and expression
L2L	Learning to learn
SIE	Sense of initiative and entrepreneurship

Evaluation

- Unit 1 End-of-unit test: Basic, Standard and Extra
- CEFR Skills Exam Generator

External exam trainer

- Speaking: A conversation

Digital material

Pulse Live! Digital Course including:
- Interactive grammar tables
- Audio visual speaking model: Asking for personal information
- Audio visual cultural material: Museums and galleries

Student's website

Digital competence

- Web quest: An urban sport
- Digital competence worksheet: Online magazines

Reinforcement material

- Basic worksheets, Teacher's Resource File pages 5–10
- Vocabulary and Grammar: Consolidation worksheets, Teacher's Resource File pages 3-4

Extension material

- Fast-finisher activity: Student's Book page 11
- Extra activities: Teacher's Book pages T10, T11, T16, T18
- Vocabulary and Grammar: Extension worksheets, Teacher's Resource File pages 5–6

Teacher's Resource File

- Translation and dictation worksheets pages 2, 12
- Evaluation rubrics pages 1–7
- Key competences worksheets pages 1–2
- Culture and CLIL worksheets pages 1–4
- Culture video worksheets pages 1–2
- Digital competence worksheets pages 1–2
- Macmillan Readers worksheets pages 1–2

THINK ABOUT IT

What do you do in your free time?

Vocabulary and Speaking
Free time activities

1 🔊 **1.08** Look at the quiz. Listen and repeat the words in blue.

2 Now do the quiz and look at your score. Do you agree with the description of you?

3 Match adjectives 1–3 with opposites a–c.

1 sociable   **a)** shy
2 sporty   **b)** unfriendly
3 friendly   **c)** lazy

LOOK!

on Monday morning
on Sunday evening
on Friday afternoon
at the weekend

EXPRESS YOURSELF

4 What do you usually do at the weekend? Copy and complete the diary.

Saturday	Sunday
morning	morning
go shopping with Mum	
afternoon	afternoon
evening	evening

5 Work in pairs. Ask and answer questions about your weekend activities from exercise 4.

💬 *What do you do on Saturday morning?*
💬 *I go shopping with my mum.*

WHAT KIND OF TEENAGER ARE YOU?

Do the quiz to find out!

1 You've got an hour of free time. Do you …
a) ring someone for a chat?
b) **play computer games**?
c) **go for a run**, walk or bike ride?

2 It's Friday night. Do you usually …
a) **watch a DVD** with a friend?
b) **surf the internet**?
c) watch the sports channel on TV?

3 On Saturday morning, do you usually …
a) **go shopping** with your friends?
b) **go to a café**?
c) **go to the gym**, park or sports centre?

4 When you go to the beach, do you …
a) just **hang out with your friends**?
b) **listen to music** or **send text messages**?
c) **play volleyball** or **do water sports**?

5 It's your birthday. Is your ideal present …
a) tickets to **go to a concert** with friends?
b) a smartphone to **chat online** all the time?
c) a new bike, skateboard or scooter?

— SCORE —

Mostly As You're sociable! You're friendly and have a good social life, but you don't go out every night. You can have fun at home too!

Mostly Bs You're a technology lover! You're shy and you like being on your own. Don't spend too many hours on your computer, though. Switch it off and go outside!

Mostly Cs You're sporty! You're very active and you get bored easily. It's great to be fit and healthy, but you must relax sometimes!

Vocabulary and Speaking
Free time activities

Warmer

Play a game of *Hangman* to introduce the topic. Use dashes to represent the letters of *free time* and write them on the board: _ _ _ _ _ _ _ _. Ask students to suggest letters of the alphabet. Continue until they have guessed the answer.

Think about it

Students work individually and write down a list of their free time activities. They work in pairs and compare their lists. They ask and answer the question. Listen to their answers as a class.

1 🔘 **1.08**

- Students look at the pictures. Elicit that they illustrate the topic of the lesson (free time activities).
- Elicit the words for the four activities in the pictures and write them on the board (*play computer games, go to a concert, go for a run, go shopping*).
- Students read the quiz.
- Play the CD. Students listen to the words in blue and repeat them.
- Make sure they pronounce *hang out* /hæŋ ˈaʊt/ correctly with the stress on *out*. Check they understand the meaning of *hang out with someone* (spend a lot of time with someone).

Language note

In phrases like *go for a run, surf the internet, go to a café, go to the gym, go to a concert*, the main stress in each phrase is on the last word, eg *surf the in<u>ter</u>net*. In phrases with compound nouns like *computer games, text messages* and *water sports*, the main stress is on the first word in the noun phrase, eg *send <u>text</u> messages*.

2
- Students read the quiz again and choose the best answer for each question.
- They check their score.
- Students compare their scores in pairs.
- Listen to students' opinions of their descriptions as a class.
- Check students understand *sociable* /ˈsəʊʃəbəl/ (a sociable person is friendly and enjoys being with other people), *shy* (a shy person is nervous and uncomfortable in the company of other people, especially people they don't know) and *switch off* (demonstrate using a switch in the classroom). Elicit that the opposite to *switch off* is *switch on*.

3
- Ask students to read the descriptions in the score for the quiz again. They then match adjectives 1–3 with their opposites a–c.
- Students compare answers in pairs.
- Check answers as a class.

Look!

Remind students that we use *on* with days of the week and *at* with *the weekend*.

 EXPRESS YOURSELF

4
- Students look at the diary page and copy it into their notebooks without the example *go shopping with Mum* unless it is true for them.
- They work individually and fill in the diary page using the activities in blue in exercise 1 or any other activities they do, eg *play tennis, go to the cinema, go swimming*.
- Monitor while they are writing and give help if necessary.

5
- Nominate two or three students to answer the example question *What do you do on Saturday morning?*
- Students work in pairs and ask and answer questions about their weekend activities.
- Listen to their ideas as a class.

Extra activity

Students look at the words in blue in the quiz and choose the three activities that they like the most. They work in groups of four. Each group has to agree on three activities that are the most popular in their group.

Vocabulary extension: Workbook page 102

T10

Reading
Text type: A magazine interview

Recommended web links

www.parkouruk.org

theiasc.org/

Warmer

Write the word *sport* on the board. Put students into teams of four. Ask them to tell you a sport beginning with a random letter, eg *b*. The first team to give a correct word, eg *basketball*, gets a point. Continue with other letters of the alphabet.

1
- Students look at the pictures and answer the question.
- Students compare answers in pairs.
- Check answers as a class.

2 1.09
- Students read the sentences carefully first.
- Play the CD.
- Students listen and follow the text in their books. They decide if the sentences are true or false and correct the false sentences.
- Students compare answers in pairs.
- Check answers as a class.

3
- Students read the five questions first.
- They look in the text and find the answers.
- Students compare answers in pairs.
- Check answers as a class.

Word check

Make sure students understand all the words and that they stress *competitive* /kəmˈpetɪtv/ correctly. Use picture b to clarify *helmet*.

Culture note

Highlight the Did you know? box. The first Go Skateboarding Day was on 21st June 2004.

4
- Give students time to think about their answer and make a few notes.
- Students work in pairs and compare their answers.
- Listen to students' ideas as a class.

Finished?

Ask fast finishers to make a list in their notebooks of any other sports they can think of.

Extra activity

Focus on the pronunciation and meaning of other vocabulary in the text, eg *exciting* /ɪkˈsaɪtɪg/, *spare time* (another expression for *free time*). Use a board drawing to illustrate the meaning of *over walls* and *down steps*.

Web quest

If your classroom has internet facilities for the class, students can be asked to do the Web quest activities in class. If not, set them as homework tasks and ask them to compare their answers at the start of the next lesson. These activities help to develop competence in processing information and use of ICT.

Students find out three interesting facts about an urban sport. Highlight the Web quest tip.

1
- Students choose an urban sport.
2
- Ask students to open an internet web browser such as Internet Explorer. Students open a search engine (eg Google) and type in the name of their urban sport.
- Students find as much information as they can, bookmarking relevant web pages and taking notes. They choose three interesting facts.
3
- Students work in pairs and swap their facts with their partner.
- Ask some pairs to report back to the class.

URBAN SPORTS: A TEEN PERSPECTIVE

DO YOU LIVE IN A CITY?

Do you want something exciting to do in your spare time?

17-year-old Jon Harrison tells us why urban sports are just what you're looking for.

REPORTER First of all, what are urban sports?

JON Activities like skateboarding, BMX biking, scootering and parkour (free running).

REPORTER Who does them?

JON Teenagers and people in their 20s, mainly. Most people who do urban sports want to have fun with their friends and do something active.

REPORTER Where do they practise?

JON Anywhere! You don't need any special facilities for urban sports. You can jump or skateboard over walls, and cycle down steps. Every city has these things – and they're free!

REPORTER Do you need any special equipment?

JON Depending on the sport, you need a skateboard, BMX bike or scooter and a helmet. Parkour is the only urban sport that you can do without any equipment.

REPORTER What do you wear?

JON We wear jeans or shorts, a T-shirt and trainers!

REPORTER Are urban sports dangerous?

JON That depends. Accidents happen when people try to do dangerous things. It's important to know what you can – and can't – do.

REPORTER Are there urban sport competitions?

JON Yes, there are.

REPORTER Do girls do urban sports?

JON Yes! Lots of girls are getting interested in them now. They are often as good as boys, or better!

Word check

urban facilities equipment helmet competitive

DID YOU KNOW?

21st June is Go Skateboarding Day. Skateboarders all over the world celebrate the sport!

Reading

A magazine interview

1 Look at the pictures. What are the sports?

2 **1.09** Read and listen to the interview. Are the sentences true or false? Correct the false sentences.

1 25-year-olds don't do urban sports.
2 You can do urban sports in any city.
3 You need a helmet for all urban sports.
4 Accidents happen for a reason.
5 You can take part in parkour competitions.
6 Boys are better at urban sports than girls.

3 Read the interview again and answer the questions.

1 How many urban sports does Jon mention?
2 Why do people do urban sports?
3 Why are urban sports easier to practise than other sports?
4 What makes parkour different from other urban sports?
5 What clothes do people wear for urban sports?

4 Do you prefer doing competitive sports or non-competitive sports? Why?

I prefer doing competitive sports because …

WEB QUEST

Find out three interesting facts about an urban sport.

1 Choose an urban sport.
2 Find some websites about your urban sport on the internet. Choose three facts.
3 Work in pairs. Tell your partner about your urban sport.

Web Quest tip!

When you research a sport, search for professional associations or information about competitions and tournaments in the sport.

FINISHED?

How many other sports can you think of? Write a list.

Tennis, …

Exercise 1

a parkour
b skateboarding

Exercise 2

False
Mainly teenagers and people in their 20s do urban sports.

True

False
You don't need a helmet for all urban sports.

True

True

False
Girls are often as good as boys at urban sports, or better!

Exercise 3

1 Four (skateboarding, BMX biking, scootering and parkour).
2 To have fun with their friends and do something active.
3 You don't need any special facilities.
4 You can do it without any equipment.
5 Jeans or shorts, a T-shirt and trainers.

Grammar

Present simple: affirmative, negative and questions

Exercise 1

1 likes
2 doesn't play
3 live

1 Copy and complete the table with the correct form of *like*, *play* and *live*.

affirmative
I / We / You / They **wear** jeans or shorts.
He / She / It (1) ... urban sports.
negative
I / We / You / They **don't need** special facilities.
He / She / It (2) ... football.
questions and short answers
Do I / we / you / they (3) ... in a city? Yes, I / we / you / they **do**.
Does he / she / it **like** parkour? No, he / she / it **doesn't**.

Exercise 2

1 does
2 don't have
3 finishes
4 worries
5 doesn't go

2 Read the spelling rules on page 19. Then complete the sentences with the present simple form of the verbs in brackets.

1 Jenna ... (do) a lot of sport in her free time.
2 We ... (not have) time to play that game now.
3 That film ... (finish) at 1am!
4 My dad ... (worry) when I come home late.
5 Jay ... (not go) to concerts very often.

Exercise 3

1 Do your friends go to the cinema? Yes, they do. / No, they don't.
2 Does your school organize interesting trips? Yes, it does. / No, it doesn't.
3 Do your parents like pop music? Yes, they do. / No, they don't.
4 Does your town have a football team? Yes, it does. / No, it doesn't.

3 Write the questions. Then write answers that are true for you.

you / belong to / any clubs?
Do you belong to any clubs?
Yes, I do. I belong to a tennis club.

1 your friends / go / to the cinema?
2 your school / organize / interesting trips?
3 your parents / like / pop music?
4 your town / have / a football team?

 **ANALYSE**

In English, the word order changes in present simple questions. Is this the same in your language?

Present continuous: affirmative, negative and questions

affirmative
I'm runn**ing**.
You / We / They**'re** jump**ing**.
He / She / It**'s** rid**ing** a bike.
negative
I (1) ... jok**ing**.
We / You / They **aren't** com**ing**.
He / She / It (2) ... listen**ing**.
questions and short answers
Am I go**ing** fast? Yes, I (3) ... !
Are we / you / they practis**ing**? Yes, we / you / they **are**.
Is he / she wear**ing** trainers? No, he / she (4) ... .

4 Copy and complete 1–4 with the correct forms of *be*. Use short forms where possible.

5 Write questions using the present continuous.

1 you / feel / hungry?
2 you / wear / jeans / today?
3 your parents / work / at the moment?
4 you / speak / English?

EXPRESS YOURSELF

6 Work in pairs. Ask and answer the questions from exercise 5.

7 Complete the dialogue with the present continuous form of the verbs in brackets.

Tom: What (1) ... (you / do)?
Anna: I (2) ... (look) at some photos.
Tom: Did you take them?
Anna: Yeah. I (3) ... (study) photography.
Tom: Well, they (4) ... (not teach) you much! I (5) ... (not joke) – these photos are bad!
Anna: What's wrong with this one?
Tom: The sun (6) ... (shine), and you (7) ... (not stand) in the right place to take the photo.
Anna: How about this one of my brother? He (8) ... (make) a funny face!

Exercise 4

1 'm not
2 isn't
3 am
4 isn't

Exercise 5

1 Are you feeling hungry?
2 Are you wearing jeans today?
3 Are your parents working at the moment?
4 Are you speaking English?

Exercise 7

1 are you doing
2 'm looking
3 'm studying
4 aren't teaching
5 'm not joking
6 's shining
7 aren't standing
8 's making

 1.10–1.11 Pronunciation lab: Third person verb endings, page 124

Grammar

Present simple: affirmative, negative and questions

Warmer

Write the sentence *You can do urban sports in any city* on the board with the words in the wrong order: *sports city you do in any can urban*. Students work in pairs and write the sentence in the correct order. Write the correct sentence on the board.

1
- Students copy the table into their notebooks.
- They complete the table with the correct forms of *like, play* and *live*.
- They compare answers in pairs.
- Check answers as a class.
- Highlight the fact that the auxiliary verb *do* is used to form negative sentences and questions in English.

2
- Ask students to look at the spelling rules on page 19. Explain the task.
- Fill in the first gap with the whole class as an example (*does*).
- Students work individually to complete the task.
- They compare answers in pairs.
- Check answers as a class. Remind students that we use the present simple to talk about habits, routines and permanent situations.

Language note

Highlight the fact that *does* in exercise 2 sentence 1 is the third person form of the main verb *do* and is different from the auxiliary verb *do* that is used to make questions and negatives. Elicit the question form: *Does Jenna do a lot of sport in her free time?*

3
- Nominate two students to read aloud the example question and answer.
- Check students understand *belong to* (if you belong to a club, you are a member).
- They work individually and write the questions and answers that are true for them.
- They compare answers in pairs.
- Check answers as a class.

Analyse

Ask students to read the information about word order in present simple questions in English and compare it with their language.

Present continuous: affirmative, negative and questions

4
- Students read the three examples in the first part of the table. Remind them that this is the present continuous and that we use this tense to talk about things that are happening now.
- Students copy the tables into their notebooks.
- They complete gaps 1–4 using the correct form of *be*.
- They compare answers in pairs.
- Check answers as a class. Point out that we usually use short forms in the present continuous except in affirmative short answers.

5
- Do the first question with the whole class as an example (*Are you feeling hungry?*).
- Students work individually and write present continuous questions using the prompts.
- They compare answers in pairs.
- Check answers as a class.

EXPRESS YOURSELF

6
- Students work in pairs and ask and answer the questions from exercise 5.
- Listen to some answers as a class.

7
- Students complete the dialogue individually.
- Check answers as a class.

Pronunciation lab: Third person verb endings, page 124

Digital course: Interactive grammar table

Study guide: page 19

Vocabulary and Listening
Skills and abilities

Warmer

Write *musical instrument* on the board. Elicit examples of musical instruments from the class and make a list on the board, eg *piano, guitar, violin, drums, keyboards*.

1 🔘 1.12
- Explain the task.
- Play the CD. Students listen and repeat the words for the different skills chorally and individually.
- Make sure they pronounce the words correctly, especially *joke* /dʒəʊk/ and *motorbike* /ˈməʊtəbaɪk/.

2 🔘 1.13
- Students read the information about the talent show contestants carefully first.
- Play the CD. Students copy and complete the introductions in their notebook using the words from the word pool in exercise 1.
- They compare answers in pairs.
- Play the CD again. Students listen and check their answers.

Look!

Highlight the expressions in the Look! box. Point out that *can / can't* are followed by the infinitive without *to* (*dance*) while *good at / not very good at* are followed by the *-ing* form. Point out the stress in *I can dance* and *I can't dance*.

👆EXPRESS YOURSELF

3 • Explain the task.
- Students work individually and write a list of things they can / can't do and things they are good at / not very good at. Encourage them to look at the word pool in exercise 1 for ideas.
- They work in pairs and compare their skills and abilities.
- Listen to their ideas as a class.

4 🔘 1.14
- Explain that students will hear talent show judges talking to some of the contestants from exercise 2. They should listen and write down the names of the contestants.
- Play the CD.
- Check answers as a class.

5 • Give students time to read the six sentences before they listen again.
- Play the CD again. Students decide if the sentences are true or false. They correct the false sentences.
- Students compare answers in pairs.
- Check answers as a class.

🔘 1.14 Audioscript, exercise 4

Judge 1: Hi, Zak.
Zak: Hi.
Judge 1: Well ... you've certainly got your own style of singing, which I like, but I think you need to work on your voice. It's not strong enough at the moment.
Judge 2: Yes, I agree with Donna. That's a beautiful song, but at the moment you aren't really expressing the feelings in it. Do you have singing lessons, Zak?
Zak: Er, no.
Judge 2: Well, you should have some. We're not saying you haven't got talent. You have. But that's not enough on its own.
Judge 1: So this time, you aren't successful ... but maybe in a few months' time you'll be one of the winners. Don't give up and good luck!
Zak: Er, thanks.
Judge 2: Well, Kelly and Jamie! That was a great performance! You move well and you look good together. Well done! Donna?
Judge 1: Mmm, I agree. How many hours a week do you train, guys?
Kelly: Two hours a day from Monday to Friday, and more on Saturdays and Sundays.
Judge 1: Well, it shows. Just one thing, though – try to relax more when you're dancing. You looked very serious, as if you weren't enjoying yourselves!
Jamie: That's because we were nervous!
Judge 1: OK, fair enough. Anyway, congratulations! You go through to the next stage of the show!

Vocabulary and Listening
Skills and abilities

1 🔊 1.12 Listen and repeat the words in the box.

> act   sing   dance   paint   draw   cook   bake a cake   play a musical instrument
> write songs   tell jokes   ride a motorbike   do tricks   drive a car   speak a language

They've got

TALENT!

Meet the contestants of tonight's show!

Read their introductions …

1 We're Kelly and Jamie and we … together.

2 I'm Ben and this is my dog Shelley. She can …!

3 We're from the Glamorgan Boys' Choir and we … in Welsh and English.

4 I'm Lara. I learned to … when I was five years old! I play the drums.

5 I'm Zak. I'm a singer and I also …

6 My name's Emma and I … I hope I can make you laugh!

Exercise 2

1 dance
2 do tricks
3 sing
4 play a musical instrument
5 write songs
6 tell jokes

---

2 🔊 1.13 Read and listen to the text. Copy and complete the introductions with words from exercise 1. Then listen and check your answers.

> **LOOK!**
>
> I can / can't **dance**.
> I'm good / not very good at **dancing**.

🔍 **EXPRESS YOURSELF**

3 Work in pairs. What skills and abilities have you got? Compare your skills and abilities.

> 🗨 *I'm good at drawing, but I can't write poetry. How about you?*
>
> 🗨 *I can …*

4 🔊 1.14 Listen to part of a TV talent show. Which contestants from exercise 1 are the judges talking to?

5 Listen again. Are the sentences true or false? Correct the false sentences.

1 The first contestant has got a strong voice.
2 Zak doesn't have singing lessons.
3 He wins this part of the competition.
4 The judges like Kelly and Jamie.
5 They don't practise every day.
6 They looked unhappy when they were performing.

Exercise 4

Zak

Kelly and Jamie

Exercise 5

1 **False**
The first contestant hasn't got a strong voice.

2 **True**

3 **False**
He doesn't win this part of the competition.

4 **True**

5 **False**
They practise every day.

6 **True**

Cultural awareness
Tourist attractions in the United Kingdom

1 Look at the pictures. Which attractions look the most fun?

FOUR
TEEN DAYS OUT IN THE UK

Are you looking for something different to do this weekend? We interviewed four teenagers at some unusual tourist attractions around the country!

BLUE PLANET AQUARIUM

If you're aged 8–15, like sharks and are good at swimming, this is the place for you. I always go swimming on Saturdays, but this weekend I'm not going to the sports centre. After a diving lesson at the aquarium, I'm going swimming with real sharks! The sharks aren't very big and they aren't dangerous. But your friends won't know that! Visiting the aquarium is quite expensive, but it's a good idea for a birthday present.

TEEN RATING 😃 😃 😃
Jack, 13, Stafford

MAGIC UNICORN THEME PARK

Unicorns are magical animals from legends, but this theme park isn't very magical. The rides and rollercoasters are OK, but nothing special. The only bit my friends and I like is the Magic Spell Academy, where they teach you to do magic tricks. We're not really enjoying our trip today!

TEEN RATING 😃
Daniel, 14, Glasgow

BEAMISH, THE LIVING MUSEUM OF THE NORTH

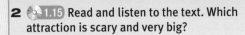

Beamish is a 'living' museum. Instead of looking at old things, I'm actually experiencing life in the past! You can have a lesson at the village school, buy things in the old-fashioned shops and learn how to cook traditional food. I usually hate museums, but Beamish is different!

TEEN RATING 😃 😃 😃 😃
Daisy, 14, Durham

GIANT SWING, ADRENALINE QUARRY

This isn't like swings you find in children's playgrounds. It's very high and really scary! I didn't think this would be so much fun, but it's better than a rollercoaster! You feel as if you are flying! The only problem is that it doesn't last very long.

TEEN RATING 😃 😃 😃
Anna, 15, Cardiff

Word check

shark old-fashioned traditional legend rollercoaster swing

Exercise 2

Giant Swing, Adrenaline Quarry

Exercise 3

1 Blue Planet Aquarium; Beamish, the Living Museum of the North; Magic Unicorn Theme Park
2 Giant Swing, Adrenaline Quarry
3 Beamish, the Living Museum of the North; Giant Swing, Adrenaline Quarry
4 Blue Planet Aquarium

---

2 🔊 1.15 Read and listen to the text. Which attraction is scary and very big?

3 Read the text again and answer the questions.

1 Which three attractions give you the chance to learn new skills?
2 Which place isn't suitable for young children?
3 Which two attractions are better than expected?
4 Which tourist attraction is expensive?

CULTURAL COMPARISON

4 Answer the questions about an interesting tourist attraction in your country.

1 What is the most popular attraction for teenagers in your country?
2 What can you do there?
3 Do you think there are more interesting attractions in the UK or in your country?

 Culture video: Museums and galleries ▶

Cultural awareness

Tourist attractions in the United Kingdom

Warmer

Books closed. Write the word *Disneyland* on the board. Ask students what it is and where it is in Europe. Elicit that it is an amusement park and that it is in France, just outside Paris. Ask students to read the Fact box about amusement parks in the UK.

1
- Students look at the pictures.
- They work in pairs and say which attractions look the most fun and why.
- Listen to their ideas as a class.

2  1.15
- Check students understand the task.
- Play the CD. Students follow the text in their books.
- Students compare the answer in pairs.
- Check the answer as a class.

 ### Culture note

Alton Towers, 80 kilometres north-west of Birmingham, is the most visited theme park in the United Kingdom and the 9th most visited in Europe.

3
- Students read the four questions carefully first.
- They read the text again and find the answers.
- Students compare answers in pairs.
- Check answers as a class.

Word check

Check students understand the words. Make sure they can pronounce them correctly with the correct stress, especially *old-fashioned, traditional* and *rollercoaster*.

CULTURAL **COMPARISON**

4
- Students read the three questions.
- They work in pairs and discuss the answers.
- Listen to their ideas as a class.

Culture video: Musuems and galleries

Grammar
Present simple and present continuous

Warmer

Books closed. Write the gapped sentences *I _____ T-shirts in the summer*. and *I'm _____ a jumper today*. on the board, changing *jumper* as necessary so that the sentence is true for you. Students work in pairs and suggest words to fill the gaps. Check answers as a class (*wear, wearing*).

1
- Students read the example sentences in the table and complete the rules.
- They compare answers in pairs.
- Highlight the difference between habits (things that we do regularly) and activities in progress (things happening right now).

2
- Make sure students understand all the time words. Check their meanings by asking students to translate them into their language.
- Students complete the sentences with either *present simple* or *present continuous*.
- Students compare answers in pairs.
- Check answers as a class.

Look!

Read the example sentences aloud to the whole class. Point out that the words *always, usually, often, sometimes* and *never* go before the main verb in affirmative sentences in the present simple. Highlight that the other time words and expressions in the table come at the end of the sentence.

Language note

Point out that the verb *be* is an exception to the first rule highlighted in the Look! box. *Always, usually, often, sometimes* and *never* go after the verb *be* in the present simple, eg *He's always late.*

3
- Students work individually to complete the exercise.
- Students compare answers in pairs.
- Check answers as a class.

4
- Make sure students understand they should use either the present simple or the present continuous to complete the dialogue, using the verbs in brackets.
- Students work individually and then compare answers in pairs.
- Check answers as a class.

Language note

Point out that some verbs are never used in the continuous form. They are usually verbs that describe states rather than actions. Examples are *know, love, sound* and *believe* in the dialogue and *belong* in the previous grammar lesson.

CLIL Grammar in context: Art

5
- This activity practises the difference between the present simple and present continuous and the correct position of time expressions.
- Ask students to read the whole text before they choose the correct answers.
- Point out that *look forward to* means to feel happy and excited about something that is going to happen.
- Students work individually to complete the exercise.
- They compare answers in pairs.

6 ● 1.16
- Play the CD. Students listen and check their answers to exercise 5.

CLIL task

Students use the internet to find the names of three other impressionist artists and the name of a painting by each artist.

Pronunciation lab: Intonation in questions, page 124

Digital course: Interactive grammar table ❯

Study guide: page 19 ❯

Grammar

Present simple and present continuous

1 Study the table and choose the correct words to complete the rules.

present simple	present continuous
I usually **hate** museums.	We **'re enjoying** this trip today!

a) We use the present simple to talk about **activities in progress / habits**.
b) We use the present continuous to talk about **activities in progress / habits**.

2 Study the time words table and complete the sentences with the correct tense.

time words + present tense
We use **now, at the moment, today** with the (1) ... . We use **always, usually, often, sometimes, never, every day, once a week / month / year** with the (2) ... .

LOOK!

Note the position of the time words and expressions.
Harry **sometimes goes** to theme parks.
Harry is playing football **at the moment**.

CLIL Grammar in context: Art

5 Read the text and choose the correct answers.

Art (1) ... my favourite subject. We (2) ... all about famous artists from the past and present and we (3) ... ourselves too. Our teacher, Mr Brown, (4) ... us lots of different techniques, but we (5) ... them properly!
Today we (6) ... on a school trip to The National Gallery, which (7) ... one of the biggest collections of art in the world.
We (8) ... Impressionism as part of our GCSE art course at the moment and I (9) ... forward to seeing some of van Gogh's work. I (10) ... his paintings.

3 Copy and complete the sentences with the correct form of the verbs in brackets. Then write the time expression in the correct place.

In July, Jo ... (go) to the beach.   **every weekend**
In July, Jo goes to the beach every weekend.

1 Sam ... (not go) swimming on Monday. **usually**
2 We ... (play) tennis. **at the moment**
3 My parents don't rent DVDs, but they ... (watch) films on TV. **sometimes**
4 I ... (not send) Matt a text message. **now**
5 My brother ... (sing) in the shower! **always**

4 Complete the dialogue with the present simple or present continuous form of the words in brackets.

Dan: Hi Kate. What (1) ... (you / do)?
Kate: I (2) ... (go) to the Chessington World of Adventures. (3) ... (you / know) what it's like?
Dan: Yeah, my brother and I (4) ... (go / sometimes) there. It's amazing!
Kate: What (5) ... (be) the best ride?
Dan: I (6) ... (love) the Dragon Falls. You (7) ... (get) wet at the end.
Kate: It (8) ... (sound) cool! Oh no! I (9) ... (not believe) it! It (10) ... (rain)!

	A	B	C
1	be	is being	is
2	are learning	learn	learning
3	paint often	often paint	are often painting
4	is teaching	teaching	teach
5	aren't always using	don't always use	always don't use
6	goes	go	are going
7	is having	have	has
8	study	are studying	being studied
9	am looking	are looking	look
10	love	am loving	loves

6 🔊 **1.16** Listen and check your answers.

CLIL TASK

Go online. Find the names of three other impressionist artists. Write the name of a painting by each artist.

🔊 **1.17** Pronunciation lab: Intonation in questions, page 124

At an activity camp

Looking for adventure?

> I like different adventures, they're very exciting! Do you like adventures?

WANTED

Teenagers looking for adventure

Are you 13–16 years old? Do you want to make new friends, do some cool activities and have fun this autumn? If the answer is yes!, then why not spend a weekend in September or October at Greenwood Activity Camp? You'll enjoy two and a half days of adventure, doing your favourite activities and learning amazing new skills!

ACTIVITIES ON OUR ADVENTURE WEEKENDS INCLUDE:

swimming	parkour	singing
sailing	painting	creative writing
skateboarding	photography	… and more!

Price of £150 includes accommodation in log cabins and all meals. Visit our website www.greenwoodcamp.com and sign up today!

Step 1: Read

1 Read the advert and answer the questions.

1 Who can sign up for an adventure weekend?
2 When are the adventure weekends?
3 How long do they last?
4 How much do they cost?
5 Where do the teenagers stay?

2 Would you like to go on an adventure weekend? Why (not)?

Exercise 1

1 Young people from 13–16 years old.
2 September or October.
3 Two and a half days.
4 £150.
5 In log cabins.

Step 2: Listen

3 🔊 1.18 Listen to a phone conversation about the Greenwood Activity Camp. Which three activities does Owen mention?

4 Listen again and choose the correct answers.

1 Owen thinks the camp will be **boring / interesting**.
2 Joe **likes / doesn't like** sport.
3 Joe thinks he won't like the **people / activities** at the camp.
4 Joe likes **photography / parkour**.
5 Owen is looking at **a website / an advert** about the camp.

Exercise 3

sailing
photography
parkour

Exercise 4

1 interesting
2 likes
3 people
4 parkour
5 a website

Integrated skills
At an activity camp

Lesson objectives

In this lesson students will:
- work on all four skills
- read an advert about an activity camp
- listen to someone registering for an adventure weekend
- write a personalized dialogue
- act out their dialogue

Warmer

Highlight the information about Chris in the speech bubble. Elicit answers to the question *Do you like adventures?* as a class. Write the word *activity camp* on the board. Ask students to work in pairs and write down what they expect to do at an activity camp, eg swimming, skateboarding, playing tennis, etc. Listen to their ideas as a class and make a list on the board.

Extra activity

Students rank the activities at an activity camp written on the board in order of preference.

Step 1: Read

1
- Explain to students that when we look at texts like this we usually have some idea of what we are looking for first. We do not usually begin at the beginning of the text and read everything. We scan the text until we find what we are looking for.
- Students read the five questions carefully first.
- They look in the advert and find the answers to the questions.
- Students compare answers in pairs.
- Check answers as a class. Make sure students understand *log cabins* (small, wooden houses).

2
- Students work in pairs and discuss the questions.
- Listen to their ideas as a class and encourage them to give reasons for their answers, eg *I would like to go because I enjoy sailing. I wouldn't like to go because I wouldn't like to sleep in a log cabin.*

Step 2: Listen

3 🔊 1.18
- Check students understand the task. Students listen and write down three activities that Owen mentions.
- Play the CD.
- Students compare answers in pairs.
- Check answers as a class.

4
- Explain the task.
- Play the CD again. Students choose the correct answers.
- They compare answers in pairs.
- Check answers as a class.

🔊 1.18 Audioscript, exercise 3

Owen: Hi Joe.
Joe: Hi Owen. How's it going?
Owen: Fine. Listen, I've just seen something that sounds really interesting.
Joe: Oh yeah? What's that?
Owen: It's an advert for adventure weekends at an activity camp for teenagers this autumn.
Joe: Ugh, sounds boring …
Owen: Why do you say that? You're into sport and stuff. It's just your kind of thing!
Joe: But doing group activities with people you don't like? Not me! We do that at school!
Owen: Oh, come on! How do you know you won't like the other people? Anyway, you don't get the chance to do things like this at school.
Joe: Yeah? So, what kind of things?
Owen: Sailing, photography, parkour …
Joe: Parkour? Can you do parkour at this place?
Owen: Yeah. And not only that – I'm looking at their website now and it says that one of the tutors is a famous parkour expert.
Joe: Oh wow! It's starting to sound interesting now. Can you give me the website address, and I'll have a look.

Integrated skills – continued

Asking for personal information

5 **1.19**

- Explain the task. Students listen to a conversation and complete the gaps.
- Ask students to look at the gaps and elicit from them the information they need to listen for (an address, a mobile phone number, an email address, a date of birth).
- Play the CD. Students write the answers in their notebooks.
- Check answers as a class.

6
- Play the CD again, pausing after each question or statement and each response for students to repeat as a class.
- Note the main stress and the falling intonation in the *wh-* questions: *What's your name? What's your address?*
- Ask students to repeat the dialogue several times both chorally and individually with the correct stress and intonation.
- Students practise the dialogue in pairs. They then swap roles and practise the dialogue again.

Skills builder

Giving your email address and phone number

Ask students to read the information in the Skills builder box. Highlight the use of *at* and *dot* when we say email addresses. Point out that in phone numbers we say individual numbers. We say *double* or *treble* for repeated numbers: 22 = *double two* and 222 = *treble two*.

Step 3: Write

7
- Students copy the questions in bold from the dialogue into their notebooks and write their answers.
- They read the advert again and choose two activities that they would like to do.

8
- Ask students to look at the Communication kit: Asking for personal information. Encourage them to use these questions in their dialogue.
- Students work individually and write their dialogue, using the dialogue in the book as a model.
- Monitor while they are writing and give help if necessary.

Step 4: Communicate

9
- Students practise their dialogues in pairs.
- For extra practice, they swap roles in both dialogues.

10
- Choose some pairs to act out their dialogue for the class.
- Make sure students say the email address and phone number correctly.

Integrated skills: Workbook page 111 ⟩⟩

ASKING FOR PERSONAL INFORMATION

Watch!

Hello. I'd like to register for one of your adventure weekends.	OK, great! I just need a few details from you. **What's your name?**
Chris Bradley.	And **what's your address,** Chris?
(1)	OK. **What's your mobile phone number?**
(2)	OK. **Have you got an email address?**
Yes, it's (3)	Can you spell that for me?
Yes. It's c-h-r-i-s at i-n-m-a-i-l dot co dot uk.	Great, thanks. Oh, I nearly forgot! **What's your date of birth?**
(4)	OK, great. Here's a leaflet for you with more information about the camp.

Exercise 5

1 21 Ash Road
2 766 892150
3 chris@ inmail.co.uk
4 The fourth of April 1999

5 🔊 1.19 **Listen to Chris registering for an adventure weekend. Copy and complete 1–4.**

6 Listen again and repeat. Practise your intonation.

🌐 SKILLS BUILDER

Giving your email address and phone number
In English, we say *at* for the @ sign and *dot* for the . mark.
We write a phone number like this: 220785.
We can say the phone number like this: *double two zero, seven eight five.*

Step 3: Write

7 Copy the questions in bold and write your answers. Then look at the advert again and choose two activities that you would like to do.

8 Write a new dialogue. Use the dialogue in exercise 5 to help you.

Hello. I'd like to register ...
OK, great! What's your name?

Step 4: Communicate

9 Work in pairs. Take turns to practise your dialogues.

💭 *Hello. I'd like to register ...*
💬 *OK, great! What's your name?*

10 Act your dialogue for the class.

COMMUNICATION KIT

Asking for personal information

What's your name? / What's your address?
What's your date of birth?
What's your mobile phone number?
Have you got an email address?

Writing
A personal profile

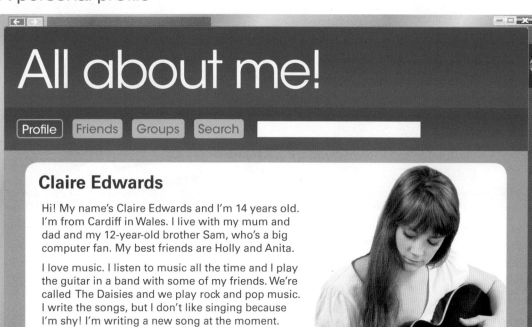

All about me!

| Profile | Friends | Groups | Search |

Claire Edwards

Hi! My name's Claire Edwards and I'm 14 years old. I'm from Cardiff in Wales. I live with my mum and dad and my 12-year-old brother Sam, who's a big computer fan. My best friends are Holly and Anita.

I love music. I listen to music all the time and I play the guitar in a band with some of my friends. We're called The Daisies and we play rock and pop music. I write the songs, but I don't like singing because I'm shy! I'm writing a new song at the moment.

I also love going shopping because I'm really into fashion. My favourite colour is green, so I've got lots of green clothes! I'm not very sporty, but I sometimes go rollerblading in the park.

Exercise 1

1 Because she is shy.
2 Because she's really into fashion.
3 Because her favourite colour is green.

Exercise 2

students' own answers

---

1 🔊 **1.20** **Read and listen to the profile. Then answer the questions.**

Why does Claire ...
1 not like singing?
2 love going shopping?
3 have lots of green clothes?

2 Look at the Writing focus. How do you say *because* and *so* in your language?

WRITING FOCUS

because and so
We use *because* when we give a reason for something.
I also love going shopping because I'm really into fashion.
We use *so* when we talk about the result of something.
My favourite colour is green, so I've got lots of green clothes.

---

3 Copy and complete the notes about Claire.

Nationality: Family members:
Friends: Likes and dislikes:

4 Read the Writing focus again. Complete the sentences with *because* or *so*.

1 I'm an animal lover ... I've got lots of pets.
2 I like dancing ... it's fun.
3 I'm into sports ... I like riding my bike.
4 I don't go to pop concerts ... I'm too young.

Writing task

Write a personal profile.

Plan   Make notes like the ones in exercise 3 about you.

Write   Write your personal profile. Use your notes and the profile in exercise 1 to help you.

Check   Check your writing.

- ✔ present simple
- ✔ present continuous
- ✔ *because* and *so*

Exercise 3

Nationality
Welsh

Family members
Mum, dad, brother Sam

Friends
Holly and Anita

Likes and dislikes
Likes: music, shopping, green clothes, rollerblading
Dislikes: singing, sport

Exercise 4

1 so
2 because
3 so
4 because

 Build your confidence: Writing reference and practice. Workbook page 120 »

Writing
A personal profile

Warmer

Write *music, free time activity, favourite colour* on the board. Ask students to guess what your favourite things are in each category.

1 **1.20**
- Remind students that *likes* are things you like and *dislikes* are things you don't like.
- Students read the questions.
- Play the CD. Students follow the text in their books and then answer the questions.
- Students compare answers in pairs.
- Check answers as a class. Point out that if you say you are *into* something, you like it very much.

2
- Students read the notes in the Writing focus box.
- Check that they understand the words *reason* and *result* and highlight the fact that we use *because* with reasons and *so* with results.
- Ask students to translate *because* and *so* into their language.

3
- Students work individually and copy and complete the notes about Claire.
- Students compare answers in pairs.
- Check answers as a class.

4
- Ask students to read the Writing focus again. They work individually and complete the sentences using *because* or *so*.
- Students compare answers in pairs.
- Check answers as a class.

Extra activity

Write two pairs of sentences on the board: *It was sunny. I went to the beach.* and *It was raining. I stayed at home.* Ask students to combine the sentences in each pair in two ways using *so* and *because*: *It was sunny so I went to the beach. I went to the beach because it was sunny. It was raining so I stayed at home. I stayed at home because it was raining.*

Writing task

The aim of this activity is for students to produce a piece of guided writing that includes the correct use of the present simple and the present continuous. It also gives them practice in using *because* and *so* correctly. Ask the students to follow the stages in the Student's Book. Encourage them to use their notes and the profile in exercise 1. At the Check stage, ask them to swap notebooks and check each other's writing.

Writing reference and practice: Workbook page 120

T18

Study guide
Grammar, Vocabulary and Speaking

Tell the students the Study guide is an important page which provides a useful reference for the main language of the unit: the grammar, the vocabulary and the functional language from the Integrated skills pages. Explain that they should refer to this page when studying for a test or exam.

Grammar

- Tell the students to look at the example sentences of the present simple: affirmative, negative, questions and short answers. Make sure they understand how to form the tense and its usage.
- Then tell students to look at the example sentences of the present continuous: affirmative, negative, questions and short answers. Make sure they understand how to form the tense and its usage. Get students to translate into their own language if necessary.
- Tell students to look at the present simple and present continuous example sentences with time words. Make sure students understand which time words are used with each tense.
- Refer students to the Grammar reference on pages 84–85 of the Workbook for further revision.

Vocabulary

- Tell students to look at the list of vocabulary and check understanding.
- Refer students to the Wordlist on page 151 of the Workbook where they can look up any words they can't remember.

Speaking

- Check that students understand the phrases to use for asking for personal information.
- Tell students to act out a conversation in pairs to exchange personal information such as email addresses, dates of birth, etc.

Additional material

Workbook

- Progress check page 14
- Self-evaluation page 15
- Grammar reference and practice pages 84–85
- Vocabulary extension page 102
- Integrated skills page 111
- Writing reference and task pages 120–121

Teacher's Resource File

- Basics section pages 5–10
- Vocabulary and grammar consolidation pages 3–6
- Translation and dictation pages 2, 12
- Evaluation rubrics pages 1–7
- Key competences worksheets pages 1–2
- Culture and CLIL worksheets pages 1–4
- Culture video worksheets pages 1–2
- Digital competence worksheets pages 1–2
- Macmillan Readers worksheets pages 1–2

Tests and Exams

- Unit 1 End-of-unit test: Basic, Standard and Extra
- CEFR Skills Exam Generator

Study guide

Grammar
Present simple: affirmative, negative and questions

affirmative
I / We / You / They **wear** casual clothes.
He / She / It **watches** films.
negative
I / We / You / They **don't study** art.
He / She / It **doesn't play** rugby.
questions and short answers
Do I / you / we / they **live** in a house?
Yes, I **do**. / No, I **don't**.
Does he / she / it **like** to sing?
Yes, he / she / it **does**. / No, he / she / it **doesn't**.

We use the present simple to talk about habits, routines and permanent situations.

Present continuous: affirmative, negative and questions

affirmative
I'm danc**ing**.
We / You / They**'re** cook**ing**.
He / She / It**'s** watch**ing** a DVD.
negative
I'm **not** talk**ing** to Jane.
We / You / They **aren't** listen**ing**.
He / She / It **isn't** swimm**ing**.
questions and short answers
Am I go**ing** fast? Yes, I **am**!
Are we / you / they eat**ing**? Yes, we **are**.
Is he / she / it play**ing** the guitar? No, he **isn't**.

We use the present continuous to talk about things that are happening now.

Present simple and present continuous

present simple
I usually **send** text messages to friends.
present continuous
We**'re going** to the cinema tonight!

time words + present tense
We use **now**, **at the moment**, **today**, **tonight** with the present continuous.
We use **always**, **usually**, **often**, **sometimes**, **never**, **every day**, **once a week** / **month** / **year** with the present simple.

Vocabulary
Free time activities

chat online	hang out with your friends
do water sports	listen to music
go for a run	play computer games
go shopping	play volleyball
go to a café	send text messages
go to a concert	surf the internet
go to the gym	watch a DVD

Skills and abilities

act	paint
bake a cake	play a musical instrument
cook	ride a motorbike
dance	sing
do tricks	speak a language
draw	tell jokes
drive a car	write songs

Third person spelling rules

- For most verbs, add -*s* to the infinitive
  draw → draws   cook → cooks

- For verbs that end in -*s*, -*sh*, -*ss*, -*ch*, -*x*, or -*o* add -*es*
  do → does   watch → watches

- For verbs that end in consonant + -*y*, omit the -*y* and add -*ies*
  fly → flies   study → studies

- Irregular verbs don't follow the rules!
  have → has   be → is

Speaking
Asking for personal information

What's your name? / What's your address?
What's your date of birth?
What's your mobile phone number?
Have you got an email address?

 LEARNING TO LEARN

Don't use the same adjectives again and again in your writing work. Find other adjectives that have a similar meaning. This makes your work more interesting to read.

Unit objectives and key competences

In this unit the student will learn …

- understand, memorize and correctly use vocabulary related to literature and professions **CLC CMST SCC CAE**
- understand and correctly use the past simple **CLC L2L**
- understand and correctly form questions and complete a text using *was / were* and *could / couldn't* **CLC L2L**
- about the Edinburgh Fringe festival in Scotland and compare with festivals in their country **CLC SCC CAE**
- about Scotland by watching a short video **CLC CMST DC CAE**

In this unit the student will learn how to …

- identify specific information in a magazine article about the mobile phone novel **CLC DC CAE**
- √ look online for information about their favourite writers, write a short biography and exchange information with their partner **CLC DC CAE SIE**
- identify specific information in a presentation about people who changed the world **CLC SCC CMST CAE**
- read information about King Arthurs labyrinth, listen to someone phoning for information and learn how to ask about an experience **CLC CAE SCC SIE**
- write a review of an interesting place **CLC SIE L2L**
- prepare for and do a matching key information exam **CLC SIE L2L**

Linguistic contents

Main vocabulary

- Literature: *autobiography, biography, detective story,* etc
- Professions: *pilot, painter, comedian,* etc

Grammar

- Past simple
- *was / were*
- *could / couldn't*

Functional language

- Phrases for asking about experiences

Pronunciation

- Past simple verb endings
- /ə/

Skills

Reading

- Read a magazine article about the mobile phone novel
- Read a text about the Edinburgh Fringe festival
- Read an information leaflet about a tourist attraction
- Read a review

Writing: Interaction and production

- Write a personalized dialogue about an experience
- Write a review in three steps: plan, write, check
- Learn how to use *also* and *too*

Listening

- Listen to an interview about people who changed the world
- Listen to someone phoning for information

Spoken interaction

- Exchange information about books you would like to read
- Ask and answer questions using *could*

Spoken production

- Prepare and act out a dialogue about an experience

Lifelong learning skills

Self-study and self-evaluation
- Study guide:
  Student's Book page 29
- Progress check and self-evaluation:
  Workbook pages 22–23
- Grammar reference and practice:
  Workbook pages 86–87
- Wordlist:
  Workbook pages 151–157

Learning strategies and thinking skills
- Using *what, why, where* and *how* for past simple questions

Cultural awareness
- A quick guide to the Edinburgh Fringe Festival
- Comparing festivals in Scotland with festivals in students' own countries and regions

Cross-curricular contents
- Literature: Charles Dickens, festivals
- Reading and writing a review
- ICT: searching the internet for information

Key competences

CLC	Competence in linguistic communication
CMST	Competence in mathematics, science and technology
DC	Digital competence
SCC	Social and civic competences
CAE	Cultural awareness and expression
L2L	Learning to learn
SIE	Sense of initiative and entrepreneurship

Evaluation
- Unit 2 End-of-unit test: Basic, Standard and Extra
- CEFR Skills Exam Generator

External exam trainer
- Listening: Matching key information

Digital material

Pulse Live! Digital Course including:
- Interactive grammar tables
- Audio visual speaking model: Asking about an experience
- Audio visual cultural material: Scotland

Student's website

Digital competence
- Web quest: your favourite writers
- Digital competence worksheet: Online biographies

Reinforcement material
- Basic worksheets, Teacher's Resource File pages 11–16
- Vocabulary and Grammar: Consolidation worksheets, Teacher's Resource File pages 7–8

Extension material
- Fast-finisher activity: Student's Book page 21
- Extra activities: Teacher's Book pages T26, T28
- Vocabulary and Grammar: Extension worksheets, Teacher's Resource File pages 9–10

Teacher's Resource File
- Translation and dictation worksheets pages 3, 13
- Evaluation rubrics pages 1–7
- Key competences worksheets pages 3–4
- Culture and CLIL worksheets pages 5–8
- Culture video worksheets pages 3–4
- Digital competence worksheets pages 3–4
- Macmillan Readers worksheets pages 1–2

Exercise 2

1 romantic novel
2 comic novel
3 autobiography
4 travel guide
5 adventure story
6 biography
7 science fiction novel

My Side and *Steve Jobs: The man who thought different* are about real people.

THINK ABOUT IT

What kind of books do you like? Do you prefer fiction or non-fiction?

Vocabulary and Speaking
Literature

1 🔊 1.21 Look at the literary genres. Listen and repeat the words.

> adventure story autobiography biography comic novel cookery book detective novel
> fairy tale historical novel poetry book romantic novel science fiction novel thriller travel guide

2 🔊 1.22 Complete the comments with words from exercise 1. Which two books are about real people? Listen and check.

This week's bestsellers! What our readers think … [home] [bestsellers]

bestsellers > *reviews*

LIFE, LOVE AND TEXTING

From the title, you'd think this was a (1) … but it's also a (2) … that really made me laugh.
Vicky, 18

Europe Essentials

This is a (4) … about some great places in Europe. There is information about lots of interesting things to see and do in Europe.
Jess, 15

Steve Jobs: The man who thought different

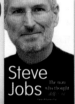

This (6) … tells the amazing life story of Steve Jobs. For technology lovers!
Maisie, 17

MY SIDE

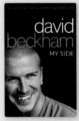

I'm not a sports fan, but I really enjoyed this (3) … of David Beckham. I'm going to buy it for my dad now!
Tom, 19

PERCY JACKSON AND THE LIGHTNING THIEF

This is an (5) … about a very clever boy called Percy. Someone stole something very important from the Greek God Zeus. It's very exciting! Children aged 10–12 will enjoy it.
Kate, 11

THE ADVENTURES OF SEAN RYANIS & THE IMPOSSIBLE CHASE

I really liked this (7) … about exciting adventures in space. Buy it!
Brad, 16

Exercise 3

1 detective novel
2 fairy tale
3 cookery book
4 thriller
5 historical novel

3 Match the definitions with words from exercise 1.

1 A story about trying to solve a crime.
2 A traditional story about magical events.
3 A book that helps you to make food.
4 An exciting story, often about danger or crime.
5 A fiction book about people and events in the past.

EXPRESS YOURSELF

4 Which of the books would you like to read? Why?

🔘 *I'd like to read 'My Side' because I like sport.*

5 Make notes about a book you enjoyed reading.

Title:	Age when you read it:
Author:	Why you liked it:
Kind of book:	

6 Work in pairs. Ask and answer questions about your books from exercise 4.

🔘 *What's the title?*   🔘 *When did you read it?*
🔘 *Who's the author?*   🔘 *Why did you like it?*
🔘 *What kind of book is it?*

Vocabulary and Speaking
Literature

Warmer

Books closed. Write *book, author* and *title* on the board with the letters in the wrong order, eg *kobo, hotaur* and *ettli*. Explain that the three words are all connected with the topic of literature. Ask students to work in pairs and write the letters in the correct order to spell the words.

Think about it

Students work individually and answer the questions. They compare answers in pairs. Get feedback from the whole class.

1 🔘 1.21
- Students look at literary genres.
- Play the CD. Students listen to the words in the word pool and repeat them.
- Check students understand the difference between an *autobiography* (a book someone writes about their own life) and a *biography* (a book about a person's life written by another person).
- Make sure they pronounce *biography* /baɪˈɒgrəfi/ correctly with the stress on the second syllable in *autobiography* and *biography*.

Language note

Point out that in compound words where both words are nouns, the first word usually carries the main stress, eg *adventure story, poetry book*. In compound nouns where the first word is an adjective, the second word is usually stressed, eg *comic novel, historical novel*.

2 1.22
- Check students understand the task.
- Students work individually and complete the comments using words from exercise 1.
- They decide which two books are about real people.
- Students compare answers in pairs.
- Play the CD for students to listen and check their answers.
- Check answers as a class.

Culture note

David Beckham was born in London, England in 1975. He is the first English footballer to win league championships in four different countries (England, Italy, the USA and France). He played 115 times for the English national team. He is married to Victoria, who was 'Posh Spice' in the 1990s all-girl pop group, The Spice Girls, and is now a fashion designer.

3
- Ask students to read the definitions.
- Students work individually and find the words in exercise 1 that match the definitions.
- They compare answers in pairs.
- Check answers as a class.

EXPRESS YOURSELF

4
- Read the example sentence aloud to the class.
- Students read the questions and answer them individually.
- They compare answers in pairs.
- Listen to their ideas as a class. Make sure they give reasons.

5
- Explain the task. Make sure they understand *kind*, meaning literary genre, eg thriller, travel guide, etc.
- Students work individually and complete the information.

6
- Read the five questions aloud to the class and ask students to repeat them chorally.
- Put students into pairs to ask and answer the questions.
- Listen to some pairs as a class.

Vocabulary extension: Workbook page 103 ▸▸

Reading

Text type: A magazine article

Recommended web links

www.handyroman.net/indexeng.html#

www.goodreads.com/group/show/103377-textnovel-cell-phone-novel-movement

litreactor.com/columns/app-tacular-writing-on-phones-smart-phones-and-tablets

Warmer

Write the word *mobile phone* on the board. Ask students to work in pairs and make a list of things they can do with a mobile phone. Listen to their ideas as a class and write the activities the board, eg *send a text message, call friends, take pictures.*

1
- Students read the two questions.
- They look at the picture and answer the questions.
- Students compare answers in pairs.
- Check answers and get feedback from the whole class.

2 1.23
- Students read the questions carefully first.
- Play the CD. Students listen and follow the article in their books.
- Students compare answers in pairs.
- Check answers as a class.

Word check

Make sure students understand the words. Ask them to translate them into their language.

Culture note

Mobile phone novels are typically very short and some only have 70 to 100 words. The biggest website for mobile phone novels has 3.5 billion visits a month. The mobile phone novel *Mika* was made into a film.
The word *emoticon* is a blend of the words *emotion* and *icon*. It's often thought that *emoticons* are a product of the computer age but, in fact, they were used in letter writing in the nineteenth century when they were commonly used in casual and humorous writing.

3
- Students read the five questions and the different possible answers.
- They read the article again and choose the correct answers.
- Students compare answers in pairs.
- Check answers as a class and highlight the information in the Did you know? box.

Finished?

Ask fast finishers to answer the question and make a list of reasons why or why not.

Web quest

Students find out about one of their favourite writers. Highlight the Web quest tip.

1
- Students choose one of their favourite writers.
- Ask students to open an internet web browser such as Internet Explorer. Students open a search engine (eg Google) and type in the name of the writer they have chosen.
- Students find as much information as they can and make notes.

2
- They write a short biography about their chosen writer using the information they have found.

3
- Students work in pairs. They tell their partner about their writer and ask and answer questions.
- Ask some students to present their biography to the class.

THE STORY OF THE MOBILE PHONE NOVEL

A few years ago, a 19-year-old Japanese girl started writing a novel about her life in a small town. She finished it in just three weeks and gave it the title *Dreams Come True*. Akiko wasn't an experienced writer and didn't expect anyone to be interested in her tale. Yet when it came out a few months later, the romantic novel was a great success. It sold over 200,000 copies.

It's an incredible story. The most amazing thing about it, though, is the fact that Akiko wrote the novel on her mobile phone! As she wrote, she posted it, chapter by chapter, on a website where readers could download it immediately. She worked on it whenever she could – mostly while she was relaxing at home. She didn't think too much about the story and she didn't rewrite anything!

Akiko was one of the first of a new generation of novelists in Japan who write novels as if they are writing a text message. They write in a simple, chatty style and use lots of abbreviations and 'emoticons'. They know how to tell a good story, but they don't worry too much about grammar and spelling.

Some people were critical of mobile phone novels at first. They thought they were a bad influence on teenage girls, who preferred them to 'proper' literature. However, they are now popular with people of all ages. Many of the best-selling paperback books in Japan were originally mobile phone novels!

DID YOU KNOW?
20% of teenage girls in Japan own two mobile phones!

Word check
post download chatty abbreviation emoticon influence paperback

Reading
A magazine article

1 Look at the picture. What is the girl doing? How much time do you spend doing this activity per day?

2 Read and listen to the article. Answer the questions with *yes* or *no*.

1 Was *Dreams Come True* about true experiences?
2 Did readers like *Dreams Come True*?
3 Did the author write the novel on her computer?
4 Is the language in a mobile phone novel always correct?
5 Do mobile phone novels sometimes become paper books?

3 Read the article again and choose the correct answers.

1 Akiko wrote her novel very …
   a) slowly.   **b)** quickly.
2 Akiko … experience of writing books.
   a) had   **b)** didn't have
3 People were first able to read *Dreams Come True* on …
   a) the internet.
   b) their mobile phones.
4 Mobile phone novelists write …
   a) the way people speak.
   b) in long sentences.
5 In Japan, mobile phone novels are …
   a) very successful.
   b) only read by teenage girls.

FINISHED?

Would you like to read a mobile phone novel? Why (not)?

I would like / wouldn't like to read a mobile phone novel because …

Exercise 1
She's texting. / She's writing a text message. / She's sending a text message.

students' own answers

Exercise 2
1 yes
2 yes
3 no
4 no
5 yes

Exercise 3
1 b
2 b
3 a
4 a
5 a

WEB QUEST
Find out about one of your favourite writers.
1 Make notes about their:
   • Name   • Nationality   • Titles of books
   • Date of birth   • Kind of books
2 Write a short biography.
3 Work in pairs. Tell your partner about your writer. Ask and answer questions.

Web Quest tip!
Find the author's official web page for their latest news and biography.

Grammar Digital
Past simple

1 Look at the affirmative examples of the past simple in the table. Which verb is regular and which is irregular?

2 How do we form the affirmative past simple tense of regular verbs?

3 Complete the rules.

   a) To make negative past simple sentences, we use ... followed by the infinitive form of the verb.

   b) We begin questions in the past simple tense with ... .

4 Write the past simple form of the verbs in the box in your notebook. Which verbs are regular?

> go like see get start read say wish
> come hate

5 Correct the sentences about the writer Suzanne Collins. Use the words in brackets.

She liked dancing when she was 11. (reading)

She didn't like dancing when she was 11. She liked reading.

1 She lived in New York for 18 years. (16 years)

2 She grew up in the same place. (different places)

3 She started writing for children's television in 1992. (1991)

4 Her books *The Hunger Games Trilogy* were successful in one country. (lots of countries)

5 She wrote a book about a character called Gregor and his little brother. (little sister)

affirmative
She **finished** the novel in 19 days.
She **wrote** the novel on a phone.
negative
They **didn't like** mobile phone novels.
They **didn't think** about the story.
questions
Did you **enjoy** the book?
Did you **find** that website?
short answers
Yes, I **did**.
No, I **didn't**.

6 Complete the book review with the past simple form of the verbs in brackets.

THE HUNGER GAMES

My brother (1) gave (give) me *The Hunger Games* by Suzanne Collins for my birthday. I (2) ... (not think) I would like it, but as soon as I (3) ... (start) reading it, I (4) ... (love) it. I (5) ... (not want) it to end! I (6) ... (think) the story, which takes place in the future, was very original. This book (7) ... (have) an unusual theme. I (8) ... (find) the main character, Katniss Everdeen, very believable and I really (9) ... (want) her to win the Hunger Games competition. The story was so exciting that I (10) ... (stay) up all night to finish it! Some people (11) ... (not like) the book because they (12) ... (say) there was too much fighting in it, but I disagree. I can't wait to read the next book in the series!

7 Rewrite the sentences so they are true for you. Change the time expressions in bold.

  1 I sent her a text message **two minutes** ago.

  2 I had something to eat **half an hour** ago.

  3 I tidied my bedroom **a few days** ago.

  4 I saw a good film **two weeks** ago.

  5 I bought some new shoes **one month** ago.

ANALYSE

In English, *ago* comes after time expressions.

That book came out two years ago.

I sent you an email a few minutes ago.

Is the word order the same in your language?

🔊 1.24–1.25 Pronunciation lab: Past simple endings, page 124

Digital course: Interactive grammar table   Study guide: page 29

Grammar

Past simple

Digital

Lesson objectives

In this lesson students will:
- learn / revise the past simple of regular and irregular verbs
- use the past simple with time expressions with *ago*

Warmer

Write the sentence *Akiko wrote a novel on her mobile phone* on the board with the words in the wrong order: *wrote Akiko novel phone her on a mobile*. Students work in pairs and write the sentence in the correct order. Write the correct sentence on the board.

1
- Read the two affirmative sentences aloud to the class.
- Ask *Which verb is regular and which is irregular?* and elicit that *finished* is regular and *wrote* is irregular.

2
- Ask *How do we form the affirmative past simple tense of regular verbs?* and elicit that it is formed by adding *-ed*.

3
- Students work individually and complete the rules.
- They compare answers in pairs.
- Check answers as a class.

4
- Students complete the exercise individually.
- They compare answers in pairs.
- Check answers as a class.
- Point out that regular verbs ending in *-e* (eg *like, hate*, etc) form the past simple by adding *-d*.
- Highlight the pronunciation of the present simple *read* /riːd/ and the past simple *read* /red/.

5
- Students look at the pictures. Elicit who the writer is (*Suzanne Collins*) and what famous books she wrote (*The Hunger Games Trilogy*).
- Students work individually and correct the sentences using the words in brackets.
- They compare answers in pairs.
- Check answers as a class.

Culture note

Suzanne Collins was born in Connecticut, the USA in 1962. She is a writer for children's television and author of *The Underland Chronicles* (a series of five books published between 2003 and 2007) and *The Hunger Games Trilogy* (published between 2008 and 2010).

6
- Explain the task.
- Students read the text carefully first.
- They work individually and complete the book review with the past simple form of the verbs in brackets.
- Students compare answers in pairs.
- Check answers as a class.

7
- Explain the task. Rewrite the first sentence as an example. Make the sentence true for you, eg *I sent her a text message five hours ago.*
- Students complete the exercise individually.
- Get feedback from the whole class.

Analyse

Students read the information. Ask them to translate the example sentences and to compare the word order in English with the word order in their language.

Pronunciation lab: Past simple endings, page 124

Digital course: Interactive grammar table

Study guide: page 29

Vocabulary and Listening
Professions

Warmer

Write *job* on the board. Put students into pairs and ask them to write a list of all the jobs they know in two minutes. Listen to their ideas as a class and make a list on the board, eg *doctor, teacher, driver, actor.*

1 🔊 **1.26**
- Explain the task.
- Play the CD. Students listen and repeat the words in blue chorally and individually.
- Elicit the names of any of the people that they know, eg 12 Barack Obama.
- Check that students understand all the different professions.

2 •
- Students match the names with the descriptions in the timeline. Point out that if they don't know, they should guess.
- Students compare answers in pairs.
- Listen to their ideas as a class but do not check the answers at this point.

3 🔊 **1.27**
- Play the CD.
- Students listen and check their answers from exercise 2.
- Check answers as a class and elicit the names of the people shown in the pictures.

4 •
- Students work individually and choose one of the people from exercise 2 or a person of their choice. They write three questions they would ask them.
- They compare their choice of person and their questions in pairs.
- Listen to their ideas as a class.

5 🔊 **1.28**
- Explain that students will hear an interview in which they will hear some of the names from exercise 2.
- Play the CD. Students write down the names from exercise 2 that they hear.
- Check answers as a class.

6 •
- Ask students to read the questions. Check that they understand all the vocabulary, especially *admire* (feel respect for someone).
- Play the CD. Students listen and answer the questions.
- Students compare answers in pairs.
- Check answers as a class.

🔊 1.28 Audioscript, exercise 5

Presenter: Tonight we're talking about important people in modern history and I'll be introducing tonight's guests in just a moment. First of all, we sent our reporter, Sam Jenkins, out and about to see what *you* had to say on the subject.

Sam: Sorry to bother you – do you mind if I ask you something?

Woman: No, of course not.

Sam: Which person in modern history do you admire the most?

Woman: Oh! That's a difficult question.

Sam: We're doing a survey to find out what people think.

Woman: I see. Can it be anyone?

Sam: Yes – a politician, a painter, an athlete ... whatever. Someone that you think has made a difference to the world.

Woman: Well then, for me it's the musician John Lennon. He was a talented singer and wrote some really beautiful songs. He believed that people should live in peace.

Sam: OK, great! Thanks a lot for your time.

Woman: No problem.

Sam: Hi there – have you got a minute? I just want to ask you a quick question.

Boy: Go ahead.

Sam: We're trying to find out which famous person from modern history people admire. Who would you choose?

Boy: Well the only person I can think of is the guy who invented Facebook ... what's his name?

Sam: Mark Zuckerberg?

Boy: That's right. I'll choose him because I think Facebook was a really clever idea. I mean, it's completely changed the way people communicate.

Sam: Right. Thanks! Er, are you two together?

Girl: Yes.

Sam: OK, so can I ask you the same question?

Girl: Yes, sure. I don't agree with Jason because I don't think Facebook is such an amazing invention.

Sam: OK ...

Girl: For me it has to be someone who really gives people hope. Like that runner, Mo Farah. He moved to the UK from Somalia when he was a boy and became a really successful athlete. He won two gold medals at the London Olympics. I think he's amazing because he shows that anything is possible when you try hard.

Sam: Great. Thanks a lot! Well, we're going back to the studio now ...

Vocabulary and Listening
Professions

PEOPLE WHO CHANGED THE W**O**RLD

1800

1 1822
An English **engineer** invented the first computer.

2 1881
1881 – A great **painter** was born in Málaga, Spain.

3 1911
An **explorer** from Norway made a trip to the South Pole.

4 1914
A young **comedian** appeared in the first of many black and white films.

9 1989
A computer **scientist** invented the World Wide Web.

8 1980
A famous **musician** was shot dead in New York.

7 1969
An American **astronaut** walked on the moon.

6 1963
A great flamenco **dancer** gave her last performance.

5 1930
A female **pilot** flew alone from Britain to Australia.

10 2003
The **inventor** of Facebook became a millionaire.

11 2007
A **writer** of children's books sold more than any other author.

12 2008
A black **politician** became president of the USA.

13 2012
An **athlete** won gold medals in the Olympic Games for both the 5,000 m and 10,000 m races.

NOW

Exercise 2

1 c
2 g
3 j
4 a
5 l
6 d
7 m
8 i
9 k
10 e
11 f
12 b
13 h

Pablo Picasso, Carmen Amaya, Mark Zuckerberg, JK Rowling, Barack Obama and Mo Farah are shown in the pictures.

1 🔊 **1.26** Look at the timeline. Listen and repeat the words in blue. Do you know who any of the people are?

2 Match the names with the descriptions in the timeline.

a) Charlie Chaplin
b) Barack Obama
c) Charles Babbage
d) Carmen Amaya
e) Mark Zuckerberg
f) J.K. Rowling
g) Pablo Picasso
h) Mo Farah
i) John Lennon
j) Roald Amundsen
k) Tim Berners-Lee
l) Amy Johnson
m) Neil Armstrong

3 🔊 **1.27** Listen and check your answers.

4 Which person from exercise 2 or the past would you most like to meet? What three questions would you ask him or her?

5 🔊 **1.28** Listen to a reporter interviewing some people. Which names from exercise 2 do they mention?

6 Listen again and answer the questions.

1 What does the woman think of the reporter's question?
2 Who does the woman admire?
3 What is the boy's opinion of Facebook?
4 Who does the girl admire? Where is he originally from?
5 What does she say the person shows?

Exercise 5

John Lennon
Mark Zuckerberg
Mo Farah

Exercise 6

1 It's difficult.
2 John Lennon.
3 It was a really clever idea and it's completely changed the way people communicate.
4 Mo Farah. He's originally from Somalia.
5 That anything is possible when you try hard.

Cultural awareness
Festivals in Scotland

Fact box

Edinburgh and Glasgow have a lot of festivals! There are film festivals, and many kinds of music festivals.

1 Look at the pictures. Which of the two performances would you like to watch?

2 🔊 1.29 Read and listen to the guide. Which famous person was once in the Edinburgh Fringe Festival?

Exercise 2

Rowan Atkinson (Mr Bean)

A quick guide to the Edinburgh

Fringe Festival

HOME   GUIDE

What is it?
It's the biggest festival of theatre, comedy, music and dance in the world. Every year there are thousands of different performers from all over the world!

Who performs in it?
Lots of young actors, comedians, musicians and dancers.

When did it start?
In 1947 – the same year that the Edinburgh International Festival started.

Why was it special?
There were rules about who could and couldn't perform at the International Festival. However, at the Fringe Festival anybody could put on a show!

Who has appeared at the festival?
Many famous people began their careers at the Edinburgh Fringe Festival. For example, Rowan Atkinson, the actor who plays Mr Bean, appeared in a play there when he was a student at Oxford University.

Where does it take place?
All over Edinburgh. Performances don't always take place in theatres, however. You can watch them outside on the street, in cafés and in people's homes. Once there was even a show on a moving bus!

When does it take place?
Every August for three weeks.

How much do tickets cost?
Most tickets cost under ten pounds, but many performances are free.

What does it offer for young people?
Lots! In the 2012 festival, for example, many events were for teenagers. They included a youth circus workshop and a musical comedy performed by American high-school pupils.

Word check
festival   perform   put on a show
take place   circus   comedy

Exercise 3

1 False
The International Festival and the Fringe Festival began in the same year, 1947.

2 True

3 False
Rowan Atkinson, the actor who plays Mr Bean, appeared in a play at one festival when he was a student at Oxford University.

4 True

5 True

3 Read the guide again. Are the sentences true or false? Correct the false sentences.

1 The International Festival began after the Fringe Festival.
2 You don't need any experience to take part in the Fringe Festival.
3 There was a Mr Bean show at one festival.
4 Performances are sometimes in strange places.
5 The Fringe Festival isn't just for adults.

CULTURAL 🌐 **COMPARISON**

4 Think of a festival in your country and answer the questions.

1 Where is it?
2 When is it?
3 Who takes part in it?
4 How much do tickets cost?

 Culture video: Scotland

Cultural awareness
Festivals in Scotland

Lesson objectives

In this lesson students will:
- read about festivals in Scotland
- talk about a festival in their country

Warmer

Write *Edinburgh* and *Glasgow* on the board. Focus students on the Fact box. Elicit from the class that Edinburgh is the capital of Scotland and any events or places to visit students know about in Edinburgh or Glasgow, eg Edinburgh: *The Military Tattoo, Edinburgh Castle, Edinburgh Zoo;* Glasgow: *the Glasgow Jazz Festival, Kelvingrove Art Gallery and Museum, the Mackintosh House,* etc.

1 • Students look at the pictures.
- They work in pairs and say which of the performances they would like to watch and why, eg *I would like to watch the drummers because I like all kinds of music.*
- Listen to their ideas as a class.

Culture note

The Edinburgh Fringe is the world's largest arts festival and about 2,000,000 tickets are sold for Fringe events every year. There are around 3,000 shows of which over a third are comedy shows.

2 🔊 1.29
- Explain the task.
- Play the CD. Students listen and follow the text in their books.
- They compare the answer in pairs.
- Check the answer as a class.

3 • Students read the sentences carefully first.
- They read the guide again and decide whether the sentences are true or false. They correct the false sentences.
- Students compare answers in pairs.
- Check answers as a class.

Word check

Make sure students understand the words, especially *take place* (happen). Ask them to translate them into their language.

CULTURAL **COMPARISON**

4 • Students read the four questions and make a note of their answers.
- They work in pairs and discuss the questions.
- Listen to their ideas as a class.

> Culture video: Scotland 》》

T24

Grammar
was / were

Warmer

Write the sentence *There was a performance on a moving bus* on the board with the words in the wrong order: *bus on was a performance there a moving.* Students work in pairs and write the sentence in the correct order. Write the correct sentence on the board.

1 • Students read the example sentences in the table.
 • They copy and complete 1–3 in their notebooks.
 • Students compare answers in pairs.
 • Check answers as a class. Highlight the contractions *wasn't* (*was not*) and *weren't* (*were not*) and their pronunciation *wasn't* /ˈwʌzənt/ (two syllables) and *weren't* /wɜːnt/ (one syllable).

2 • Do the first example with the class to demonstrate the task (*Were the* Harry Potter *films good? Yes, they were. / No, they weren't.*).
 • Students work individually to complete the questions and write short answers.
 • They compare answers in pairs.
 • Check answers as a class.

Culture note

Sherlock Holmes first appeared in a story by Sir Arthur Conan Doyle in 1887 and featured in four novels and fifty-six short stories.

Look!

Read the two example sentences aloud to the class. Point out that we can contract the present simple form *there is* to *there's* but that we cannot do this with the past simple form.

could / couldn't

3 • Students study the table.
 • They choose the correct words to complete the rules.
 • Students compare answers in pairs.
 • Check answers as a class. Highlight that *could* refers to both ability and possibility in the past.

4 • Encourage students to read the whole dialogue first before they begin the activity.
 • Students work individually and complete the conversation using *could* or *couldn't*.
 • Check answers as a class.

5 • Demonstrate how the prompts are used to make the question with *Could you* and *were*.
 • Students work individually to write the full questions.
 • They compare answers in pairs.
 • Check answers as a class.
 • Remind students that the short answers are *Yes, I could.* and *No, I couldn't.*
 • Students work in pairs and ask and answer the questions.

CLIL Grammar in context: Literature

6 • This activity gives further practice in the past simple of regular and irregular verbs.
 • Ask students to read the whole text before they complete the text with the past simple form of the verbs in brackets.
 • Students work individually to complete the exercise.
 • They compare answers in pairs.

7 1.30
 • Play the CD. Students listen and check their answers.

CLIL task

Students use the internet to find out which of the novels were written by Charles Dickens (*Bleak House, Great Expectations*). *Jane Eyre* was written by Charlotte Brontë and *Emma* was written by Jane Austen.

Pronunciation lab: /ə/, page 124

Digital course: Interactive grammar table

Study guide: page 29

Grammar
was / were

could / couldn't

Exercise 1

1 were
2 wasn't
3 Was

1 Study the table. Copy and complete 1–3 with *was*, *wasn't* and *were*.

affirmative
He **was** a student in Madrid. Many events (1) … for teenagers.
negative
It (2) … a good play. They **weren't** from Scotland.
questions
(3) … I / he / she / it a famous actor? **Were** we / you / they in the show?
short answers
No, I / he / she / it **wasn't**. Yes, we / you / they **were**.

Exercise 2

1 Were the *Harry Potter* films good? Yes, they were. / No, they weren't.
2 Was Sherlock Holmes a real person? No, he wasn't.
3 Were any of Shakespeare's plays comedies? Yes, they were.

2 Complete the questions with *was* or *were*. Then write short answers.

Were you interested in books five years ago?
No, I wasn't.

1 … the *Harry Potter* films good? …
2 … Sherlock Holmes a real person? …
3 … any of Shakespeare's plays comedies? …

> **LOOK!**
>
> there's / there are → there was / there were
> There's a film festival this week.
> There was a film festival last week.

Exercise 6

1 was
2 was
3 lived
4 wrote
5 did he write
6 were
7 didn't have
8 didn't think
9 tried
10 did people like
11 had
12 loved
13 couldn't
14 paid

CLIL Grammar in context: Literature

6 Complete the text with the past simple form of the verbs in brackets.

7 🔊 1.30 Listen and check your answers.

> **CLIL TASK**
>
> Which of these novels were written by Charles Dickens?
> *Jane Eyre   Bleak House   Emma
> Great Expectations*

3 Study the table. Choose the correct words to complete the rules.

affirmative
You **could watch** unknown performers.
negative
They **couldn't perform** at that festival.
questions
Could she **sing**?
short answers
Yes, she **could**. / No, she **couldn't**.

a) The **infinitive / past simple** form of the main verb follows *could*.
b) We use *could* and *couldn't* to talk about ability and possibility in the **present / past**.

Exercise 3

a infinitive
b past

4 Complete the conversation with *could* or *couldn't*.

Jenny: Was the play good last night?
John: Yes, but I (1) … see very well. We (2) … get seats near the front.
Jenny: (3) … you understand it, though? I think Shakespeare's difficult.
John: Yes, we (4) … . This play was in modern English so we (5) … easily follow it.

Exercise 4

1 couldn't
2 couldn't
3 Could
4 could
5 could

5 Write questions with *could*. Then work in pairs and ask and answer the questions.

read / when / four?

Could you read when you were four?

1 ride a bicycle / when / six?
2 use a computer / when / eight?
3 speak English / when / ten?
4 cook / when / 12?

Exercise 5

1 Could you ride a bicycle when you were six?
2 Could you use a computer when you were eight?
3 Could you speak English when you were ten?
4 Could you cook when you were 12?

Who (1) … (be) Charles Dickens?
He (2) … (be) an English writer who (3) … (live) from 1812 to 1870. He (4) … (write) 15 novels, including *A Christmas Carol* and *Oliver Twist*.
What (5) … (he / write) about?
A lot of his books (6) … (be) about poor people. They (7) … (not have) an easy life in the 19th century. Dickens (8) … (not think) people should live in bad conditions and he (9) … (try) to make people think about these problems.
Why (10) … (people / like) his books?
Because they (11) … (have) exciting stories and interesting characters. Everyone (12) … (love) them — even people who (13) … (can not) read! They (14) … (pay) other people to read the books to them!

🔊 1.31–1.32 Pronunciation lab: /ə/, page 124

Digital course: Interactive grammar table   Study guide: page 29   **25**

A visit to King Arthur's Labyrinth

I had a fantastic weekend with my family. What did you do at the weekend?

The tourist attraction that brings the
legend to life!

Travel into the past to the times of King Arthur at one of the most unusual tourist attractions in Wales.

But who was King Arthur?

He was a legendary king from medieval times. He was a hero who won many battles and even fought dragons!

King Arthur's Labyrinth isn't a museum: it's an underground adventure! First, you descend underground into a large cave. Then, you can explore the cave with a guide, who tells you the story of King Arthur and his exciting life.

The experience is interactive. You don't just hear about the tale of King Arthur – you can see and hear his adventures too! And you might also see a Welsh dragon … but don't be scared!

Don't forget to wear comfortable shoes for walking. This attraction is suitable for all the family. It's lots of fun for children, teenagers and adults.

Step 1: Read

Exercise 1

1 In Wales.
2 He was a legendary king from medieval times.
3 A guide.
4 A Welsh dragon.
5 Comfortable shoes for walking.
6 All the family.

1 Read the information about King Arthur's Labyrinth. Then answer the questions.

1 Where is King Arthur's Labyrinth?
2 Who was King Arthur?
3 Who can you explore the cave with?
4 What might you see in the cave?
5 What must you wear?
6 Who is the attraction suitable for?

2 Would you like to visit King Arthur's Labyrinth? Why (not)? Give reasons for your answer.

I would really like to visit King Arthur's Labyrinth because …

Step 2: Listen

3 🔊 1.33 Listen to someone phoning for information about King Arthur's Labyrinth. Copy and complete the notes.

King Arthur's Labyrinth
Open every day 10am to (1) …
Tickets: Children (2) £…   Adults (3) £…
Where to buy tickets: at the Labyrinth or (4) …
Food available at the (5) …

4 Listen again and answer the questions.

1 When is the boy going to visit King Arthur's Labyrinth?
2 Who is he going with?
3 How is he going to travel there?

Exercise 3

1 5pm
2 £5.95
3 £8.95
4 online
5 café

Exercise 4

1 Next weekend.
2 His younger sister and his parents.
3 By car.

26

Integrated skills
A visit to King Arthur's Labyrinth

Warmer

Ask students to read the information about Chris in the speech bubble. Then write the question *What did you do at the weekend?* on the board. Students answer the question in pairs. Listen to answers as a class.

Step 1: Read

1
* Remind students that when we look at texts like this we usually have some idea of what we are looking for first. We do not usually begin at the beginning of the text and read everything. We scan the text until we find what we are looking for.
* Students read the six questions carefully first.
* They look in the text and find the answers to the questions.
* Students compare answers in pairs.
* Check answers as a class. Make sure students understand *cave* (a large hole in the side of a hill or under the ground) and *dragon* (a mythical animal that breathes out fire).

2
* Students work individually and think about their answers to the questions.
* They compare answers in pairs.
* Listen to students' ideas as a class. Make sure they give reasons.

Step 2: Listen

3 1.33
* Check students understand the task. Elicit the type of information they should listen for (a time in gap 1, a price in gaps 2 and 3, a place in gaps 4 and 5).
* Students copy the notes into their notebooks.

* Play the CD. Students complete the notes with the missing information.
* They compare answers in pairs.
* Check answers as a class.

4
* Students read the three questions carefully first.
* Play the CD again. Students write the answers.
* They compare answers in pairs.
* Check answers as a class.

Extra activity

Focus on some of the vocabulary in the dialogue, eg *in advance* (before a particular event or time in the future) and *brilliant* /ˈbrɪljənt/ (meaning *fantastic* or *wonderful*).

1.33 Audioscript, exercise 3

Woman: Wales Tourist Information. How can I help?
Boy: Oh hello. I'd like some information about King Arthur's Labyrinth, please.
Woman: OK. What would you like to know?
Boy: Well, I'm interested in visiting next weekend. Can you tell me the opening times?
Woman: Yes, it's open from 10am until 5pm every day.
Boy: Great. And how much are the tickets?
Woman: Well, how old are you?
Boy: I'm fourteen and I'm coming with my younger sister and my parents.
Woman: OK, well our children's tickets are £5.95 and our adults' tickets are £8.95. You can buy them at the Labyrinth on the day, or you can buy them in advance online.
Boy: Great, thanks. Is there anywhere we can buy something to eat?
Woman: Yes, you can eat at the café. It's also open all day.
Boy: Brilliant! Oh, I nearly forgot … We'll be travelling by car – is there a car park?
Woman: Yes, there is.
Boy: OK. Thanks very much for your help.
Woman: You're welcome.
Boy: Bye.

Integrated skills – continued
Asking about an experience

5 🔊 1.34

- Students look at the picture. Check that they understand the situation and the task.
- Play the CD. Students write the answers in their notebooks.
- They compare answers in pairs.
- Check answers as a class.

6
- Play the CD again, pausing after each question or statement and each response for students to repeat as a class.
- Note the main stress and the falling intonation in the *wh-* questions: *What did you <u>do</u> there? Why was it so much <u>fun</u>? What did you enjoy <u>most</u>?*
- Ask students to repeat the dialogue several times both chorally and individually with the correct stress and intonation.
- Students practise the dialogue in pairs. Then swap roles and practise the dialogue again.

Skills builder

***What*, *Why*, *Where* and *How* for past simple questions**
Read aloud the four questions beginning with the *wh-* words. Ask students to translate the sentences into their language. Highlight the importance of these key words in communication.

Step 3: Write

7
- Students choose a tourist attraction they have visited.
- They copy the phrases and questions in bold from the dialogue into their notebooks.
- They write their own answers to the questions.

8
- Ask students to look at the questions and responses in the Communication kit: Asking about an experience. Encourage them to use these expressions in their dialogue.
- Students work individually and write their dialogue, using the dialogue in the book as a model.
- Monitor while they are writing and give help if necessary.

Step 4: Communicate

9
- Students practise their dialogues in pairs.
- For extra practice, they swap roles in both dialogues.

10
- Choose some pairs to act out their dialogue for the class.
- Students raise their hand if another pair has the same tourist attraction as the tourist attraction they have chosen. This will encourage them to listen carefully to their classmates.

Integrated skills: Workbook page 112 ⟫

ASKING ABOUT AN EXPERIENCE

Watch!

So, **did you have a good time** in Wales?	Yes, thanks. **It was amazing**!
What did you do there?	We went to King Arthur's Labyrinth in the (1) ... . It was really exciting!
Really? Why was it so much fun?	We went underground and explored a cave with a (2) ... . He was so funny!
That sounds great! **What did you enjoy most?**	Well, I really liked hearing about King Arthur's adventures, but I thought the interactive parts were best. Look at this photo of me with a (3) ... !
It looks quite (4) ... ! **I'm glad you enjoyed it**, though.	You should go one day!

Exercise 5

1 mountains
2 guide
3 dragon
4 scary

5 🔊 1.34 Listen to Chris telling Nina about his trip to King Arthur's Labyrinth. Complete 1–4 in your notebook.

6 Listen again and repeat. Practise your intonation.

SKILLS BUILDER

What, Why, Where and **How** for past simple questions
What did you do?
Why was / wasn't it fun?
Where did you go?
How did you get there?

Step 3: Write

7 Think of a tourist attraction you have visited. Then copy the phrases and questions in bold and write your answers to the questions.

8 Write a new dialogue about visiting your tourist attraction. Write both parts. Use the dialogue in exercise 5 to help you.

Step 4: Communicate

9 Work in pairs. Take turns to practise your dialogues.

💬 *So, did you have a good time in / at …?*
💬 *Yes, thanks. It was …*

10 Act your dialogue for the class.

COMMUNICATION KIT

Asking about an experience

Did you have a good time in / at … ?
It was amazing / interesting / awful / boring.
What did you do?
What did you enjoy most?
I'm glad you enjoyed it.
It's a pity you didn't enjoy it.

Writing
A review

THE SHERLOCK HOLMES MUSEUM

1 Last weekend my family and I visited the Sherlock Holmes Museum in London. It's small but interesting. It's got a shop for visitors too.

2 The museum is like the home of Sherlock Holmes, the main character from the famous detective stories. You could look around the different rooms. You could see lots of his possessions too. You could also meet characters from the books – but they were really actors!

3 My favourite thing was the museum shop, which was very good value. There were also some good books to buy. The only problem was that the museum was very busy. We waited half an hour to buy tickets!

1 🔊 1.35 **Read and listen to the review. In which paragraph does Penelope ...**

a) give details about what you can do at the museum?
b) say what she liked and didn't like about the museum?
c) give some general information about the museum?

2 Read the Writing focus. How do you say *too* and *also* in your language?

WRITING FOCUS
also and *too*
We use *also* and *too* to give more information about something.
We use *also* after the verb *be*, but before main verbs.
You could look around the different rooms. You could also meet characters from the books.
We use *too* at the end of sentences.
It's small but interesting. It's got a shop for visitors too.

3 Read the review again. Find more examples of sentences with *also* and *too*.

4 Rewrite the second sentences using the words in brackets.

1 You could have a drink. You could have a meal. (also)
2 Young children will enjoy it. Teenagers will enjoy it. (too)
3 The tickets were expensive. The café was expensive. (also)
4 We enjoyed exploring the castle. We enjoyed exploring the gardens. (too)

Writing task
Write a review of an interesting place you visited recently.

Plan Choose an interesting place and make notes.

Write Write your review. Write there paragraphs. Use your notes and the review in exercise 1 to help you.

Check Check your writing.

- ✔ *also* and *too*
- ✔ past simple verbs
- ✔ *could / couldn't*

Writing
A review

Lesson objectives

In this lesson students will:
- read a review
- use *also* and *too* to give additional information
- write a review of a place

Warmer

Tell students that you have written the name of a famous fictional character on a piece of paper. They should try to guess what you have written by asking questions. You can only answer *yes* or *no*, eg *Is it a man? Yes. Is he a detective? Yes. Is it Sherlock Holmes? Yes!*

1 🔘 1.35
- Students read the three questions carefully first.
- Play the CD. Students follow the text in their books.
- They read the text again and find the answers.
- Check answers as a class.

2
- Students read the notes in the Writing focus box.
- Ask students to translate *also* and *too* into their language.
- Highlight the fact that *also* comes after *be* but before main verbs and write two example sentences on the board, eg *He also speaks French. She is also a dancer.*
- Highlight the position of *too* at the end of sentences.

3
- Students read the review again.
- They work individually and find more examples of sentences with *also* and *too*.
- Students compare answers in pairs.
- Check answers as a class.

4
- Do the first question with the whole class as an example (*You could also have a meal*).
- Students work individually to rewrite the second sentences using the words in brackets. Encourage them to look at the Writing focus box help them.
- Students compare answers in pairs.
- Check answers as a class.

Extra activity

Write *I play tennis.* and *I like watching films.* on the board. Ask students to write two more sentences beginning with *I play* and *I like* using *too* and *also*, eg *I also play basketball. I like playing computer games too.*

Writing task

The aim of this activity is for students to produce a piece of guided writing that includes the correct use of *also* and *too*. It also gives them practice in using the past simple and *could / couldn't* correctly. Ask the students to follow the stages in the Student's Book. At the Check stage, ask them to swap notebooks and check each other's writing.

> Writing reference and practice: Workbook page 122 ❯❯

Study guide
Grammar, Vocabulary and Speaking

Tell the students the Study guide is an important page which provides a useful reference for the main language of the unit: the grammar, the vocabulary and the functional language from the Integrated skills pages. Explain that they should refer to this page when studying for a test or exam.

Grammar

- Tell the students to look at the example sentences of the past simple: affirmative, negative, questions and short answers. Make sure they understand how to form the tense and its usage.
- Then tell students to look at the example sentences of *was / were* and *could / couldn't* (affirmative, negative, questions and short answers). Ensure they know when to use each set of words.
- Refer students to the Grammar reference on pages 86–87 of the Workbook for further revision.

Vocabulary

- Tell students to look at the list of vocabulary and check understanding.
- Refer students to the Wordlist on page 151 of the Workbook where they can look up any words they can't remember.

Speaking

- Check that students understand the phrases to use for asking about an experience.
- Tell students to act out a conversation in pairs asking each other about a recent exciting experience.

Additional material

Workbook

- Progress check page 22
- Self-evaluation page 23
- Grammar reference and practice pages 86–87
- Vocabulary extension page 103
- Integrated skills page 112
- Writing reference and task pages 122–123

Teacher's Resource File

- Basics section pages 11–17
- Vocabulary and grammar consolidation pages 7–10
- Translation and dictation pages 3, 13
- Evaluation rubrics pages 1–7
- Key competences worksheets pages 3–4
- Culture and CLIL worksheets pages 5–8
- Culture video worksheets pages 3–4
- Digital competence worksheets pages 3–4
- Macmillan Readers worksheets pages 1–2

Tests and Exams

- Unit 2 End-of-unit test: Basic, Standard and Extra
- CEFR Skills Exam Generator

Study guide

Grammar
Past simple

affirmative
I **read** the book in class. They **enjoyed** the autobiography.

negative
I **didn't see** the film adaptation. They **didn't want** to read the ending.

questions
Did I **finish** the book? **Did** you **like** the main character?

short answers
Yes, I / you / he / she / it / we / they **did**. No, I / you / he / she / it / we / they **didn't**.

We use the past simple for finished actions in the past.

was / were

affirmative
He **was** an actor. Many events **were** free.

negative
It **wasn't** a good performance. They **weren't** in the show.

questions
Was I / he / she / it an explorer? **Were** we / you / they critical about the novel?

short answers
No, I / he / she / it **wasn't**. Yes, we / you / they **were**.

could / couldn't

affirmative
You **could visit** many places.

negative
We **couldn't see** the stage.

questions
Could they **perform**?

short answers
Yes, they **could**. / No, they **couldn't**.

 LEARNING TO LEARN

Make a list of irregular past simple verbs in your notebook. Everytime you learn a new one, add it to the list.

Vocabulary
Literature

adventure story	historical novel
autobiography	poetry book
biography	romantic novel
comic novel	science fiction novel
cookery book	thriller
detective novel	travel guide
fairy tale	

Professions

astronaut	musician
athlete	painter
comedian	pilot
dancer	politician
engineer	scientist
explorer	writer
inventor	

Speaking
Asking about an experience

Did you have a good time in / at … ?
It was amazing / interesting / awful / boring.
What did you do?
What did you enjoy most?
I'm glad you enjoyed it.
It's a pity you didn't enjoy it.

UNIT 3 WILD WEATHER

Unit objectives and key competences

In this unit the student will learn ...

- understand, memorize and correctly use vocabulary related to weather and natural disasters **CLC CMST SCC CAE**
- understand and correctly use the past continuous **CLC L2L**
- understand and correctly use adverbs **CLC L2L**
- understand when to use the past simple or the past continuous, draw parallels to **L1** and use them in a short speaking activity **CLC SCC SIE L2L**
- about a natural disaster in New Zealand and compare with natural disasters in their country **CLC CMST SCC CAE**
- about charities by watching a short video **CLC SCC DC CAE**

In this unit the student will learn how to...

- identify specific information in a news report about lightning **CLC CMST SCC**
- look online for information about what you should and shouldn't do if lightning strikes **CLC CMST DC SIE**
- identify specific information in a presentation about natural disasters **CLC CMST SCC**
- read short news paper reports, listen to a weather report and learn how to react to news **CLC CMST SCC**
- write a fictional narrative about an eventful day **CLC SCC SIE L2L**
- prepare for and do a speaking exam discussing a topic **CLC CMST L2L SIE**

Linguistic contents

Main vocabulary
- Weather: *sunny, stormy, cloudy,* etc
- Activities that go with different kinds of weather
- Words for natural disasters: *earthquake, hurricane,* etc

Grammar
- Past continuous
- Adverbs
- Past continuous and past simple

Functional language
- Phrases for reacting to news
- Phrases to use when discussing a topic in an exam
- Phrases for activities and weather in an exam context

Pronunciation
- *was* and *were*

Skills

Reading
- Read a news report about lightning
- Read a text about an earthquake in New Zealand
- Read news reports about different kinds of weather
- Read a fictional narrative

Writing: Interaction and production
- Write a personalized dialogue about how to react to a news story
- Write a fictional narrative in three steps: plan, write, check
- Learn how to use sequencing words and expressions

Listening
- Listen to a TV programme about natural disasters
- Listen to a weather report

Spoken interaction
- Ask and answer questions about activities and weather
- Exchange information about an emergency you have experienced

Spoken production
- Prepare and act out a dialogue about how to react to news
- Prepare and do a speaking exam where you discuss a topic

Lifelong learning skills

Self-study and self-evaluation
- Study guide:
  Student's Book page 39
- Progress check and self-evaluation:
  Workbook pages 30–31
- Grammar reference and practice:
  Workbook pages 88–89
- Wordlist:
  Workbook pages 151–157

Learning strategies and thinking skills
- Matching headings with paragraphs

Cultural awareness
- A natural disaster in New Zealand
- Comparing earthquakes in New Zealand with earthquakes in students' own countries and regions

Cross-curricular contents
- Natural disasters, famous disasters, a natural disaster in New Zealand
- Language and literature: reading news reports and reacting to news
- ICT: searching the internet for information

Key competences

CLC	Competence in linguistic communication
CMST	Competence in mathematics, science and technology
DC	Digital competence
SCC	Social and civic competences
CAE	Cultural awareness and expression
L2L	Learning to learn
SIE	Sense of initiative and entrepreneurship

Evaluation
- Unit 3 End-of-unit test: Basic, Standard and Extra
- CEFR Skills Exam Generator
- End-of-term test, Units 1–3: Basic, Standard and Extra

External exam trainer
- Speaking: Discussing a topic

Digital material

Pulse Live! Digital Course including:
- Interactive grammar tables
- Audio visual speaking model: Reacting to news
- Audio visual cultural material: Charities

Student's website

Digital competence
- Web quest: Find out what you should and shouldn't do if lightning strikes
- Digital competence worksheet: Video clips

Reinforcement material
- Basic worksheets, Teacher's Resource File pages 17–22
- Vocabulary and Grammar: Consolidation worksheets, Teacher's Resource File pages 11–12

Extension material
- Fast-finisher activity: Student's Book page 31
- Extra activities: Teacher's Book pages T31, T33
- Vocabulary and Grammar: Extension worksheets, Teacher's Resource File pages 13–14

Teacher's Resource File
- Translation and dictation worksheets pages 4, 14
- Evaluation rubrics pages 1–7
- Key competences worksheets pages 5–6
- Culture and CLIL worksheets pages 9–12
- Culture video worksheets pages 5–6
- Digital competence worksheets pages 5–6
- Macmillan Readers worksheets pages 1–2

UNIT 3 WILD WEATHER

 THINK ABOUT IT

What kind of weather do you like best?
How does it make you feel?

Vocabulary and Speaking
Weather

1 🔊 1.36 Listen and repeat the different kinds of weather. What's the weather like today?

> sunny   rainy   windy   snowy   stormy   cloudy   damp   icy   foggy   warm   wet   dry
> thunder and lightning   blizzard   heatwave   hailstones

2 Look at the pictures. What's the weather like in ...

London?   Tokyo?   Sydney?   Athens?   Madrid?   New York?

In London it's cold and foggy.

Today 10am ATHENS 27 degrees

Today 11am LONDON 5 degrees

Today 1pm MADRID 18 degrees

Today 2pm NEW YORK -1 degrees

Today 4pm SYDNEY 38 degrees

Today 8pm TOKYO 14 degrees

3 In which city ...

1 is there a heatwave?
2 could you hear thunder and see lightning?
3 could you get caught in a blizzard?

> **LOOK!**
>
> **in** spring   **in** summer
> **in** autumn   **in** winter

🔎 **EXPRESS YOURSELF**

4 Read about the weather in Sydney, Australia. Then change the red words to make the sentences true for your country.

In spring it's usually sunny and dry. In summer it's very hot and windy. In autumn it's sometimes rainy and foggy.
In winter it's warm, but often stormy.

5 In what kind of weather do you do these activities? Ask and answer in pairs.

> go windsurfing   go skiing   play volleyball   play computer games

💬 *When do you go windsurfing?*
💬 *I go windsurfing on windy days.*

Exercise 2

Possible answers

In Tokyo it's stormy.

In Sydney it's hot and sunny.

In Athens it's warm and cloudy.

In Madrid, it's wet and rainy.

In New York it's cold and snowy.

Exercise 3

1 Sydney
2 Tokyo
3 New York

30

Vocabulary extension: Workbook page 104 ▸

Vocabulary and Speaking
Weather

Warmer

Write *weather* on the board. Students work in pairs and write down all the words they know that are related to *weather*, eg *hot, cold, rain, sun.* Listen to their ideas as a class and make a list of relevant words on the board.

Think about it

Students work individually. They read the two questions and write their answers. They compare ideas in pairs. Get feedback from the whole class.

1 🔘 **1.36**
- Write the question *What's the weather like today?* on the board. Elicit the meaning.
- Play the CD. Students listen to the words and repeat them chorally and individually.
- Make sure they pronounce *icy* /ˈaɪsɪ/ correctly.
- Elicit the answer to the question.

Language note

We use the question *What is … like?* to ask about whether something is good or bad in some way, eg *What's London like? It's a very interesting city.* It can also be used to ask about people, eg *What's Helen like? She's very friendly.* The word *like* in these questions is a preposition and has no connection with the verb *like*.

2
- Ask students to look at the pictures.
- Students write about the weather in the different cities using the information in the pictures and the vocabulary from exercise 1.
- Students work individually to complete the task.
- They compare answers in pairs.

- Check answers as a class. Point out that because the last four expressions in the list of words in exercise 1 are nouns, if we use these expressions we must use *There is / There are* with them, eg *There is a heatwave. There are hailstones.*

Culture note

Fog is now relatively rare in London, but in the 19th and first half of the 20th centuries a combination of damp winter weather and the burning of fossil fuels in millions of houses often produced thick fog, called *pea soup*. In 1952, there was a particularly thick fog and up to 4,000 people died from respiratory diseases. This led to the Clean Air Act of 1956, which controlled the burning of fossil fuels in London and some other large towns and cities in the UK.

3
- Students read the questions carefully first.
- They look at the pictures and find the answers.
- Students compare answers in pairs.
- Check answers as a class.

Look!

Make sure students remember the words for the four seasons of the year. Remind them that *autumn* is pronounced /ˈɔːtəm/ and that the final *n* is silent. Highlight the use of the preposition *in* with the seasons.

 EXPRESS YOURSELF

4
- Check students understand the task.
- Nominate a student to read aloud the sentences about Sydney.
- Students work individually and change the red words to make the sentences true for their country.
- Listen to their ideas as a class.

5
- Check students understand the task. Make sure they pronounce *skiing* /ˈskiːɪŋ/ correctly.
- Students work in pairs and ask and answer the questions.
- Listen to some pairs as a class.

Vocabulary extension: Workbook page 104 ▶▶

Reading

Text type: A news report

Recommended web links

www.metoffice.gov.uk/weather/uk/advice/
lightning.html

www.mcofs.org.uk/lightning.asp

Warmer

Ask students to work in pairs and say which types of weather they like and why, eg *I like sunny weather because I like going to the beach. I like snowy weather because I like winter*. Listen to their ideas as a class.

1 🔘 1.37
- This exercise gives students practice in listening and reading for gist – to get the general idea of a piece of text from key words. This is an important skill for effective listening and reading, especially when listening to or reading longer pieces of authentic text.
- Students look at the pictures.
- Ask what students think happened to the girl. Elicit ideas from the class.
- Play the CD. Students listen and follow the text in their books.
- They compare answers in pairs.
- Check the answer as a class.

2
- Students read through the five events carefully first.
- They read the report again.
- Students work individually and put the events in the correct order.
- They compare answers in pairs.
- Check answers as a class.

3
- Students read the six questions first.
- They look in the text and find the information to answer the questions.
- Check answers as a class and highlight the information in the Did you know? box.

Word check

Make sure students understand the words. Ask them to translate them into their language.

4
- Students read the questions and work individually to think of their answers.
- They discuss their answers in pairs.
- Listen to their ideas as a class.

Finished?

Ask fast finishers to think what other kinds of weather are sometimes dangerous and why.

Extra activity

Focus on some of the other vocabulary in the text, eg *unexpected, strike / struck, underneath*. Make sure students understand the words and can pronounce them. Check understanding by asking them to translate into their language.

Web quest

Students find out about what you should / shouldn't do if lightning strikes. Highlight the Web quest tip.

1
- Ask students to open an internet web browser such as Internet Explorer. Students open a search engine (eg Google) and type in the subject of their search.
- Students find as much information as they can.
- They make notes on three things you should do and three things you shouldn't do if lightning strikes.

2
- Students work in pairs and compare their information.

3
- Students make a class fact sheet about lightning.

SAVED BY AN MP3 PLAYER!

Sophie Frost, a schoolgirl from England, felt very lucky when her grandmother gave her an MP3 player as a present. She didn't know just how lucky she was, however. When an unexpected accident happened a few days later, the MP3 player probably saved her life!

14-year-old Sophie was going for a walk with her boyfriend, Mason Billington, when it started raining. The young couple took shelter from the rain under a tree and were sitting together when lightning struck. The lightning hit them both and they lost consciousness. Then Mason woke up and carried Sophie to the nearest road in order to get help. A car stopped and took them to hospital. Sophie had some burns on her chest and legs. She also had some damage to her eyes and ears, but fortunately she quickly recovered.

How did Sophie's MP3 player prevent her from having serious injuries? When the accident happened, she wasn't listening to music on the player, but was wearing it around her neck. Doctors believe that the lightning travelled through the wire of the MP3 player instead of through Sophie's body. Even though she was lucky this time, one thing's for sure. The next time there's a storm, she and her boyfriend won't sit underneath a tree!

Word check

take shelter   consciousness   burn   damage   recover   injury   wire

DID YOU KNOW?
Lightning can travel at 150,000 km per second!

3 Answer the questions.

1 What did Sophie's grandma give her?
2 Where were Sophie and her boyfriend when lightning struck?
3 How did Sophie go to hospital?
4 Where was Sophie hurt?
5 Where was Sophie's MP3 player when the accident happened?
6 What part of the MP3 player did the lightning go through?

4 Have you ever been in a very bad storm? What happened?

Yes, I have. My mum and I were in the car and it started raining …

Reading
A news report

1 1.37 Look at the pictures. What do you think happened to the girl? Read, listen and check.

2 Read the report again and put the events in order.

a) It started raining.
b) Sophie went to hospital.
c) Sophie and her boyfriend went for a walk.
d) Sophie's grandmother gave her a present.
e) An accident happened.

FINISHED?
What other kinds of weather are sometimes dangerous? Why?

Foggy weather is dangerous because it causes car accidents.

WEB QUEST

Search the internet to find out what you should / shouldn't do if lightning strikes.

1 Find three things you should do and three things you shouldn't do.
2 Work in pairs. Compare your information.
3 Make a class fact sheet about lightning.

Web Quest tip!
When you use a search engine to find information, just enter the main words the search box – don't write words like *the* or *and*.

Exercise 1

Her MP3 player probably saved her life when she was struck by lightning. / Her MP3 player probably saved her life when lightning hit her.

Exercise 2

1 d
Sophie's grandmother gave her a present.

2 c
Sophie and her boyfriend went for a walk.

3 a
It started raining.

4 e
An accident happened.

5 b
Sophie went to hospital.

Exercise 3

1 An MP3 player.
2 Under a tree.
3 By car.
4 Sophie's chest, legs, eyes and ears were hurt.
5 Around her neck.
6 The wire.

 31

Grammar Digital
Past continuous

affirmative
I / He / She / It **was** go**ing** for a walk. We / You / They (1) ... under a tree.

negative
I / He / She / It (2) ... to music. We / You / They **weren't** stand**ing** in the rain.

questions
(3) ... it ...? **Were** we / you / they talk**ing**?

short answers
Yes, it **was**. No, we / you / they **weren't**.

1 Copy and complete the table with the past continuous form of *rain*, *sit* and *listen*.

2 Read the table and choose the correct words to complete rules a) and b).

   a) We use the past continuous to talk about **actions in progress / completed actions** in the past.

   b) We form the past continuous with *was / were* + the **-ing / infinitive** form of the verb.

3 Read the spelling rules on page 39. Then write the *-ing* form of the verbs in the box.

> tell   do   lie   get   come   run

4 What were they doing? Write complete questions and answers.

   he ski / ice-skate

   Was he skiing?   No, he wasn't. He was ice-skating.

   1 they swim in the sea / swim in a pool
   2 she sleep / read
   3 they fight / play
   4 it lie on the bed / lie on the sofa
   5 he watch TV / play computer games
   6 she go windsurfing / play volleyball

 **ANALYSE**

In English, we usually use the past continuous to talk about temporary situations. When do you use it in your language?

5 Complete Tom's email with the past continuous form of the verbs in brackets.

Hi Emma!
Something really strange happened to me today. I (1) ... (walk) home from school and suddenly lots of apples started falling out of the sky. I couldn't believe it! It (2) ... (rain) apples! Where (3) ... they ... (come) from? I went home and told my mum and brother, but they said I (4) ... (not tell) the truth. However, that evening, my mum and dad (5) ... (watch) the news on TV and they heard the story. Nobody knows why the apples fell out of the sky, but they did. I (6) ... (not lie)!
See you soon,
Tom

Adverbs

LOOK!

We use adjectives to tell us more about nouns.
We use adverbs to tell us more about verbs.
It was a bright, sunny day.
The sun was shining brightly.

6 Look at the Study guide on page 39. Then copy and complete the table with the adverbs of the adjectives in the box.

> noisy   bad   easy   hard   careful   good

regular (*-ly*)	regular (*-ily*)	irregular
	noisily	

7 Choose the correct words to complete the advice.

   1 The roads are icy. Drive **careful / carefully**!
   2 It was raining **hard / hardly** yesterday.
   3 There's a storm. Come inside **quick / quickly**!
   4 The sun was shining very **bright / brightly** today.
   5 It's snowing! Dress **warm / warmly**!
   6 When it's foggy you want drivers to see you **easy / easily.** Wear bright clothes!

 1.38–1.39 Pronunciation lab: Weak forms: *was* /wəz/ and *were* /wɜ:/, Page 124

Exercise 1

1 were sitting
2 wasn't listening
3 Was it raining?

Exercise 2

a actions in progress
b *-ing*

Exercise 3

telling
doing
lying
getting
coming
running

Exercise 4

1 Were they swimming in the sea? No, they weren't. They were swimming in a pool.
2 Was she sleeping? No, she wasn't. She was reading.
3 Were they fighting? No, they weren't. They were playing.
4 Was it lying on the bed? No, it wasn't. It was lying on the sofa.
5 Was he watching TV? No, he wasn't. He was playing computer games.
6 Was she going windsurfing? No, she wasn't. She was playing volleyball.

Exercise 5

1 was walking
2 was raining
3 were they coming
4 wasn't telling
5 were watching
6 wasn't lying

Exercise 6

regular (*-ly*)
badly
carefully
regular (*-ily*)
easily
irregular
hard
well

Exercise 7

1 carefully
2 hard
3 quickly
4 brightly
5 warmly
6 easily

Grammar

Past continuous

Lesson objectives

In this lesson students will:
- learn / revise the past continuous
- learn / revise a set of adverbs

Warmer

Write the sentence *Sophie was wearing an MP3 player around her neck* on the board with the words in the wrong order: *around Sophie an neck was MP3 player wearing her*. Students work in pairs and write the sentence in the correct order. Write the correct sentence on the board.

1.
   - Students copy the table into their notebooks.
   - They read the example sentences.
   - Students work individually and complete the table with the past continuous form of *rain, sit* and *listen*.
   - They compare answers in pairs.
   - Check answers as a class.

2.
   - Explain the task.
   - Students look at the table again and choose the correct words to complete the rules.
   - Check answers as a class.

Language note

Point out that the present continuous refers to actions in progress in the present and the past continuous refers to actions in progress in the past.

3.
   - Students read the spelling rules on page 39.
   - They complete the exercise individually.
   - Students compare answers in pairs.
   - Check answers as a class. Make sure they understand the two meanings of *lie*, eg *lying in bed* and *lying* (not telling the truth) as these are both used in later exercises in the lesson.

4.
   - Nominate two students to read aloud the example question and answer.
   - Students work individually to write questions and answers for each of the situations.
   - They compare answers in pairs.
   - Check answers as a class.

Analyse

Students read the information. Ask them to compare the usual use of the past continuous in English to talk about temporary situations with when they use the past continuous in their language.

5.
   - Students read the whole email first.
   - They work individually and fill the gaps using the past continuous form of the verbs in brackets.
   - Students compare answers in pairs.
   - Check answers as a class.

Adverbs

Look!

Focus students on the Look! box. Highlight that adjectives tell us more about nouns, and adverbs tell us more about verbs. Read the example sentences aloud to the class.

6.
   - Students look at the Study guide on page 39.
   - They copy the table into their notebooks.
   - Students work individually to write the adverb forms of the adjectives in the correct column in the table.
   - They compare answers in pairs.
   - Check answers as a class.

7.
   - Explain the task. Students choose the correct words to complete the different pieces of advice.
   - They complete the exercise individually.
   - Check answers as a class.

Language note

Hard is the irregular adverb form of the adjective *hard*. It can be used to modify various verbs, eg *work hard, study hard, rain hard*. The word *hardly* does exist but it means *almost not*, eg *It was so foggy I could hardly see.*

 Pronunciation lab: Weak forms: *was* /wəz/ and *were* /wɜː/, page 124

Digital course: Interactive grammar table

Study guide: page 39

Vocabulary and Listening
Natural disasters

Warmer

Play a game of *Hangman* to introduce the topic. Use dashes to represent the letters of *disaster* and write them on the board: _ _ _ _ _ _ _ _. Ask students to suggest letters of the alphabet. Only accept letters that are pronounced correctly. Continue until students have guessed the word.

1 🔘 1.40
- Play the CD.
- Students listen and repeat the words chorally and individually.
- Students work individually. They answer the question and complete the explanations using the words in the box.
- Students compare answers in pairs. Listen to their ideas but do not correct them at this stage.

2 🔘 1.41
- Play the CD.
- Students listen and check their answers to exercise 1.
- Point out that a *landslide* is when a large amount of earth falls down a mountain and a *famine* happens when people can't grow enough food to eat. Highlight the pronunciation of *drought* /draʊt/.

3
- Check students understand the task.
- Students do the quiz individually and compare answers in pairs.
- Listen to their ideas as a class but do not correct them at this stage.

4
- Explain the task. Read the example sentences aloud to the class.
- Students work individually and write about a disaster in their country.
- They compare answers in pairs.
- Listen to their ideas as a class.

5 🔘 1.42
- Play the CD.
- Students check their answers from exercise 3.
- Students compare answers in pairs.
- Check answers as a class.

6
- Students read the questions carefully first.
- Play the CD again. Students write the answers.
- Check progress. If necessary, play the CD again.
- Check answers as a class.

Extra activity

Focus on some of the vocabulary in the audioscript, eg *crashing down, occur, behave, cry, special ability*. Make sure students understand the words and can pronounce them.

🔘 1.42 Audioscript, exercise 5

Presenter: Hello and welcome to *Mysteries of the Earth*. This week we're talking about natural disasters. Did you know that there are some areas of the world where more natural disasters happen than others? For example, 75% of volcanoes are in the countries on the Pacific Ocean – like Japan and New Zealand. Most of the world's big earthquakes also happen here. And the USA has more tornadoes than any other country – over a thousand a year!
Some natural disasters happen more often than you think. For example, there's actually one earthquake every thirty seconds somewhere in the world – that's two a minute! However, most of these earthquakes are so small that we can't feel them.
Unfortunately, sometimes one disaster can cause another one. For example a tsunami sometimes happens after there is an earthquake in the middle of the sea. And a wildfire on a mountain can sometimes cause a landslide. We know that trees can stop landslides happening. That's because trees help to keep the earth in place. But when there aren't any trees, the earth can move more easily – and it can come crashing down onto a town or city.
The big problem with many natural disasters is that nobody knows when they will happen. However, some people believe that animals can *feel* when a disaster is about to occur. There are many stories about animals behaving unusually just before a volcano or an earthquake – dogs cry and birds stop singing, for example. Why does this happen? Who knows! Maybe they have a special ability, which human beings don't have, to understand how nature works!

Vocabulary and Listening
Natural disasters

A hurricane is a storm with very strong winds.

1 An ... is a large amount of snow which falls down a mountain.

2 A ... happens in hot weather when an area of forest is very dry.

3 A ... happens when it rains a lot.

4 A ... is a mountain that erupts and releases hot liquid.

5 An ... makes the ground move.

6 A ... is a very big sea wave.

7 A ... happens when there isn't enough rain.

8 A ... is a very strong wind that goes round and round.

Exercise 1

1 avalanche
2 wildfire
3 flood
4 volcano
5 earthquake
6 tsunami
7 drought
8 tornado

Landslide and *famine* are not shown in the pictures.

Exercise 3

1 False
2 True
3 True
4 True

1 🔊 1.40 Listen and repeat the words in the box. Which two words can't you see in the pictures? Complete the explanations 1–8.

> volcano   earthquake   avalanche   hurricane
> flood   wildfire   tornado   tsunami   landslide
> drought   famine

2 🔊 1.41 Listen and check your answers.

3 What do you know about natural disasters? Look at the quiz. Are the sentences true or false?

NATURAL DISASTERS QUIZ

1 Most of the world's volcanoes are in Europe.
2 There are over 1,000 tornadoes in the USA every year.
3 An earthquake happens somewhere in the world every 30 seconds.
4 Landslides can happen because of wildfires.

4 Write three sentences about a disaster that happened in your country. Use words from exercise 1.

There was a flood in Córdoba. Some people lost their homes. My family and I were safe.

5 🔊 1.42 Listen to a TV programme about natural disasters and check your answers to exercise 3.

6 Listen again and answer the questions.

1 Which two kinds of disaster often happen near the Pacific Ocean?
2 Why don't we always feel earthquakes?
3 Where do some tsunamis start?
4 What can stop a landslide?
5 What do birds sometimes do before a disaster?

Exercise 6

1 Volcanoes and earthquakes.
2 Because they are too small.
3 In the middle of the sea.
4 Trees.
5 They stop singing.

Cultural awareness
A natural disaster in New Zealand

Earthquake in Christchurch

A few years ago, a terrible earthquake happened in the city of Christchurch in New Zealand. It killed 185 people, but Jay Watson had a lucky escape.

Reporter What were you doing when the earthquake happened?

Jay I wasn't at school that day because I was sick. I was sitting on my bed when I heard a terrible noise and the whole house started shaking.

Reporter What did you do?

Jay I realized it was an earthquake so I quickly got down on the floor between my bed and the wall. I thought that was the safest place. At school, we often have earthquake drills, so we know what to do in an emergency.

Reporter What happened next?

Jay Suddenly the wall of my bedroom collapsed and I fell out of the house! I fell about ten metres, from the second floor of the house into the front garden!

Reporter Were you hurt?

Jay At first I thought I was seriously injured, but I actually only had a few scratches and bruises on my back. I was really lucky!

Reporter How did you feel?

Jay Scared! And not just because of the fall. Lots of bricks fell on top of me while I was lying on the ground. Our next-door neighbour, who's a firefighter, pulled me out from under the bricks. My mum couldn't believe that I was alive!

Reporter How did your life change because of the earthquake?

Jay Well, we had to move to a new house because there was so much damage to our old one. It's in a different area, but I still go to the same school. And it's only got one floor, so I feel a bit safer!

Word check

shake | drill | emergency | collapse | scratch | bruise | brick

Exercise 1

He was at home in his bedroom sitting on his bed.

Exercise 3

1 protect himself
2 through a wall
3 not badly
4 someone he knew
5 lives in the same area

1 Look at the pictures of Jay and his house after an earthquake. Can you guess where he was when the earthquake happened?

2 🔊 1.43 Read and listen to Jay's story. Check your answer to exercise 1.

3 Read the interview again and choose the correct words.

Jay ...
1 tried to **escape** / **protect himself**.
2 fell **out of a window** / **through a wall**.
3 was **badly** / **not badly** hurt in the earthquake.
4 was helped by **someone he knew** / **a team of firefighters**.
5 no longer **lives in the same area** / **goes to the same school**.

CULTURAL  **COMPARISON**

4 Answer the questions.

1 Do earthquakes ever happen in your country?
2 When and where was the most recent earthquake?
3 Do earthquakes happen more in some places?

 Culture video: Charities

Cultural awareness
A natural disaster in New Zealand

Culture note

Christchurch is the largest city in the South Island of New Zealand, with a population of 375,000. On February 22nd 2011, it was struck by an earthquake of a magnitude of 6.3 on the Richter scale, killing 185 people and destroying numerous buildings. The cost of the damage to the New Zealand economy has been estimated at around £20 billion.

Lesson objectives

In this lesson students will:
- read about a natural disaster in New Zealand
- talk about earthquakes in their country

Warmer

Write *New Zealand* on the board. Focus students on the Fact box. Students work in pairs and discuss any other information they know about this country. Listen to their ideas as a class and make a list on the board, eg *They speak English there. It's made up of two large islands and many smaller ones. They are sometimes called 'The Shaky Islands'.*

CULTURAL **COMPARISON**

4
- Students read the three questions and make a note of their answers.
- They work in pairs and discuss the questions.
- Listen to their ideas as a class.

Culture video: Charities

1
- Check students understand the task.
- They look at the pictures and answer the question.
- Students compare their ideas in pairs.
- Listen to their ideas as a class but do not correct them at this stage.

2 1.43
- Play the CD. Students follow the text in their books and check their answer to the question in exercise 1.
- Students compare their answer in pairs.
- Check the answer as a class. Make sure students understand *next-door neighbour* (someone who lives in the house next to yours).

3
- Students read the questions carefully first.
- Students look in the text and choose the correct words to complete the sentences.
- They compare answers in pairs.
- Check answers as a class.

Word check

Make sure students understand the words and can pronounce them correctly, especially *bruise* /bruːz/. Ask them to translate them into their language.

Grammar
Past simple and past continuous

Lesson objectives

In this lesson students will:
- contrast the use of the past simple and the past continuous
- ask and answer questions about an emergency
- read a quiz about historical events

Warmer

Write *hit, say, lie, sit, put, come, hope, run, die, have* on the board. Put students into pairs to write the *-ing* form of the verbs without referring to the spelling rules on page 39. Invite students to the board to write the answers (*hitting, saying, lying, sitting, putting, coming, hoping, running, dying, having*).

1 • Students look at the table and complete the rules with *when* and *while*.
- Students compare answers in pairs.
- Check answers as a class. Highlight the use of *when* with the past simple (the single action) and *while* with the past continuous (the action in progress).

2 • Students work individually to write full sentences from the prompts.
- Students compare answers in pairs.
- Check answers as a class.

3 • Students complete the email individually.
- They compare answers in pairs.
- Check answers as a class.

EXPRESS YOURSELF

4 • Students work in pairs and ask and answer questions about an emergency they have experienced.
- Listen to their ideas as a class.

CLIL Grammar in context: Famous disasters

5 • This activity gives students more practice in the difference between the past continuous and the past simple and also practises adverbs.

- Ask students to read the whole text before they choose the correct words and answer the questions.
- Students work individually to complete the exercise.
- They compare answers in pairs.

6 **1.44**
- Play the CD. Students listen and check their answers to exercise 5.

CLIL task

Students use the internet to answer the question.

Digital course: Interactive grammar table

Study guide: page 39

1.44 Audioscript, exercise 6

Dinosaurs were living on Earth when they suddenly disappeared. Many scientists believe that a natural disaster killed them. How many years ago did it happen?
a) 5 million, b) 15 million, c) 65 million.
The answer is c) – it happened 65 million years ago.
In the year 79 AD, there was a terrible volcanic eruption near an Italian city. Many people were trying to escape when they died. Where was it?
a) Rome, b) Pompeii, c) Venice.
The answer is b) – the volcano was near Pompeii.
In September of this year, London was burning! The fire started by accident and it quickly destroyed large areas of the city. What was the year?
a) 1444, b) 1555, c) 1666.
The answer is c) – the Great Fire of London was in 1666.
On 1st November 1755, a terrible disaster destroyed the beautiful city of Lisbon in Portugal. However, the people rebuilt their city and made it beautiful again. What was the disaster?
a) an earthquake, b) a tornado, c) a flood.
The answer is a) – there was a terrible earthquake in Lisbon.
On 15th April 1912, a ship was crossing the Atlantic Ocean to the USA when it suddenly hit an iceberg. The ship sank. What was the ship's name?
a) The *Golden Hind*, b) The *Titanic*, c) The *Santa María*.
The answer is b) – the ship was called the *Titanic*.

Grammar Digital
Past simple and past continuous

1 Look at the table. Then copy and complete the rules with *when* and *while*.

past continuous and past simple
I was sitting on my bed **when** I heard a noise.
I heard a noise **while** I was sitting on my bed.

a) We usually use the past simple after … .
b) We usually use the past continuous after … .

2 Make sentences about Jay's family using the past simple and past continuous.

His mum / cook / when / she / hear a shout.

His mum was cooking when she heard a shout.

1 His brother / eat / when / the lights / go out.
2 His dad / walk down the street / when / the ground / move.
3 Jay's sister / talk to her friends / when / somebody / shout 'Earthquake!'
4 His grandparents / watch TV / when / everything / fall off the shelves.

3 Copy and complete the email with the correct form of the verbs in brackets.

> ✉ Send ◁ Reply
>
> Hi Ingrid!
>
> We're having lots of adventures on our holiday. While we (1) … (stay) at a campsite near a river, we (2) … (have) a terrible experience. There (3) … (be) a flood while we (4) … (sleep). When we (5) … (wake up), we (6) … (be) wet.
>
> Hope you're having a good summer!
>
> Jack

EXPRESS YOURSELF

4 Work in pairs. Think of an emergency you have experienced. Ask and answer the questions.

What were you doing when it happened?
What did you do next?
How did you feel while it was happening?
What did you do afterwards?

CLIL Grammar in context: Famous disasters

5 Read the text and choose the correct words. Then answer the questions.

6 🔊 1.44 Listen and check your answers.

Dinosaurs (1) **lived** / **were living** on Earth when they suddenly (2) **disappeared** / **were disappearing**. Many scientists believe that a natural disaster killed them. How many years ago did it happen?

a) 5 million **b)** 15 million **c)** 65 million

In the year 79 AD, there was a terrible volcanic eruption near an Italian city. Many people were trying to escape (3) **while** / **when** they died. Where was it?

a) Rome **b)** Pompeii **c)** Venice

In September of this year, London (4) **was** / **were** burning! The fire started by accident and it (5) **quick** / **quickly** destroyed large areas of the city. What was the year?

a) 1444 **b)** 1555 **c)** 1666

On 1st November 1755, a terrible disaster destroyed the beautiful city of Lisbon in Portugal. However, the people (6) **were rebuilding** / **rebuilt** their city and made it beautiful again. What was the disaster?

a) an earthquake **b)** a tornado **c)** a flood

On 15th April 1912, a ship was crossing the Atlantic Ocean to the USA when it (7) **sudden** / **suddenly** hit an iceberg. The ship sank. What was the ship's name?

a) The *Golden Hind* **b)** The *Titanic*
c) The *Santa María*

CLIL TASK
Can you name a natural disaster from the past 10 years?

In the news

It's so cold here at the moment! Do you prefer hot or cold weather? I definitely prefer hot weather!

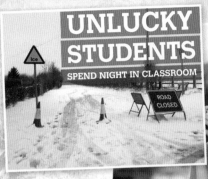
UNLUCKY STUDENTS
SPEND NIGHT IN CLASSROOM

LOCAL GIRL'S PHOTO SUCCESS

SCHOOLS CLOSE AS BLIZZARDS CONTINUE

1 Students and teachers at Grange Secondary School in the village of Hepworth near Dundee were unable to get home last night because heavy snow was blocking the roads. 'We had to sleep on the floor – it wasn't very comfortable,' said 13-year-old Jamie Banks. But it wasn't all bad. 'The teachers let us play games on the school computers,' Jamie added.

2 Icy conditions were still causing problems all over the country today. However, in the north of England some students were celebrating when their school was closed because of the bad weather. 'This is great! Now I can go and play snowballs with my friends,' said Jessica Watson, a Year 8 student from Durham.

3 A student from Mortimer School, Coventry, has come first in a national photography competition. 14-year-old Lucy Preston used her mobile phone to take her winning photo of a frozen lake in winter. What is she going to do with her £500 prize? 'I'm going to use it to buy a camera!' she laughed.

Exercise 1

1 Unlucky students spend night in classroom
2 Schools close as blizzards continue
3 Local girl's photo success

Step 1: Read

1 Match the headlines with newspaper articles 1–3.

SKILLS BUILDER

Matching headings with paragraphs
When trying to match headings with paragraphs, look for words that have similar meanings.
photo success = has won

Exercise 2

1 Jamie Banks
2 Lucy Preston
3 Jessica Watson
4 Lucy Preston
5 Jessica Watson

2 Read the articles and answer the questions. Who ...

1 said he had fun in a difficult situation?
2 won something?
3 felt happy when she heard some news?
4 plans to spend some money?
5 didn't expect to have a holiday?

Step 2: Listen

3 🔊 1.45 Listen to a weather report. Write missing words and phrases 1–7 in your notebook.

WEATHERVIEW

Today it is very cold in Scotland, the north and south of England, and in (1) ... . Snow is falling and there is deep snow lying in some parts of the country. It is more than (2) ... deep in some places. There are blizzards in the south of England. The heavy snow has made conditions on the roads very (3) ... , and many (4) ... are not running. Some roads are blocked by snow, while other roads are very (5) ... . The police have asked people not to travel by car if their journey isn't important. Twenty people spent the night in a local (6) ... when blizzards on the M25 motorway closed the road.
The weather will (7) ... tomorrow, but it will remain very cold until the weekend.

4 Listen again. What have the police asked people to do?

Exercise 3

1 Wales
2 one and a half metres
3 dangerous
4 trains
5 icy
6 sports centre
7 get better

Exercise 4

Not to travel by car if their journey isn't important.

Integrated skills

In the news

Warmer

Revise some of the weather vocabulary from the first lesson in this unit. Write *blizzard, thunder, lightning, foggy, stormy, heatwave* on the board with the letters in the wrong order: *zdrazilb, derunth, nngithlig, gofgy, mortys, wvehatea*. Students work in pairs and write the words with the correct spelling.

Step 1: Read

1. • Highlight Lucy's speech bubble. Elicit answers to the question from the class.
   • Students read the headlines carefully.
   • Make sure they understand *unlucky* (unfortunate).
   • Students read the short articles and match them with the headlines.
   • They compare answers in pairs.
   • Check answers as a class.

Skills builder

Matching headings with paragraphs
Focus students on the Skills builder box. Elicit the phrases in article 3 that show the girl was successful (*come first, winning photo*). Point out that it is an important skill to recognize key words and to use extra information such as headings or headlines in order to get the general idea of the context of a text and understand it.

2. • Students read the questions carefully first.
   • They look at the articles again and find the answers.
   • Students compare answers in pairs.
   • Check answers as a class.

Step 2: Listen

3. 🔊 1.45
   • Students read the whole weather forecast first.
   • Play the CD. Students write the missing words and phrases in their notebooks.
   • Check progress. If necessary, play the CD again.
   • Check answers as a class.

4. • Check students understand the task.
   • Play the CD again. Students follow the weather report in their books.
   • Students answer the question.
   • They compare the answer in pairs.
   • Check the answer as a class.

Integrated skills – continued
Reacting to news

5 🔘 1.46
- Students read the dialogue first.
- Play the CD. Students listen and choose the correct words.
- They compare answers in pairs.
- Check answers as a class.

6
- Play the CD again, pausing after each question or statement and each response for students to repeat as a class.
- Note the main stress and the falling intonation in the *wh-* questions: *What happened? What was it?*
- Ask students to repeat the dialogue several times both chorally and individually with the correct stress and intonation.
- Students practise the dialogue in pairs. Then swap roles and practise the dialogue again.

Step 3: Write

7
- Students work individually.
- They choose a news story from exercise 1 or choose a news story of their own.
- They copy the questions and phrase in the box into their notebooks.
- They write answers to the questions and complete the phrase.

8
- Ask students to look at the questions and responses in the Communication kit: Reacting to news. Encourage them to use these expressions when writing their dialogue.
- Students work individually and write their dialogue, using the dialogue in the book as a model and their notes from exercise 7.
- Monitor while they are writing and give help if necessary.

Step 4: Communicate

9
- Students practise their dialogues in pairs.
- For extra practice, they swap roles in both dialogues.

10
- Choose some pairs to act out their dialogue for the class.
- Students raise their hand if another pair has the same news story as the news story they have chosen. This will encourage them to listen carefully to their classmates.

Integrated skills: Workbook page 113 ›››

REACTING TO NEWS

Watch!

Hi Chris! Guess what happened (1) **yesterday** / **last night** during the storm?	I don't know, what happened?
Well, I was watching TV when I heard a loud noise ...	What was it?
A huge tree fell down in our (2) **road** / **street**! It fell in our garden.	No way! That's (3) **terrible** / **bad** news. Was anybody hurt?
No, luckily everybody was OK. We were all inside because of the awful weather.	Great, I'm really pleased about that.
Well, I've got some good news too! A reporter from the local TV station came and interviewed us about what happened. I'm going to be on TV (4) **tonight** / **tomorrow**!	Wow, that's (5) **amazing** / **fantastic**! I'm definitely going to watch it.

Exercise 5

1 last night
2 street
3 terrible
4 tonight
5 amazing

5 1.46 Listen to the dialogue. Choose the correct words.

6 Listen again and repeat. Practise your intonation.

Step 3: Write

7 Choose a news story from exercise 1 or use your own ideas. Then copy the questions and phrase in the box. Write answers and complete the phrase.

> What happened? When did it happen?
> Why did it happen? How did it happen?
> That's ... !

8 Prepare a new dialogue. Write both parts. Use your notes from exercise 7 to help you.

Step 4: Communicate

9 Work in pairs. Take turns to practise your dialogues.

🔵 Hi Sara! Guess what happened ...?
⚪ I don't know, what happened?

10 Act your dialogue for the class.

COMMUNICATION KIT

Reacting to news

What ... ?
Where ... ?
When ... ?
Why / Why not?
No way! / I can't believe it!
That's amazing / great / terrible news!
I'm really sorry / pleased.
Congratulations!
Well done!

Writing
A fictional narrative

LOST!

(1) … my friend Rosie and I decided to go for a walk in the mountains. The sun was shining when we set off, but (2) … the weather changed. It was very foggy and we couldn't see where we were going. (3) … we were lost.

We didn't know what to do. (4) … I remembered I had my mobile phone in my bag! I tried to phone my dad, but my phone wasn't working. (5) … it was getting dark and we were cold and frightened.

Suddenly we heard the sound of a helicopter. We couldn't believe our luck! It was coming to rescue us.

Everything was alright (6) … – but we learned our lesson. Next time, we'll check the weather forecast before we go for a walk in the mountains!

Exercise 1

1 One day
2 later
3 Soon
4 Then
5 By then
6 in the end

1 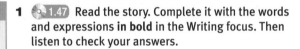 **1.47** Read the story. Complete it with the words and expressions **in bold** in the Writing focus. Then listen to check your answers.

WRITING FOCUS
Sequencing words and expressions

We use the following words and expressions to show the order in which events happened.

One day *Sam woke up early and went swimming …*
Soon *it was time for breakfast.*
Then *he went back to the campsite.*
By then *his family were eating.*
Later *they all went to the beach.*
In the end *they stayed at the beach until 10 p.m.*

2 Look again at the Writing focus. How do you say the words and phrases in your language?

Exercise 3

1 One day
2 In the end
3 By then
4 the past simple

3 Read the story again and answer the questions about sequencing words and phrases.

  1 Which phrase often goes at the beginning of a story?
  2 Which phrase often goes at the end of a story?
  3 Which phrase is often followed by the past continuous?
  4 What tense do we usually use with the other words?

4 Rewrite the sentences with the words in the correct position. More than one answer is possible.

  1 She **soon** was tired so she sat down to have a rest.
  2 Sam didn't want to go on the trip, but he **in the end** enjoyed it.
  3 I was feeling **by then** hungry because it was lunchtime.
  4 It went cloudy and it started **then** raining.

Writing task

Write a fictional narrative about an eventful day trip.

Plan Think of an idea for your story. Then make notes:
- who it is about – you or somebody else?
- how will the story begin and end?

Write Write three paragraphs – an introduction, the main part of the story, and the end.

Check Check your writing.

> ✔ past simple and past continuous verbs
> ✔ sequencing words

Exercise 4

1 Soon she was tired so she sat down to have a rest. / She was soon tired so she sat down to have a rest.

2 Sam didn't want to go on the trip, but in the end he enjoyed it. / Sam didn't want to go on the trip, but he enjoyed it in the end.

3 By then I was feeling hungry because it was lunchtime. / I was feeling hungry by then because it was lunchtime.

4 It went cloudy and then it started raining. / It went cloudy and it then started raining.

Writing
A fictional narrative

Lesson objectives

In this lesson students will:
- read a short narrative
- use sequencing words and expressions
- write a fictional narrative

Warmer

Write the word *mountains* on the board. Ask students to look at the picture and tell you why mountains can be dangerous. Elicit some possible answers from the class and write them on the board, eg *You can lose your way. You might fall. The weather can change very quickly.*

1 🔊 **1.47**
- Students read the information in the Writing focus box first. Check students understand the term *sequencing word* (a word that helps the story have a logical order).
- They read the text and use the words and expressions in bold to complete the text.
- They compare answers in pairs.
- Play the CD. Students check their answers.

2
- Students look at the sequencing words and expressions in the Writing focus box.
- They translate them into their language.

3
- Students read the questions and find the answers in the text.
- They compare answers in pairs.
- Check answers as a class.

4
- Explain the task. Make sure students understand that the sequencing words and expressions are in the wrong position in the sentences.
- They work individually to rewrite the sentences in the correct order. Encourage them to refer back to the story and to the Writing focus box to help them.
- Students compare answers in pairs.
- Check answers as a class.

Language note

The expression *in the end* is used to mean *finally* or *after a period of time or thought*. The expression *at the end* cannot be used in this way. It must be followed by *of*, eg *at the end of the lesson, at the end of the film* and refers to a specific point of time.

Writing task

The aim of this activity is for students to produce a piece of guided writing that includes the correct use of the past simple and the past continuous. It also gives them practice in using sequencing words appropriately. Ask the students to follow the stages in the Student's Book. At the Check stage, ask them to swap notebooks and check each other's writing.

> Writing reference and practice: Workbook page 124

Study guide
Grammar Vocabulary and Speaking

Tell the students the Study guide is an important page which provides a useful reference for the main language of the unit: the grammar, the vocabulary and the functional language from the Integrated skills pages. Explain that they should refer to this page when studying for a test or exam.

Grammar

- Tell the students to look at the example sentences of the past continuous: affirmative, negative, questions and short answers. Make sure they understand how to form the tense and its usage.
- Then tell students to look at the example sentences with adverbs. Ensure they understand how to use adverbs in sentences. Get students to translate into their own language if necessary.
- Tell students to look at the example sentences with *when* and *while*. Make sure they understand that we usually use the past simple after *when* and the past continuous after *while*.
- Refer students to the Grammar reference on pages 88–89 of the Workbook for further revision.

Vocabulary

- Tell students to look at the list of vocabulary and check understanding.
- Refer students to the Wordlist on page 151 of the Workbook where they can look up any words they can't remember.

Speaking

- Check that students understand the phrases to use for reacting to news.
- Tell students to act out a conversation between two people who are discussing an interesting piece of recent news.

Additional material

Workbook

- Progress check page 30
- Self-evaluation page 31
- Grammar reference and practice pages 88–89
- Vocabulary extension page 104
- Integrated skills page 113
- Writing reference pages 124–125

Teacher's Resource File

- Basics section pages 18–22
- Vocabulary and grammar consolidation pages 11–14
- Translation and dictation pages 4, 14
- Evaluation rubrics pages 1–7
- Key competences worksheets pages 5–6
- Culture and CLIL worksheets pages 9–12
- Culture video worksheets pages 5–6
- Digital competence worksheets pages 5–6
- Macmillan Readers worksheets pages 1–2

Tests and Exams

- Unit 3 End-of-unit test: Basic, Standard and Extra
- CEFR Skills Exam Generator
- End-of-term test: Basic, Standard and Extra

Study guide

Grammar

Past continuous

affirmative
I / He / She / It **was** talk**ing** with friends.
We / You / They **were** do**ing** their homework.

negative
I / He / She / It **wasn't** tidy**ing** her room.
We / You / They **weren't** eat**ing** lunch.

questions
Was it snow**ing**?
Were we / you / they walk**ing**?

short answers
Yes, it **was**.
No, we / you / they **weren't**.

We use the past continuous to talk about things that were in progress in the past.

Adverbs

It's cold. Dress warm**ly**!
It's foggy. Drive careful**ly**!
It's raining hard today.
I can easi**ly** do this exercise.
She speaks English well.

Past simple and past continuous

past continuous and past simple
His mum was cooking dinner **when** she heard a shout.
Lots of brick fell on me **while** I was lying on the ground.

Past continuous spelling rules

- For most verbs, add -*ing* to the infinitive
  go → going   play → playing

- For verbs that end in -*e*, omit the -*e* and add -*ing*
  come → coming   give → giving

- For one syllable verbs that end in vowel + consonant (except *w*, *x* or *y*), double the consonant and add -*ing*

- For verbs that end in -*ie*, omit the -ie and add -*ying*
  die → dying   lie → lying

Vocabulary

Weather

blizzard	rainy
cloudy	snowy
damp	stormy
dry	sunny
foggy	thunder and lightning
hailstones	warm
heatwave	wet
icy	windy

Natural disasters

avalanche	landslide
drought	tornado
earthquake	tsunami
famine	volcano
flood	wildfire
hurricane	

Speaking

Reacting to news

What … ?
Where … ?
When … ?
Why / Why not?
No way! / I can't believe it!
That's amazing / great / terrible news!
I'm really sorry / pleased.
Congratulations!
Well done!

 LEARNING TO LEARN

Practise weather vocabulary by keeping a weather diary. Write a short description of the weather every day.

Giving a talk

TASK

Work in groups of three to prepare and give a talk about a famous person in history.

Step 1: Think

1 Look at the materials for giving a talk below. Find ...

1 a picture of the person
2 a video clip
3 an overview of the talk
4 questions for the people listening to the talk
5 quotes by the famous person

2 Look at the equipment for giving a talk in the box. What are the advantages and disadvantages of each item?

> computer   internet connection   DVD player
> board   projector   speakers   poster
> photocopies

@ DIGITAL LITERACY

When you give a talk, remember to:
- plan the talk and make a list of the equipment you will need.
- be creative – use search engines to look for different photos and video clips to make your talk more attractive.
- check the pronunciation of difficult words in an online dictionary.

> The stars don't look bigger, but they do look brighter.

> Yes, I did feel a special responsibility to be the first American woman in space.

> I didn't really decide that I wanted to be an astronaut until the end of college.

quotes by the famous person

an overview of the talk

questions for the people listening to the talk

Sally Ride was the first American woman in space. How much do you know about her?

Where was she born?

Sally joined NASA (North American Space Agency) in 1978. How many people saw the advert in the newspaper and applied to join the space programme?

When was her first space flight?

Sally was an astronaut and physicist. What else did she do?

Which of these awards did Ride win?

a picture of the person

a video clip

Collaborative project 1
Giving a talk

Warmer

Ask students to work in teams. Tell them to write a name of a famous person from history for each letter of the alphabet, eg A (Jane) Austen, B (Napoleon) Bonaparte, C Cleopatra, D (Charles) Darwin, E (Albert) Einstein. Elicit answers from the class and write all the names on the board. The team with the most names wins. Elicit one or two facts about each person, eg why they are famous, what they achieved, etc.

TASK

Read the task with the class and check students understand.

Step 1: Think

1 • Briefly discuss giving a talk with the class. What makes a talk interesting? What types of information can you include? What equipment could you use?
 • Read the list of items students have to identify and help with any vocabulary. Remind students that *a quote* is something a person says.
 • Ask students to read the information and find an example of each item.
 • Check answers as a class. Ask if there are any other items which could be included in the list.
 • Read the Digital literacy box with the class and check students understand. Discuss why it is important to plan the talk and what equipment you need.
 • Point out that talks are more interesting when you include photos and video clips and that it is important to check the pronunciation of difficult words.

2 • Students work in pairs and discuss the advantages and disadvantages of using each piece of equipment for giving a talk.
 • Listen to students' ideas as a class.
 • Point out the importance of knowing how to use any equipment selected for a talk.

Step 2: Listen and plan

3 1.48
- Ask students to read the questions carefully.
- Play the CD. Students listen and answer the questions.
- Check the answers as a class.

4
- Students read the sentences carefully first.
- Play the CD again.
- Students decide if the sentences are true or false and correct the false sentences.
- Students compare answers in pairs.
- Check answers as a class.

5
- Students read the conversation extract and complete it in pairs.
- Play the CD of the whole conversation again. Students listen and check their answers.
- Check answers as a class. Students practise the converstion extract in groups.

6
- Read the Useful language box with the class and help with any vocabulary. Practise as necessary.
- Elicit other examples of each phrase, eg *We need a computer with an internet connection for our talk. Instead of a poster, let's draw a cartoon.*
- Students work in groups of three and plan their talks.

Step 3: Create

7
- Read the three steps with the class to give students a clear idea of what they have to do.
- Monitor while they are working and give help if necessary.

Share information
Students share their information in their groups. They discuss their work and how to improve it. They check for errors.

Create the talk
Each group creates their talk. Encourage them to be creative and try to make the talk as interesting as possible. Remind them to use their own words and to check for errors.

Show and tell
Each group gives their talk. Allow time for the other students to ask questions. If you like, the class can vote for their favourite talk.

Step 4: Evaluate

8
- Look at the evaluation grids with the class.
- Read through the different options and help with any vocabulary as necessary.
- Students complete their self-evaluation. Give help if necessary.

Extra activity

In pairs, students write an interview with a famous person from history. They can practise and act out their interview.

1.48 Audioscript, exercise 3

Sonia: OK, so we decided to do our talk about Sally Ride, the astronaut who was the first American woman in space. We're all looking for information. Shall I check all the facts and write a plan? Then I can write the overview, too.
Edu: We have to participate equally. We can all write a plan. Sonia, you can check the facts and then I can organize the information.
Mario: I can write the overview, find photos and quotes … and look for a good video clip.
Edu: But we're not giving a Powerpoint presentation … We can't show a video clip.
Mario: What about putting the video clip on a DVD? We can use a projector for the photos.
Edu: So we need a DVD player and a projector. I'm not sure. I think that's too much equipment.
Sonia: But we want the talk to be creative and interesting!
Edu: Wait a minute! We don't need lots of equipment to make the talk interesting.
Mario: That's true. We can make a poster with the photos and quotes, and write the overview on the board.
Sonia: I've got an idea. Instead of a video clip, we can write an interview with Sally Ride and act it out. What do you think?
Edu: That's brilliant! And what about writing a quiz? We can divide the class into teams and give them a photocopy of the questions. They listen to the talk and then answer the questions.
Sonia: Yes, I love that idea. We can have a prize for the best team. Do you agree?
Mario: Yes, I think that's a good idea. So our talk includes an interview, a photo with quotes and a fun quiz.
Edu: And we only need the board and some photocopies. We don't need any other equipment!
Mario: OK, so shall we write the plan?

Exercise 3

1 computer, internet connection
2 a poster, the board and photocopies

Exercise 4

1 False
They do participate equally.
2 False
They aren't all happy to use lots of equipment for the talk.
3 True
4 True

Exercise 5

1 need
2 minute
3 true
4 Instead
5 brilliant
6 idea
7 Yes

Step 2: Listen and plan

3 ◉ 1.48 **Listen to Sonia, Mario and Edu doing the task about the items in the box in exercise 2. Answer the questions.**

1 Which two items don't they mention?
2 Which items do they decide to use?

4 Listen again. Are the sentences true or false? Correct the false sentences.

1 They don't participate equally because Sonia does all the work.
2 They are all happy to use lots of different equipment for the talk.
3 They make a poster with photos and some quotes.
4 They decide not to show a video clip of an interview with Sally Ride.

5 Complete the conversation extract with the words in the box. Listen again and check your answers.

minute idea instead true yes
brilliant need

Edu: So we (1) ... a DVD player and a projector? I'm not sure. I think that's too much equipment.

Sonia: But we want the talk to be creative and interesting!

Edu: Wait a (2) ... ! We don't need lots of equipment to make the talk interesting.

Mario: That's (3) ... . We can make a poster with the photos and quotes, and write the overview on the board.

Sonia: I've got an idea. (4) ... of a video clip, we can write an interview with Sally Ride and act it out. What do you think?

Edu: That's (5) ... ! And what about writing a quiz? We can divide the class into teams and give them a photocopy of the questions. They listen to the talk and then answer the questions.

Sonia: Yes, I love that (6) ... . We can have a prize for the best team. Do you agree?

Mario: (7) ..., I think that's a good idea. So our talk includes an interview, a photo with quotes and a fun quiz.

6 Work in groups. Plan your talk. Use the Useful language box to help you.

- Choose a famous person in history to do your talk about.
- Decide how to structure the talk and what equipment you need.
- Decide how to share the work. Make sure everyone contributes.
- Decide when to meet again to share your information.

Step 3: Create

7 Follow the steps to create your talk.

Share information
Read and listen to each other's work. Discuss your work. Check these things.
- Is it in your own words?
- Have you got all the information you need?
- Have you got photos, video clips, etc?
- Is the grammar and vocabulary correct?
- Is the spelling and punctuation correct?

Create the talk
Plan the talk and what information you will include. Decide what equipment you will need. Add your photos and video clips. Then, check the grammar, vocabulary, spelling and punctuation.

Show and tell
- Give your talk to the class.

Step 4: Evaluate

8 Now ask your teacher for the group and individual assessment grids. Then complete the grids.

USEFUL LANGUAGE

What equipment (do we need)?
We need (a DVD player).
That's true.
I've got an idea. Let's (play some music). What do you think?
That's brilliant! / Yes, I love that idea. / OK.
That's boring. / I don't really like that idea.
Instead of (a video clip), let's ...

Unit objectives and key competences

In this unit the student will learn …
- understand, memorize and correctly use vocabulary related to geography, landscape and animals **CLC CMST SCC**
- understand and correctly use comparatives and superlatives and draw parallels to L1 **CLC L2L**
- understand and correctly use countable and uncountable nouns **CLC L2L**
- about safaris in South Africa and compare with animals in their country **CLC CMST CAE SCC**
- about animals by watching a short video **CLC CMST SCC DC**

In this unit the student will learn how to …
- identify specific information in an online news article about a Scottish island **CLC CMST DC CAE**
- look online for information about Scottish islands **CLC CMST DC CAE SIE**
- identify specific information in a dialogue about a project **CLC CMST SCC**
- read a web page about a day as a volunteer, listen to conversations about volunteering and learn how to express preferences **CLC CMST SCC CAE**
- write a geographical description **CLC CMST SIE L2L**
- prepare for and do a listening exam with multiple-choice answers **CLC L2L SIE**

Linguistic contents

Main vocabulary
- Geography and landscape: *canyon, desert, forest*, etc
- Animals: *butterfly, gorilla, owl,* etc

Grammar
- Comparatives and superlatives
- Countable and uncountable nouns

Functional language
- Phrases for expressing preferences

Pronunciation
- /ɪ/ in comparatives and superlatives
- Difficult sounds: /g/ and /dʒ/

Skills

Reading
- Read an online news article about a small Scottish island
- Read a text about safaris in South Africa
- Read a web page about a day as a volunteer
- Read a geographical description

Writing: Interaction and production
- Write a personalized dialogue about expressing preferences
- Write a geographical description in three steps: plan, write, check
- Learn how to order adjectives correctly

Listening
- Listen to a dialogue about a project
- Listen to short conversations about volunteering

Spoken interaction
- Exchange information about natural wonders

Spoken production
- Prepare and act out a dialogue about preferences

Lifelong learning skills

Self-study and self-evaluation

- Study guide:
  Student's Book page 51
- Progress check and self-evaluation:
  Workbook pages 38–39
- Grammar reference and practice:
  Workbook pages 90–91
- Wordlist:
  Workbook pages 151–157

Learning strategies and thinking skills

- Scanning a text when reading

Cultural awareness

- Thula Thula Wildlife Reserve
- Comparing wild animals in South Africa with wild and endangered animals in students' own countries

Cross-curricular contents

- Natural science, endangered animals, safaris in South Africa
- Language and Literature: reading and writing a geographical description
- ICT: searching the internet for information

Key competences

CLC	Competence in linguistic communication
CMST	Competence in mathematics, science and technology
DC	Digital competence
SCC	Social and civic competences
CAE	Cultural awareness and expression
L2L	Learning to learn
SIE	Sense of initiative and entrepreneurship

Evaluation

- Unit 4 End-of-unit test: Basic, Standard and Extra
- CEFR Skills Exam Generator

External exam trainer

- Listening: Multiple-choice answers

Digital material

Pulse Live! Digital Course including:
- Interactive grammar tables
- Audio visual speaking model: Expressing preferences
- Audio visual cultural material: Animals

Student's website

Digital competence

- Web quest: Scottish islands
- Digital competence worksheet: Audioblogs

Reinforcement material

- Basic worksheets, Teacher's Resource File pages 23–28
- Vocabulary and Grammar: Consolidation worksheets, Teacher's Resource File pages 15–16

Extension material

- Fast-finisher activity: Student's Book page 43
- Extra activities: Teacher's Book pages T43, T50
- Vocabulary and Grammar: Extension worksheets, Teacher's Resource File pages 17–18

Teacher's Resource File

- Translation and dictation worksheets pages 5, 15
- Evaluation rubrics pages 1–7
- Key competences worksheets pages 7–8
- Culture and CLIL worksheets pages 13–16
- Culture video worksheets pages 7–8
- Digital competence worksheets pages 7–8
- Macmillan Readers worksheets pages 3–4

THINK ABOUT IT
Which place on Earth would you most like to visit? Why?

Vocabulary and Speaking
Geography and landscape

1 🔊 1.49 Look at the information about seven places. Listen and repeat the words in **blue**.

WHAT ARE THE SEVEN NATURAL WONDERS OF THE WORLD?

THESE ARE THE PLACES OUR READERS CHOSE!

1 THE GRAND CANYON, USA
This **canyon** in the middle of a **desert** is nearly 2 km deep! You can go rafting down the Colorado **River** at the bottom of the **valley**.

2 THE GREAT BARRIER REEF, AUSTRALIA
In the Pacific **Ocean**, near the **coast** of Queensland, this coral **reef** has over 1,500 different kinds of fish!

3 THE AMAZON RAINFOREST, ECUADOR
The world's biggest **forest** is full of plants and animals, which are disappearing as people cut trees down.

4 THE DEAD SEA, JORDAN
This is a **lake** of salty water which you can float in. On the **beach**, there is a special kind of mud which people put on their bodies!

5 THE NIAGARA FALLS, CANADA
At Niagara there are three different **waterfalls**. About 5 million litres of water go through them every second!

6 TABLE MOUNTAIN, SOUTH AFRICA
This **mountain**, which is flat on top, has steep **cliffs** you can climb, and all kinds of wildlife.

7 THE BLUE CAVE, GREECE
Inside this **cave** on the Greek **island** of Kastelorizo the water is a beautiful deep blue.

Exercise 2

land
desert
valley
coast
forest
beach
mountain
cliffs
cave
island

water
ocean
reef
lake
waterfalls

LOOK!

The names of mountains, rivers, etc have a capital letter.
Table Mountain, Everest, the Mississippi

2 Copy and complete the table with the blue words from exercise 1.

land	water
canyon	river

LOOK!

Adjectives to describe places
beautiful   dangerous   amazing   unusual
boring   interesting

---

3 Which place in the list do you most / least want to visit?

I'd love to visit the Dead Sea because it's amazing.
I don't want to visit the Niagara Falls because …

👆 EXPRESS YOURSELF

4 Write a list of natural wonders in your country.

1 The Tabernas Desert

5 Work in pairs. Talk about your list of natural wonders.

💬 *Montserrat is more beautiful than the Tabernas Desert.*
💬 *No, I don't agree. I think …*

Vocabulary and Speaking
Geography and landscape

Warmer

Write *Everest, Amazon, Sahara* on the board with the letters in the wrong order: *reveste, zomana, hasaar*. Tell students that one of these is a well-known desert, one an enormous river and one a very high mountain. Students work in pairs and write the correct spelling for each word.

Think about it

Students work in pairs and discuss the questions. Get feedback from the whole class.

1 🔘 1.49
- Students read the text.
- Play the CD. Students repeat the words in blue chorally and individually.
- Make sure they pronounce *island* /ˈaɪlənd/ correctly and point out that the *s* is silent.

Language note

In two-syllable nouns, the stress usually falls on the first syllable, eg *canyon, desert, river, valley, ocean, forest, mountain, island.*

Look!

Point out that the names of geographical features like mountains, rivers, oceans, deserts, etc have a capital letter in English.

2
- Students copy the table into their notebooks.
- Explain the task. Students sort the words in blue from exercise 1 into two columns.
- They compare answers in pairs.
- Check answers as a class.

Culture note

The surface of the Dead Sea is 438 metres below sea level. With 33.7% salinity, it is one of the saltiest lakes in the world. Table Mountain, which overlooks the city of Cape Town, is just 1,084 metres high but the climb up from the city is steep and the paths are narrow. Fortunately, there is also a cable car to take you to the top!

Look!

- Focus students on the list of adjectives to describe places and check that they understand them.

3
- Students read the question carefully.
- They work individually and write their answers.
- Students compare answers in pairs.
- Listen to their ideas as a class.

👆 **EXPRESS YOURSELF**

4
- Explain the task. Point out that the Tabernas Desert is one example of a natural wonder. Others might include mountains, lakes, caves, etc.
- They work individually and write their lists.
- Monitor while they are writing and give help if necessary.

5
- Students work in pairs and talk about their list of natural wonders.
- Listen to their ideas as a class.

Vocabulary extension: Workbook page 105 ▶▶

Reading

Text type: An online news article

Recommended web links

www.isleofmuck.com/

www.visitscotland.com

Warmer

Write the word *island* on the board. Students work in pairs and write the names of as many islands as possible in two minutes. Listen to their ideas as a class and make a list on the board. Ask what is good about living on an island and what is not so good.

1 • Students look at the pictures.
- They guess what country the island is in (*Scotland*).
- Ask students to give reasons for their answers, eg *The dancers are wearing kilts*.
- Highlight the information in the Did you know? box.

2 [1.50]
- This exercise gives students practice in listening for key information.
- Students read the notes. They copy them into their notebooks.
- Check that they understand *facilities* (things in a place that people can use such as shops, schools, transport, entertainment).
- Play the CD. Students listen and follow the text in their books.
- They complete the notes.
- Students compare answers in pairs.
- Check answers as a class.

Word check

Make sure students understand the words. Ask them to translate them into their language.

3 • Explain the task.
- Students look at the positive and negative aspects already listed. Check that they understand *wildlife* (animals and birds).
- They read the text again and add two more positive things and two more negative things to the lists.
- Students compare answers in pairs.
- Check answers as a class. Note that there are several possible answers.

4 • Students work individually and write three differences between their town or city and the island in the article.
- Students compare answers in pairs.
- Listen to their ideas as a class.

Finished?

Ask fast finishers to read the article and the two comments again and decide which comment they agree with and why.

Extra activity

Focus on some of the vocabulary in the text, eg *attractions, seabirds, attend*. Make sure that students understand the words and that they can pronounce them correctly.

Web quest

Students find out information about another Scottish island. Highlight the Web quest tip.

1 • Students work in pairs and choose one of the Scottish islands.
2 • Ask students to open an internet web browser such as Internet Explorer. Students open a search engine (eg Google) and type in the subject of their search.
- Students find as much information as they can.
- They make notes about: the climate, the population, the history, the typical food and getting to the island.
3 • They present their findings to the class.

Family wanted to live on an island

The owners of a small Scottish island are looking for a new family to live there. The Isle of Muck, which is only 4 km long, is one of the smallest islands in Scotland. It's only got 16 houses and a population of 30 people!

Life on the island is quieter than in most places. There aren't many facilities: there's no post office on the island and there's only one shop. As for entertainment, there's one café, but it isn't open in the evenings! Technology lovers might have a problem because there isn't any electricity between 11am and 5pm. Its location also means it isn't easy to use your mobile phone.

The Isle of Muck has other attractions, however. It's the most beautiful place you can imagine, with white sandy beaches and clear sea. There's lots of wildlife, including seabirds and dolphins. It's also possibly the friendliest and safest place in the world. The last crime happened here in the 1960s, and nobody locks their doors!

The residents of Muck hope that the chosen family will play an active part in island life. The most important thing, however, is that they have children, so that they can attend the island's primary school. It's only got eight pupils at the moment and they'd like it to be bigger!

COMMENTS:

I can't think of anything worse than living on a small island. Imagine seeing the same people all the time! And what do they do there in the evenings?
cityboy

It's true that islands are more boring than cities, but city people aren't as friendly as island people. Island life is also healthier than city life!
Lara17

DID YOU KNOW?
There are 787 islands in Scotland.

Word check
owner facilities location sandy wildlife dolphin lock

Reading
An online news article

Exercise 1

Scotland

1 Look at the pictures. Can you guess what country this island is in?

Exercise 2

1 the Isle of Muck
2 Scotland
3 4 km long
4 30
5 café

2  **1.50** Read and listen to the article. Then copy and complete the notes.

Name of island: (1) ...
Country: (2) ...
Size: (3) ...
Number of people: (4) ...
Facilities: shop, (5) ...,
school

3 Write two positive things and two negative things about living on the Isle of Muck.

Positive ☺	Negative ☹
1 beautiful place	5 not many facilities
2 lots of wildlife	6 not much entertainment
3 ...	7 ...
4 ...	8 ...

4 Compare your town or city with the Isle of Muck. Write three differences.

There are a lot of shops in my town.

FINISHED?

Read the article and the comments again. Which comment do you agree with? Why?

I agree with cityboy because ...

Exercise 3

Possible answers

Positive

white sandy beaches
clear sea
friendly
safe
no crime

Negative

no post office
only one shop
café closed in the evenings
no electricity between 11am and 5pm
not easy to use a mobile phone

WEB QUEST

Find out information about another Scottish island.

1 Decision making: in pairs, choose one of these Scottish islands.
 • Orkney • Skye • Mull • Lewis
2 Make notes about: the climate, the population, the history, the typical food and getting to the island.
3 Share your knowledge with the rest of the class.

Web Quest tip!

You can use an online encyclopaedia to find information about most things.

Grammar Digital

Comparatives and superlatives

affirmative	comparative	superlative
small	smaller	the smallest
big	bigger	the biggest
friendly	friendlier	the friendliest
interesting	more interesting	the most interesting
good	better	the best
bad	worse	the worst

1 Study the table. Then copy and complete the sentences.

a) It's … (beautiful) place you can imagine.
b) Island life is … (healthy) than city life.

2 Which sentence in exercise 1 compares …

one thing with another thing?
one thing with many other things?

3 Write sentences using the comparative form of the adjectives in brackets.

the Mediterranean / the Atlantic (cold)
The Atlantic is colder than the Mediterranean.

1 Spain / Scotland (hot)
2 cities / villages (busy)
3 swimming / running (enjoyable)
4 winter / summer (bad)
5 Iceland / Egypt (cold)
6 the Mississippi / the Thames (long)

> **LOOK!**
>
> We also use *as … as* + adjective to compare things.
> Scotland is **as beautiful as** England. (they are equally beautiful)
> Islands aren't **as dirty as** cities. (cities are dirtier)

4 Rewrite the sentences from exercise 3 in your notebook using *isn't / aren't as … as.*

The Mediterranean isn't as cold as the Atlantic.

 ANALYSE

In English, we use *than* to compare two things.
The Atlantic is colder **than** the Mediterranean.
Reading is more interesting **than** watching TV.
How do you compare two things in your language?

5 Order the words to make superlative sentences.

wettest / is / England / place / the / in / The Lake District .
The Lake District is the wettest place in England.

1 city / the / Tokyo / world / biggest / the / in / is .
2 in / popular / most / is / Sydney / the / beach / Bondi Beach .
3 the / the Maldives / country / flattest / the / is / world / in .
4 in / lake / famous / most / the / Loch Ness / Scotland / is .
5 country / the / smallest / world / is / Vatican City / in / the .

6 Compete the questions with the superlative form of the adjectives in brackets. Then answer the questions about your country.

WHAT IS …

(1) … (high) mountain?
(2) … (long) river?
(3) … (big) lake?
(4) … (beautiful) beach?
(5) … (near) island?
(6) … (expensive) city?

 1.51–1.52 Pronunciation lab: /ə/ in comparatives and superlatives, page 124

  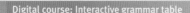

Grammar

Comparatives and superlatives

Lesson objectives

In this lesson students will:
- learn / revise comparatives and superlatives
- write about geographical features in their country

Warmer

Write the sentence *Muck is the safest place in the world* on the board with the words in the wrong order: *safest world the in place Muck the i*s. Students work in pairs and write the sentence in the correct order.

1 • Students work individually. They study the table and copy and complete the sentences using comparative and superlative forms. Encourage students to look back at the text in the previous lesson to help them.
  • They compare answers in pairs.
  • Check answers as a class.
  • Point out that two-syllable adjectives ending in *-y* change to *-ier* in the comparative form and *-iest* in the superlative form.
  • Highlight the use of *more* and *the most* with long adjectives (more than two syllables). Emphasize that we always use *the* with the superlative form.
  • Highlight the irregular forms of *good* and *bad*.

Language note

Two-syllable adjectives usually form their comparative forms by adding *-er* and their superlative forms by adding *-est*. There are exceptions to this rule, however. In particular, two-syllable adjectives ending in *-ful* form their comparatives and superlatives like long adjectives, eg *careful, more careful, most careful*.

2 • Students work individually and answer the questions.
  • They compare answers in pairs.
  • Check answers as a class.

3 • Read the example sentence aloud to the class.
  • Students work individually and complete the sentences using the comparative form of the adjectives in brackets.
  • They compare answers in pairs.
  • Check answers as a class. Point out that with short adjectives ending in vowel + consonant, eg *hot*, the consonant is doubled in the comparative and superlative forms, eg *hotter, the hottest*.

Look!

Highlight the use of *as ... as* to compare things that are equal and *not as ... as* to show that something has less of a positive or negative quality than something else. Read the two example sentences aloud to the class.

4 • Students read the example sentence from exercise 3 again and compare it with the *not as ... as* example sentence in exercise 4.
  • Students work individually and complete the sentences using *isn't / aren't as ... as.*
  • They compare answers in pairs.
  • Check answers as a class.

Analyse

Students read the information. Ask them how they compare two things in their language.

5 • Students look at the picture. Ask students to guess the place.
  • They read the example sentence. Elicit that the photo shows the Lake District in England.
  • Students work individually and order the words to make superlative sentences.
  • They compare answers in pairs.
  • Check answers as a class.

6 • Students work individually to write the questions and answer them.
  • They compare answers in pairs.
  • Check answers as a class.

Pronunciation lab: /ə/ in comparatives and superlatives, page 124

Digital course: Interactive grammar table

Study guide: page 51

Vocabulary and Listening
Animals

Lesson objectives

In this lesson students will:
- learn the words for different animals
- listen for specific information

Warmer

Write *animal* on the board. Students work in pairs and make a list of all the animal words they know in English in two minutes. Listen to their ideas as a class and make two lists on the board – domestic and wild animals.

1 🔘 2.02

- Check students understand *endangered species* (a type of animal that may soon disappear from the world).
- Play the CD. Students repeat the words chorally and individually. Make sure they pronounce *rhinoceros* /raɪˈnɒsərəs/, *giraffe* /dʒəˈrɑːf/ and *penguin* /ˈpengwɪn/ correctly and with the correct word stress.
- Check the answer to the question as a class.

2 🔘 2.03

- Students copy and complete the descriptions with the animal words from exercise 1.
- They compare answers in pairs.
- Play the CD. Students listen and check their answers.

Language note

We sometimes use the definite article with the names of animals to refer to the species, eg *The tiger lives in India.* The plural form can also be used with the same meaning, eg *Tigers live in India.*

3
- Ask students to translate the headings into their language.
- Point out that *mammal*, *reptile* and *insect* are all stressed on the first syllable.
- Students copy the table into their notebooks.

4
- Students work individually and write the animal words from exercise 1 in the correct column in the table.
- They compare answers in pairs.
- Check answers as a class.

5 🔘 2.04

- Explain the task. Make sure students understand that the first time they listen they only have to answer this one question.
- Play the CD. Students listen and write the answer in their notebooks.
- They compare answers in pairs.
- Check the answer as a class.

6
- Students read the five questions carefully first.
- Play the CD. Students write the answers in their notebooks.
- Check progress and if necessary, play the CD again.
- Students compare answers in pairs.
- Check answers as a class.

🔘 2.04 Audioscript, exercise 5

Chris: Which endangered animal are you going to do your project on?
Lucy: Whales, I think. I found this article about them on the internet and they're really amazing animals, you know.
Chris: What's so amazing about them?
Lucy: Well, first of all, they're really intelligent. For one thing, they've got their own language.
Chris: What do you mean? Fish can't talk!
Lucy: They aren't fish! Honestly, Chris, don't you listen to anything in biology? They're mammals!
Chris: OK, if you say so!
Lucy: Anyway, whales make sounds under the ocean in order to communicate with other whales.
Chris: Really? I didn't know that!
Lucy: Yes, and they're very friendly animals too. When people go whale watching, the whales swim near the boats and look at the people!
Chris: Wow! I'd love to see a real whale.
Lucy: Me too. But soon there might not be any.
Chris: Why not? Whale hunting isn't allowed any more, is it?
Lucy: No, but they still do it in some countries. Another problem is ships.
Chris: Ships?
Lucy: Yes, sometimes ships hit whales and kill them by mistake.
Chris: That's terrible!
Lucy: I know. Anyway, what are you doing your project on?
Chris: Er, I haven't decided yet. Maybe snakes.
Lucy: Snakes? They aren't an endangered species, are they?
Chris: No, but I know a lot about them. My brother's got a pet snake, you see.
Lucy: You're joking! Yuk!

TOP TEN ENDANGERED SPECIES

These animals are in danger! Find out why below.

7 People hunt the ... for its horn, which is very valuable.

1 Hotter summers and colder winters are making it difficult for this Monarch ... to survive.

4 Tourists are disturbing the leatherback sea ..., which lays its eggs on beaches.

8 In some parts of the world the ... can't find enough fish to eat.

2 People are destroying the forest where the mountain ... lives.

5 It's illegal, but people still hunt the ... for its skin.

9 People are building houses and roads in areas where the ... lives.

3 Large areas of ice where the ... hunts for food are melting.

6 People in some countries eat ... meat.

10 Hunters kill this animal because ... tusks are worth a lot of money.

Exercise 4

mammal
elephant
whale
rhinoceros
polar bear
giraffe
tiger

reptile
crocodile
snake
turtle

bird
owl
penguin

insect
butterfly
bee

Vocabulary and Listening
Animals

Exercise 1

owl
snake
giraffe
bee

1 🔊 2.02 Listen and repeat the animals. Which four animals do you think aren't endangered species?

> gorilla elephant crocodile owl whale
> rhinoceros polar bear snake turtle butterfly
> giraffe penguin tiger bee

2 🔊 2.03 Copy and complete the descriptions with words from the box. Then listen and check.

3 Look at the headings in the table. How do you say the words in your language?

mammal	reptile	bird	insect
gorilla			

4 Copy and complete the table with the animals in exercise 1.

5 🔊 2.04 Listen to Chris and Lucy talking about a project they have to do. What mistake does Chris make?

6 Listen again and answer the questions.

1 Why does Lucy think whales are intelligent?
2 What do whales do when people watch them from boats?
3 What does Chris say people aren't allowed to do any more?
4 Why are ships dangerous to whales?
5 Which animals does Chris want to write about?

Exercise 2

1 butterfly
2 gorilla
3 polar bear
4 turtle
5 tiger
6 whale
7 rhinoceros
8 penguin
9 crocodile
10 elephant

Exercise 5

He thinks whales are fish.

Exercise 6

1 They've got their own language.
2 They swim near the boats and look at the people.
3 Hunt whales.
4 They hit them and kill them by mistake.
5 Snakes.

Cultural awareness
Safaris in South Africa

Fact box

When people visit South Africa, most of them hope to see some wild animals. The most popular ones are the elephant, the rhinoceros, the lion, the buffalo and the leopard.

THULA THULA WILDLIFE RESERVE

ABOUT THULA THULA

Thula Thula is a private wildlife reserve and hotel. Thula Thula means 'peace' in Zulu, the language of a famous South African tribe. Thula Thula is in Kwazulu Natal province in South Africa. This is where the Zulu tribe comes from.

WILDLIFE

The area is home to hundreds of species of animals, including rhinoceros, leopards, crocodiles and giraffes.

RESCUED ANIMALS

In 1999, the owner of Thula Thula, Lawrence Anthony, rescued a herd of seven elephants and brought them to his wildlife reserve. Since then, the family has grown to 25 elephants! The story of his experiences with the elephants is the subject of his book, *The Elephant Whisperer*.

The owners of Thula Thula adopted Thabo, a baby rhino, in 2009 when he was just a few days old. He now lives on the wildlife reserve.

ACCOMMODATION

Guests stay in luxury tents with beds and showers. There are some outdoor showers too if you don't mind monkeys watching you from the trees!

MEALS

A lot of guests say the food is the best thing at Thula Thula! Don't forget to try a traditional African 'braai' (barbecue).

ACTIVITIES

Local guides, who have a lot of knowledge about the area, take groups of guests on safaris. You can also go on organized walks and learn about unusual plants that only grow in South Africa.

WHEN TO VISIT

Thula Thula is open all year. In winter (April–August) the temperature is usually warm in the day and cool at night. In summer (September–March) the days are hot and the nights are warm.

Word check

wildlife reserve | rescue | herd | adopt

Exercise 1

gnu
giraffes
zebra
antelope
rhinoceros
elephants

Exercise 2

rhinoceros
leopards
crocodiles
giraffes
elephants
monkeys

Exercise 3

1 a
2 a
3 a
4 b
5 b

1 Look at the pictures. Which animals can you name?

2 2.05 Read and listen. Which animals live at Thula Thula?

3 Read the text again and choose the correct answers.

1 'Thula Thula' is …
   a) a Zulu word. **b)** a South African tribe
2 Lawrence Anthony wrote a book about …
   a) elephants. **b)** his wildlife reserve.

3 A lot of guests …
   a) like the food. **b)** don't like the food.
4 Guests can observe wild animals …
   a) on their own. **b)** with other people.
5 The hottest time of the year at Thula Thula is …
   a) the winter. **b)** the summer.

CULTURAL COMPARISON

4 Answer the questions.

1 Think of three kinds of wild animals in your country.
2 Where do they live and are they endangered?

 Culture video: Animals

Cultural awareness
Safaris in South Africa

CULTURAL COMPARISON

4 • Students read the two questions and make a note of their answers.
   • They work in pairs and discuss their answers.
   • Listen to their answers as a class.

Culture video: Animals ❯❯

Lesson objectives

In this lesson students will:
• read about safaris in South Africa
• talk about wildlife in their country

Warmer

Draw a map of Africa on the board. Ask students to tell you the name of the country at the bottom of the continent (South Africa). Highlight the Fact box and the pronunciation of *buffalo* /ˈbʌfələʊ/ and *leopard* /ˈlepəd/. Ask students what other information they know about South Africa.

---

1 • Students look at the pictures.
   • They use the animal words from the Fact box and from exercise 1 of the previous lesson to identify as many of the animals in the pictures as possible. Give help with vocabulary (*gnu, zebra, antelope*) if necessary.

2 🔘 2.05
   • Explain the task.
   • Students listen to the CD and follow the text in their books.
   • They write the answer to the question in their notebooks.
   • They compare answers in pairs.
   • Check the answer to the question as a class and make sure students understand *monkey*.

3 • Students read the questions and the different possible answers carefully first.
   • They read the text again and choose the correct answers.
   • They compare answers in pairs.
   • Check answers as a class.

Word check

Make sure students understand the words. Ask them to translate them into their language.

Grammar

a / an, some, any

Warmer

Write *animal, tent, guests* on the board. Then write the indefinite article *a* to the left of the words on the board. Ask students which of the three words we can use *a* with. Elicit that it is *tent*. Ask which word can go before *animal*. Elicit the other indefinite article form *an*. Check that students understand why we say *an animal* (because *animal* begins with a vowel sound). Ask why we cannot use *a* with *guests*. Elicit that it is because *guests* is plural.

1
- Students study the example sentences in the tables carefully.
- They copy and complete the rules for *some* and *any*.
- They compare answers in pairs.
- Check answers as a class.

2
- Complete the first sentence with the class as an example to demonstrate the task (*some*).
- Students work individually to choose the correct words to fill the gaps.
- They compare answers in pairs.
- Check answers as a class.

much, many, a lot

3
- Students read the example sentences in the table carefully.
- They choose the correct words to complete the rules.
- They compare answers in pairs.
- Check answers as a class.

Language note

We very rarely use *many* and *much* in affirmative sentences. There are some examples, such as *Many people say …* or *Much of the time …* but the best advice for students is to use *a lot of* instead of *many* and *much* in affirmative sentences.

4
- Students look at the picture.
- Explain the task. The sentences contain factual errors (see the picture).
- Students work individually to correct the sentences.
- They compare answers in pairs.
- Check answers as a class.

CLIL Grammar in context: Natural science

5
- This activity gives students more practice in comparatives and superlatives and in using *a / an*, *some*, *any*, *a lot of*, *many* and *much*.
- Students read the information about four different vertebrates.
- They work individually to choose the correct words.
- They compare answers in pairs.

6 2.06
- Play the CD. Students listen and check their answers to exercise 6. Make sure students understand *actually* as it may be a false friend. In English *actually* means *in fact*.

CLIL task

Students use the internet to do the task.

Pronunciation lab: Difficult sounds: /g/ and /dʒ/, page 125

Digital course: Interactive grammar table ❯❯

Study guide: page 51 ❯❯

Grammar

a / an, some, any

1 Study the table and copy and complete the rules.

countable nouns
He wrote **a** book. That's **an** elephant!
It's home to **some** rescued animals.
I haven't got **a** camera.
There aren't **any** lions.
Is that **a** crocodile? Are there **any** giraffes?

uncountable nouns
Try **some** traditional African food.
There wasn't **any** time to go on a safari.
Did you see **any** wildlife?

a) In affirmative sentences, we use ... with plural countable nouns and uncountable nouns.

b) In negative sentences and questions, we use ... with plural countable nouns and uncountable nouns.

2 Copy and complete the sentences with *a / an, some* or *any*.

1 I'd like ... information please.
2 Is there ... airport near the wildlife reserve?
3 Shall I bring ... camera?
4 Will I see ... wild animals?
5 Do I need ... warm clothes?

much, many, a lot of

3 Study the table. Then choose the correct words to complete rules a–c.

countable nouns
There are **a lot of** things to do.
We didn't see **many** wild animals.
How **many** endangered species live there?

uncountable nouns
We had **a lot of** fun on holiday.
There isn't **much** water in the river.
How **much** time will we have?

a) In affirmative sentences, we use **much / a lot of** with plural countable nouns and uncountable nouns.

b) In negative sentences and questions, we use **many / much** with plural countable nouns.

c) In negative sentences and questions, we use **a lot of / much** with uncountable nouns.

4 Look at the picture. Then correct the sentences. Use *a lot of, many* and *much*.

She hasn't got many clothes.
She has got a lot of clothes.

1 She hasn't got much sun cream.
2 She's got a lot of mosquito bites.
3 There's a lot of space in the room.
4 There aren't any mosquitoes.

CLIL Grammar in context: Natural science

5 Read the text about four different vertebrates and choose the correct answers.

What is a vertebrate? It's (1) **a / an** animal with a backbone. Read about these four different types of vertebrates.

1 Dolphin: this animal looks like (2) **the / a** fish, but it is actually (3) **a / an** mammal.
2 Penguin: this animal (4) **doesn't have any / has** feathers and it spends (5) **much / a lot of** time in water.
3 Human being: although this animal doesn't have (6) **much / many** hair on its body, it is (7) **any / a** mammal. Scientists believe it is the (8) **more / most** intelligent animal on Earth!
4 Crocodile: this reptile is one of the (9) **older / oldest** animals on Earth. It appeared on this planet as early (10) **than / as** the dinosaurs, more than 200 million years ago!

6 2.06 Listen and check your answers.

CLIL TASK

Go online. Find the names of four more vertebrates.

2.07–2.08 Pronunciation lab: Difficult sounds: /g/ and /dʒ/, page 125

A day as a volunteer

Volunteering is a great way to help the local community, learn new skills and make new friends.

HAVE FUN AND DO SOMETHING USEFUL THIS WEEKEND!

Are you aged 14–16? We need you for these great volunteer days!

WORK WITH WILDLIFE
Find out what it's like to work in a zoo! You can help the zookeepers for a day. Duties include feeding some of the animals or cleaning the penguin pool. More activities available!
Location: Chester Zoo

BE A FRIEND TO A BLIND TEENAGER
Accompany a blind teenager on holiday in London and let him or her see the sights through your eyes.
Location: London

CLEAN A BEACH!
Join one of our 'green' teams at your local beach on Saturday and help to pick up litter.
Location: all over the UK

HELP SOME INSECTS
Bees and butterflies are disappearing from the countryside. Plant flowers that will help to bring them back!
Location: Dartmoor National Park

🔍 **Search the website to find out more about voluntary work in your area.**

Step 1: Read

 Exercise 1

1 Be a friend to a blind teenager
2 Clean a beach! Help some insects
3 Work with wildlife

1 **Read the web page and answer the questions.**

Which activity or activities lets you …
1 help another person?
2 do something positive for the environment?
3 care for animals?

2 **Which activity do you think sounds the most interesting? Why?**

 SKILLS BUILDER

Reading: Scanning a text
When reading a web page, you don't need to read all of the information. Learn how to scan a text, in other words, to read a text quickly to find out what the main ideas are. This will save you a lot of time.

Step 2: Listen

3 🔊 **2.09** **Listen to three short conversations. Which of the activities from the web page are the teenagers doing?**

4 **Listen again and answer the questions.**

Conversation 1
1 What does the boy want to do?
2 What does he see?
Conversation 2
3 Where will the girl and boy get off the bus?
4 What will they do there?
Conversation 3
5 What food is the boy giving the giraffes?
6 Where are the people going next?

Exercise 3

1 Clean a beach!
2 Be a friend to a blind teenager
3 Work with wildlife

Exercise 4

1 Have a break.
2 Some cans.
3 Oxford Street.
4 Go to a café.
5 Some carrots.
6 The elephant house.

Integrated skills

A day as a volunteer

Lesson objectives

In this lesson students will:
- work on all four skills
- read a web page
- listen to three short conversations
- write a personalized dialogue
- act out their dialogue

Warmer

Write the word *wildlife* on the board. Ask students to discuss in pairs or small groups what they can do to help wildlife in their country and around the world. Listen to their ideas as a class.

Step 1: Read

1
- Highlight Lucy's speech bubble.
- Students read the questions carefully first.
- They read the text and find the answers.
- Students compare answers in pairs.
- Check answers as a class.

2
- Explain the task.
- Students work individually and think about their answers. They write notes in their notebooks.
- They compare answers in pairs.
- Listen to their ideas as a class.

Skills builder

Reading: Scanning a text
Ask students to read the information in the Skills builder box. Highlight the importance of learning how to scan a text when reading a web page.

Step 2: Listen

3 2.09
- Explain the task.
- Play the CD. Students listen and match conversations 1–3 with the activities from the web page.
- Students compare answers in pairs.
- Check answers as a class.

4
- Students read all the questions carefully first.
- Play the CD again.
- Check progress. If necessary, play the recording again.
- Students compare answers in pairs.
- Check answers as a class.

2.09 Audioscript, exercise 3

Conversation 1
Boy 1: The sand looks much cleaner now! Can we have a break? It's hot!
Girl 1: We can soon, but there's still plenty of rubbish to pick up!
Boy 1: Oh yeah, there are some cans over there … Let's go and get them. Bring the rubbish bag over here, Tina!

Conversation 2
Girl 2: We're getting on the bus now, John. Careful! That's it. One to Oxford Street, please.
Boy 2: And one ticket to Oxford Street for me too, please.
Driver: There you go.
Girl 2: Thanks. Let's sit here.
Boy 2: What are we going to do now?
Girl 2: I'm going to take you to my favourite café. It's got the best sandwiches in London! Are you hungry?
Boy 2: Yes!

Conversation 3
Woman: Right, Anthony – here's the food for the giraffes. You can feed it to them by hand if you like.
Boy 3: OK. Like this?
Woman: Yes. Don't worry – they're very friendly. They're enjoying those carrots! Right, in a minute we're going to go over to the elephant house. The elephants like playing with water, so you might get a bit wet!
Boy 3: Sounds fun!
Woman: Yes, it is! Here, I've got this waterproof jacket for you.
Boy 3: Great. Thanks.

Integrated skills – continued
Expressing preferences

5 🔘 2.10
- Students read the dialogue first.
- Play the CD. Students listen and choose the correct words.
- They compare answers in pairs.
- Check answers as a class.

6
- Play the CD again, pausing after each question or statement and each response for students to repeat as a class.
- Note the main stress and the rising intonation in the *yes / no* questions: *Could I feed the animals? Could you please fill in this form?*
- Ask students to repeat the dialogue several times both chorally and individually with the correct stress and intonation.
- Students practise the dialogue in pairs. Then swap roles and practise the dialogue again.

Look!

Point out that *I'd rather* and *I'd prefer to* mean the same thing. Highlight the difference in form with *to* following *prefer*.

Step 3: Write

7
- Students work individually.
- They choose one of the activities.
- They make a list of reasons why it is better than the other activities.
- Monitor while they are writing and give help if necessary.

8
- Ask students to look at the Communication kit: Expressing preferences. Encourage them to use these expressions when writing their dialogue.
- Students work individually and write their dialogue, using the dialogue in the book as a model.
- Monitor while they are writing and give help if necessary.

Step 4: Communicate

9
- Students practise their dialogues in pairs.
- For extra practice, they swap roles in both dialogues.
- Choose some pairs to act out their dialogue for the class.

10
- Students raise their hand if another pair has the same activity as the activity they have chosen. This will encourage them to listen carefully to their classmates.

Integrated skills: Workbook page 114

UNIT 4

EXPRESSING PREFERENCES

Watch!

Hello there, how can I help?	Hello, I'd like to sign up for the volunteer day.
Great! Do you want to help in the zoo (1) **gift shop / ticket hall**?	That's a (2) **nice / great** idea, but I want to help wildlife. I'd rather do something with the animals.
OK. How about cleaning the penguin pool?	Well, I (3) **do / don't** mind cleaning, but I don't really like water! Could I feed the animals?
Yes, maybe that's a better idea for you. You can help one of the zookeepers feed the (4) **elephants / giraffes**.	Thanks! That sounds more interesting than the other (5) **tasks / activities**.
No problem!	Do you need any details from me?
Yes, could you please fill in this form?	OK!

Exercise 5
1 gift shop
2 nice
3 don't
4 elephants
5 activities

5 🔊 2.10 Listen to the dialogue and choose the correct answers for 1–5.

6 Listen again and repeat. Practise your intonation.

LOOK!
We use *I'd rather* + infinitive.
I'd rather help animals.
We use *I'd prefer* + to + infinitive.
I'd prefer to help a person.

Step 3: Write

7 Look again at the web page on page 48. Which volunteer day activity is best for you? Make a list of reasons why one activity is better than the others.

I prefer to work with people.
I like flowers and plants, but I'm scared of insects.

8 Write a dialogue to sign up for a volunteer day activity. Use the dialogue in exercise 5 to help you.

Step 4: Communicate

9 Work in pairs. Take turns to practise your dialogues.

💬 *Hello. I'd like to sign up for the volunteer day.*
💬 *Great! Do you want to work with people?*

10 Act your dialogue for the class.

COMMUNICATION KIT

Expressing preferences

I'd like to …
It's a nice idea but …
I'd rather … / I'd prefer to …
I don't mind …
Maybe … is a better idea.
That is / sounds more interesting / fun / than …

My country

Greece is a small country in southern Europe. It has a population of about 10 million. Many tourists visit Greece every year because of its warm climate, beautiful scenery and friendly people.

1 ...

Greece has long dry summers and short winters. July and August are the hottest months of the year, but temperatures are warm from May to October.

2 ...

Greece has hundreds of islands, which have beautiful sandy beaches and clear blue sea. However, a lot of people don't know that Greece also has many forests and mountains with a lot of wildlife.

3 ...

Athens, the capital of Greece, is famous for its amazing ancient monuments, but the islands are the best place to go if you just want to relax. In winter, you can go walking, climbing and even skiing on Mount Olympus, which according to legend was the home of the gods!

Eleni, 14

Writing
A geographical description

Exercise 1

1 Climate
2 Landscape
3 Places to visit

1 🎵 2.11 Read and listen to the description. Match the subheadings with paragraphs 1–3.

> Landscape   Places to visit   Climate

2 Read the Writing focus. Find four examples of two adjectives together in the description.

Exercise 2

long dry
beautiful sandy
clear blue
amazing ancient

WRITING FOCUS
Order of adjectives

When we use two or more adjectives together, we use the following order:
opinion size age shape colour origin material + noun
a picturesque little village (opinion, size)
a long sandy beach (shape, material)

3 Rewrite the sentences with the adjectives in brackets in the correct places.

1 There is a cave that you can only reach by boat. (white, big)
2 There aren't many hotels. (ugly, modern)
3 You can explore the streets. (narrow, old)
4 It is famous for its restaurants, where you can eat fish. (fresh, delicious)

Writing task
Write a description of your country.

Plan Use the paragraph subheadings from exercise 1. Make notes about what you will include under each subheading.

Write Write your description. Use your notes and the description in exercise 1 to help you.

Check Check your writing.

- ✔ layout – paragraphs with subheadings
- ✔ order of adjectives

Exercise 3

1 There is a big white cave that you can only reach by boat.
2 There aren't many ugly modern hotels.
3 You can explore the narrow old streets.
4 It is famous for its restaurants where you can eat delicious fresh fish.

 Build your confidence: Writing reference and practice. Workbook page 126 »

Writing
A geographical description

Lesson objectives

In this lesson students will:
* read a description
* study adjectival order
* write a description of their country

Warmer

Write *Greece* on the board. Put students into pairs and ask them to discuss what they know about this country. Listen to their ideas as a class, eg *It's got a lot of islands. There are a lot of classical buildings. The capital city is Athens.*

1 🔊 2.11
* Explain the task. Check students understand *landscape* (geographical appearance of a place).
* Play the CD.
* Students listen and follow the text in their books.
* They match the subheadings with the paragraphs.
* Students compare answers in pairs.
* Check answers as a class.

2 • Make sure students understand the task. They should find four places where there are two adjectives together.
* Students complete the task individually.
* They compare answers in pairs.
* Check answers as a class.
* Read aloud to the class the information in the Writing focus box. Tells students that we usually only use two or three adjectives in a row but, in theory, it is possible to use more.
* Point out that this order is very useful as a reference when they are writing a description.

3 • Students work individually to complete the exercise.
* They compare answers in pairs.
* Check answers as a class.

Extra activity

For further practice of adjectival order, write these phrases on the board: *a (little, beautiful) town; an (old, interesting) picture; a (brown, leather, big) suitcase.* Students write the adjectives in the correct order. Check answers as a class (*a beautiful little town; an interesting old picture; a big brown leather suitcase*).

Writing task

The aim of this activity is for students to write a short description that includes the correct use of paragraphs with subheadings and adjectival order. Ask the students to follow the stages in the Student's Book. At the Check stage, ask them to swap notebooks and check each other's writing.

> Writing reference and practice: Workbook page 126 ▷▷

Study guide
Grammar, Vocabulary and Speaking

Tell the students the Study guide is an important page which provides a useful reference for the main language of the unit: the grammar, the vocabulary and the functional language from the Integrated skills pages. Explain that they should refer to this page when studying for a test or exam.

Grammar
- Tell the students to look at the examples of comparative and superlative adjectives. Make sure they understand the spelling rules.
- Then tell students to look at the example sentences of *a / an, some, any, much, many* and *a lot of*. Ensure they understand when to use each item correctly with countable or uncountable nouns. Get students to translate into their own language if necessary.
- Refer students to the Grammar reference on pages 90–91 of the Workbook for further revision.

Vocabulary
- Tell students to look at the list of vocabulary and check understanding.
- Refer students to the Wordlist on page 151 of the Workbook where they can look up any words they can't remember.

Speaking
- Check that students understand the phrases to use when expressing preferences.
- Tell students to act out a conversation between two people expressing preferences about a place to visit at the weekend.

Additional material
Workbook
- Progress check page 38
- Self-evaluation page 39
- Grammar reference and practice pages 90–91
- Vocabulary extension page 105
- Integrated skills page 114
- Writing reference page 126–127

Teacher's Resource File
- Basics section pages 23–28
- Vocabulary and grammar consolidation pages 15–18
- Translation and dictation pages 5, 15
- Evaluation rubrics pages 1–7
- Key competences worksheets pages 7–8
- Culture and CLIL worksheets pages 13–16
- Culture video worksheets pages 7–8
- Digital competence worksheets pages 7–8
- Macmillan Readers worksheets pages 3–4

Tests and Exams
- Unit 4 End-of-unit test: Basic, Standard and Extra
- CEFR Skills Exam Generator

Study guide

Grammar
Comparatives and superlatives

adjective	comparative	superlative
fast	faster	the fastest
hot	hotter	the hottest
funny	funnier	the funniest
expensive	more expensive	the most expensive
good	better	the best
bad	worse	the worst

a / an, some, any

countable nouns
He climbed **a** mountain. There's **an** elephant! There are **some** great beaches.
I haven't got **a** car. There aren't **any** animals on the island.
Is that **a** waterfall? Are there **any** owls?
uncountable nouns
I need **some** information about volunteering.
There isn't **any** clean water in some countries.
Did you try **any** special food?

much, many, a lot of

countable nouns
There are **a lot of** volunteering projects.
I didn't go to **many** boring places.
How **many** people were there?
uncountable nouns
We had **a lot of** time to explore the city.
There isn't **much** rain in summer.
How **much** food will we need?

Vocabulary
Geography and landscape

beach	desert	ocean
canyon	forest	reef
cave	island	river
cliff	lake	valley
coast	mountain	waterfalls

Animals

bee	gorilla	snake
butterfly	owl	tiger
crocodile	penguin	turtle
elephant	polar bear	whale
giraffe	rhinoceros	

Speaking
Expressing preferences
I'd like to …
It's a nice idea but …
I'd rather … / I'd prefer to …
I don't mind …
Maybe … is a better idea.
That is / sounds more interesting / fun / than …

 LEARNING TO LEARN

Think about word order when translating from your language to English as this can be different in both languages.

UNIT 5 — LET'S EXPERIMENT

Unit objectives and key competences

In this unit the student will learn …

- understand, memorize and correctly use vocabulary related to science and science in the classroom **CLC CMST SCC**
- understand and correctly use *will / won't*, draw parallels to L1, and use both in a short speaking activity **CLC L2L SIE**
- understand and correctly use the first conditional **CLC L2L**
- learn about a day in the life of an American astronaut and compare US space exploration with space exploration and astronauts in their country **CLC CMST CAE SCC SIE**
- about technology by watching a short video **CLC CMST DC**

In this unit the student will learn how to …

- identify specific information in a magazine article about predictions for the future **CLC CMST CAE**
- look online for predictions about science **CLC CMST DC SIE**
- identify specific information about science and a classroom experiment **CLC CMST SIE**
- read information about making a time capsule, listen to classroom instructions and learn how to make suggestions **CLC CMST L2L CAE**
- write an opinion essay **CLC L2L SIE**
- prepare for and do a speaking exam describing a photo **CLC SIE L2L**

Linguistic contents

Main vocabulary
- Science: *DNA, clone, vaccine,* etc
- Science in the classroom: *test tube, pressure,* etc

Grammar
- *will / won't*
- First conditional

Functional language
- Phrases for making suggestions
- Phrases for describing a photo in an exam

Pronunciation
- Short form of *will: 'll*

Skills

Reading
- Read a magazine article about predictions for the future
- Read a text about a day in the life of an astronaut
- Read about making a time capsule
- V Read an opinion essay about the future

Writing: Interaction and production
- Write a personalized dialogue about making suggestions
- Write an opinion essay in three steps: plan, write, check
- Learn how to use *on the one hand* and *on the other hand*

Listening
- Listen to a science teacher carrying out an experiment in class
- Listen to a teacher giving classroom instructions about a time capsule

Spoken interaction
- Ask and answer questions about science in the future
- Ask and answer questions about your life in the next ten years

Spoken production
- Prepare and act out a dialogue about a time capsule
- Prepare and do a speaking exam about describing a photo

Lifelong learning skills

Self-study and self-evaluation

- Study guide:
  Student's Book page 61
- Progress check and self-evaluation:
  Workbook pages 46–47
- Grammar reference and practice:
  Workbook pages 92–93
- Wordlist:
  Workbook pages 151–157

Learning strategies and thinking skills

- Learn how to listen to instructions

Cultural awareness

- Space exploration
- Comparing space exploration missions in the US with missions in students' own country

Cross-curricular contents

- Science, space exploration, predictions about the future
- Language and literature: reading and writing an opinion essay
- ICT: searching the internet for information

Key competences

CLC	Competence in linguistic communication
CMST	Competence in mathematics, science and technology
DC	Digital competence
SCC	Social and civic competences
CAE	Cultural awareness and expression
L2L	Learning to learn
SIE	Sense of initiative and entrepreneurship

Evaluation

- Unit 5 End-of-unit test: Basic, Standard, and Extra
- CEFR Skills Exam Generator

External exam trainer

- Speaking: Describing a photo

Digital material

Pulse Live! Digital Course including:
- Interactive grammar tables
- Audio visual speaking model: Making suggestions
- Audio visual cultural material: Technology

Student's website

Digital competence

- Web quest: Predictions by scientists about the future
- Digital competence worksheet: Online adverts

Reinforcement material

- Basic worksheets, Teacher's Resource File pages 29–34
- Vocabulary and Grammar: Consolidation worksheets, Teacher's Resource File pages 19–20

Extension material

- Fast-finisher activity: Student's Book page 53
- Extra activities: Teacher's Book pages T58
- Vocabulary and Grammar: Extension worksheets, Teacher's Resource File pages 21–22

Teacher's Resource File

- Translation and dictation worksheets pages 6, 16
- Evaluation rubrics pages 1–7
- Key competences worksheets pages 9–10
- Culture and CLIL worksheets pages 17–20
- Culture video worksheets pages 9–10
- Digital competence worksheets pages 9–10
- Macmillan Readers worksheets pages 3–4

THINK ABOUT IT

In your opinion, what is the best scientific invention?

Vocabulary and Speaking
Science

1 🔊 **2.12** Read the museum guide. Then listen and repeat the words in blue.

THE SCIENCE MUSEUM
Explore the world and have fun!

WHO AM I?
Find out how your **DNA** makes you different from other people and how a scientist would make a **clone** of you!

FOOD OF THE FUTURE
Millions of people around the world go hungry every day. But are **genetically modified crops** really the answer?

JOURNEY INTO SPACE
Experience space in 3D in our amazing IMAX cinema! Travel by **spacecraft** to the **planet** Mars and see the view from a **satellite** flying round the Earth.

HEALTHY EARTH
Watch a **wind turbine** and a **solar panel** make electricity. And see what happens to a **battery** when you throw it away.

THE SECRETS OF MEDICINE
How does a scientist find a **cure** for a **disease**? And how can a **vaccine** stop you getting ill? Learn the answers to these questions and more.

Exercise 3

space
planet
satellite
medicine
DNA
clone
cure
disease
vaccine
environment
genetically modified crops
wind turbine
solar panel
battery

2 Which part of the museum would you like to visit? Why?

3 Copy and complete the table with the correct words from exercise 1.

space	medicine	environment
spacecraft		

EXPRESS YOURSELF

4 What do you want to know about science in the future? Write one question for each of the three subheadings in exercise 3.

Will people live on other planets?

5 Work in pairs. Ask and answer your questions from exercise 4.

💬 *Will people live on other planets?*
💬 *Yes, I think so. / No, I don't think so.*

Vocabulary extension: Workbook page 106 ›

Vocabulary and Speaking
Science

Lesson objectives

In this lesson students will:
- learn / revise words related to space, medicine and the environment
- ask and answer questions about science

Warmer

Play a game of *Hangman* to introduce the topic. Use dashes to represent the letters of *museum* and write them on the board: _ _ _ _ _ _ . Ask students to suggest letters of the alphabet. Continue until students have guessed the word. Make sure they pronounce *museum* /mjuːˈziːəm/ correctly.

Think about it

Students work individually and write down what they think is the best scientific invention. They compare answers in pairs. Get feedback from the whole class.

1 🔘 **2.12**

- Students read the museum guide.
- Play the CD. Students listen to the words in blue and repeat them chorally and individually.
- Make sure they pronounce the words correctly with the correct stress, especially *disease* /dɪˈziːz/, *vaccine* /ˈvæksiːn/ and *turbine* /ˈtɜːbaɪn/.

Language note

In abbreviations like *DNA*, the main stress falls on the final letter. Other examples are *GM*, *BBC*, *USA* and *EU*.

Culture note

The Science Museum in London was founded in 1857. It contains over 300,000 exhibits, including the world's oldest steam locomotive and the world's first jet engine. More than 2.7 million people visit the Science Museum each year.

2
- Students work individually and answer the questions.
- They compare answers in pairs.
- Listen to their ideas as a class.

3
- Explain the task.
- Students copy the table into their notebooks. They sort the words in blue from exercise 1 into three categories and write the words in the correct columns.
- They compare answers in pairs.
- Check answers as a class.

🔘**EXPRESS YOURSELF**

4
- Explain the task.
- Give students a couple of minutes to think about their questions and to make a few notes.

5
- Put students into pairs to ask and answer their questions from exercise 4.
- Listen to questions from different pairs and elicit answers from the class.

Vocabulary extension: Workbook page 106 ▶▶

Reading

Text type: A magazine article

Recommended web links

www.bbc.co.uk/news/magazine-24331106

www.wfs.org/node/920

www.futuretechnology500.com/

Warmer

Write *spacecraft, satellite, planet, Mars* on the board with all the letters removed apart from the first and last letters: *s_ _ _ _ _ _ _ _ t, s_ _ _ _ _ _ e, p _ _ _ _ t, M _ _ s*. Tell students they all refer to space. Students work in pairs and complete the words. Invite students to come to the board and write in the missing letters.

1 2.13

- Explain the task. Students read the five topics carefully first. Point out that there are six predictions so one of the topics is mentioned twice.
- Play the CD. Students listen and follow the text in their books.
- Check answers as a class. Point out that the ability to get the gist of a piece of text quickly by recognizing key words, eg the predictions about travel and transport include the words *cars, space*, is an important skill when reading efficiently.

Word check

Make sure students understand the words. Ask them to translate them into their language.

2
- Students read the six questions carefully first.
- They work individually and find the answers in the text.
- They compare answers in pairs.
- Check answers as a class.

3
- Read the example sentence aloud to the class.
- Make sure students understand the task.
- They work individually and write answers to the questions in their notebooks.
- They compare answers in pairs.
- Listen to their ideas as a class.

Finished?

Ask fast finishers to write answers to the questions.

Web quest

Students find three more predictions by scientists about the future. Highlight the Web quest tip.

1
- Ask students to open an internet web browser such as Internet Explorer. Students open a search engine (eg Google) and type in the subject of their search.
- Students find three more predictions by scientists about the future.
- They write down the three predictions and add one of their own that is extremely improbable, eg *People will live under the sea.*

2
- Put students into pairs. They guess which three of their partner's predictions are scientific and which one is improbable.

3
- Students tell the class about their predictions.

6 Amazing predictions for the future!

Will the world be very different 20 years from now? Futurologist Mark Mann gives us his view of life in the future.

1 Many people who are born in the 2040s will live until they are 150! That's because there will be vaccines for most serious diseases, including cancer.

2 Cars will drive themselves! Our cars will take us wherever we want to go, safely and easily – and we'll be able to relax and enjoy the ride!

3 Learning a second language won't be necessary. We'll be able to buy tiny computers that fit in our ear and translate what we hear into our own language.

4 There will be genetically modified crops that are very healthy. For example, sweets will have vitamins in them! We'll also be able to buy square fruit and vegetables that fit in the fridge more easily.

5 People will go on holiday to space. Thousands of us will work in space stations, which will have hotels, restaurants and sports stadiums.

6 We'll be able to play video games just by thinking! The games will be advanced enough to 'understand' what move we want to make. It will make the move for us – we won't need to touch anything!

Reading
A magazine article

Word check

safely square advanced

Exercise 1

a 2, 5
b 1
c 6
d 4
e 3

1 🔊 2.13 Read and listen to the article. Which predictions are about ...

a) travel and transport?   d) eating?
b) medicine?   e) education?
c) entertainment?

2 Read the article again and answer the questions about the future.

1 What age will people live to?
2 Why won't people learn to drive?
3 How will computers help people who can't speak foreign languages?
4 How will fruit and vegetables be different?
5 Where will people stay on a space station?
6 What won't people have to do when they play video games?

3 Do you disagree with any of the predictions in the article? Which one(s)? Why?

I don't think genetically modified crops will be healthy because they aren't natural.

🏁 **FINISHED?**

Do you think the future will be better than the present? Why (not)?

Exercise 2

1 150.
2 Because cars will drive themselves.
3 They will translate what we hear into our own language.
4 They will be square.
5 In hotels.
6 Touch anything.

WEB QUEST

Find three more predictions by scientists about the future.

1 Go online and find the predictions. Write them down. Then add one prediction of your own that is unlikely to happen!

2 Work in pairs. Look at each other's lists. Can you say which are the three scientists' predictions and which one is the unlikely one?

3 Tell the class about your predictions.

Web Quest tip!

Find more English-language websites by searching websites with .co.uk in the address.

Grammar Digital
will / won't

Exercise 1

1 'll
2 won't
3 won't
the infinitive without *to*

1 Copy and complete the table with short forms of *will* and *will not*. What form of the verb do we use after *will*?

affirmative
Sweets **will have** vitamins. We (1) ... **be able to** relax and enjoy the ride!
negative
Learning a second language (2) ... **be** necessary.
questions
Will the world **be** very different in 20 years from now?
short answers
Yes, it **will**. / No, it (3) ... .

Exercise 2

students' own answers

2 Complete the sentences with *will* or *won't* to make predictions about the future.

1 People ... stop smoking.
2 Trees ... disappear completely.
3 E-books ... replace paper books.
4 Crime ... increase.
5 Computers ... become cheaper.

 ANALYSE

In English, we use *will* / *won't* to talk about future events. Can you translate this meaning of *will* / *won't* in your language?

Exercise 3

1 Will I get up early?
2 Will the weather be good?
3 Will we have an English test?
4 Will I play computer games?
5 Will anyone send me a text message?

3 Order the words to make questions about your day tomorrow.

1 get up / I / Will / early ?
2 weather / good / be / Will / the ?
3 English test / have / we / Will / an ?
4 Will / computer games / play / I ?
5 anyone / me / send / text message / Will / a ?

4 Read the advert. Then complete the sentences with *will* or *won't*. Use short forms where possible.

1 You ... drive it.
2 It ... be good for the environment.
3 It ... be intelligent.
4 Lots of things ... fit in it.
5 It ... be expensive.
6 You ... have an accident in it.

Exercise 4

1 won't
2 'll
3 'll
4 will
5 won't
6 won't

THE CAR OF THE FUTURE ...
• will have lots of space.
• won't need a driver!
• will understand what you say.
• won't cost a lot of money.
• won't use petrol.
• will be fast, but safe!

 EXPRESS YOURSELF

5 What will happen in your life in the next ten years? Write sentences about topics 1–4.

I'll learn another language.
I won't study science at university.

1 go to university
2 get married
3 learn Chinese
4 travel round the world

6 Work in pairs. Ask and answer questions about topics 1–4 from exercise 5.

● *Will you go to university?*
● *Yes, I will.*

2.14–2.15 Pronunciation lab: Short form of *will*: *'ll*, page 125

Grammar

will / won't

Lesson objectives

In this lesson students will:

- learn / revise *will / won't* to make predictions
- talk about their life in the next ten years

Warmer

Write the question *Will people go on holiday to space?* on the board with the words in the wrong order: *will holiday people space go to on ?* Students work in pairs and write the question in the correct order. Invite a student to come to the board to write the question. If there are errors, invite other students to come to the board and correct them.

1 • Students copy and complete the table in their notebooks with short forms of *will* and *will not* and answer the question.
- They compare answers in pairs.
- Check answers as a class. Point out that *will* is often contracted to *'ll* in the affirmative, especially in spoken English.
- Emphasize that we do not contract the affirmative short answer, *Yes, I will.*
- Highlight the fact that *won't* is the contracted form of *will not.* Point out that we usually say *won't* in negative short answers and not *will not.*

2 • They read the five sentences carefully first.
- They work individually and complete the sentences using *will* or *won't.*
- They compare answers in pairs.
- Check answers as a class. Note that both *will* and *won't* are possible in all the sentences. The answers depend on personal opinions.
- Find out which sentences most students agree about. Are there any they do not agree about?

Analyse

Students read the information and answer the question.

3 • Write the question *Will it rain tomorrow?* and highlight that we use questions beginning with *will* when we are not sure what will happen.
- Students work individually and put the words in the correct order to make questions beginning with *will.*
- They compare answers in pairs.
- Check answers as a class.

4 • Students read the advert carefully.
- They work individually and complete the sentences with *will* or *won't.*
- Encourage them to refer back to the table in exercise 1 if necessary.
- Student compare answers in pairs.
- Check answers as a class.

EXPRESS YOURSELF

5 • Students read the example sentences and topics 1–4.
- Remind students that *won't* is the contracted form of *will not.*
- Students work individually and write sentences about topics 1–4 beginning with either *I'll* or *I won't.*

6 • Focus on the question form *Will you …?* and point out that we use this to ask another person to predict what will happen to them in the future.
- Put students into pairs to ask and answer questions about topics 1–4 from exercise 5. Remind them to answer using *Yes, I will* or *No, I won't.*
- Listen to some pairs as a class.

Finished?

Add some extra topics to topics 1–4 in exercise 5, eg become a scientist; buy a house; have children; visit Australia; learn to play the violin / piano / guitar; do a parachute jump. Students write sentences using *I'll, I won't.*

Pronunciation lab: Short form of *will*: *'ll,* page 125

Digital course: Interactive grammar table

Study guide: page 61

Vocabulary and Listening
Science in the classroom

Warmer

Write the lesson heading *Science in the classroom* on the board. Elicit from the class examples of different kinds of science that you can study and make a list on the board, eg *chemistry, physics, biology, botany, zoology, geology.*

1 2.16
- Play the CD. Students listen and repeat the words chorally and individually.
- Make sure they pronounce the words correctly with the correct stress, especially *thermometer* /θɜːˈmɒmɪtə/, *pressure* /ˈpreʃə/ and *liquid* /ˈlɪkwɪd/.
- They read the list of words and say which words are pieces of equipment that a scientist uses.
- They compare answers in pairs.
- Check answers as a class.

Language note

Words ending in *-ometer* are usually stressed on the *o*, eg, *thermometer, barometer.*

2 2.17
- Explain the task.
- Students fill the gaps in the instructions using words from the word pool in exercise 1.
- They compare answers in pairs.
- Play the CD.
- Students listen and check their answers.

3
- Students read the sentences carefully first.
- They complete the sentences about the experiment with the words in the box.
- Check answers as a class. Point out that *fizz* is what happens when you shake a bottle of lemonade or cola.

4 2.18
- Make sure students understand the task.
- They look at the five pictures carefully first.
- Play the CD.
- Students put the steps in the correct order 1–5.
- Check progress. If necessary, play the CD again.
- Check answers as a class.

5
- Students read the sentences carefully first.
- Play the CD. Students decide if the sentences are true or false.
- Play the CD again. Students correct the false sentences.
- Check answers as a class.

2.18 Audioscript, exercise 4

Mr Marston: If you turn a glass of water upside down, what happens?
Simon: It goes all over the floor.
Mr Marston: That's right. Thank you, Simon. And why does it go all over the floor?
Ruby: Because water is heavier than air.
Mr Marston: Exactly. And gravity makes the water fall. But that doesn't always happen. Here's a glass. Tom, can you fill it with water from the jug for me, please?
Tom: Yes, Mr Marston. Here you are.
Mr Marston: Thank you, Tom. So, we have the jug and the glass. The only other equipment I need is this piece of cardboard. Now, I'm going to put this cardboard on top of the glass of water and turn it upside down. Then I'll take my hand away, but none of the water will go on the floor. Do you believe me?
Students: No!
Mr Marston: OK, watch. Now this is the difficult bit. When I put the cardboard on top of the glass, I have to make sure no air gets inside. If there are any air bubbles in the water, it won't work. Right, I think that's OK. Now watch! Look. I've taken my hand away and the water has stayed in the glass! Amazing, isn't it?
Students: Mmmm.
Mr Marston: OK. So, can anyone explain why that happened? Why didn't the water go all over my feet? I'll give you a clue. It's to do with air pressure. Yes, Emily?
Emily: Well, because there was no air inside the glass, the air pressure from outside the glass was greater than the pressure of water inside the glass. That's why the water stayed where it was.
Mr Marston: Exactly! Well done, Emily! Did you all get that? The reason the water stayed in the glass was because …

Vocabulary and Listening
Science in the classroom

Exercise 1

test tube
thermometer
jug

1 🔊 2.16 Listen and repeat the science words in the box. Which words are pieces of equipment that a scientist uses?

2 🔊 2.17 Complete the instructions for a chemical experiment with words from the box. Then listen and check.

laboratory test tube
thermometer explosion
pressure jug gas liquid gravity
temperature air bubbles acid
chemical reaction

Exercise 2

1 laboratory
2 jug
3 temperature
4 liquid
5 gas
6 bubbles
7 explosion

THE EXPLODING BAG!

In the school (1)... you can try this fun experiment!
You will need the following equipment:
A plastic bag with a zip   A measuring (2) ...   Warm water   Vinegar   Baking soda

First, put 100 ml of warm water and 200 ml of vinegar into the bag. The (3) ... of the water shouldn't be higher than 60°C.

Next, add three spoons of baking soda to the bag of (4) ...

Quickly close the bag with the zip. Watch as a (5) ... called carbon dioxide is produced inside the bag. Can you see the (6) ...?

Now here's the fun bit! The bag will get bigger and bigger until there is an (7) ...!

Exercise 3

1 reaction
2 bubbles
3 gas
4 laboratory
5 thermometer

3 Complete the sentences about the experiment with the words in the box.

bubbles thermometer
laboratory gas reaction

1 If you mix vinegar and baking soda, there is a chemical ... .
2 The mixture of vinegar and baking soda fizzes and produces ... .
3 A ... like carbon dioxide needs a lot of space.
4 Experiments like these should be done in a safe environment such as a ... .
5 Check the temperature of water with a ... .

4 🔊 2.18 Listen to a science teacher carrying out a classroom experiment. Put the steps in order.

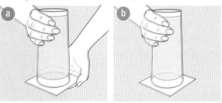  

Exercise 4

1 e
2 c
3 d
4 a
5 b

5 Listen again. Are the sentences true or false? Correct the false sentences.

1 The teacher fills the glass with water.
2 He makes sure there is air inside the glass.
3 The water doesn't come out of the glass.
4 The experiment is successful.
5 Emily's explanation is wrong.

Exercise 5

1 **False**
   Tom fills the glass with water.
2 **False**
   He makes sure there is no air inside the glass.
3 **True**
4 **True**
5 **False**
   Emily's explanation is correct.

Cultural awareness
Space exploration

1 What problems do you think astronauts have with washing and eating when they go to space?

2 🔊 2.19 Read and listen to the blog post. Were your answers from exercise 1 correct?

Fact box

The International Space Station (ISS) was built so that people could live and do research in space. It is 354 km from Earth and it takes two days to get to it. It travels around the Earth at a speed of 28,000 km per hour, so it goes round the Earth 16 times a day!

Exercise 2

They can't have showers because they use too much water. Nothing tastes very nice in space and they aren't allowed any fresh fruit because it makes the whole space station smell.

A DAY IN THE LIFE OF AN ASTRONAUT

Hi! I'm Serena Hughes and I'm an American astronaut on the International Space Station. This is my day.

8.00 am: I wake up to the sound of one of my favourite songs. Mission Control Center in Houston plays a different song for each crew member every morning!

8.15 AM: I get up and have a wash. We have to transport water from Earth to the space station. This means we can't have showers because they use too much water. If we use too much water for washing, we won't have enough to drink!

8.30 AM: I have breakfast with the rest of the crew. Today it's pancakes. Usually I love pancakes, but nothing tastes very nice in space!

9.00 AM: I try to 'fly' to my work station to switch on my computer. Everyone is weightless in space because there is no gravity, so moving around is difficult!

1.00 PM: It's lunchtime and I'm hungry! I'd love some fresh fruit, but it isn't allowed. If someone eats a banana, the whole space station will smell of bananas!

2.00 PM: Now it's time for some housework! In space, we have to take the rubbish out – just like we do at home! We load it into a spacecraft, which will take it down to Earth.

3.00 PM: I spend half an hour on the exercise bike. You don't use your muscles in space because everything is weightless. If I don't do daily exercise, my body will become very weak.

4.00 PM: I go to the laboratory to check on an experiment we're doing. We're trying to see if we can grow vegetables in space!

7.00 PM: I have dinner, then I send some emails to my friends and family on Earth. They'll worry about me if they don't hear from me!

10.00 PM: It's bedtime! I get into my sleeping bag and lie down in my little cabin. There will be another day in space tomorrow!

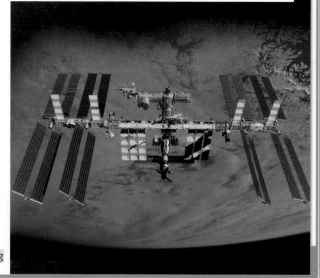

Word check

gravity housework muscles weightless sleeping bag

Exercise 3

1 Because everyone is weightless.

2 They load it into a spacecraft, which will take it down to Earth.

3 Because if she doesn't do daily exercise, her body will become very weak.

4 She sends emails.

3 Read the blog post again. Then answer the questions.

1 Why is it difficult to get from one place to another inside the space station?

2 Where do astronauts send their rubbish?

3 Why does Serena do exercise?

4 How does Serena communicate with people she knows on Earth?

CULTURAL COMPARISON

4 Answer the questions.

1 Has there been a space exploration mission from your country?

2 What are the names of some astronauts from your country?

Cultural awareness
Space exploration

4 • Students read the two questions and make a note of their answers.
   • They work in pairs and discuss their answers.
   • Listen to their answers as a class.

Culture video: Technology ▷▷

Lesson objectives

In this lesson students will:
• read about the International Space Station
• talk about their country's involvement in space exploration missions

---

Warmer

Books closed. Write the words *orbit* and *Earth* on the board. To check the meaning of *orbit*, draw a picture to show something *orbiting the Earth*. Elicit from the class different things that orbit the Earth, eg the Moon, communications satellites, the International Space Station.

---

1 • Students read the information in the Fact box. Point out that *go round* is another way of saying *orbit*.
   • Explain the task. Students work individually and answer the question with their ideas.
   • They compare answers in pairs.
   • Listen to their ideas as a class.

2 🔘 2.19
   • Play the CD. Students listen and follow the blog post in their books.
   • They check whether their answers from exercise 1 were correct.
   • Check the answer as a class.

3 • Students read the questions carefully first.
   • They read the blog post again and find the answers.
   • Students compare answers in pairs.
   • Check answers as a class.

Word check

Make sure students understand the words and can pronounce them correctly, especially *muscles* /ˈmʌsəlz/. Ask them to translate them into their language.

Grammar
First conditional

Warmer

Write *water, banana, moving around* on the board. Ask students to say what the problem is with each of these in space. Elicit answers from the class, eg *There isn't enough water for showers. You can't eat bananas because they will smell. Moving around is difficult because everyone is weightless.*

1 • Check students understand the task.
- Students read the headings and the example sentences in the table.
- Ask students to translate the example sentences into their language.
- They answer the questions.
- Students compare answers in pairs.
- Check answers as a class. Emphasize that we never use *will / won't* in the *if* clause.

Look!

Highlight the use of the comma when we write the *if* + conditional situation first.

2 • Do the first example with the whole class to demonstrate the activity (*If you go to the space station, the journey will take two days.*).
- Highlight the use of the comma and point out that all the sentences begin with *If*.
- Students work individually to match the sentence beginnings and endings.
- They compare answers in pairs.
- Check answers as a class.

Finished?

Students rewrite the sentences beginning with a–e and matching them with 1–5. Remind students that there is no comma if the second part of the sentence is the clause beginning with *if.*

3 • Students copy the sentence beginnings into their notebooks.
- They use their own ideas to finish each sentence.
- Encourage students to refer back to the table to help them choose the correct form of the verb in each clause.
- Students work individually to complete the task.
- Listen to their ideas as a class. Correct any errors in the use of present simple in the *if* clause and *will / won't* in the result clause.

CLIL Grammar in context: Science

4 • Do the first example with the whole class (*mix*). Explain that this is the *if* part of the sentence so the present simple must be used.
- Check students remember *lightning* (the flash you see during an electric storm) and *thunder* (the sound you hear during an electric storm) from Unit 3.
- Students complete the exercise individually.
- They compare answers in pairs.

5 🔘 2.20
- Play the CD. Students listen and check their answers to exercise 4.

CLIL task

Students use the internet to find three other science facts about the natural world.

Digital course: Interactive grammar table

Study guide: page 61

Grammar Digital
First conditional

situation	result
If we **use** too much water for washing,	we **won't have** enough to drink!

result	situation
They**'ll worry** about me	if I **don't keep** in touch with them!

LOOK!

When we write *If* + conditional situation first, we use a comma between the two parts of the sentence.

Exercise 1

a the present simple
b the *will / won't* form of the future

1 Look at the sentences in the table. In first conditional sentences, what tense do we use ...

  a) after *if* to talk about a conditional action?
  b) to talk about the result of the conditional action?

Exercise 2

1 c
2 e
3 a
4 b
5 d

2 Match 1–5 with a–e to make sentences. Don't forget to use a comma!

  1 If you go to the space station
  2 If you miss your family
  3 If you drink too much water
  4 If you feel sick
  5 If you go on the exercise bike

  a) you won't have enough for later.
  b) the doctor will give you some medicine.
  c) the journey will take two days.
  d) your muscles will stay strong.
  e) you'll be able to send them emails.

Exercise 3

students' own answers

3 Copy and complete the sentences with your own ideas.

  1 If I live to the age of 150, I ...
  2 We'll travel to other planets if ...
  3 If someone buys me a smartphone, ...
  4 Everybody will use bicycles if ...
  5 If I have my own robot, I ...

CLIL Grammar in context: Science

4 Penny is testing Matt about science. Complete the dialogues with the correct forms of the verbs in brackets.

Matt If you (1) ... (mix) red and yellow, it (2) ... (make) purple.
Penny No, it (3) ... (not make) purple!
Matt (4) ... (it / make) orange?
Penny Yes, it will!

Matt A worm (5) ... (not die) if you (6) ... (cut) it in half.
Penny What (7) ... (happen)?
Matt It (8) ... (become) two worms!
Penny Good!

Matt If lightning (9) ... (strike), you (10) ... (hear) thunder.
Penny OK. (11) ... (you / see) the lightning before or after you hear the thunder?
Matt Before.
Penny That's right!

5 2.20 Listen and check your answers.

CLIL TASK

Go online. Find three other science facts about the natural world.

Exercise 4

1 mix
2 will / 'll make
3 won't make
4 Will it make
5 won't die
6 cut
7 will happen
8 will / 'll become
9 strikes
10 will / 'll hear
11 Will you see

Making a time capsule

What will the world be like in 100 years time? What are your predictions?

Tell people in the future about your life now!

Here's how to make a time capsule. Choose some everyday things, put them in a box and leave them in a secret place for someone in the future to find! The person who finds the box will learn about what life is like now by looking at the things.

You will need:

- five to six things
- paper, a pen and some pencils
- a box
- a plastic bag
- strong tape
- a permanent marker pen

1 Choose five to six things that show what life is like now. Avoid things that need electronic equipment to work. Don't forget, CD players and computers will be very different in the future!

2 Write a letter to the finder of the time capsule.

3 Put the things and the letter in a box.

4 Put the box in a plastic bag and seal it with strong tape.

5 Write your name, today's date and the date you want the box to be opened on the bag. Use a permanent marker pen so that people will be able to read it in 50 years' time!

6 Make a hole in the garden and bury your time capsule.

7 Draw a map to show where your time capsule is. Keep it somewhere safe.

8 Now try to forget about it!

Step 1: Read

1 **Read the information about making a time capsule. Look at the pictures. Which thing wouldn't you put in a time capsule? Why not?**

2 **Read the text again and answer the questions.**

1 If you make a time capsule, what will it show people in the future?
2 What will you put in the box with your chosen objects?
3 What will you put the box into?
4 What two dates will you write on it?
5 Why will you need a special kind of pen to write on it?
6 How will people in the future find the time capsule?

Step 2: Listen

3 🔊 2.21 **Listen to a teacher talking to her class about a time capsule project. How many time capsules will the class make?**

SKILLS BUILDER

Listening to instructions
These time words and phrases will help you understand the order of instructions.
first   then   next   in a minute   finally

4 **Listen again and choose the correct answers.**

1 The students will work ...
a) alone.
b) in pairs.
2 They will ...
a) talk together and write two things.
b) write lots of interesting things.
3 The homework task is for ...
a) Monday.
b) Wednesday.
4 The class will put ... things in the box.
a) 6
b) 16
5 The students are going to bury the time capsule on ...
a) Monday.
b) Wednesday.

Exercise 1

students' own answers

Exercise 2

1 What life is like now.
2 A letter.
3 A plastic bag.
4 Today's date and the date you want the box to be opened.
5 So that people will be able to read it in 50 years' time.
6 From a map.

Exercise 3

One.

Exercise 4

1 b
2 a
3 a
4 a
5 b

Integrated skills
Making a time capsule

Lesson objectives

In this lesson students will:
- work on all four skills
- read a set of instructions
- listen to a conversation between a teacher and her students
- write a personalized dialogue
- act out their dialogue

Warmer
Highlight Nina's speech bubble. Elicit answers to the questions from the class.

Step 1: Read

1
- Students read the first paragraph of the text. Check that they understand *time capsule*.
- They read the rest of the text.
- Students look at the pictures. They decide which item they would not put in a time capsule and think of a reason.
- They compare answers in pairs.
- Listen to their ideas as a class.

Culture note

The world's first time capsule is believed to be the one created at Oglethorpe University, Atlanta, Georgia in 1936. It was called the Crypt of Civilization and was intended to be opened in the year 8113!

2
- Students read the questions carefully first.
- They read the text again and find the answers.
- They compare answers in pairs.
- Check answers as a class.

Extra activity

Make sure students understand the vocabulary in the text, eg *seal, tape, hole* and *bury*.

Step 2: Listen

3   2.21
- Students read the question.
- Play the CD. Students write the answer in their notebooks.
- Check the answer as a class.

Skills builder

Listening to instructions
Focus on the information in the Skills builder box. Highlight that recognizing time words and phrases will help students understand the order of instructions.

4
- Students read the sentence beginnings and the different possible endings.
- Play the CD again. Students choose the correct answers.
- They compare answers in pairs.
- Check answers as a class.

2.21 Audioscript, exercise 3

Teacher: Right, for this week's project we're going to make a time capsule. First, can you all remember what a time capsule is? Come on, everyone, we talked about time capsules last lesson. Yes, Lizzie?

Girl: It's when we put some things in a box and hide it somewhere so that people in the future can find it.

Teacher: That's right. The idea is that many years from now people will find what we put in the box and learn more about our life now, at the beginning of the 21st century. So in a minute, you're going to work in pairs. In your pairs, you're going to talk together about the things you think would show people what life is like today. And then each pair is going to write down the two best things from the ones you have discussed. Then your homework is to find one of the things you chose together and to bring it to the next lesson on Monday. You'll have to decide together who is going to bring what, so that you don't both bring the same thing! Then on Monday we'll choose the six most interesting things and we'll put them in our time capsule.

Boy: Will we bury it somewhere, miss?

Teacher: Yes, but not on Monday. On Monday, we'll look at the things you bring in, choose the six most interesting, and put them in the box. Finally, in Wednesday's lesson, we'll bury our time capsule. That will be something else for you to think about – the best place to bury our time capsule. But don't worry about that at the moment. OK. Now, you've got 15 minutes to talk about and decide on your two things. You can make notes if you want, but you don't have to.

T58

Integrated skills – continued
Making suggestions

5 🔘 2.22
- Students read the dialogue first.
- Play the CD. Students listen and follow the text in their books. They write answers 1–5 in their notebooks.
- They compare answers in pairs.
- Check answers as a class.

6
- Play the CD again, pausing after each question or statement and each response for students to repeat as a class.
- Ask students to repeat the dialogue several times both chorally and individually with the correct stress and intonation.
- Students practise the dialogue in pairs. Then swap roles and practise the dialogue again.

Step 3: Write

7
- Students work individually. They copy the phrases in bold into their notebooks.
- Give them a few minutes to think about the items they would put in a time capsule.
- Encourage them to use the phrases in bold to write suggestions, eg *What about a photo of our class?* Make sure they also give reasons.
- Monitor while they are writing and give help if necessary.

8
- Ask students to look at the Communication kit: Making suggestions. Encourage them to use these expressions when writing their dialogue.
- Students work individually and write their dialogue, using the dialogue in the book as a model.
- Monitor while they are writing and give help if necessary.

Step 4: Communicate

9
- Students practise their dialogues in pairs.
- For extra practice, they swap roles in both dialogues.

10
- Choose some pairs to act out their dialogue for the class.
- Students raise their hand if another pair has the same two items as they have chosen. This will encourage them to listen carefully to their classmates.

Integrated skills: Workbook page 115 ⟫

MAKING SUGGESTIONS

Watch!

So, **what shall we** put in the time capsule?	How about a (1)... ? Then people in the future will know what kind of music we listened to.
But people in the future probably won't be able to (2)... . There won't be CD players then.	Yes, you're right. I didn't think of that.
I know! **What about** a (3) ... from a restaurant?	What's interesting about that?
It'll show people in the future (4) ... we ate.	**That's a good idea!** Maybe they won't have (5) ... in 50 years' time!
Exactly!	We could also put in a copy of today's newspaper so people can see what happened in the world.
Great! That's two things, now let's think of one more.	How about a photo of us?

Exercise 5

1 CD
2 play CDs
3 menu
4 what food
5 pizza

5 ◗ 2.22 Read and listen to the dialogue. Complete 1–5 in your notebook.

6 Listen again and repeat. Practise your intonation.

Step 3: Write

7 Copy the phrases in bold. What two things would you put in a time capsule? Write your suggestions and the reasons why you think they will tell people in the future about life now.

8 Write a new dialogue. Write both parts. Use the dialogue in exercise 5 to help you.

Step 4: Communicate

9 Work in pairs. Take turns to practise your dialogues.

- What shall we put in the time capsule?
- How about a mobile phone? Then people in the future will …

10 Act your dialogue for the class.

COMMUNICATION KIT

Making suggestions

What shall we …?
What / How about a …?
Why don't we …?
Let's …
Maybe we could …
Then … will …

Writing
An opinion essay

1 🔊 **2.23** Read and listen to the essay. Do you agree with the opinion in paragraph B or C?

Will people ever live on the Moon?

A Many people like the idea of going on holiday to the Moon, but will anyone actually live there in the future? Scientists have different opinions on this subject.

B On the one hand, the number of people on Earth is growing and we are destroying our natural environment. If we aren't careful, one day we won't have any food or energy. If this happens, we will need to find a new place to live.

C On the other hand, the Moon isn't a very comfortable place for human beings. There isn't any air or water, and the temperature is too hot or too cold. Maybe we will be able to improve conditions on the Moon, but it will be very difficult.

D In conclusion, I don't think people will ever live on the Moon. In my opinion, the Earth is a better place for human beings.

2 Look at the Writing focus. How do you say *On the one hand* and *On the other hand* in your language?

> ## WRITING FOCUS
> ### *On the one hand* and *On the other hand*
> In an opinion essay, we can make the two possible opinions clear with the phrases *On the one hand* and *On the other hand*. We often use them at the beginning of paragraphs.
> *On the one hand, computers are already very intelligent.*
> *On the other hand, they haven't got feelings like human beings.*

Exercise 3

1 C
2 B
3 D
4 A

3 Look at the essay again. In which paragraph does the writer ...

1 give reasons why people probably won't live on the Moon?
2 give reasons why people might live on the Moon?
3 give a personal opinion on the subject?
4 ask a question?

4 Copy and complete the notes for paragraphs B and C of a different essay with your own 'yes' and 'no' reasons.

> **'Will computers ever think like human beings?'**
>
> B Yes, maybe they will because ...
>   1 they are already very intelligent.
>   2 ...
>   3 ...
>
> C No, they probably won't because ...
>   1 they don't have feelings.
>   2 ...
>   3 ...

> ## Writing task
> **Write an essay with the title:**
> **Will computers ever think like human beings?**
>
> **Plan** First decide what your opinion is. This will be the main point of your conclusion. Then plan your two middle paragraphs, using your ideas from exercise 4.
>
> **Write** Write four paragraphs: your introduction with a question, your two middle paragraphs with the two possible opinions with reasons, and your conclusion with your personal opinion. Use the essay in exercise 1 to help you.
>
> **Check** Check your writing.
>
> ✔ layout – introduction, two main paragraphs, conclusion
> ✔ *On the one hand* and *On the other hand*
> ✔ the opinions are clear

Writing
An opinion essay

Lesson objectives

In this lesson students will:
- read a short essay
- use *on the one hand* and *on the other hand* to show contrasting opinions
- write a short essay

Warmer

Write *The Moon* on the board. Ask students if they would like to travel to the Moon and to say why or why not.

1 💿 **2.23**
- Students read the question first.
- Play the CD. Students listen and follow the text in their books.
- They compare answers in pairs.
- Listen to their answers as a class.

2
- Focus on the information in the Writing focus box. Highlight the use of *On the one hand* and *On the other hand* to introduce contrasting ideas.
- Students translate *On the one hand* and *On the other hand* into their language.

3
- Explain the task.
- Students work individually and match the questions with the paragraphs.
- They compare answers in pairs.
- Check answers as a class.

Culture note

The first manned Moon landing took place on 20th July 1969, when the American spacecraft Apollo XI landed on the Moon. The astronauts Neil Armstrong and Buzz Aldrin were the first people to walk on the Moon's surface. Between 1969 and 1972 there were a total of six manned flights to the Moon and a total of 12 people have walked on the Moon's surface. The last person to walk on the Moon was Eugene Cernan on 14th December 1972.

4
- Check that students understand the task. Highlight the fact that paragraph B is a positive response to the question *Will computers ever think like human beings?* and paragraph C a negative response.
- Students work individually to write more reasons.
- They compare answers in pairs.
- Listen to their ideas as a class.

Writing task

The aim of this activity is for students to write a short essay with an introduction, two main paragraphs and a conclusion that includes the correct use of *On the one hand* and *On the other hand*, and that makes the opinions of the writer clear. Ask the students to follow the stages in the Student's Book. At the Check stage, ask them to swap notebooks and check each other's writing.

Writing reference and practice: Workbook page 128

Study guide
Grammar, Vocabulary and Speaking

Tell the students the Study guide is an important page which provides a useful reference for the main language of the unit: the grammar, the vocabulary and the functional language from the Integrated skills pages. Explain that they should refer to this page when studying for a test or exam.

Grammar
- Tell the students to look at the example sentences of *will / won't*. Make sure they understand how to form the affirmative, negative, questions and short answers. Get students to translate into their own language if necessary.
- Then tell students to look at the example sentences of the first conditional. Ensure they understand how to use the first conditional correctly.
- Refer students to the Grammar reference on pages 92–93 of the Workbook for further revision.

Vocabulary
- Tell students to look at the list of vocabulary and check understanding.
- Refer students to the Wordlist on page 151 of the Workbook where they can look up any words they can't remember.

Speaking
- Check that students understand the phrases to use for making suggestions.
- Tell students to act out a conversation between two students making suggestions. The two students' homework is to think in pairs of a simple scientific experiment for their next science class.

Additional material
Workbook
- Progress check page 46
- Self-evaluation page 47
- Grammar reference and practice pages 92–93
- Vocabulary extension page 106
- Integrated skills page 115
- Writing reference and task pages 128–129

Teacher's Resource File
- Basics section pages 29–34
- Vocabulary and grammar consolidation 19–22
- Translation and dictation pages 6, 16
- Key competences worksheets pages 9–10
- Evaluation rubrics pages 1–7
- Culture and CLIL worksheets pages 17–20
- Culture video worksheets pages 9–10
- Digital competence worksheets pages 9–10
- Macmillan Readers worksheets pages 3–4

Tests and Exams
- Unit 5 End-of-unit test: Basic, Standard and Extra
- CEFR Skills Exam Generator

Study guide

Grammar
will / won't

affirmative
Robots **will work** for humans. We **will be able to** do more things we enjoy!

negative
Learning a second language **won't be** necessary.

questions
Will humans **be able to** fly?

short answers
Yes, they **will**. / No, they **won't**.

First conditional

first conditional: order of verbs
We use the first conditional to talk about possible actions in the future and their results. We can put the possible action first in the sentence and the result second, or we can put the result first and the action second.

situation	result
If scientists **continue** to experiment,	we **will find** cures for more diseases.
result	**situation**
There **will be** more explosions in our science class	if we **aren't** careful with the chemicals!

Vocabulary
Science

battery	planet
clone	satellite
cure	solar panel
disease	spacecraft
DNA	vaccine
genetically modified crops	wind turbine

Science in the classroom

acid	jug
air	laboratory
bubbles	liquid
chemical reaction	pressure
explosion	temperature
gas	test tube
gravity	thermometer

Speaking
Making suggestions
What shall we …?
What / How about a …?
Why don't we …?
Let's …
Maybe we could …
Then … will …

LEARNING TO LEARN
Organize your vocabulary notes into different topics in a notebook. This will help you to find what you need more quickly when you're revising for an exam.

UNIT 6
MONEY

Unit objectives and key competences

In this unit the student will learn...

- understand, memorize and correctly use vocabulary related to jobs and chores and money and shopping **CLC CMST SCC**
- understand and correctly use *be going to*, draw parallels to **L1** and use it in a short speaking activity **CLC L2L SIE**
- understand and correctly use *will* and *would like* **CLC L2L**
- how to form phrases using future time expressions **CLC L2L**
- about second-hand shopping in the United Kingdom and compare second-hand shopping in the United Kingdom with second-hand shopping in their country **CLC SCC CAE**
- about shopping by watching a short video **CLC SCC DC**

In this unit the student will learn how to ...

- identify specific information in an online message board about tips for making money **CLC SCC DC**
- look online for information about part-time and temporary jobs in students' country **CLC DC CMST SIE**
- identify specific information in a street interview **CLC SCC**
- read a magazine article about British teenagers and money, listen to a radio programme about pocket money and learn how to ask for a favour **CLC SCC CAE CMST**
- write an informal letter **CLC SCC SIE L2L**
- prepare for and do a listening exam about completing a table **CLC SIE L2L**

Linguistic contents

Main vocabulary
- Jobs and chores: *wash cars, lay the table*, etc
- Money and shopping: buy, sell, earn, etc

Grammar
- *be going to*
- *will* and *be going to*
- Future time expressions + *will*, *when* + *will* and *would like*

Functional language
- Phrases for asking for a favour

Pronunciation
- Difficult sounds: /w/
- Difficult sounds: /s/ at the beginning of words

Skills

Reading
- Read an online message board about tips for making money
- Read a text about second-hand shops in the UK
- Read a magazine article about British teenagers and money
- Read an informal letter

Writing: Interaction and production
- Write a personalized dialogue about asking for a favour
- Write an informal letter in three steps: plan, write, check
- Learn how to use pronouns correctly

Listening
- Listen to a street interview
- Listen to a radio programme about pocket money

Spoken interaction
- Exchange information about chores you can do
- Ask and answer questions using *be going to*

Spoken production
- Prepare and act out a dialogue about asking for a favour

Lifelong learning skills

Self-study and self-evaluation

- Study guide:
Student's Book page 71
- Progress check and self-evaluation:
Workbook pages 54–55
- Grammar reference and practice:
Workbook pages 94–95
- Wordlist:
Workbook pages 151–157

Learning strategies and thinking skills

- Expressing numbers as percentages or fractions

Cultural awareness

- A quick guide to second-hand shopping
- Comparing second-hand shopping in the UK with second-hand shopping in students' own countries and regions

Cross-curricular contents

- Maths, charity shops, percentages and fractions
- Language and literature: reading and writing an informal letter
- ICT: searching the internet for information

Key competences

CLC	Competence in linguistic communication
CMST	Competence in mathematics, science and technology
DC	Digital competence
SCC	Social and civic competences
CAE	Cultural awareness and expression
L2L	Learning to learn
SIE	Sense of initiative and entrepreneurship

Evaluation

- Unit 6 End-of-unit test: Basic, Standard and Extra
- CEFR Skills Exam Generator
- End-of-term test, Units 4–6: Basic, Standard and Extra

External exam trainer

- Listening: Completing a table or diagram

Digital material

Pulse Live! Digital Course including:
- Interactive grammar tables
- Audio visual speaking model: Asking for a favour
- Audio visual cultural material: Shopping
Student's website

Digital competence

- Web quest: part-time and temporary jobs in students' own country.
- Digital competence worksheet: Online cartoon strips

Reinforcement material

- Basic worksheets, Teacher's Resource File pages 35–40
- Vocabulary and Grammar: Consolidation worksheets, Teacher's Resource File pages 23–24

Extension material

- Fast-finisher activity: Student's Book page 63
- Extra activities: Teacher's Book pages T62, T70
- Vocabulary and Grammar: Extension worksheets, Teacher's Resource File pages 25–26

Teacher's Resource File

- Translation and dictation worksheets pages 7, 17
- Evaluation rubrics pages 1–7
- Key competences worksheets pages 11–12
- Culture and CLIL worksheets pages 21–24
- Culture video worksheets pages 11–12
- Digital competence worksheets pages 11–12
- Macmillan Readers worksheets pages 3–4

 THINK ABOUT IT

Who does which chores in your house?

Vocabulary and Speaking

Jobs and chores

1 🎧 2.24 Listen and repeat the jobs and chores.
Which jobs are the most enjoyable? Which are the least enjoyable?

> wash cars   babysit   pet sit   deliver newspapers   take dogs for walks   do the ironing
> clean the windows   do the washing-up   lay the table   tidy your room   make the beds
> do the gardening

Community noticeboard

Too busy to cut the grass and water the flowers? No problem – I can (1) … for you! Call Alex on 2678 933300

Animal Lover
wanted to (2) … and (3) … when we go on holiday. Contact Mr Briggs on Hepworth 233856

Boy or girl wanted to (4) … Weekdays 7.30–8.30 am. £5 per hour. Must have own bicycle. Contact Smiths Newsagent's 23, Clee Road.

Spend your summer working in a seaside hotel! We need someone in August to tidy the rooms and (5) … For more information, contact the manager of the Blue Beach Hotel.

17-year-old girl who loves children wants to (6) … 2–3 evenings a week. Ring Mandy on 87220996

Exercise 2

1 do the gardening
2 pet sit
3 take dogs for walks
4 deliver newspapers
5 make the beds
6 babysit

Alex and Mandy are looking for work.

---

2 Complete the adverts with words from exercise 1. Which two people are looking for work?

3 🎧 2.25 Listen and check your answers.

👆 **EXPRESS YOURSELF**

4 Think about the chores you do at home. Complete the sentences.

I always lay the table.

1 I always …
2 I usually …
3 I sometimes …
4 I never …

5 Work in pairs. Ask and answer questions about the chores you do.

🔵 *Do you do the washing–up?*
🔵 *Yes, sometimes.*

Vocabulary and Speaking
Jobs and chores

Lesson objectives

In this lesson students will:
- learn / revise words related to jobs and chores
- ask and answer questions about chores they do at home

Warmer

Write the word *jobs* on the board. Put the students into pairs and ask them to make a list of all the jobs they know. Set a time limit of two minutes. Listen to their ideas as a class and make a list of jobs on the board. The pair with the most correct words wins.

Think about it

Students work individualy and answer the question. They compare answers in pairs. Get feedback with the whole class.

1   2.24
- Explain the word *chore* (an ordinary job that must be done regularly, eg washing-up).
- Play the CD. Students repeat the words chorally and individually.
- Make sure they pronounce the words correctly with the correct stress, especially *ironing* /ˈaɪənɪŋ/.
- Students work in pairs and discuss their answers to the questions.
- Listen to their ideas as a class.

Language note

Highlight that in the three-word expressions beginning with a verb and ending with a noun, the main stress falls on the noun: *do the ironing, clean the windows, lay the table, tidy your room, make the beds, do the gardening*.

Extra activity

Ask the class which of the activities they think young people do for money and which they do to help around the home. Listen to their ideas as a class. (In the UK, young people often wash cars, babysit, pet sit and deliver newspapers for money.)

2
- Students work individually and use words from exercise 1 to complete the adverts on the Community noticeboard.
- They answer the question.
- Students compare answers in pairs.

3   2.25
- Play the CD. Students listen and check their answers to exercise 2.
- Check the answer to the question *Which two people are looking for work?* as a class and elicit that Alex and Mandy are looking for work.

EXPRESS YOURSELF

4
- Students work individually and complete the sentences using the vocabulary from exercise 1.

5
- Nominate two students to read aloud the example question and answer.
- Put students into pairs.
- They ask and answer questions about the chores they do.
- Listen to some pairs as a class.

Vocabulary extension: Workbook page 107

Reading

Text type: An online message board

Recommended web links

www.hse.gov.uk/youngpeople/law/

www.adviceguide.org.uk/england/work_e/
work_young_people_e/young_people_and_
employment.htm

Warmer

Write the word *money* on the board. Put students into pairs. Set a time limit of two minutes for them to make a list of the money that is used in different countries. Listen to their ideas as a class and make a list on the board (*euro, pound, dollar, peso*, etc).

1 🔘 2.26
- Explain the task. Check students understand the question. Point out that this exercise gives students practice in getting the gist (general idea) of a text from listening to it for general meaning and / or reading it quickly.
- Play the CD. Students listen and follow the text in their books.
- They compare answers in pairs.
- Check the answer as a class and highlight the information in the Did you know? box.

2
- Students read the questions carefully first.
- They read the text again and find the answers. They note down the answers in their notebooks.
- Students compare answers in pairs.
- Check answers as a class.

3
- Students read the questions carefully first.
- They read the text again and find the answers. They note down the answers in their notebooks.
- Students compare answers in pairs.
- Check answers as a class.

Word check

Make sure students understand the words. Ask them to translate them into their language. You could also check *auction* (a sale when things are sold to the people who offer the most money for them – an example of an *online auction* is eBay).

4
- Read the example sentence aloud to the class.
- Students work in pairs and discuss what they think is the best tip and why.
- Listen to their ideas as a class.

Finished?

Students work in groups of 3–4 and think of more tips for saving money. Listen to their ideas as a class. Which group has the best ideas for saving money?

Web quest

Students find out information about a part-time or temporary job in their country. Highlight the Web quest tip.

1 • Ask students to open an internet web browser such as Internet Explorer. Students open a search engine (eg Google) and type in the subject of their search.
  • Students find information about a job they would like to do.
2 • Students make notes about the pay, working hours and duties.
3 • Students work in pairs and tell each other about their jobs.
  • Ask some students to report on the information they have found to the class.

MESSAGE BOARD

HOME   FORUM   LOG IN   REGISTER

USERNAME: PENNYLESS

Tips for making money?   by **PennyLess**   17/08   11:43

Hi! I'm 14 and I want to buy a smartphone. There's only one problem – it's expensive! Has anyone got any tips for making and saving money?

RE: Tips for making money?   by **Cinderella**   Fri 17/08   13:30

My parents sometimes pay me to do chores around the house. I wash the car or do the ironing – whatever needs doing! It gives me a bit of extra pocket money!

Re: Tips for making money?   by **owen99**   17/08   15:55

Why don't you get a job in the school holidays? I'm going to work in a hotel so I'll have enough money to go on holiday in August. Maybe you could try babysitting?

RE: Tips for making money?   by **KittyB**   18/08   10:14

Think about your skills. Maybe you're good with children, so you could babysit for families in your area. Or if you like animals, how about pet sitting while the owners are on holiday? Put an advert in a shop window that says what you can do.

Re: Tips for making money?   by **smartAlec**   20/08   21:21

I know a way to make money. Sort out all the things you don't use any more (clothes, CDs or toys) and put an advert for them on an online auction website. Other people really will want to buy your old things! And it's much better to recycle them than throw them away!

RE: Tips for making money?   by **TrendyGirl**   20/08   13:45

Instead of earning money, why not try to spend less? Do what I do – buy your clothes at markets and in second-hand shops. You can find some really nice things at great prices!

Re: Tips for making money?   by **PennyLess**   21/08   14:07

Thanks for your advice. ☺ I've seen an advert for a babysitting job, so I'm going to apply! I'm also going to visit the second-hand shops in my area to look for bargains.

Word check

tip   pocket money   sort out   second-hand   apply   bargain

---

DID YOU KNOW?

On average, UK teenagers receive £6 every week from their parents.

Reading
An online message board

1 🔊 2.26   Read and listen to the message board. Who doesn't suggest a way of making money?

2 Answer the questions.

1 Why does PennyLess need some money?
2 What kind of jobs does Cinderella do?
3 What is owen99 going to do in August?
4 How can PennyLess help the environment?
5 Where does TrendyGirl go shopping?

3 Read the text again and answer the questions.

1 Who suggests PennyLess sells some things?
2 Who is planning to do a temporary job?
3 How can PennyLess advertise herself?

4 Which do you think is the best tip? Why?

I think the best tip is to do chores in the house because it's an easy way to make money.

FINISHED?

Can you think of more tips for saving money?
Walk or cycle instead of using public transport.

WEB QUEST

Search for a website with adverts for part-time and temporary jobs in your country.

1 Look for a job that you would like to do.
2 Read the information about the job and make notes about the pay, working hours and duties.
3 Work in pairs. Tell each other about your jobs.

Web Quest tip!

Work in pairs and share your tasks for the web quest. This helps to save time and focuses your search even more.

Exercise 1

TrendyGirl

Exercise 2

1 To buy a smartphone.
2 Chores around the house.
3 Go on holiday.
4 By selling and recycling her old things.
5 At markets and in second-hand shops.

Exercise 3

1 smartAlec
2 owen99
3 By putting an advert in a shop window.

Grammar

be going to

affirmative
I (1) ... **going to work** in a hotel.
negative
You (2) ... **going to find** work easily.
questions
(3) ... you **going to be** free this summer?
short answers
Yes, I **am**. / No, I'**m not**.

LOOK!

We use *be going to* to talk about future plans and intentions.
I'm going to tidy my room tomorrow.

1 Copy and complete the table with the correct form of *be*.

2 Complete the sentences with the correct form of *be going to* and the verbs in brackets.
1 Adam ... (not go) to university.
2 He and his best friend ... (design) computer games.
3 They ... (sell) them to big companies.
4 His parents ... (not be) happy.
5 Adam thinks he ... (make) lots of money!

3 Write the questions using *be going to*.
1 you / go shopping on Saturday?
2 anyone / give you money for your birthday?
3 you / save your pocket money?
4 your parents / let you get a job?
5 you / be a millionaire in the future?

ANALYSE

In English, the *going to* part of *be going to* never changes form depending on the person who is speaking. Is this the same in your language?

EXPRESS YOURSELF

4 Work in pairs. Ask and answer the questions from exercise 3.

🗨 *Are you going to go shopping on Saturday?*

🗨 *No, I'm not. I'm going to take my dog for a walk.*

will and be going to

5 Copy and complete the rules with *be going to* or *will*.

a) We use ... to talk about future predictions or decisions we make at the moment of speaking.
I'll do the washing-up!
b) We use ... to talk about future plans and intentions.
I'm going to buy a new jacket.

6 Complete the sentences with the correct form of *be going to* or *will*.

① I ... help you carry those bags.

② He ... buy an ice cream.

③ It ... grow a lot.

④ They ... rob a bank.

⑤ You ... be a scientist, live on the Moon and be very happy!

Exercise 1
1 'm
2 aren't
3 Are

Exercise 2
1 isn't going to go
2 are going to design
3 're going to sell
4 aren't going to be
5 's going to make

Exercise 3
1 Are you going to go shopping on Saturday?
2 Is anyone going to give you money for your birthday?
3 Are you going to save your pocket money?
4 Are your parents going to let you get a job?
5 Are you going to be a millionaire in the future?

Exercise 5
a will
b be going to

Exercise 6
1 'll
2 's going to
3 'll
4 're going to
5 'll

2.27–2.28 Pronunciation lab: Difficult sounds: /w/, page 125

Grammar

be going to

 Digital

Lesson objectives

In this lesson students will:
- learn / revise *be going to* for future plans and intentions
- contrast *will* and *be going to*

Warmer

Write the word *weekend* on the board. Put students into pairs and ask them to discuss their plans for the coming weekend. Listen to their ideas as a class. At this stage, don't correct them if they make errors with *be going to* as this is the subject of this lesson.

1 • Students copy the table into their notebooks.
- They read the example sentences and complete the table using contractions if possible.
- Check answers as a class. Point out that *going to* doesn't change in different persons in the affirmative, negative and question forms but that the verb *be* does.
- Highlight the short answers and emphasize that we do not use *going to* in the short answers.

Look!

Highlight the use of *be going to* to talk about future plans and intentions and read the example sentence aloud to the class.

2 • Do the first sentence with the whole class as an example (*isn't going to go*).
- Students copy the sentences into their notebooks.
- Students work individually and complete the sentences using the correct form of *be going to* and the verbs in brackets.
- They compare answers in pairs.
- Check answers as a class.

3 • Do the first question with the whole class as an example (*Are you going to go shopping on Saturday?*).
- Students complete the exercise individually.
- They compare answers in pairs.
- Check answers as a class.

Analyse

Ask students to read the information about the *going to* part of *be going to* in English and compare it with their own language.

EXPRESS YOURSELF

4 • Nominate two students to read the example question and answer aloud to the class.
- Students work in pairs and ask and answer the questions. They give answers that are true for them.
- Listen to some pairs as a class.

Finished?

Ask fast finishers to write answers that are not true for them to each of the questions in exercise 3.

will and *be going to*

5 • Students copy the rules into their notebooks.
- They use *be going to* and *will* to complete the rules.
- They compare answers in pairs.
- Check answers as a class.

6 • Explain the task.
- Students work individually and use the correct forms of *be going to* and *will* to fill the gaps. Remind them that they will need to use the correct form of *be* in the sentences with *be going to*.
- They compare answers in pairs.
- Check answers as a class.

 Pronunciation lab: Difficult sounds: /w/, page 125

Digital course: Interactive grammar table

Study guide: page 71

Vocabulary and Listening
Money and shopping

Warmer

Write *spend money* on the board. Ask students to work in pairs and discuss the three things they spend most money on each week. Listen to their ideas as a class by asking them to report back on what their partner said, eg *Sara spends a lot of money on DVDs. David buys a lot of clothes.*

1 🔘 2.29
- Play the CD. Students listen and repeat the words in the word pool.
- Make sure they pronounce the words correctly, especially *earn* /ɜ:n/.
- Check students understand all the words by asking them to translate them into their language.
- Students answer the question. Make sure they understand that when you *lend* money, you give it to another person and when you *borrow* money, you take it from another person.

2
- Students work individually and fill the gaps in the text using the words from exercise 1.
- They answer the question.
- Students compare answers in pairs.

3 🔘 2.30
- Play the CD. Students listen and check their answers from exercise 2.
- Check the answer to the question as a class and elicit that Clare prefers to spend money.

4
- Students read the questions carefully first.
- They work individually and think about their answers.
- They compare answers in pairs.
- Listen to their ideas as a class.

5 🔘 2.31
- Explain the task.
- Play the CD. Students listen and note down the answer to the question.
- Students compare answers in pairs.
- Check the answer as a class.

6
- Students read the questions carefully first.
- Play the CD again. Students listen and choose the correct words.
- They compare answers in pairs.
- Check answers as a class. Point out that another word for *used* is *second-hand*.

🔘 **2.31 Audioscript, exercise 5**

Reporter: Hi and welcome to *The Style Show*. This week, we're coming to you live from Camden Market, where some of the most fashionable people in London do their shopping! Let's talk to a few of them … Hi! What's your name?
Anna: Anna.
Reporter: Do you live in London, Anna?
Anna: No, I'm on holiday here. I've come to Camden today to visit the market because I want to buy some presents for my friends in Poland.
Reporter: And have you bought anything yet?
Anna: Yes, I have. These earrings.
Reporter: How much did you pay for them?
Anna: They were only three pounds.
Reporter: Well, I hope you find lots more bargains!
Anna: Thanks!
Reporter: Hi there. Can I talk to you for a minute?
Boy: Sure.
Reporter: Do you often come to Camden?
Boy: About once a week. Yeah, I love this area. It's really lively. And the market sells really interesting things.
Reporter: Tell me something about your style. Do you always wear black?
Boy: Most of the time, yeah. I don't like bright colours.
Reporter: What have you got in your bag?
Boy: A T-shirt. I bought it from that stall over there. And yes, it's black!
Reporter: Excuse me?
Girl: Yeah?
Reporter: We're from *The Style Show*. Can I ask you a few questions?
Girl: OK.
Reporter: I love your look. Do you spend a lot of money on clothes?
Girl: No, I don't. I haven't got much money because I'm a student. I buy most of my clothes from second-hand shops. Sometimes I borrow clothes from other people too.
Reporter: That's a great jacket. Did it cost a lot?
Girl: I don't know. A friend of mine lent it to me.
Reporter: Cool! Thank you. Right, now we've got an interesting report on a new …

Vocabulary and Listening
Money and shopping

1 2.29 Listen and repeat the money words in the box. Do you ever lend or borrow money?

> buy sell cost spend save earn pay for borrow lend lose swap win collect

MY SHOPPING TRIP

I've got some money for my birthday! Mum thinks I should put it in the bank and (1) … it, but I want to go shopping!

Camden Market in London is a great place to (2) … clothes and jewellery.

Some stalls (3) … second-hand things, so you don't need to (4) … a lot of money.

I really like these bags! How much does this (5) …, please?

Let's have a rest now! I'll (6) … the coffees.

Not everyone comes to Camden to go shopping. Some people (7) … money by entertaining the shoppers!

Other people (8) … money for charity, like this one for sick children.

I haven't got any money left now! I'll have to (9) … some money from my friend to buy my bus ticket!

2 Read the text and complete it with words from exercise 1. Does Clare prefer to spend money or to save it?

3 2.30 Listen and check your answers to exercise 2.

4 Think about a shop or market in your town and answer the questions.

1 What's the name of the shop?
2 What does it sell?
3 How often do you go shopping there?
4 What's the last thing you bought there?
5 How much did it cost?

5 2.31 Listen to a reporter interviewing people in the street for a TV programme. What's the name of the programme?

6 Listen again and choose the correct words.

1 Anna comes from **London** / **Poland**.
2 Anna's earrings were **cheap** / **expensive**.
3 The boy prefers **black** / **bright colours**.
4 He's got a new **bag** / **T-shirt**.
5 The girl usually buys **new** / **used** clothes.
6 She has **bought** / **borrowed** a jacket.

Cultural awareness
The United Kingdom

Fact box

There are about 7,000 charity shops in the UK!

A QUICK GUIDE TO **SECOND-HAND SHOPPING**

Even if you haven't got lots of money to spend, you can still go shopping!
Read on to find out where to find the best bargains.

HOME

NEWS

GUIDES

LINKS

CHARITY SHOPS

Why do people in Britain like shopping in charity shops? First, because of the low prices, and second, because when you buy something, the money is used to help people in need. For example, Oxfam, which has shops all over the UK, works to stop poverty in countries around the world. What can you find in a charity shop? Used clothes, shoes, books, toys, DVDs and kitchen equipment. It might take a while to find what you want, but it's fun looking!

CAR BOOT SALES

What do British people do with their old or unwanted possessions? Take them to a car boot sale! Every Saturday and Sunday, people all over Britain fill the boot of their car with things they don't want and take them to one of these sales. Car boot sales attract hundreds of people, so get there early for the best bargains. You never know what you might find. Recently, someone bought an old picture frame at a car boot sale for one pound and later found it was worth £500,000!

SWAP SHOPS

Do you want to get some new clothes without spending any money? The answer is a swap shop! Swap shops are events where you and other people can exchange clothes that you don't want. The clothes have to be good quality and look new. You can then choose clothes of the same value that other people have brought to the swap shop. Swap shops are popular with fashionable people who have lots of nice clothes that they never wear. Swapping clothes is also better for the environment than buying new ones!

Word check

charity poverty frame exchange good quality value

Exercise 2

In swap shops.

Exercise 3

1 They use it to help people in need.

2 Oxfam.

3 Things they don't want.

4 One pound.

5 Good quality clothes that look new.

6 You don't spend any money and swapping clothes is better for the environment than buying new ones.

---

1 Do you like shopping? Why (not)?

2 🔊 2.32 Read and listen. Where can you shop for free?

3 Read the guide again and answer the questions.

1 How do charity shops use the money they make?
2 Which charity has a lot of shops?
3 What do people sell at car boot sales?
4 How much did a valuable picture frame cost at a car boot sale?
5 What kind of clothes can you find at swap shops?
6 What are two advantages of swapping?

CULTURAL 🌐 **COMPARISON**

4 Answer the questions about your country.

1 Do people like buying second-hand things? Why (not)?
2 Are there any charity shops in your town or city?
3 What do people do with things that they don't want any more?
4 Can you go shopping on a Sunday? If so, where?
5 Do young people ever swap clothes with each other?

Cultural awareness

The United Kingdom

Warmer

Highlight the information in the Fact box and write *charity* on the board. Check that students understand the meaning (a *charity* is an organization to which you give money so that it can give money and help to people who are poor or ill, or who need help and support). Elicit from the class different charities, eg *the Red Cross*.

1
- Students work in pairs and ask and answer the questions.
- Listen to their ideas as a class.

2 2.32
- Check students understand the task.
- Play the CD. Students listen and follow the text in the books.
- They write the answer in their notebooks.
- Check the answer as a class.

Culture note

Oxfam was originally founded in Oxford, in 1942 as the *Oxford Committee for Famine Relief*. Today, Oxfam has the largest network of charity shops in the UK. Items donated to Oxfam chartiy shops are sold or recycled, to make money for development and campaigningwork to help improve lives around the world.

3
- Students read the questions carefully first.
- They look in the text and find the answers.
- They compare answers in pairs.
- Check answers as a class.

Word check

Make sure students understand the words. Ask them to translate them into their language. Other words you could check include *kitchen equipment* and *car boot* (the part of a car where you put your luggage).

CULTURAL **COMPARISON**

4
- Put students into pairs and ask them to discuss the questions.
- Listen to their ideas as a class.

Culture video: Shopping ⟩⟩

Grammar
Future time expressions

Lesson objectives

In this lesson students will:
- learn a set of future time expressions
- learn / revise *would like / wouldn't like*
- read a short text about maths problems

Warmer

Write the sentence *It will grow a lot* on the board with the words in the wrong order: *lot it a grow will*. Students work in pairs and write the sentence with the words in the correct order. Remind students that *will* can also be contracted.

1
- Students read the information in the table and answer the question.
- They compare answers in pairs.
- Check the answer as a class. Point out that we never use *will* after *when*.

2
- Complete the first sentence with the whole class to demonstrate the activity (*When we're in Paris, we'll go shopping.*).
- Point out that not all the sentences contain *when* so the present simple is not always the correct form of the verb. Highlight that all the sentences are predictions about a trip to Paris.
- Students work individually to complete the sentences with the correct form of the verbs in brackets.
- They compare answers in pairs.
- Check answers as a class.

3
- Students complete the task individually.
- They compare answers in pairs.
- Listen to their ideas as a class. Make sure they use *I'll*.

would like

4
- Students read the information in the table and the example sentences.
- Explain the task. A tick means an affirmative sentence and a cross means a negative sentence.
- Students work individually to complete the exercise.
- They compare answers in pairs.
- Check answers as a class.

CLIL Grammar in context: Maths

5
- Students work individually and choose the correct answers.
- They compare answers in pairs.

6 2.33
- Students work individually and solve the three maths problems.
- They compare answers in pairs.
- Play the CD. Students listen and check their answers. (The answers are also given at the bottom of the page.)

CLIL task

Students use the internet to do the task.

Pronunciation lab: Difficult sounds: /s/ at the beginning of words, page 125

Digital course: Interactive grammar table

Study guide: page 71

 2.33 Audioscript, exercise 6

Boy: Problem A. Bananas are 1.20 euros a kilo, apples are 2.50 euros a kilo, and pears are 2.20 euros a kilo. You are going to buy half a kilo of bananas, a kilo of apples, and a kilo of pears. Will a five-euro note be enough to pay for them?
Girl: No, five euros won't be enough to pay for the fruit. Half a kilo of bananas cost 60 cents. The cost of all the fruit is 60 cents plus 2.50 plus 2.20 equals 5.30 euros.
Boy: Problem B. Sue gets 100 euros for her birthday. She's going to spend 36.99 euros on a camera and 12.50 euros on a DVD. How much change will she have?
Girl: Sue spends 36.99 plus 12.50 which equals 49.49 euros. Her change from a hundred euros is a hundred minus 49. 49 which equals 50.51 euros.
Boy: Problem C. You're going to go on holiday to the USA and you'd like to change 200 euros into dollars. 1 euro equals 1.5 dollars. How many dollars will you get when you change this number of euros?
Girl: When you change 200 euros into dollars, you'll get 200 times 1.5 which equals 300 dollars.

Grammar
Future time expressions

time expressions + *will*, *when* + *will*

When we make predictions about the future with *will*, we often use time expressions like:

tomorrow   next week   this summer   one day   soon

I'll be rich one day!

We use phrases with *when* like this:

*When I **go** shopping, I'll buy some new shoes.* ✔

When I'll go shopping, I'll buy some new shoes. ✘

Exercise 1

the present simple

1 Study the table. In sentences about the future, which tense do we use after *when*?

2 Copy and complete the sentences with the correct form of the verbs in brackets.

  1 When we … (be) in Paris, we … (go) shopping.
  2 I … (try) lots of different clothes on, but I … (not buy) them all!
  3 When we … (feel) tired, we … (find) a café.
  4 I … (have) a drink and a sandwich.

Exercise 2

1 When we're in Paris, we'll go shopping.
2 I'll try lots of different clothes on, but I won't buy them all!
3 When we feel tired, we'll find a café.
4 I'll have a drink and a sandwich.

3 Make predictions about your future. Use these phrases to help you.

> get a job go to university buy a car
> travel round the world get married   learn to drive

  1 When I'm 18, I …
  2 When I'm 20, I …
  3 When I'm 25, I …
  4 When I'm 30, I …

Exercise 3

students' own answers

would like

would like + infinitive

We use *would like* to mean *want*. We use the infinitive with *to* after it.

affirmative and negative

I**'d like to borrow** your pen.

Tom **wouldn't like to miss** the concert.

questions and short answers

Would you **like to take** the dog for a walk?

Yes, I **would**. / No, I **wouldn't**.

Exercise 4

1 He wouldn't like to have short hair.
2 Sarah would like to play the guitar.
3 Mrs Smith wouldn't like to go on a rollercoaster.
4 Neil and Liz would like to get married.

4 Study the table. Write sentences using *would like* (✔) or *wouldn't like* (✘).

I / forget your birthday ✘
I wouldn't like to forget your birthday.

  1 He / have short hair ✘
  2 Sarah / play the guitar ✔
  3 Mrs Smith / go on a rollercoaster ✘
  4 Neil and Liz / get married ✔

 **2.34–2.35** Pronunciation lab: Difficult sounds: /s/ at the beginning of words, page 125

CLIL Grammar in context: Maths

5 Read the maths problems and circle the correct answers for 1–8.

A Bananas are 1.20 euros a kilo, apples are 2.50 euros a kilo, and pears are 2.20 euros a kilo. You are going **(1) a buy / to buy / buying** half a kilo of bananas, a kilo of apples, and a kilo of pears. Will a five euro note **(2) it is / it be / be** enough to pay for them?

B Sue gets 100 euros for her birthday. She **(3) will to / going to / 's going to** spend 36.99 euros on a camera and 12.50 euros on a DVD. How much change **(4) she will have / will she have / will have she**?

C You **(5) going / going to go / 're going to go** on holiday to the USA and you'd **(6) like / like to / would like** change 200 euros into dollars. 1 euro = 1.5 dollars. How many dollars **(7) will you get / you'll get / will get** when you **(8) will change / are going to change / change** this number of euros?

6 **2.33** Can you solve the three maths problems? Listen and check your answers.

Answers

A: No, five euros won't be enough. Half a kilo of bananas cost 0.60 euros. The cost of the fruit is 0.60 + 2.50 + 2.20 = 5.30 euros.
B: 100 − (36.99 + 12.50) = 50.51 euros
C: 200 x 1.5 = 300 dollars

CLIL TASK
Go online. Find three maths problems. Can you do them?

Exercise 5

1 to buy
2 be
3 's going to
4 will she have
5 're going to go
6 like to
7 will you get
8 change

All about pocket money

Doing odd jobs around the house is a great way to earn extra money.

WHERE DO BRITISH TEENAGERS GET THEIR MONEY FROM?

* Parents and neighbours pay some children to do 'odd jobs'. These are chores such as doing the ironing, cutting the grass or washing the car.
** Many British children over the age of thirteen have got Saturday jobs in places like shops or sports centres.

20%
10%
60%
10%

● Saturday jobs**   ◑ presents
● odd job earnings*   ● parents

HOW DO THEY SPEND THEIR MONEY?

1 Boys and girls spend two-thirds of their pocket money on sweets and chocolate.
2 Girls buy more clothes, magazines and cosmetics than boys.
3 Boys buy more food and drink, computer games, DVDs and CDs than girls.
4 Girls spend 50% more on mobile phones than boys.

SKILLS BUILDER

Expressing numbers as percentages or fractions

Amounts can be given as percentages. Percentages can be expressed in the following ways.

10% = a tenth   50% = (a) half
25% = a quarter   75% = three-quarters
33.3% = a third   100% = all

Step 1: Read

1 Look at the magazine article. On what day of the week do some teenagers work?

2 Are the sentences true or false? Correct the false sentences.

1 Teenagers only get money from their parents.
2 Children aged 11 and 12 have part-time jobs.
3 Teenagers spend most of their pocket money on sweets and chocolate.
4 More girls buy computer games than boys.
5 Boys spend less money on mobile phones than girls.

Step 2: Listen

3 ● 2.36 Listen to a radio programme about pocket money. Who doesn't get money from his or her parents?

4 Listen again. Copy and complete the table in your notebook.

name	age	way of making money	what he / she does with money
Ben			buys sweets and computer games
Lily	16		
Harry		does odd jobs for people	

Exercise 1

Saturday

Exercise 2

1 False
Many teenagers have Saturday jobs.
2 False
Children over the age of 13 have part-time jobs.
3 True
4 False
More boys buy computer games than girls.
5 True

Exercise 3

Lily

Exercise 4

age
Ben: 13
Harry: 15

way of making money
Ben: does chores around the house
Lily: works in a restaurant

what he / she does with money
Lily: buys clothes
Harry: saves it

Integrated skills
All about pocket money

Lesson objectives

In this lesson students will:
- work on all four skills
- read a magazine article
- listen to a radio programme about pocket money
- write a personalized dialogue
- act out their dialogue

Warmer

Ask students to look at the pictures of what teenagers in the UK spend their money on. Elicit as much vocabulary from the class as possible to describe the items in the pictures and write the words on the board (*sweets, a computer game, nail polish, shoes*). Ask students what other things they think British teenagers spend their money on and write their suggestions on the board.

Skills builder

Expressing numbers as percentages or fractions

Focus on the information in the Skills builder box. Highlight that amounts can be given as percentages or fractions. Books closed. Write *25%, a half, three-quarters, 10%* on the board. Ask students to express the percentages as fractions and the fractions as percentages (*a quarter, 50%, 75%, a tenth*). Then ask them what *20%* and *33.3%* are in fractions and elicit a *fifth* and a *third*.

Step 1: Read

1
- Students read the question carefully first.
- They read Lucy's speech bubble and the text. They find the answer to the question.
- Check the answer as a class.

2
- Students read the sentences first.
- They look in the text and decide if the statements are true or false.
- They compare answers in pairs and correct the false statements.
- Check answers as a class.

Step 2: Listen

3 ⊙ 2.36
- Play the CD. Students listen and write the answer in their notebooks.
- Check the answer as a class.

4
- Students copy the table into their notebooks.
- Play the CD again. Students listen and complete the table.
- Students compare answers in pairs.
- Check answers as a class.

2.36 Audioscript, exercise 3

Presenter: Hi and welcome to the *Money Show!* This week we're talking about pocket money – how much you get, how you get it and what you spend it on. We're going to take some calls from listeners now and, to start with, I think we've got Ben on line 1. Hi Ben.
Ben: Hi.
Presenter: You're 13 years old, right?
Ben: Yeah.
Presenter: Do you get any pocket money from your parents?
Ben: Yes, I do. But my mum and dad also pay me for doing chores around the house sometimes.
Presenter: I see. What do you spend your money on?
Ben: Sweets and computer games mainly. My parents buy all my clothes.
Presenter: OK. Thanks a lot, Ben. Let's go to line 2 now, where we've got our next caller – Lily, who's 16. Do your parents give you pocket money, Lily?
Lily: No, they don't. But I have a Saturday job in a restaurant and I get £20 a week from that.
Presenter: Do you save your money or spend it?
Lily: Spend it – on clothes usually.
Presenter: So you don't put any money in the bank?
Lily: No!
Presenter: OK. Now we've got another caller on line 3. Harry, you're 15 years old and you've found a great way to earn money in your free time. Can you tell us about it?
Harry: Yes. I do odd jobs for other people – shopping, posting letters … that kind of thing.
Presenter: What made you start doing odd jobs?
Harry: My parents didn't give me enough pocket money!
Presenter: I see! Do you spend the money you earn?
Harry: No, I don't. I save it.
Presenter: Very sensible! Now it's time for some music …

T68

Integrated skills – continued
Asking for a favour

5   🔘 2.37
- Students read the dialogue first.
- Play the CD. Students listen and follow the text in their books. They write answers 1–4 in their notebooks.
- They compare answers in pairs.
- Check answers as a class.

6
- Play the CD again, pausing after each question or statement and each response for students to repeat as a class.
- Note the main stress and the rising intonation in the *yes / no* questions: *Can I ask you a favour? Could you lend me three <u>pounds</u>?*
- Note the falling tone in the *wh-* questions: *What <u>is</u> it? Why don't you <u>earn</u> the money instead?*
- Ask students to repeat the dialogue several times both chorally and individually with the correct stress and intonation.
- Students practise the dialogue in pairs. Then swap roles and practise the dialogue again.

Step 3: Write

7
- Students work individually. They copy the phrases and questions in bold from the dialogue into their notebooks.
- They think of something they want to buy (not a CD) and a different way of earning money.

8
- Ask students to look at the Communication kit: Asking for a favour. Encourage them to use these questions when writing their dialogue.
- Students work individually and write their dialogue, using the dialogue in the book as a model.
- Monitor while they are writing and give help if necessary.

Step 4: Communicate

9
- Students practise their dialogues in pairs.
- For extra practice, they swap roles in both dialogues.

10
- Choose some pairs to act out their dialogue for the class.
- Students raise their hand if another pair has the same thing they want to buy as the item they have chosen. This will encourage them to listen carefully to their classmates.

Integrated skills: Workbook page 116 ›

UNIT 6

ASKING FOR A FAVOUR

Watch!

Hi Dad. **Can I ask you a favour?**	OK. What is it?
Could you lend me (1) … , please?	Why?
I want to buy a (2) …	How much does it cost?
(3) … , but I've already got 10.	I've got an idea. **Why don't you earn the money instead?**
How can I do that?	**I'll pay you** three pounds **to** (4) … .
OK, it's a deal! I'll do it when I finish my homework.	Great! Thanks.

Exercise 5

1 three pounds
2 CD
3 Thirteen pounds
4 wash the car

5 🔊 2.37 Listen to Lucy talking to her dad. Complete 1–4 in your notebook.

6 Listen again and repeat. Practise your intonation.

Step 3: Write

7 Copy the phrases and questions in bold in your notebook. Then think of something else you want to buy and another way of earning the money to buy it.

8 Write a new dialogue. Write both parts. Use the dialogue in exercise 5 to help you.

Hi … Can I ask you a favour?
OK. What is it?

Step 4: Communicate

9 Work in pairs. Take turns to practise your dialogues.

🔵 *Hi … Can I ask you a favour?*
⚪ *OK. What is it?*

10 Act your dialogue for the class.

COMMUNICATION KIT

Asking for a favour

Can I ask you a favour?
Could / Can you … ?
Is it OK if I … ?
Would you mind doing / cleaning / helping me with … ?

Writing
An informal letter

3 Bennett Road
Bolton
BL7 4PJ
Friday 15 April

Dear Grandma and Grandad,

Thank you very much for my birthday present! I love my new trainers. I'm wearing them right now! They fit me perfectly.

I'm going to have my birthday party tomorrow because it's Saturday. First, ten of my friends are coming to my house in the afternoon. Then, we're going to go to the bowling alley in the town centre. My brother isn't going to come because he hates bowling – I think that's because he isn't very good at it! I'll invite him to join us later though. We're going to eat at my favourite burger bar. In the evening, we'll probably watch a film at my house. Mum and Dad bought me some great new DVDs for my birthday, so I'd like to watch one of them.

I'll see you next month! Thanks again for the present.

Love from,
Paul

Exercise 1

Paul and ten of his friends are going to a bowling alley in the afternoon. Then they're going to eat at a burger bar. In the evening they're probably going to watch a film at Paul's house.

Exercise 2

1 Paul's new trainers
2 Paul
3 bowling
4 Paul's brother
5 Paul, ten of his friends and Paul's brother
6 Paul's grandmother and grandfather

Exercise 3

1 he
2 they
3 you
4 it

1 🔊 2.38 **Read and listen to the letter. What is Paul going to do for his birthday party?**

2 Look at the sentences from the letter. What or who do the words in blue refer to?

1 I'm wearing **them** right now!
2 **I**'m going to have my birthday party tomorrow.
3 He isn't very good at **it**!
4 I'll invite **him** to join us.
5 **We**'ll probably watch a film.
6 I'll see **you** next month!

3 Copy and complete the sets of pronouns in the Writing focus.

WRITING FOCUS

Using pronouns
We use pronouns to avoid repeating names and nouns.

Subject pronouns:
I   you   (1) ...   she   it   we   (2) ...

Object pronouns:
me   (3) ...   him   her   (4) ...   us   them

Molly hates shopping. **She** prefers playing computer games.
*That's a nice **t-shirt**. Why don't you buy **it**?*

4 Change the words in blue to subject or object pronouns.

1 If I find some cheap DVDs, I'm going to buy **the DVDs**.
2 Lucy doesn't like football because she isn't very good at **football**.
3 I want to buy a CD for Tim's birthday, but I don't know what music **Tim** likes.
4 Amy didn't know where to go swimming, but someone told **Amy** about the new sports centre.

Exercise 4

1 them
2 it
3 he
4 her

Writing task:
Write an informal letter.

Plan   Imagine that it was your birthday yesterday and you're writing to thank a relative for their birthday present and tell them about your birthday party. Decide what present they bought you and think of three plans for your party.

Write   Write an informal letter to your relative to thank them and tell them about your plans. Write three paragraphs.

Check   Check your writing.

- ☑ subject and object pronouns
- ☑ use of future verb forms
- ☑ 'Dear ...' at the start, your name at the end

Writing
An informal letter

Warmer

Write *birthday party* on the board. Elicit from the class ideas of things to do for a birthday party, eg *going to a concert*. Write students' suggestions on the board and ask them to vote for their favourite suggestion.

1 🔊 2.38
- Read the question aloud to the class.
- Play the CD. Students listen and follow the text in their books.
- Check the answer as a class.

2
- Explain that this exercise focuses on pronouns and how we can use them to avoid repeating names and nouns.
- Students read the sentences, look in the text and say what or who the pronouns refer to.
- They compare answers in pairs.
- Check answers as a class.

3
- Read the example sentences in the Writing focus box aloud to the class and highlight that we use pronouns to avoid repeating names and nouns.
- Students work individually and complete the sets of subject and object pronouns.
- They compare answers in pairs.
- Check answers as a class.

4
- Explain the task.
- Students change the words in blue to subject or object pronouns.
- They compare answers in pairs.
- Check answers as a class.

Extra activity

Write these sentences on the board: *1 Lucy is my best friend. I'm going to buy Lucy a present. 2 Peter wants to buy a new bike. He doesn't know where to buy a new bike. 3 I watched a good film last night. The film was really scary.* Students rewrite the second sentences using pronouns (*her, it, It*).

Writing task

The aim of this activity is for students to write an informal letter with *Dear …* at the start and the writer's name at the end that includes the correct use of subject and object pronouns and future verb forms. Ask the students to follow the stages in the Student's Book. At the Check stage, ask them to swap notebooks and check each other's writing.

Writing reference and practice: Workbook page 130

Study guide
Grammar, Vocabulary and Speaking

Tell the students the Study guide is an important page which provides a useful reference for the main language of the unit: the grammar, the vocabulary and the functional language from the Integrated skills pages. Explain that they should refer to this page when studying for a test or exam.

Grammar

- Tell the students to look at the example sentences of *be going to*. Make sure they understand how to form the affirmative, negative, questions and short answers.
- Then tell students to look at the example sentences of *will* and *be going to*. Ensure they understand when to use each structure. Get students to translate into their own language if necessary.
- Tell students to look at the example sentence for time expressions with *will* and the example sentence for *when + will*. Make sure students understand how to use time expressions with *will* and how to use *when + will* to make predictions about the future.
- Tell students to look at the example sentences of *would like* and make sure they understand the meaning of *would like* and how to form the affirmative, negative, questions and short answers.
- Refer students to the Grammar reference on pages 94–95 of the Workbook for further revision.

Vocabulary

- Tell students to look at the list of vocabulary and check understanding.
- Refer students to the Wordlist on page 151 of the Workbook where they can look up any words they can't remember.

Speaking

- Check that students understand the phrases to use for asking for a favour.
- Tell students to act out a conversation between two people who are asking each other for a favour.

Additional material

Workbook

- Progress check page 54
- Self-evaluation page 55
- Grammar reference and practice pages 94–95
- Vocabulary extension page 107
- Integrated skills page 116
- Writing reference and task pages 130–131

Teacher's Resource File

- Basics section pages 35–40
- Vocabulary and grammar consolidation pages 23–26
- Translation and dictation pages 7, 17
- Evaluation rubrics pages 1–7
- Key competences worksheets pages 11–12
- Culture and CLIL worksheets pages 21–24
- Culture video worksheets pages 11–12
- Digital competence worksheets pages 11–12
- Macmillan Readers worksheets pages 3–4

Tests and Exams

- Unit 6 End-of-unit test: Basic, Standard and Extra
- CEFR Skills Exam Generator
- End-of-term test: Basic, Standard and Extra

Study guide

Grammar
be going to

affirmative
I'm going to buy a magazine with my pocket money.

negative
We aren't going to go on holiday this year.

questions
Are you going to get a part-time job?

short answers
Yes, I am. / No, I'm not.

will and be going to

We use *will* to talk about future predictions or decisions we make at the moment of speaking.
I'll take the bus home!
We use *be going to* to talk about future plans and intentions.
I'm going to the cinema with Jack tomorrow.

time expressions + *will, when + will*
tomorrow next week this summer one day soon I'll see you tomorrow! When I **go** on holiday, I'll **buy** some souvenirs.

would like

would like + infinitive
We use *would like* to mean *want*. We use the infinitive with *to* after it.

affirmative
I'd like to visit Canada.

negative
Jess wouldn't like to babysit.

questions
Would you like to go shopping at the weekend?

short answers
Yes, I would. / No, I wouldn't.

Vocabulary
Jobs and chores

babysit	lay the table
clean the windows	make the beds
deliver newspapers	pet sit
do the gardening	take dogs for walks
do the ironing	tidy your room
do the washing-up	wash cars

Money and shopping

borrow	lend	spend
buy	lose	swap
collect	pay for	win
cost	save	
earn	sell	

Speaking
Asking for a favour
Can I ask you a favour?
Could / Can you … ?
Is it OK if I … ?
Would you mind doing / cleaning / helping me with … ?

LEARNING TO LEARN
Study with a friend and practise the role-plays on the Integrated Skills pages. Try inventing your own dialogues too.

Making a poster

TASK

Work in groups of three to make a poster about endangered animals.

Step 1: Think

1 Look at the poster below. Find ...

1. a photo
2. facts about an endangered animal
3. a description of an endangered animal
4. a map
5. a link to more information

facts about an endangered animal

@ DIGITAL LITERACY

When you make a poster, remember to:

- include images to make your poster look interesting.
- use different fonts and colours.
- look up words in an online dictionary.

2 Read the task. Which information would you include in a poster about endangered animals?

- links to organizations that protect endangered animals
- facts about endangered animals
- facts about zoos
- reasons why the animals are in danger
- photos of endangered animals
- maps
- a list of endangered animals

a description of an endangered animal

The *Iberian lynx* is Europe's most endangered mammal.

IBERIAN LYNX FACTS

- They are a kind of wild cat.
- The head and body are 85–110 cm long. They weigh 9–13 kg.
- There are only about 300 lynx now.
- They are yellow and they have got brown spots.
- They eat meat.
- They live in Spain.

Why are they in danger?

- Many lynxes die from hunger. They eat rabbits, but there aren't as many rabbits now.
- People kill them.
- People build houses and farms. They are destroying many of the places where the lynxes live.

a photo

a map

This is the *loggerhead turtle*. It is an endangered animal.

LOGGERHEAD TURTLE FACTS

- They are 90–240 cm long and they can weigh 450 kg.
- They live in the Atlantic, Pacific and Indian Oceans, and in the Mediterranean Sea.
- Turtles can live for 67 years.
- They eat plants and fish – they are omnivorous.
- They come onto the land to have babies. They lay eggs.

Why are they in danger?

- Humans kill turtles for their shells and their eggs.
- Tourists disturb the turtles when they are laying their eggs.
- Many baby turtles die before they get to the sea.
- Many turtles die in fishing nets.

When you make a poster, remember to:

- research the topic and decide what information to include
- use your own words
- include different types of information – photos, maps, facts, useful links, graphs ...

For more information see:
www.redlist.org – 2000 IUCN Red List of Threatened Species
www.wildaid.org – WildAid – Protecting and Educating

a link to more information

Collaborative project 2
Making a poster

Warmer

Play a guessing game with the class. Tell students you are thinking of an animal. They have to ask questions to find out what it is, but you can only answer *yes* or *no.* Elicit examples of questions and write them on the board, eg *Has it got a tail? Does it live in a hot country? Does it walk on four legs? Does it live in the sea? Is it an insect?* After playing a few rounds as a class, students continue the game in pairs or groups.

TASK

Read the task with the class and check students understand.

Step 1: Think

1
- Briefly discuss making posters with the class. What makes a poster interesting? What types of information can you include? What things can you include, eg photos, graphs, maps? How can you organize the information?
- Read the list of items students have to identify and help with any vocabulary.
- Ask students to read the information and find an example of each item.
- Check answers as a class. Ask if there are any other items which could be included in the list.
- Read the Digital literacy box with the class and check students understand.
- Point out that posters are more interesting when you include different types of information and that it is important to make the poster look attractive and edit the material carefully.

2
- Check students understand all the items.
- Briefly discuss the advantages or disadvantages of using each item, eg links to organizations that protect endangered animals would enable people to find out more information after reading the poster.

Step 2: Listen and plan

3 💿 2.39

- Ask students to read the questions carefully.
- Play the CD. Students listen and answer the questions.
- Check the answers as a class.

4
- Students read the conversation extract and complete it in pairs.
- Play the CD again. Students listen and check their answers.
- Check answers as a class. Students practise the conversation in groups.

5
- Read the Useful language box with the class and help with any vocabulary.
- Practise as necessary. Elicit other examples of each phrase, eg *How shall we find information? Let's put the information in speech bubbles from the animals.*
- Students work in groups of three and plan their posters. Ask one or two groups to report back to the class to explain their plans.

Step 3: Create

6
- Read the three steps with the class to give students a clear idea of what they have to do.
- Monitor while they are working and give help if necessary.

Share information
Students share their information. They look at the original sources and check they haven't copied any information directly. They discuss if they need to change anything and how to improve their work. They check they have everything they need and they check for errors.

Create the poster
Each group creates their poster. Encourage them to be creative and try to make the poster as interesting as possible. Remind them to use their own words and to check for errors. Help as necessary.

Show and tell
Each group shows their poster to the class. Allow time for the other students to ask questions. If you prefer, a few groups can show their posters over several different classes or you can display all the posters on the class walls as an exhibition. If you like, the class can vote for their favourite poster.

Step 4: Evaluate

7
- Look at the evaluation grids with the class.
- Read through the different options and help with any vocabulary as necessary.
- Students complete their self-evaluation. Give help if necessary.

Extra activity

In pairs or groups, students make a wordmap of vocabulary related to endangered animals. They discuss how to organize the vocabulary and what vocabulary to include. They then make a poster of the wordmap.

💿 2.39 Audioscript, exercise 3

Edu: OK, let's choose an animal each. I'd like to write about the Javan rhinoceros.
Sonia: I'd like to do the giant panda.
Mario: And the western lowland gorilla for me.
Sonia: OK. What information shall we include?
Mario: Let's give some facts about each animal.
Edu: Good idea! And let's give reasons why each animal is in danger. What do you think, Sonia?
Sonia: Yes, that's a good idea. Let's include some facts about zoos and the work they do.
Mario: No, that's too difficult.
Sonia: OK. What about adding photos of the animals? And we can have maps to show where they live.
Mario: Great idea! So, we've got three tasks – finding facts about animals, finding reasons why they are in danger, and finding photos and maps.
Edu: How shall we share the tasks?
Mario: I can find some facts about the three animals.
Sonia: I know – why don't we do each task for our own animal? Then the work is equal.
Mario: Yes, I think that's more interesting. Do you agree, Edu?
Edu: OK, let's do that.
Sonia: OK, so when shall we meet to share our information?
Edu: Tomorrow?

Exercise 3

1 Javan rhinoceros

giant panda

western lowland gorilla

2 They decide to include facts about endangered animals, reasons why the animals are in danger, photos of endangered animals and maps.

Exercise 4

1 shall
2 Let's
3 think
4 idea
5 What
6 Great

Step 2: Listen and plan

3 🔘 2.39 Listen to Sonia, Mario and Edu doing the task. Answer the questions.

> Western Lowland Gorilla   Iberian lynx
> Siberian tiger   loggerhead turtle   giant panda
> Javan rhinoceros

1 Which three animals do they choose?
2 Which items from exercise 2 do they decide to include?

4 Complete the conversation extract with the words in the box. Listen again and check.

> think   idea   shall   great   let's   what

Sonia: OK. What information (1) ... we include?

Mario: (2) ... give some facts about each animal.

Edu: Good idea! And let's give reasons why each animal is in danger. What do you (3) ... , Sonia?

Sonia: Yes, that's a good (4) ... . Let's include some facts about zoos and the work they do.

Mario: No, that's too difficult.

Sonia: OK. (5) ... about adding photos of the animals? And we can have maps to show where they live.

Mario: (6) ... idea!

5 Work in groups. Plan your poster.

- Choose which endangered animals you want to make your poster about
- Decide what information to include and how to organize it.
- Make a list of tasks and decide how to share the work.
- Decide when to meet again to share your information.

Step 3: Create

6 Follow the steps to create your poster.

Share information
Read or listen to each other's work. Discuss your work. Check these things.
- What can you improve?
- Have you got all the information you need?
- Have you got photos, maps, etc?
- Is the grammar and vocabulary correct?
- Is the spelling and punctuation correct?

Create the poster
Put all your information on the poster. Add any photos or maps. Decide the final layout. Then check the grammar, punctuation and spelling again.

Show and tell
- Show the rest of the class your poster. Answer any questions.

Step 4: Evaluate

7 Now ask your teacher for the group and individual assessment grids.

USEFUL LANGUAGE

What do you think?
I think ...
Yes, that's a good idea. /
No, that's too difficult / boring.
What (facts) shall we include?
How shall we (share the tasks)?
Let's (give some facts).
Why don't we (add a video clip)?
When shall we (meet)?

UNIT 7 — JOURNEYS

Unit objectives and key competences

In this unit the student will learn ...

- understand, memorize and correctly use vocabulary related to transport and verbs of movement (1) **CLC CMST SCC**
- understand and correctly use the present perfect, draw parallels to L1, ask questions and give short answers using the present perfect, and produce a short speaking activity **CLC L2L SIE**
- about journeys in the USA and compare with journeys in their country **CLC SCC CAE CMST**
- about transport by watching a short video **CLC CMST SCC DC**

In this unit the student will learn how to ...

- identify specific information in a feature article about Amish teenagers **CLC CAE SCC**
- look online for information about the Amish and share with the class **CLC DC CAE SIE**
- identify specific information in a presentation about electric bicycles **CLC CMST SCC**
- read information about trams in Manchester, listen to short dialogues about transport and learn how to ask for travel information **CLC CMST SCC CAE**
- write a blog post **CLC DC SIE L2L**
- prepare for and do a speaking exam about a prepared topic **CLC SIE L2L**

Linguistic contents

Main vocabulary
- Transport: *bicycle, plane, shop,* etc
- Verbs of movement (1): *sail, climb, fly,* etc

Grammar
- Present perfect: affirmative, negative, questions and short answers

Functional language
- Phrases for asking for travel information
- Phrases for answering questions about a prepared topic

Pronunciation
- Difficult sounds: /I/ and /i:/

Skills

Reading
- Read a feature article about Amish teenagers
- Read a text about Route 66
- Read information about trams in Manchester
- Read a blog post

Writing: Interaction and production
- Write a personalized dialogue about asking for travel information
- Write a blog post in three steps: plan, write, check
- Learn how to use *really* and *a bit*

Listening
- Listen to a TV programme about electric bicycles
- Listen to short dialogues about journeys

Spoken interaction
- Ask and answer questions about different forms of transport you use
- Exchange information about activities you have done

Spoken production
- Prepare and act out a dialogue about asking for travel information
- Prepare and do a speaking exam talking about a prepared topic

Lifelong learning skills

Self-study and self-evaluation

- Study guide:
  Student's Book page 83
- Progress check and self-evaluation:
  Workbook pages 62–63
- Grammar reference and practice:
  Workbook pages 96–97
- Wordlist: Workbook pages 151–157

Learning strategies and thinking skills

- Listening for key words

Cultural awareness

- Journeys in the USA – Route 66
- Comparing long car journeys in the USA with long car journeys in students' own country

Cross-curricular contents

- The Amish, electric bikes, Route 66
- Language and literature: reading and writing a blog post
- ICT: searching the internet for information

Key competences

CLC	Competence in linguistic communication
CMST	Competence in mathematics, science and technology
DC	Digital competence
SCC	Social and civic competences
CAE	Cultural awareness and expression
L2L	Learning to learn
SIE	Sense of initiative and entrepreneurship

Evaluation

- Unit 7 End-of-unit test: Basic, Standard and Extra
- CEFR Skills Exam Generator

External exam trainer

- Speaking: Talking about a prepared topic

Digital material

Pulse Live! Digital Course including:
- Interactive grammar tables
- Audio visual speaking model: Asking for travel information
- Audio visual cultural material: Transport

Student's website

Digital competence

- Web quest: The Amish
- Digital competence worksheet: Presentations

Reinforcement material

- Basic worksheets, Teacher's Resource File pages 41–46
- Vocabulary and Grammar: Consolidation worksheets, Teacher's Resource File pages 27–28

Extension material

- Fast-finisher activity: Student's Book page 75
- Extra activities: Teacher's Book pages T82
- Vocabulary and Grammar: Extension worksheets, Teacher's Resource File pages 29–30

Teacher's Resource File

- Translation and dictation worksheets pages 8, 18
- Evaluation rubrics pages 1–7
- Key competences worksheets pages 13–14
- Culture and CLIL worksheets pages 25–28
- Culture video worksheets pages 13–14
- Digital competence worksheets pages 13–14
- Macmillan Readers worksheets pages 5–6

JOURNEYS

 THINK ABOUT IT

What's your favourite form of transport? Why?

Vocabulary and Speaking
Transport

1 🔘 **2.40** Listen and repeat the different forms of transport. Which do you use the most?

> bicycle   motorbike   plane   ship   horse and carriage   coach   tram   lorry   yacht
> caravan   the Underground   helicopter   ferry   hot-air balloon

7 COOL WAYS TO GET AROUND!

The Amish people don't use cars. They prefer to travel the old-fashioned way by (1) ... .

Lisbon is famous for its green form of public transport – the (2) ... .

The best way to see the Greek islands is by (3) ... .

You get a great view of the Sahara Desert in a (4) ... !

These Irish travellers live in a (5) ... and take it with them wherever they go!

In London, the quickest way to get around is on (6) ... , which is also called the Tube.

Chinese people like travelling by (7) ... because it's cheap and healthy.

Exercise 2

1 horse and carriage
2 tram
3 yacht
4 hot-air balloon
5 caravan
6 the Underground
7 bicycle

2 🔘 **2.41** Read and listen. Complete the sentences with words from exercise 1.

3 Answer the questions.

Which form or forms of transport ...
1 carries large, heavy things from one place to another?
2 transports people by air in an emergency?
3 is a fast, noisy vehicle for one or two people?
4 carry people and cars on short journeys across the sea?
5 takes large groups of passengers on long journeys by road?

LOOK!

I love travelling **by** ship.
My mum goes to work **by** bus.

Exercise 3

1 lorry
2 helicopter
3 motorbike
4 ferry
5 coach

⟳ EXPRESS YOURSELF

4 Which form of transport do you use in these situations? Write sentences.

I go to school by bicycle.
1 go to school
2 go shopping
3 go to the beach
4 visit your friends
5 go on holiday

5 Work in pairs. Ask and answer questions about the different forms of transport you use.

💬 *How do you go to school?*
💬 *I go to school by bicycle.*

Exercise 4

students' own answers

Vocabulary and Speaking
Transport

Warmer

Write the word *transport* on the board. Students work in pairs and make a list of all the forms of transport they know. Set a time limit of two minutes. Listen to their ideas as a class and make a list on the board (*car, bus, train*, etc).

Think about it

Students work in pairs and discuss the questions. Get feedback from the whole class.

1 🔊 **2.40**
- Students read the words in the word pool.
- Play the CD. Students listen to the different forms of transport and repeat them.
- They answer the question.
- Listen to their ideas as a class.

Language note

The Underground almost always refers to the London underground railway. Other cities around the world (eg Madrid, Paris, Moscow, Budapest) have *a metro*. The New York underground railway system is called *the subway*. In British English *a subway* is a passage for pedestrians under a road or railway line.

2 🔊 **2.41**
- Students work individually.
- Play the CD. Students listen and follow the text in their books.
- They complete the sentences using the words from exercise 1.
- They compare answers in pairs.
- Check answers as a class. Note the pronunciation of *yacht* /jɒt/.

3
- Students work individually and answer the questions using the words from exercise 1.
- They compare answers in pairs.
- Check answers as a class. Note that a coach is used for long-distance journeys while a bus is used for short journeys and journeys within a city.

Look!

Ask students to read the example sentences in the Look! box. Highlight that we use the preposition *by* with forms of transport: *by car, by plane*, etc. Point out that the only exception to this is *on foot*, which is used to mean *walk*, eg *I go to school on foot*.

EXPRESS YOURSELF

4
- Students work individually and write sentences.

5
- Nominate two students to read aloud the example question and answer.
- Students work in pairs and ask and answer the questions in exercise 4.
- Listen to some pairs as a class.

Vocabulary extension: Workbook page 108 ▶▶

Reading

Text type: A feature article

Recommended web links

www.channel4.com/programmes/living-with-the-amish

www.bbc.co.uk/religion/religions/christianity/subdivisions/amish_1.shtml

Warmer

Write on the board *What's the quickest form of transport from London to Paris?* Elicit from the class possible forms of transport between the two capital cities from the previous lesson. Students discuss the answer to the question in pairs. Listen to their ideas as a class. Then explain that it's quicker by train. If you go by plane, you have to travel a long way to the airport, then you have to check in and wait to board the plane. The train goes from central London to central Paris.

1 🔘 2.42

- Students look at the picture of the people.
- Listen to students' ideas about who the people in the photo are.
- Play the CD. Students listen, follow the text in their books and check their ideas.
- Check the answer as a class.
- Focus on the Did you know? box. Make sure students understand *rollerblades* and the phrasal verb *get around*. Here it means to move from one place to another.

Language note

Highlight that *Great Britain* (England, Scotland and Wales) is often referred to as *Britain*. Remind students that *the UK* (the *United Kingdom*) includes England, Scotland, Wales and Northern Ireland.

Word check

Make sure students understand the words. Ask them to translate them into their language. Note that in this context *get on* is used to talk about how well someone has done a particular activity.

2
- This exercise gives students practice in reading to locate specific information.
- Students read the beginnings of the notes and copy them into their notebooks.
- They look in the text and find the information to complete the notes.
- Students compare answers in pairs.
- Check answers as a class.

3
- Students read the sentences carefully first.
- Students look in the text and decide whether the sentences are true or false. They correct the false sentences.
- Students compare answers in pairs.
- Check answers as a class.

4
- Explain the task. Read the example sentence aloud to the class.
- Students work individually and write five sentences about how Andrew is different from most teenagers.
- Listen to their ideas as a class.

Finished?

Encourage fast finishers to write three or four sentences to answer the questions about Andrew's visit to Britain. They should begin by using the prompt in the book.

Web quest

Students find out more information about the Amish. Highlight the Web quest tip.

1 • Ask students to open an internet web browser such as Internet Explorer. Students open a search engine (eg Google) and type in the subject of their search.
  • Students find information about the Amish and make notes.
2 • They work in pairs and make a list of information they have found.
  • They present their findings to the class.

T75

Reading
A feature article

1 🔊 2.42 **Who do you think the people in the picture are? Read and listen to check your ideas.**

JOURNEY INTO THE MODERN WORLD

Channel 4 follows a group of Amish teenagers as they leave their homes in the USA for the first time to travel to Britain.

WHO ARE THE AMISH?

The Amish are a group of people in the USA who live very simply, often on farms, far away from big cities. They prefer the old-fashioned way of life and avoid using a lot of modern gadgets. They don't have cars and usually travel around by horse and carriage. Amish teenagers spend most of their time with their families. Girls do a lot of household chores, like cooking and cleaning, while the boys help their fathers with jobs outside.

MEET ANDREW MILLER

Andrew is 18. He's never used a computer, had a TV in his home or owned a mobile phone. He doesn't wear fashionable clothes or listen to rock music. He prefers hunting with his bow and arrow and ice-fishing. Andrew has lived in the state of Mississippi all his life and hasn't been to a big city before. He's never been to school either. His father taught him at home with his 12 brothers and sisters.

Along with four other Amish teenagers, Andrew is about to go on a journey to Britain which will change his life forever. Andrew's curious to find out what life in Britain is really like. 'I've read about the history of England in books, but I've heard terrible things about the English,' he says. When he goes back home, he will decide whether or not he wants to continue living in the Amish society.

THE TRIP

First, Andrew is going to stay in London. He'll stay with the family of a British teenager who is interested in fashion and rap music and likes playing video games. During the rest of his stay in Britain, Andrew will have the chance to visit a night club, go to a music festival and try some traditional British sports.

Watch Channel 4 on Friday at 8pm to see how Andrew gets on!

2 Copy and complete the notes about Andrew.

> Name: Andrew Miller
> Age: (1) ...
> Comes from: (2) ...
> Family: (3) ...
> Hobbies: (4) ...
> Reason for visiting Britain: (5) ...

Word check

old-fashioned gadget household chore hunting bow and arrow curious get on

DID YOU KNOW?

Lots of Amish teenagers use rollerblades to get around!

3 Read the text again. Are the sentences true or false? Correct the false sentences.

1 Amish children help their parents at home.
2 Amish people don't use any transport.
3 Andrew likes watching TV.
4 Andrew has been to Britain before.
5 Andrew is going to stay with a British family.

4 How is Andrew different from most teenagers? Write five differences.

He doesn't listen to rock music.

 FINISHED?

Do you think Andrew will enjoy his trip to Britain? Why (not)?

I think he will enjoy his trip to Britain because ...

WEB QUEST

Find out more information about the Amish.

1 **Make notes about:**
- The history of Amish people
- Population
- Interesting facts
- Their homes

2 **Work in pairs. Share your information with the rest of the class.**

Web Quest tip!

When you find a website with interesting information, add it to your favourites.

Grammar

Present perfect: affirmative and negative

use of the present perfect
We use the present perfect to talk about things in the past, when we don't say exactly when they happened.

affirmative
I**'ve read** about England in books.
He / She / It**'s had** lessons at home.
You / We / They**'ve lived** all their life in the USA.

negative
I **haven't visited** a big city.
He / She / It **hasn't used** a computer.
You / We / They **haven't travelled** by plane.

Exercise 1

a have, has
b -ed

1 Look at the table and answer the questions.

  a) What are *'ve* and *'s* short for?
  b) What do we add to the end of regular verbs in the present perfect?

Exercise 2

gone
made
seen
done
laughed
come
given
wanted
thought

2 Read the spelling rules on page 83 and look at the Irregular verbs list on page 126. Then write the past participles of these verbs.

> go make see do laugh come give
> want think

3 Read the sentences about Andrew Miller and choose the correct words.

  1 His parents **has / have** allowed him to go to Britain.
  2 **He've / He's** tried English food.
  3 He hasn't **seen / saw** a football match.
  4 He **isn't / hasn't** called his parents in the USA.
  5 His family are sad because **they've / they's** missed him!

Exercise 3

1 have
2 He's
3 seen
4 hasn't
5 they've

> ### LOOK!
> Andrew has **gone** to Britain. (He's still there.)
> Andrew has **been** to Britain. (He went there in the past, but he isn't there now.)

Exercise 4

1 gone
2 been
3 been
4 gone

4 Complete the sentences with *gone* or *been*.

  1 Fiona isn't here. She's … for a walk.
  2 I haven't … to Paris, but I'd love to go!
  3 We've … in a hot-air balloon. It was great!
  4 Scott hasn't … to school yet. He's still here.

5 2.43 Complete the paragraph with the present perfect form of the verbs in brackets. Then listen and check.

LIVING WITH THE AMISH

Charlotte is an 18-year-old student from Devon in England. A TV producer (1) … (choose) her and five other British teenagers to take part in a programme called *Living with the Amish*. Charlotte (2) … (live) away from home before, but she (3) … (not be) to the USA. She (4) … (just / arrive) at the airport in Ohio and is very excited! Some members of the Amish family that she will be staying with (5) … (come) to meet her. Charlotte hasn't got much luggage with her. She (6) … (leave) her fashionable clothes, her laptop computer and her mobile phone at home. She (7) … (not bring) her make-up with her either because Amish women don't wear make-up.

Exercise 5

1 has chosen
2 has lived
3 hasn't been
4 has just arrived
5 have come
6 has left
7 hasn't brought

6 What have you done in your life so far? What haven't you done? Write sentences.

I've watched an English film.
I haven't been abroad.

  1 go abroad
  2 eat Chinese food
  3 travel by plane
  4 meet a famous person
  5 ride a motorbike

> ### ANALYSE
> We don't use the present perfect with past time expressions like *yesterday* and *last year*. What about in your language?

 2.44–2.45 **Pronunciation lab: Difficult sounds: /ɪ/ and /iː/, page 125**

Grammar
Present perfect: affirmative and negative

Lesson objectives

In this lesson students will:
- learn / revise the present perfect affirmative and negative
- compare the use of *gone* and *been* in the present perfect

Warmer

Write the sentence *Andrew has never used a computer* on the board with the words in the wrong order: *computer Andrew never a used has*. Students work in pairs and write the sentence in the correct order. Invite students to come to the board and write the correct sentence. If there are any mistakes, invite other students to correct them. Point out that we can also used the contracted form: *Andrew's never used a computer*.

1
- Students read the information and the example sentences in the table.
- Students work individually and answer the questions.
- They compare answers in pairs.
- Check answers as a class.

Language note

Highlight that we use the present perfect to talk about past experiences when we do not say exactly when they happened. Compare *He's been to Paris* (at some point in his life) and *He went to Paris in 2013* (a specific time is mentioned so the past simple is used).

2
- Remind students that some verbs in English have irregular past participle forms, eg *read, read, read; have, had, had*.
- Elicit the past participle form of a regular verb, eg *visit, visited* and highlight that the past simple and past participle of regular verbs are the same.
- Students work individually. They read the spelling rules and look at the Irregular verbs list. They then write the past participle forms.
- They compare answers in pairs.
- Check answers as a class.

3
- Point out that the correct sentences use the present perfect form.
- Students choose the correct words individually.
- They compare answers in pairs.
- Check answers as a class.

Look!

Students read the information in the Look! box. Highlight the difference between *gone* and *been* by writing *Andrew has gone to Britain* on the board. Ask where he is now to elicit that he is in Britain. Write *Andrew has been to Britain* on the board. Ask where he isn't now to elicit that he isn't in Britain.

4
- Students complete the sentences using *gone* or *been*.
- They compare answers in pairs.
- Check answers as a class.

5 **2.43**
- Point out that some of the verbs in this exercise have irregular past participles.
- Students work individually to complete the paragraph.
- They compare answers in pairs.
- Play the CD. Students listen and check their answers.

6
- Read the example sentences aloud to the class.
- Students work individually to write sentences about what they have and haven't done in their lives so far using *I've* or *I haven't*.
- Listen to their sentences as a class.

Analyse

Ask students to read the information about English and compare it with their own language.

Pronunciation lab: Difficult sounds: /ɪ/ and /iː/, page 125

Digital course: Interactive grammar table

Study guide: page 83

Vocabulary and Listening
Verbs of movement (1)

Warmer

Write *car* and *bicycle* on the board. Ask students to think of a verb or verbs that can go with each word. Elicit answers from the class and write them on the board, eg *drive a car, ride a bicycle.*

1 **2.46**
- Play the CD. Students listen and repeat the verbs of movement.
- Students look at the list of verbs.
- They write down which of the verbs they can do without any equipment.
- They compare answers in pairs.
- Listen to their answers as a class.

2
- Explain the task.
- Students work individually and complete the sentences using the verbs from exercise 1.
- They compare answers in pairs.

3 **2.47**
- Play the CD. Students listen and check their answers to exercise 2.

Culture note

Situated about 100 kilometres south-west of Tokyo, Mount Fuji is the highest mountain in Japan at 3,776 metres. It is an active volcano but it hasn't erupted since 1708!

4
- Check that students understand the task.
- Give them a couple of minutes to make notes.
- They compare ideas in pairs.
- Listen to their ideas as a class.

5 **2.48**
- Students read the notes carefully first.
- Play the CD. Students work individually and copy and complete the notes.
- Check progress. If necessary, play the CD again.
- Check answers as a class.

6
- Ask students to read the questions carefully first.
- Play the CD again. Students write their answers.
- They compare answers in pairs.
- Check answers as a class.

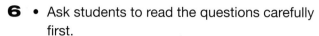

2.48 Audioscript, exercise 5

Now, I'm not very fit and I don't really like cycling. So what am I doing on a bicycle? Well, this isn't a normal bicycle. It's actually an electric bicycle, or e-bicycle for short. It's got a battery, and can go up to 25 kilometres an hour. And although you can use your own power, just as you can for a normal bicycle, if you're feeling tired – or, like me, you're just a bit lazy – you can relax and let the bicycle do the hard work.

Now in China, electric bicycles are really popular, with about 125 million of them on the road. In Europe, however, it's a different story. People still prefer to use their cars to get around, even though they're more expensive to buy and run and are very bad for the environment.

But are electric bicycles really as easy to use as they sound? Today I'm going to find out. I've left my car at home and am on my way to work in the centre of London on an e-bicycle! Well, it's a bit scary riding any kind of bicycle in central London with all this traffic. Oh, there's a hill coming up now – I'm going to switch the power on. This is great – I'm overtaking all the other cyclists now! I bet they think I'm really fit! If I was on a normal bicycle, I would definitely have to get off it and push it up the hill now. Right, here we are. I made it to work! Phew!

Well, I definitely think electric bicycles are a great invention and they really make cycling possible for everyone. It doesn't matter how old you are or how fit you are, e-bicycles are a great way to get around. They aren't cheap, though. Prices start at about £600. But with petrol prices going up, who knows? Maybe they'll soon be as fashionable here as they are in China.

Vocabulary and Listening
Verbs of movement (1)

1 🔊 2.46 Listen and repeat the verbs of movement in the box. Which can you do without any equipment?

> sail fly climb drive cross fall crash carry pull
> push follow arrive take off land

AROUND THE WORLD BY BICYCLE

Guim Valls Teruel from Spain has become the first person to cycle around the world on an electric bicycle! Here are some photos of what he saw on his trip.

It's easy to (1) … things with an electric bicycle!

The great thing about an electric bicycle is that you never need to (2) … it up hills!

Cycling isn't much fun when everyone else prefers to (3) … .

It's so relaxing to (4) … across the ocean.

Guim managed to (5) … to the top of Mount Fuji in Japan – without his bicycle!

It took Guim weeks to (6) … Australia in the heat!

2 Read the text and complete the sentences with words from exercise 1.

3 🔊 2.47 Listen and check your answers to exercise 2.

4 How do you think electric bicycles are different from normal bicycles?

5 🔊 2.48 Listen to a TV programme about electric bicycles and copy and complete the notes.

> Electric bikes
> - also called (1) …
> - power comes from a (2) …
> - fastest speed: (3) …
> - popular in (4) …
> - cost in the UK: from (5) £…

6 Listen again and answer the questions.

1 Where do people still prefer cars?
2 How does the man usually travel to work?
3 What is the problem with cycling in the centre of London?
4 Which part of the man's journey is easier for him than for other cyclists?
5 Give one advantage of e-bicycles.
6 Give one disadvantage of e-bicycles.

Cultural awareness
Journeys in the USA

Fact box
In 1945, the very first McDonald's fast food restaurant opened on Route 66 in San Bernadino, California. The Disney film *Cars* also takes place on Route 66.

 ROUTE 66

FREQUENTLY ASKED
QUESTIONS

HOME   FAQ

WHAT IS ROUTE 66?
It is a road that goes from Chicago in the Midwest to Los Angeles on the West Coast. It crosses eight states and is 3,940 km long. People sometimes call it 'The Main Street of America'.

HOW LONG HAS IT EXISTED?
Since 1926. Now, however, there are newer, longer highways and Route 66 no longer appears on most maps.

HAVE PEOPLE STOPPED USING IT NOW?
No! Many people, especially tourists, still travel on it because it is an important part of American history.

WHAT'S SO IMPORTANT ABOUT IT?
Route 66 was one of the very first highways in the USA. Cars were a new invention then, and wide roads like Route 66 made it much easier to get from one place to another.

WHY HAS IT BECOME SO FAMOUS?
In 1946 Bobby Troup wrote a song about Route 66 which became a big hit. Since then, many performers have recorded versions of the song.

HAS THE ROAD CHANGED A LOT OVER THE YEARS?
Yes, it has, but you can still see what it was like in the past. Herman's Gas Station in Thoreau, New Mexico, first started selling petrol in 1935. The Wigwam Motel in Holbrook, where you can stay in a Native American tent, has also been there since the 1930s.

HAS ANYONE EVER TRAVELLED ALONG ROUTE 66 ON FOOT?
Yes, they have! In 1928 there was a race which went from one end of Route 66 to the other and then continued to New York! The route was 5,507 km long, making it the longest race in history!

WHAT IS THERE TO SEE ON ROUTE 66?
The road passes through beautiful scenery, including the Arizona Desert and the Black Mountains. There are also lots of interesting towns and sights on the way, such as the Grand Canyon.

Word check
state   hit   version   Native American   scenery

1 Look at the map and the picture. Which two American cities does Route 66 connect?

2 🔊 3.02 Read and listen. What's the connection between the songwriter Bobby Troup and Route 66?

3 Read the text again. Are the sentences true or false? Correct the false sentences.
  1 Route 66 is the longest road in America.
  2 You can still drive along Route 66 today.
  3 Route 66 existed before anyone had a car.
  4 The Wigwam Motel has now closed.
  5 The 1928 race stopped at the end of Route 66.

4 Find American words in the text that mean ...
  1 a big road.
  2 petrol.
  3 a hotel.

CULTURAL 🌐 COMPARISON

5 Think of a long car journey that you have made in your country and answer the questions.
  1 Where did you go?
  2 What did you see?
  3 What did you enjoy about the journey?
  4 What didn't you enjoy about it?

Exercise 1
Chicago and Los Angeles

Exercise 2
He wrote a song about Route 66 which became a big hit.

Exercise 3
1 **False**
There are newer, longer highways today.
2 **True**
3 **False**
Route 66 was one of the very first highways in the USA when cars were a new invention.
4 **False**
You can still stay at the Wigwam Motel.
5 **False**
The 1928 race continued to New York.

Exercise 4
1 highway
2 gas
3 motel

Culture video: Transport

Cultural awareness
Journeys in the USA

Warmer

Write *USA* on the board. Put students into pairs. Ask them to make a list of US cities. Set a time limit of two minutes. The pair with the most cities wins.

1
- Check students understand the task.
- They look at the map and the picture and find the answer.
- Check the answer as a class.

Culture note

Route 66 passes through eight states on its way from Chicago to Los Angeles: Illinois, Missouri, Kansas, Oklahoma, Texas, New Mexico, Arizona and California.

2 3.02
- Explain the task.
- Play the CD. Students listen and follow the text in their books.
- They compare their answer in pairs.
- Check the answer as a class.

Culture note

Bobby Troup's rhythm and blues song *Route 66* was first recorded by Nat King Cole in 1946. Many artists have recorded the song, including Chuck Berry, the Rolling Stones and Depeche Mode.

3
- Students read the sentences carefully first.
- They read the text again and decide if the sentences are true or false.
- They compare answers in pairs and correct the false sentences.
- Check answers as a class and highlight the information in the Fact box.

4
- Point out that some words are different in British English and American English. Common examples include *shop* and *store* and *trainers* and *sneakers*.
- Students work individually and find the American words for the three items.
- They compare answers in pairs.
- Check answers as a class. Point out that *motel* is short for *motor hotel* and is always found next to a road.

Word check

Make sure students understand the words. Ask them to translate them into their language. Highlight that a *hit* is a very successful song, film, play, show, television programme, etc.

CULTURAL COMPARISON

5
- Students read the questions and make a note of their answers.
- Put them into pairs to ask and answer the questions.
- Listen to some pairs as a class.

Culture video: Transport ▶▶

Grammar

Present perfect: questions and short answers

Warmer

Write the sentence *She has been to San Francisco* on the board. Ask students to turn the statement into a question. Elicit that the question is *Has she been to San Francisco?* and point out that we begin questions in the present perfect with *Has* or *Have*.

1
- Students copy the table into their notebooks.
- They complete the table using *driven, has* and *haven't*.
- They compare answers in pairs.
- Check answers as a class. Point out that we contract the negative short answers (*hasn't, haven't*) but we never contract the affirmative short answers.

2
- Check students understand the task. Show how the words are reordered to make the question.
- Students work individually to write the question forms and the short answers to the questions.
- They compare answers in pairs.
- Check answers as a class. Highlight the irregular past participle of *sing* (*sung*).

Look!

Highlight the information in the Look! box. Point out that *No, I haven't* can also be used as the short answer to the question. We use the full answer with *never* to emphasize the answer.

3
- Explain the task. Make sure students remember to use the past participle of the verbs in brackets.
- Check answers as a class. Highlight the irregular verb *ride, rode, ridden*.

4
- Put students into pairs.
- They ask and answer the questions from exercise 3.
- Listen to some pairs as a class.

CLIL Grammar in context: Transport

5
- Check students understand the task. Students work individually to complete the project with the present perfect form of the verbs in brackets.
- They compare answers in pairs.

Culture note

Concorde was a supersonic passenger aircraft jointly developed by the UK and France. In all, 20 aircraft were built and they operated for 27 years on routes such as London to New York. While regular flights take about 7 hours to reach New York from London, Concorde could fly this route in 3 hours 30 minutes.

6 🔊 3.03
- Play the CD. Students listen and check their answers to exercise 5.

CLIL task

Students use the internet to answer the questions.

Digital course: Interactive grammar table ⟩

Study guide: page 83 ⟩

Grammar

Present perfect: questions and short answers

questions
Have I / we / you / they (1) ... along Route 66?
(2) ... he / she / it **been** in a song?
short answers
Yes, I **have**. / No, I (3) ... .
Yes, it **has**. / No, it **hasn't**.

1 Copy and complete the table with *driven*, *has* and *haven't*.

2 Order the words to make questions about Route 66. Then write true short answers.

Route 66 / famous / become / Has ?

Has Route 66 become famous? Yes, it has.

1 hotels / all / closed / the / Have / old ?
2 in / Has / been / film / it / a ?
3 about / sung / it / people / Have ?
4 longer roads / Have / they / built ?
5 walked / anyone / Has / Route 66 / along ?

LOOK!

We often use *ever* in present perfect questions to mean 'at some time in your life'.
The negative of *ever* is *never*.
Have you **ever** driven a car?
Yes, I have. / No, I've **never** driven a car.

3 Write questions using the present perfect and *ever*.

(travel) across America?

Have you ever travelled across America?

1 (see) the film *Cars*?
2 (ride) a motorbike?
3 (stay) in a hotel?
4 (eat) fast food?
5 (climb) a mountain?

4 Work in pairs. Ask and answer the questions from exercise 3.

🗨 *Have you ever travelled across America?*
🗨 *No, I haven't.*

CLIL Grammar in context: Transport

5 Complete the project with the present perfect form of the verbs in brackets.

A journey through the history of transport

by James Preston, aged 13

(1) ... (you ever / think) about the transport you use every day? (2) ... (people / use) cars, bikes and trains for hundreds of years or are they a modern invention? Read my project to find out!

It's 1783: the Montgolfier brothers (3) ... (fly) for the first time – in a hot-air balloon!

It's 1814: George Stevenson's invention is going to change the world. (4) ... (he / invent) the car, the bus or the train?

It's 1863: London (5) ... (become) the first city in the world with an underground railway. At the moment there is only one line! The other lines (6) ... (not / start) running yet.

It's 1870: lots of people are riding bicycles like this! Cycling (7) ... (never / be) so difficult!

It's 1903: the Wright brothers (8) ... (design) the first plane with an engine.

It's 1908: Henry Ford (9) ... (open) the first car factory. Now people can own a car!

It's 1976: for the first time passengers (10) ... (travel) by Concorde, a new kind of plane. It's faster than the speed of sound.

It's 1995: the UK and France (11) ... (finish) building the Channel Tunnel. There is now a railway line between the two countries which goes under the sea!

Finally, in case you're wondering, George Stevenson invented the train!

Exercise 5
1 Have you ever thought
2 Have people used
3 have flown
4 Has he invented
5 has become
6 haven't started
7 has never been
8 have designed
9 has opened
10 have travelled
11 have finished

6 🔊 3.03 Listen and check your answers.

CLIL TASK

What was the most popular form of transport 100 years ago? What is the most popular form of transport now?

All about transport

Public transport is a great way to travel around a big city. Do you have a tram or metro station near where you live?

The Manchester Metrolink

The Metrolink is a tram system. It has 37 stations which connect different parts of Manchester with the city centre.

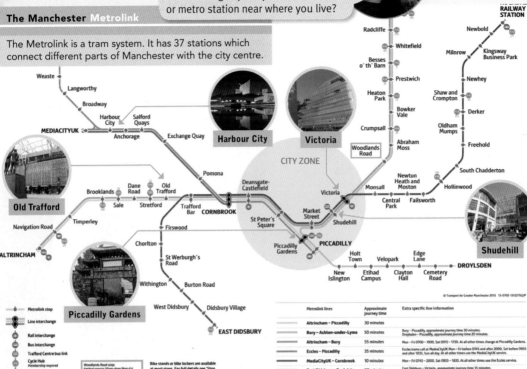

Metrolink lines	Approximate journey time	Extra specific line information
Altrincham – Piccadilly	30 minutes	
Bury – Ashton-under-Lyme	50 minutes	Bury – Piccadilly, approximate journey time 30 minutes. Droylsden – Piccadilly, approximate journey time 20 minutes.
Altrincham – Bury	55 minutes	Mon – Fri 0700 – 1930, Sat 0915 – 1730. At all other times change at Piccadilly Gardens.
Eccles – Piccadilly	35 minutes	Eccles trams call at MediaCityUK Mon – Fri before 0745 and after 2000, Sat before 0855 and after 1835, Sun all day. At all other times use the MediaCityUK service.
MediaCityUK – Cornbrook	10 minutes	Mon – Fri 0745 – 2000, Sat 0955 – 1835. At all other times use the Eccles service.
East Didsbury – Rochdale Railway Station	80 minutes	East Didsbury – Victoria, approximate journey time 35 minutes. Rochdale Railway Station – Victoria, approximate journey time 45 minutes.

Ticket information

1 Ticket prices depend on how long the journey is and when you travel.
2 Children aged 5–16 pay about half of the adult fare, but children under five can travel free.
3 If you make more than five return journeys a week by tram, a season ticket will save you money. You can buy season tickets for a week, a month or a year.

Step 1: Read

Exercise 1

a season ticket

1 Look at the information about trams in Manchester. What is the best kind of ticket for someone who travels by tram every day?

Exercise 2

1 two
2 purple
3 Victoria or Cornbrook
4 It's direct.

2 Answer the questions.

1 You are at St Peter's Square and want to go to Piccadilly. How many stops is it on the pink line?
2 You are at Market Street and want to go to Freehold. What colour line will you use?
3 You want to go from Central Park to Old Trafford. Where will you change onto the green line?
4 You want to go from Piccadilly Gardens to Victoria. Is it direct or do you need to change trams?

Step 2: Listen

SKILLS BUILDER

Listening for key words

Before a listening task, read the questions and find the key words. Listen carefully for words which have a similar meaning as the key words.
For example, you read:
They arrive **late** at the station. (late = key word)
In the listening you hear:
'Quick! Hurry up! Oh no, our train has already gone.'

Exercise 3

2

3 🔊 3.04 Listen to three dialogues. Which dialogue takes place in Manchester?

4 Listen again and write the number of the dialogue in your notebook.

Exercise 4

a 3
b 1
c 3
d 2
e 1

a) They want to buy some tickets.
b) They arrive late at the station.
c) Something is broken.
d) The boy and girl don't know each other.
e) It isn't possible to make the journey by train.

Integrated skills
All about transport

Lesson objectives

In this lesson students will:
- work on all four skills
- read information about tram journeys
- listen to dialogues about travel
- write a personalized dialogue
- act out their dialogue

Warmer

Write the word *Manchester* on the board. Ask students to work in pairs and say what they know about this city. Listen to their ideas as a class, eg *It has two famous football teams, Manchester City and Manchester United. It's in the north of England. It rains a lot. It's an industrial city.*

Step 1: Read

1
- Explain the task.
- Students look at the information about trams in Manchester. They answer the question.
- They compare answers in pairs.
- Check the answer as a class.
- Highlight Nina's speech bubble. Elicit answers to the question from the class.

2
- Students read the questions carefully first.
- They look at the information again and find the answers.
- They compare answers in pairs.
- Check answers as a class.

Step 2: Listen

Skills builder

Listening for key words
Highlight the information in the Skills builder box and emphazise the importance of focusing on key words.

3 🔘 3.04
- Read the question aloud to the class.
- Play the CD.
- Students listen and note down the answer.
- Check the answer as a class.

4
- Explain the task. Encourage students to find the key words in sentences a–e before they listen.
- Play the CD again.
- Students compare answers in pairs.
- Check answers as a class.

🔘 **3.04 Audioscript, exercise 3**

1
Girl 1: Quick, Zak! Hurry up!
Boy 1: Don't worry. It's not going yet.
Girl 1: Yes, it is! Look! The doors are closing!
Boy 1: Oh well, we'll just have to wait for the next one.
Girl 1: But there isn't another one. That was the last train tonight.
Boy 1: Oh no!
Girl 1: We'll have to get a taxi now …
Boy 1: Yes … or walk home.

2
Boy 2: Excuse me … can I help you with that?
Girl 2: Oh, yes please! That's very kind of you.
Boy 2: Phew! It's very heavy. What have you got in it?
Girl 2: Too many things for a week in Manchester!
Boy 2: Yeah, right. Well, here we are.
Girl 2: Thank you. I'm glad it's got wheels … it was just the stairs that were a problem. Thanks again for you help.
Boy 2: No problem. Enjoy the rest of your stay!

3
Boy 3: Oh no … Look at all the people waiting to buy tickets at the ticket office.
Girl 3: Don't worry. We can use the ticket machine.
Boy 3: But I haven't got any change.
Girl 3: That's OK. The machine gives change. Look, you choose the station you're going to, like this, and then the kind of ticket you want, like this, and then you put the money in here.
Boy 3: What's the matter?
Girl 3: It isn't working.
Boy 3: What isn't working?
Girl 3: The ticket machine. That's why all those people are waiting at the ticket office!

Integrated skills – continued
Asking for travel information

5 🔘 3.05
- Students read the dialogue first.
- Play the CD. Students listen and follow the text in their books. They write answers 1–4 in their notebooks.
- They compare answers in pairs.
- Check answers as a class.

6
- Play the CD again, pausing after each question or statement and each response for students to repeat as a class.
- Ask students to repeat the dialogue several times both chorally and individually with the correct stress and intonation.
- Students practise the dialogue in pairs. Then swap roles and practise the dialogue again.

Step 3: Write

7
- Students work individually. They copy the questions in bold into their notebooks.
- They look at the information on page 80 again and choose a different place from Nina to get to in Manchester.
- Students write answers to the questions.

8
- Ask students to look at the Communication kit: Asking for travel information. Encourage them to use these questions when writing their dialogue.
- Students work individually and write their dialogue, using the dialogue in the book as a model.
- Monitor while they are writing and give help if necessary.

Step 4: Communicate

9
- Students practise their dialogues in pairs.
- For extra practice, they swap roles in both dialogues.

10
- Choose some pairs to act out their dialogue for the class.
- Students raise their hand if another pair has the same destination as they do. This will encourage them to listen carefully to their classmates.

Integrated skills: Workbook page 117 〉〉

ASKING FOR TRAVEL INFORMATION

Watch!

Hello. **Could you tell me how to get to the (1) ... , please?**	Yes, of course. The nearest station is (2) ... . Shall I show you on the map?
Yes, please.	OK, we're here at Cornbrook. Take the (3) ... line to Piccadilly Gardens, then take the blue line to Shudehill.
Where do I change trains?	At Piccadilly Gardens.
Great! Thanks. **How much is it?**	Are you under 16?
Yes.	That's just (4) ... , please.
OK. Here you are.	Thanks. Bye!

Exercise 5

1 Arndale shopping centre
2 Shudehill
3 pink
4 a pound

5 🔊 3.05 Listen to Nina asking about travelling in Manchester. Complete 1–4 in your notebook.

6 Listen again and repeat. Practise your intonation.

Step 3: Write

7 Copy the questions in bold into your notebook. Then look at the information on page 80 again. Choose a different place in Manchester and write your answers to the questions.

8 Imagine you want to travel to the place you have chosen. Write a new dialogue. Write both parts. Use the dialogue in exercise 5 to help you.

Hello. Could you tell me how to get to ...?
Yes, of course. The nearest station is ...

Step 4: Communicate

9 Work in pairs. Take turns to practise your dialogues.

🔵 *Hello. Could you tell me how to get to ...?*
🔵 *Yes, of course. The nearest station is ...*

10 Act your dialogue for the class.

COMMUNICATION KIT

Asking for travel information

Could you tell me how to get to ... ?
How do I get to?
Where do I change (trains)?
How much is it?
What time does it leave?

Writing
A blog post

Posted on 8th July, 10.14am

SEEING THE SIGHTS IN LONDON

This is the second day of my holiday in London! I've never been here before, so I'm really excited! Yesterday we went to Buckingham Palace, but we didn't see the Queen! We also went to the London Eye. It was fun, but Mum thought it was a bit scary. Today we're shopping in Harrods, the biggest shop in the world! We came here by Tube, but we got a bit lost. The London Underground is really busy – and there are a lot of stations!

We've still got lots of things to do! We haven't been to Madame Tussauds or the Natural History Museum yet. I hope we'll have time to go there tomorrow because it's our last day!

Exercise 1

1 The writer has been to Buckingham Palace and the London Eye, been shopping, travelled by Tube and got a bit lost.

2 The writer hasn't been to Madame Tussauds or the Natural History Museum.

Exercise 2

1 a little
2 very

Exercise 3

really excited
a bit lost

Exercise 4

1 The museum was a bit boring.
2 It's a bit cold today.
3 The people were a bit unfriendly.
4 The meal was a bit expensive!

Exercise 5

1 We had a really great time.
2 I was really tired after the journey.
3 I think Berlin is a really amazing city.
4 There was a really long queue for the museum.
5 It's a really big shop.

---

1 🔊 3.06 **Read and listen to the blog post. Answer the questions.**

What has the writer …
1 already done?
2 not done yet?

2 Look at the sentences from the blog post. What is the meaning of the words in blue?

1 Mum thought it was **a bit** scary.
2 The London Underground is **really** busy.

3 Read the Writing focus. Then find more examples of *really* and *a bit* in the blog.

WRITING FOCUS

really* and *a bit

We can use *really* and *a bit* before adjectives in informal writing, such as in a blog or an email.
really = very
a bit = a little
I'm really hungry!
Sam is a bit sad.

4 Rewrite the sentences using *a bit* and the words in brackets.

The buses weren't very fast. (slow)
The buses were a bit slow.

1 The museum wasn't very interesting. (boring)
2 It isn't very warm today. (cold)
3 The people weren't very friendly. (unfriendly)
4 The meal wasn't very cheap! (expensive)

5 Rewrite the sentences using *really*.

It was hot on the train.
It was really hot on the train.

1 We had a great time.
2 I was tired after the journey.
3 I think Berlin is an amazing city.
4 There was a long queue for the museum.
5 It's a big shop.

Writing task

Write a blog post.

Plan   Imagine you are on holiday. Make notes about:
• where you are and how you feel.
• what you've already done.
• what you're doing now.
• what you haven't done yet.

Write   Write two short paragraphs based on your notes.

Check   Check your writing.

- ☑ present perfect
- ☑ other verb tenses
- ☑ *really* and *a bit* + adjective

Writing
A blog post

Warmer

Write *London* on the board. Elicit from the class what they know about the city, eg famous sights (*Buckingham Palace, Tower Bridge*), museums (*the Science Museum, the Victoria and Albert Museum of Childhood*), things to do (*shopping in Oxford Street, walking in the parks*).

1   🔊 3.06
- Make sure students understand the task.
- Play the CD. Students listen and follow the text in their books.
- They answer the questions.
- They compare answers in pairs.
- Check answers as a class.

2
- Students read the sentences.
- They translate them into their language.
- Check answers as a class. Highlight that *a bit* is a less formal way of saying *a little* and that *really* is a less formal way of saying *very*.

3
- Students read the information in the Writing focus box. Point out that both these adverbial expressions come before adjectives.
- They work individually and find more examples of *really* and *a bit* in the text.
- They compare answers in pairs.
- Check answers as a class.

4
- Explain the task. Focus on the example and show how the first sentence is transformed using the adjective in brackets and the adverbial phrase *a bit*.
- Students work individually and rewrite the sentences using *a bit* and the words in brackets.
- They compare answers in pairs.
- Check answers as a class.

Extra activity

Write *1 The hotel wasn't very comfortable. (uncomfortable) 2 The journey wasn't very easy. (difficult)* on the board. Students rewrite the sentences using *a bit* as in exercise 4: *1 The hotel was a bit uncomfortable. 2 The journey was a bit difficult.*

5
- Make sure students understand the task. Remind them that *really* comes before the adjective.
- Students work individually and rewrite the sentences using *really*.
- They compare answers in pairs.
- Check answers as a class.

Writing task

The aim of this activity is for students to write a blog post that includes the correct use of the present perfect and other tenses, *really* and *a bit* + adjective. Ask the students to follow the stages in the Student's Book. At the Check stage, ask them to swap notebooks and check each other's writing.

Writing reference and practice: Workbook page 132

Study guide
Grammar, Vocabulary and Speaking

Tell the students the Study guide is an important page which provides a useful reference for the main language of the unit: the grammar, the vocabulary and the functional language from the Integrated skills pages. Explain that they should refer to this page when studying for a test or exam.

Grammar

- Tell the students to look at the example sentences of the present perfect: affirmative and negative. Make sure students understand how to use the tense.
- Then tell students to look at the example sentences of the present perfect: questions and short answers. Ensure they understand how to form the tense correctly. Get students to translate into their own language if necessary.
- Refer students to the Grammar reference on pages 96–97 of the Workbook for further revision.

Vocabulary

- Tell students to look at the list of vocabulary and check understanding.
- Refer students to the Wordlist on page 151 of the Workbook where they can look up any words they can't remember.

Speaking

- Check that students understand the phrases to use for asking for travel information.
- Tell students to act out a conversation between someone asking for travel information and the other person giving the information.

Additional material

Workbook

- Progress check page 62
- Self-evaluation page 63
- Grammar reference and practice pages 96–97
- Vocabulary extension page 108
- Integrated skills page 117
- Writing reference and task pages 132–133

Teacher's Resource File

- Basics section pages 41–46
- Vocabulary and grammar consolidation pages 27–30
- Translation and dictation pages 8, 18
- Evaluation rubrics pages 1–7
- Key competences worksheets pages 13–14
- Culture and CLIL worksheets pages 25–28
- Culture video worksheets pages 13–14
- Digital competence worksheets pages 13–14
- Macmillan Readers worksheets pages 5–6

Tests and Exams

- Unit 7 End-of-unit test: Basic, Standard and Extra
- CEFR Skills Exam Generator

Study guide

Grammar

Present perfect: affirmative and negative

use of the present perfect
We use the present perfect to talk about things in the past, when we don't say exactly when they happened.

affirmative
I**'ve seen** lots of monuments. He / She / It**'s visited** interesting places. You / We / They**'ve lived** in many different countries.

negative
I **haven't read** the new novel. He / She / It **hasn't been** on a yacht. We / You / They **haven't flown** by helicopter.

Present perfect: questions and short answers

questions
Have I / you / we / they **been** to the USA? **Has** he / she / it **seen** the TV programme?

short answers
Yes, I **have**. / No, I **haven't**. Yes, he **has**. / No, he **hasn't**.

Present perfect spelling rules

- For most verbs, add -*ed* to the infinitive to form the past participle
  walk → walked   jump → jumped

- Some past participles are irregular, but the same as the past simple
  have → had   say → said

- Some past participles are irregular and different from the past simple
  do → did → done
  give → gave → given

Check the Irregular verbs list on page 126.

Vocabulary

Transport

bicycle	lorry
caravan	motorbike
coach	plane
ferry	ship
helicopter	the Underground
horse and carriage	tram
hot-air balloon	yacht

Verbs of movement (1)

arrive	drive	pull
carry	fall	push
climb	fly	sail
crash	follow	take off
cross	land	

Speaking

Asking for travel information

Could you tell me how to get to ... ?
How do I get to?
Where do I change (trains)?
How much is it?
What time does it leave?

LEARNING TO LEARN

When you are reading in English and find a word you don't know, try using a monolingual dictionary instead of a bilingual one. Monolingual dictionaries contain a lot of useful information about new words.

UNIT 8
GOOD LUCK, BAD LUCK

Unit objectives and key competences

In this unit the student will learn ...
- understand, memorize and correctly use vocabulary related to sport and competitions **CLC CMST SCC**
- understand, memorize and correctly use vocabulary related to verbs of movement (2) **CLC L2L**
- understand and correctly use the present perfect + *for* and *since*, the difference between the present perfect and the past simple and draw parallels to L1 **CLC L2L**
- about superstitions in Ireland and compare with superstitions in their country **CLC CMST SCC CAE**
- about Ireland by watching a short video **CLC DC CMST CAE**

In this unit the student will learn how to ...
- identify specific information in an online magazine article about superstition and sport **CLC DC CAE SCC**
- look online for information about a famous athlete **CLC DC CAE SIE**
- identify specific information in a radio programme about superstitions **CLC CAE SCC**
- read a leisure centre timetable, listen to four announcements and learn how to make arrangements **CLC SCC L2L**
- write an email **CLC DC SIE L2L**
- prepare for and do a listening exam about answering open questions **CLC SIE L2L**

Linguistic contents

Main vocabulary
- Sports and competitions: *winner, loser, champion,* etc
- Verbs that go with different sports: *play, do, go*
- Verbs of movement (2): *carry, cross, spill,* etc

Grammar
- Present perfect + *for* and *since*
- *How long* with the present perfect
- Present perfect and past simple

Functional language
- Phrases for making arrangements

Pronunciation
- Linking words: final consonant + vowel sound

Skills

Reading
- An online magazine article about superstition in sport
- Read a text about superstitions in Ireland
- Read a leisure centre timetable
- Read an email

Writing: Interaction and production
- Write a personalized dialogue about making arrangements
- Write an email in three steps: plan, write, check
- Learn how and where to use adjectives

Listening
- Listen to part of a radio programme about superstitions
- Listen to announcements at a leisure centre

Spoken interaction
- Ask and answer questions about the sport you do

Spoken production
- Prepare and act out a dialogue about making arrangements for an activity

Lifelong learning skills

Self-study and self-evaluation

- Study guide:
  Student's Book page 93
- Progress check and self-evaluation:
  Workbook pages 70–71
- Grammar reference and practice:
  Workbook pages 98–99
- Wordlist:
  Workbook pages 151–157

Learning strategies and thinking skills

- Understanding timetables

Cultural awareness

- Superstitions in Ireland
- Comparing superstitions in Ireland with superstitions in students' own countries and regions

Cross-curricular contents

- The history of superstitions, Irish beliefs and superstitions
- Language and literature: writing an email
- ICT: searching the internet for information

Key competences

CLC	Competence in linguistic communication
CMST	Competence in mathematics, science and technology
DC	Digital competence
SCC	Social and civic competences
CAE	Cultural awareness and expression
L2L	Learning to learn
SIE	Sense of initiative and entrepreneurship

Evaluation

- Unit 8 End-of-unit test: Basic, Standard and Extra
- CEFR Skills Exam Generator

External exam trainer

- Listening: Open questions

Digital material

Pulse Live! Digital Course including:
- Interactive grammar tables
- Audio visual speaking model: Making arrangements
- Audio visual cultural material: Ireland

Student's website

Digital competence

- Web quest: A famous athlete
- Digital competence worksheet: Online collaborative speaking

Reinforcement material

- Basic worksheets, Teacher's Resource File pages 47–52
- Vocabulary and Grammar: Consolidation worksheets, Teacher's Resource File pages 31–32

Extension material

- Fast-finisher activity: Student's Book page 85
- Vocabulary and Grammar: Extension worksheets, Teacher's Resource File pages 33–34

Teacher's Resource File

- Translation and dictation worksheets pages 9, 19
- Evaluation rubrics pages 1–7
- Key competences worksheets pages 15–16
- Culture and CLIL worksheets pages 29–32
- Culture video worksheets pages 15–16
- Digital competence worksheets pages 15–16
- Macmillan Readers worksheets pages 5–6

GOOD LUCK, BAD LUCK

THINK ABOUT IT

Why do people do sports?

Vocabulary and Speaking
Sport and competitions

Exercise 1

winner, loser, champion, supporter, opponent, captain, coach

1 3.07 Check the meaning of the words in the box. Then listen and repeat. Which ones can be a person?

> winner loser champion tournament supporter team
> opponent captain race match goal stadium coach

OUR LUCKY YEAR!

It's been a fantastic year for sport at Swallow School.

SEPTEMBER
Jake Matthews scored a brilliant (1) … in the football (2) … against Healey School. Well done, Jake!

NOVEMBER
Iris Carter in Year 9 beat William Lee to become the local under-16s chess (3) … . Congratulations to you Iris!

JANUARY
The (4) … of the girls' under-16 basketball (5) … shakes hands with her (6) … from Lindsey School. Swallow School won the game!

APRIL
Eight students from Swallow School took part in a (7) … Between them they raised £650 for charity. A wonderful achievement!

JUNE
Swallow School's Angus Hill got to the final of a national tennis (8) … Here is Angus with Mrs Jones, his tennis (9) … .

Exercise 2

1 goal
2 match
3 champion
4 captain
5 team
6 opponent
7 race
8 tournament
9 coach

2 Read the picture diary. Complete it with words from exercise 1.

3 3.08 Listen and check your answers.

LOOK!

We use *play* + ball sports such as football, tennis or basketball.
Ben **plays** tennis on Saturday.
We use *do* + activities such as judo, archery or gymnastics.
Kate **does** judo at school.
We use *go* + *-ing* words such as swimming or running.
I **go** running in the park.

EXPRESS YOURSELF

4 Which sports do you do? Write four sentences.

I play tennis. I don't do gymnastics.

5 Work in pairs. Ask and answer questions about the sports you do. Use the prompts to help you.

💬 *Are you in a school team?*
💬 *Yes, I am. I'm in the chess team.*

- be in a school team
- be captain of a team
- take part in tournaments
- win a match or competition
- have a difficult game

Vocabulary and Speaking

Sport and competitions

Lesson objectives

In this lesson students will:
- learn / revise words related to sport and competitions
- discuss the sports they do

Warmer

Books closed. Write *sport* on the board. Put students into pairs. Ask them to make a list of all the sports they know in English. Set a time limit of two minutes. The pair with the most sports wins.

Think about it

Students read the question. They discuss their answers in pairs. Listen to their ideas as a class.

1 🔘 3.07
- Students read the words in the word pool. Make sure they understand all the words. If necessary, ask them to translate into their language.
- Play the CD. Students listen to the words and repeat them.
- Make sure they pronounce the words correctly with the correct stress, especially *tournament* /ˈtɔːnəmənt/ and *opponent* /əˈpəʊnənt/.
- Students work individually and answer the question.
- They compare answers in pairs.
- Check answers as a class.

Language note

Remind students that two-syllable nouns are almost always stressed on the first syllable, eg *winner*, *loser* and *captain*.

2
- Explain the task.
- Students work individually and fill the gaps in the photo diary using words from exercise 1.
- They compare answers in pairs.

3 🔘 3.08
- Play the CD.
- Students listen and follow the text in their books. They check their answers to exercise 2.

Look!

Ask students to read the information in the Look! box. Elicit other sports for each category and write them on the board, eg *play:* volleyball, table tennis, rugby, golf, squash; *do:* karate, taekwondo, aerobics; *go:* skiing, jogging, walking, climbing, sailing.

Language note

Boxing and *wrestling* are two sports which do not fit into any of the three categories in the Look! box. In the case of these two sports, the verb is used, eg *He boxes* and *They wrestle*.

EXPRESS YOURSELF

4
- Explain the task. Read the example sentences aloud to the class.
- Students work individually and write four sentences.
- Listen to some students as a class.

5
- Nominate two students to read aloud the example question and answer to the class.
- Elicit the questions for the prompts from the class.
- Put students into pairs. They ask and answer the questions.
- Listen to some pairs as a class.

Vocabulary extension: Workbook page 109 ▶

Reading

Text type: An online magazine article

Recommended web links

www.historic-uk.com/CultureUK/British-Superstitions/

www.bbc.com/future/story/20120327-why-do-we-have-superstitions

sportsmedicine.about.com/od/sportspsychology/a/superstitions.htm

Warmer

Write *football, athletics, tennis, basketball, motor racing, golf* and *swimming* on the board. Put students into pairs. Students write the name of a well-known sportsman or sportswoman in each category from another country, not their own. The first pair to write seven names wins.

1
- Students look at the picture.
- Elicit what they know about Rafa Nadal and write it on the board.

2 🔘 3.09
- This exercise gives students practice in reading and listening to locate specific information. This is an important skill for effective reading and listening, especially when reading or listening to longer pieces of authentic text.
- Explain the task.

3
- If necessary, tell the students that four different kinds of athletes are mentioned including the example, *tennis player*.
- Play the CD. Students listen and follow the text in their books.
- They compare answers in pairs.
- Check answers as a class. Highlight the fact that we say *tennis player* and *basketball player* but *golfer* and *footballer*.

- Students read the questions and the different possible answers first.
- They work individually and choose the correct answers.
- They compare answers in pairs.
- Check answers as a class and highlight the *Did you know?* box.

Culture note

Goran Ivanisevic won Wimbledon in 2001 when he ate fish soup, lamb and chips and ice cream with chocolate sauce every night at the same table in the same restaurant during the tournament.

Word check

Make sure students understand the words. Ask them to translate them into their language.

4
- Students work individually and read the questions.
- Give them two or three minutes to think about their answers and make notes.
- Listen to their ideas as a class.

Finished?

Ask fast finishers to make a list of famous tennis players and golfers from their country.

Web quest

Students choose a famous athlete to find out about. Highlight the Web quest tip.

1 • Students write three things they want to know about the famous athlete they have chosen.
2 • Students work in pairs. They swap questions.
  • Ask students to open an internet web browser such as Internet Explorer. Students open a search engine (eg Google) and type in the subject of their search.
  • Students find the answers to their partner's questions.
3 • They report on the information they have found to their partner.
  • They present their findings to the class.

Reading
An online magazine article

1 Who is the athlete in the picture? What do you know about him?

2 🔊 3.09 Read and listen. The article mentions different kinds of athletes. Find them and write them in your notebook.

tennis player

3 Read the article again and choose the correct answers.

1 For Tiger Woods, it is sometimes important to play golf ...
a) on a particular day.
b) in a particular colour.

2 Michael Jordan always wore ...
a) two different pairs of shorts.
b) one long pair of shorts.

3 In the past, athletes ...
a) weren't superstitious.
b) were as superstitious as athletes today.

4 The writer of the article ...
a) isn't superstitious about anything.
b) is a bit superstitious.

5 People sometimes repeat the same behaviour because ...
a) they are scared of changing it.
b) they want to be like athletes.

6 The word *them* in **blue** refers to ...
a) footballers.
b) athletes.

4 Are you superstitious? Have you got any particular habits you have to do when you do sport? What do you do?

🏁 FINISHED?

How many famous tennis players and golfers from your country do you know?

SUPERSTITION *and* SPORT

Many sportspeople are superstitious. Did you know that tennis player, Rafa Nadal always takes two identical bottles of water with him to a tennis match? He puts them next to the court before he plays. Golfer, Tiger Woods always wears red on the last day of a golf tournament. And what about the famous basketball player Michael Jordan? He always wore his old college basketball shorts under his team shorts for luck, so the team shorts on top had to be very long!

Superstitions like these have been part of sport since it began. The superstitions don't make much sense, but many sports champions believe they bring them luck and help them succeed in competitions.

When it comes to superstition, athletes aren't the only ones, of course. Many of us have our own little habits. Personally, I always have to drink my coffee from the same cup, which drives my family crazy!

According to psychologists, following the same routine makes people feel safe. When we do something and everything goes OK, it seems like a good idea to

do it the same way next time – we don't want to behave differently in case things go wrong! Another possible explanation for the athletes' behaviour is that following the same routine helps them relax before a game. Some of **them** go too far, however. There are stories of footballers who have worn the same pair of socks for many weeks because they thought they were lucky! Yuck!

Word check

superstition identical habit drive someone crazy behaviour routine

DID YOU KNOW?

During a tournament, Croatian tennis star Goran Ivanisevic ate the same meal at the same restaurant every night for two weeks!

WEB QUEST

Choose a famous athlete to find out about.

1 Write three things you want to know about him or her.

2 Work in pairs. Swap your questions and find the answers to your partner's questions.

3 Share your information with your partner and then with the rest of the class.

Web Quest tip!

Use a variety of search engines to look for information, not just one.

Grammar

Present perfect + *for* and *since*

present perfect + *for* and *since*

We use *for* and *since* with the present perfect to talk about a period of time up to the present.
We use *for* when we are talking about the **length of time** up to the present.
I've been in the team **for three years**.
We use *since* when we state the **starting point** of the period of time up to the present.
I've been in the team **since 2012**.
I've been in the team **since I was 13**.

Exercise 1

1 since
2 for

1 Study the table. Complete the sentences with *for* or *since*. Look at the article on page 85 to check your answers.

1 Superstitions have been part of sport … it began.
2 Some footballers have worn the same pair of socks … many weeks.

Exercise 2

time expressions with *since*

last week
10th June
1995
my birthday
she was a student

time expressions with *for*

five minutes
a few days
many years
a long time

2 Copy the table into your notebook. Complete it with the time expressions in the box.

> two hours   yesterday   five minutes   last week
> a few days   10th June   many years   1995
> my birthday   she was a student   a long time

time expressions with *since*	time expressions with *for*
yesterday	two hours

🔍 ANALYSE

Look at the sentence and answer the questions.
Anna and Jack have been friends since they were four.
When did Anna and Jack first become friends? Are they still friends now?

Exercise 3

1 since
2 for
3 since
4 since
5 for

3 Complete the sentences with *for* or *since*.

1 The modern Olympic Games have existed … 1896.
2 England hasn't won the World Cup … a long time.
3 Table tennis has been an Olympic sport … 1988.
4 Our town has had a sports stadium … last year.
5 Juan has been a Málaga supporter … seven years.

LOOK!

How long …? with the present perfect
How long has Jo been a swimming teacher?
She's been a swimming teacher for ten years.
She's been a swimming teacher since she was 18.

4 Write questions using *How long …?* and the present perfect.

you / be at this school?
How long have you been at this school?

1 you / have a mobile phone ?
2 you / live in your town ?
3 your parents / know each other ?
4 computers / exist ?

5 Complete the answers to the questions in exercise 4.

1 I've been at this school since …
2 I've had a mobile phone for …
3 I've lived in this town for …
4 My parents have known each other for …
5 Computers have existed since …

6 Circle the correct answers.

Lucy: You look happy. What (1) **'s** / **'ve** happened?
Nina: I've (2) **won** / **win** a game of chess against Adam Green!
Lucy: Who's Adam Green?
Nina: He's (3) **been** / **was** the school chess champion (4) **since** / **for** two years.
Lucy: How long (5) **you've** / **have you** been in the chess team?
Nina: Only (6) **for** / **since** January.
Lucy: Well done!
Nina: Oh look … he's (7) **send** / **sent** me a message.
Lucy: What does it say?
Nina: Congratulations! You (8) **got** / **'ve got** better since we last (9) **have played** / **played**!

Exercise 4

1 How long have you had a mobile phone?
2 How long have you lived in your town?
3 How long have your parents known each other?
4 How long have computers existed?

Exercise 5

students' own answers

Exercise 6

1 's
2 won
3 been
4 for
5 have you
6 since
7 sent
8 've got
9 played

🔊 3.10–3.11 Pronunciation lab: Linking words: final consonant + vowel sound, page 125

Grammar

Present perfect + *for* and *since*

Lesson objectives

In this lesson students will:
- use the present perfect with *for* and *since*
- make questions using *How long?*

Warmer

Write the sentence *He ate the same meal every night for two weeks* on the board with the words in the wrong order: *for meal every ate two same night the weeks he*. Students work in pairs and write the sentence with the words in the correct order.

1 • Students read the rules and example sentences in the table carefully.
- They complete the sentences using *for* or *since*.
- They compare answers in pairs.
- They check answers in the article on page 85.
- Highlight the fact that *for* is used for a number of *minutes, hours, weeks, months, years*, etc and that these words are often in the plural. *For* is also used in the expressions *for a long time* and *for ages*.
- *Since* is used to refer to the point in time where the action started and is usually a date (a day, a month, a year) or a phrase, eg *I was young, I was a student*.

2 • Explain the task.
- Students copy the table into their notebooks.
- They write the time expressions in the correct column.
- They compare answers in pairs.
- Check answers as a class.

Analyse

Focus students' attention on the Analyse box. Ask the two questions and elicit the answers (*When they were four. Yes.*).

3 • Make sure students understand the task.
- They complete the exercise individually.
- They compare answers in pairs.
- Check answers as a class.

Look!

Focus students on the example sentences and highlight that we use *How long ...?* with the present perfect to ask questions about a period of time up to the present time.

4 • Students work individually and write the questions.
- They compare answers in pairs.
- Check answers as a class.

5 • Explain the task.
- Students complete the sentences with answers that are true for them.
- They compare answers in pairs.
- Listen to students' answers as a class. Accept any answers that are possible (see the Culture note for answers to question 5), but make sure students use *for* and *since* correctly.
- Using your knowledge of your students, ask individual students appropriate questions with *How long has ...?*, eg *How long has your mother been a teacher?*

Culture note

The first mechanical computer was invented by Charles Babbage in 1822. The first electromechanical computer was developed by IBM and Harvard in 1944 and the first completely electronic computer was not developed until the 1960s.

6 • Make sure students understand the task. Encourage them to read the whole dialogue before they choose the correct words.
- Students work individually and choose the correct answers.
- They compare answers in pairs.
- Check answers as a class. Point out that the past simple is correct in answer 9 because Adam is referring to a definite time in the past, the last time he and Nina played.

Pronunciation lab: Linking words: final consonant + vowel sound, page 125

Digital course: Interactive grammar table ❯❯

Study guide: page 93 ❯❯

Vocabulary and Listening
Verbs of movement (2)

Lesson objectives

In this lesson students will:
- learn a set of verbs related to movement
- listen for specific information

Warmer

Write a verb of movement from the word pool box on page 77 on the board, eg *sail*. Ask students to work in pairs and write down all the verbs of movement they know in English. Set a time limit of two minutes. The pair with the most verbs wins.

1 🔘 3.12
- Play the CD. Students listen and repeat the words.
- Students repeat the words chorally and individually. Point out that the *l* in *walk* /wɔːk/ is silent.
- Make sure students understand all the words. If necessary, ask students to translate then into their language.

2
- Students read the article and complete the sentences using the verbs from exercise 1.
- They compare answers in pairs.

3 🔘 3.13
- Play the CD. Students listen and follow the text in their books.
- They check their answers to exercise 2.

4
- Explain the task.
- Students work individually and complete the sentences.
- They compare answers in pairs.
- Listen to their ideas as a class.

5 🔘 3.14
- Play the CD. Students write the answers in their notebooks.
- They compare answers in pairs.
- Check answers as a class.

6
- Students read the six sentences carefully.
- Play the CD. Students listen and decide if the sentences are true or false.
- Play the CD again. Students correct the false sentences.
- Check answers as a class.

🔘 **3.14 Audioscript, exercise 5**

Gavin: Hi, this is Gavin Healy, and you're listening to *Cool FM*. Today we're talking about superstitions. With me in the studio is psychologist Selma Hughes, but first of all I'd like to take a few calls from listeners. We've got our first call here from Becky. Hi Becky. Are you a superstitious person?
Becky: No, not at all.
Gavin: So you never say things like 'Touch wood' and you never cross your fingers for good luck?
Becky: No, never! I don't believe in luck. Yesterday my friend Helen said, 'Oh, a black cat walked in front of me this morning; that's really bad luck. That's why I did so badly in the maths test.' But I think that's silly. You do badly in the maths test because you don't work hard, not because you see a black cat!
Gavin: I see what you mean, yeah. Thanks, Becky. We've got another caller on the line now. Hi, is that Darren?
Darren: Yes, it is. Hello.
Gavin: What do you think about superstitions, Darren?
Darren: Well, I always thought superstitions were stupid, but I had an experience recently that made me not so sure.
Gavin: Oh? What happened exactly?
Darren: I was on my way to school and there was a ladder on the pavement. I didn't think twice about it and just walked under it. But after that I had a really bad day! I missed the bus and was late for school. Then I had an argument with my girlfriend. Everything went wrong!
Gavin: And you think that's all because you walked under the ladder?
Darren: Er … I don't know … Maybe it was just chance. But since then, I haven't walked under any ladders!
Gavin: Hmm, I'm not surprised! OK, let's take our third and final call now. Hello Tina! What have you got to say about superstitions, Tina?
Tina: Well, my problem is that I'm too superstitious!
Gavin: Why? What kind of things do you do?
Tina: Well, I'm always worrying about breaking mirrors or doing anything that might bring me bad luck. When I lost my lucky charm last year, I really thought something terrible was going to happen to me!
Gavin: And did anything terrible happen?
Tina: No, it didn't actually, but that didn't stop me from being superstitious. It's become a bad habit and I need some help to stop it but I don't know what to do!
Gavin: Well, stay on the line, Tina, because Selma will have some advice for you right after this next song. I've been waiting to play this all morning! It's *Superstition* by Stevie Wonder …

Vocabulary and Listening
Verbs of movement (2)

1 🔊 **3.12** Listen and repeat the words in the box.

> touch carry break drop spill walk cross open pick scratch meet put

Good (and bad) luck with British superstitions!

1 Before an exam or other important event, … your fingers for good luck.

2 Don't … your nose, or you'll have an argument with someone.

3 To make sure that something you say with confidence won't bring you bad luck, … something made of wood as you say it.

4 Don't … your shoes on the table, or you'll have bad luck for the rest of the day.

5 Try to … a black cat, because it's lucky. But be careful – it's unlucky if it walks in front of you!

6 Never … under a ladder, or somebody will have an accident.

7 And never … an umbrella indoors. It's unlucky.

8 … a four-leaf clover and you'll have love, health, money and fame!

9 If you … some salt, throw some of it over your shoulder to make sure you don't have bad luck.

10 Expect something good to happen if you … a glass and it breaks.

11 But don't … a mirror, or you'll have bad luck for seven years.

12 … a lucky charm with you to make sure you **always** have good luck!

2 Read the article and complete the sentences with words from exercise 1.

3 🔊 **3.13** Listen and check your answers.

4 Are there any superstitions in your country? What superstitions do people have? Complete the sentences.

People say it's lucky to …
People say it's unlucky to …

5 🔊 **3.14** Listen to part of a radio programme about superstitions. Who …

1 believes in superstitions?
2 doesn't believe in superstitions?
3 isn't certain that he or she believes in superstitions?

6 Listen again. Are the sentences true or false? Correct the false sentences.

1 Becky said she had a bad experience when she saw a black cat.
2 Becky doesn't believe in bad luck.
3 In the past, Darren wasn't a superstitious person.
4 Darren sometimes walks under ladders now.
5 Tina lost something special last year.
6 Tina is superstitious because she is always having bad luck.

Exercise 2

1 cross
2 scratch
3 touch
4 put
5 meet
6 walk
7 open
8 Pick
9 spill
10 drop
11 break
12 Carry

Exercise 5

1 Tina
2 Becky
3 Darren

Exercise 6

1 **False**
Becky's friend Helen said she had a bad experience when she saw a black cat.
2 **True**
3 **True**
4 **False**
Darren doesn't walk under ladders now.
5 **True**
6 **False**
Tina is superstitious because it's a habit.

Cultural awareness
Superstitions in Ireland

IRISH BELIEFS
AND SUPERSTITIONS

Hi, I'm Will. I've written this information page about Irish beliefs and superstitions. I hope you enjoy reading it.
The Irish people have kept a lot of their old superstitions and traditions. Many of these come from the Celts, who lived in Ireland and other parts of Britain about 2,000 years ago.

FAIRIES

In the past, nearly everyone in Ireland believed in fairies! According to legend, fairies are little people who can do magic and bring people good or bad luck. A common name for fairies is 'the Good People', but they aren't always good! There are many different kinds of fairy. One well-known kind of fairy is the leprechaun, who likes to play tricks on people.

STONE CIRCLES

There are rings of stones all over the Irish countryside. According to legend, these are fairy rings, and if you destroy one, you'll have an accident before the end of the year. Local people have avoided them for centuries for this reason. However, archaeologists think that Stone Age people, not fairies, made them!

RAINBOWS

In Ireland we say that leprechauns keep a pot of gold at the end of the rainbow. If you catch a leprechaun, you can make him give you his treasure! Leprechauns are difficult to catch, though, because they are very clever!

THE BLARNEY STONE

This is a stone in the walls of Blarney Castle near Cork. People say that if you kiss the stone, you will get 'the gift of the gab' and become a good speaker. Most Irish people have this gift already. We love to talk and are very good at it!

Thank you for reading this information page! I wish you all 'the luck of the Irish'!

Will, age 15

Word check

...end centuries archaeologist Stone Age rainbow treasure

1 Look at the web page. Pictures a–d are in the wrong place. Match them with the correct subheadings.

2 ⬤ 3.15 Read and listen. What is a leprechaun?

3 Read again and choose the correct words.

1 The Celts lived **only in Ireland** / **all over Britain**.
2 The Irish believe that fairies are **good and bad** / **usually good**.
3 Some Irish **people** / **archaeologists** think it's dangerous to destroy stone circles.
4 Leprechauns can show people where to find **rainbows** / **money**.
5 Irish people have a talent for **speaking** / **kissing**.

CULTURAL ⬤ COMPARISON

4 Compare superstitions in your country with superstitions in Ireland. Think about ...

- fairies
- ghosts
- UFOs
- the evil eye

In my country we don't believe in fairies, but some people believe in ghosts.

Exercise 1

a Rainbows
b Fairies
c The Blarney Stone
d Stone circles

Exercise 2

A kind of fairy.

Exercise 3

1 all over Britain
2 good and bad
3 people
4 money
5 speaking

Cultural awareness
Superstitions in Ireland

4
- Explain the task.
- Students work individually and think about their answers. They make notes in their notebooks.
- They compare ideas in pairs.
- Listen to their ideas as a class.

Culture video: Ireland ▷▷

Lesson objectives

In this lesson students will:
- read about Irish beliefs and superstitions
- compare superstitions in their country with superstitions in Ireland

Warmer

Focus students on the Fact box. Write *Ireland* on the board and draw a shamrock (a four-leaf clover) next to the name of the country. Point out that the harp is another symbol of Ireland. Put students into pairs and ask them to make a list of as many countries and their symbols as they can. Set a time limit of two minutes. Listen to their ideas as a class and make a list on the board, eg *England: rose, lion; Wales: daffodil, dragon; Scotland: thistle, bagpipes.*

1
- Make sure students understand the task.
- Students read the text and match the pictures with the subheadings.
- They compare answers in pairs.
- Check answers as a class.

2 ◉ 3.15
- Read the question aloud to the class.
- Play the CD. Students listen and follow the text in their books.
- They compare their answer in pairs.
- Check the answer as a class.

3
- Students read the sentences carefully.
- They read the text again and choose the correct words.
- Students compare answers in pairs.
- Check answers as a class.

Word check

Make sure students understand the words.
Ask them to translate them into their language.
Note the pronunciation and stress of
archaeologist /ɑːkɪˈɒlədʒɪst/.

Grammar
Present perfect and past simple

Warmer

Write the sentence *The modern Olympic Games have existed since 1896* on the board with the words in the wrong order: *existed modern since Games the have Olympic 1896.* Students work in pairs and write the sentence in the correct order. Invite students to come to the board and write their sentence. If there are mistakes, ask other students to correct them.

1
- Ask the class to say which sentence has a verb in the past simple (*sentence 2*) and which has a verb in the present perfect (*sentence 1*).

2
- Students read the information carefully in the table. They copy the table into their notebooks and complete the rules.
- They compare answers in pairs.
- Check answers as a class. Highlight the fact that we use the present perfect to talk about past actions when no time is mentioned, eg *I've been to Paris*, and the past simple when an action is completed in the past, eg *I went to Paris in 2013*.

Look!

Focus on the information in the Look! box. Highlight that we use *just* with the present perfect for something that happened a few moments earlier.

3
- Explain the task.
- Students work individually and choose the correct words.
- They compare answers in pairs.
- Check answers as a class.

4
- Do the first example with the whole class to demonstrate the activity (*'ve been*). Elicit that it is present perfect because it is followed by *since Saturday*.
- Students work individually and fill the gaps using either the past simple or the present perfect of the verbs in brackets.
- They compare answers in pairs.
- Check answers as a class.

CLIL Grammar in context: History

5
- Students work individually. Ask them to read the whole text before they complete the essay with the correct form of the verbs in brackets.
- They compare answers in pairs.

6 3.16
- Play the CD. Students listen and check their answers to exercise 5.
- Highlight the irregular verb *wear, wore, worn*.

CLIL task

Students use the internet to find out about three superstitions in two different countries.

Digital course: Interactive grammar table

Study guide: page 93

Grammar
Present perfect and past simple

1 Look at sentences 1 and 2. Are the verbs past simple or present perfect?

1 The Irish have kept their traditions.
2 In the past, everyone believed in fairies.

2 Read the table. Copy and complete the rules with the present perfect or the past simple.

present perfect and past simple

We use the (1) ... to talk about:
- actions that happened in the past, but we don't specify when they happened.
- actions that began in the past and continue now.
- recent actions.

We use the (2) ... to talk about:
- completed actions in the past.
- states or repeated actions in the past.

LOOK!

We use *just* with the present perfect when we want to emphasize that we have done something very recently.
I **have just spoken** to him.
They**'ve just left**.

3 Choose the correct words.

1 Look! I**'ve found** / **found** a four-leaf clover!
2 It**'s been** / **was** Jo's birthday last week!
3 Dan's cat **had** / **has had** four black kittens last night.
4 Oh no! Somebody **broke** / **'s broken** the mirror!
5 Jo **gave** / **'s given** me this charm yesterday.

4 Complete the postcard with the past simple or present perfect form of the verbs in brackets.

Dear Beth,
We (1) ... (be) in Ireland since Saturday and we're having a great time! Yesterday morning we (2) ... (go) to Blarney Castle and I (3) ... (kiss) the Blarney Stone! In the afternoon we (4) ... (have) a picnic in the countryside. The weather isn't good – it (5) ... (rain) four times since we (6) ... (arrive).
Love Katie
PS I (7) ... (see) a rainbow yesterday, but I (8) ... (not catch) a leprechaun yet!

CLIL Grammar in context: History

5 Complete the essay with the correct form of the verbs in brackets.

The history of superstitions

How long (1) ... people ... (have) superstitions? Probably since the world (2) ... (begin)! For thousands of years, people (3) ... (look) for ways to explain why certain things happen.

The evil eye
The superstition of the evil eye (4) ... (exist) in Greece since ancient times. The ancient Greeks (5) ... (believe) that some people could have a bad effect on others just by looking at them. Since then, Greek people (6) ... (wear) special bracelets with a blue 'eye' on them to protect them from evil.

Cats
For centuries, people (7) ... (think) that cats have magical powers. For this reason, the ancient Egyptians (8) ... (keep) cats in their homes and (9) ... (not allow) anyone to treat them badly.

The number 13
Why (10) ... this number ... (become) an unlucky number? Some people say it is because there (11) ... (be) 13 people at Christ's last meal. Friday the 13th (12) ... (not always be) an unlucky date. People only (13) ... (start) being superstitious about it in the 20th century, but no one really knows why.

6 ▶ 3.16 Listen and check your answers.

CLIL TASK
Go online. Find out about three superstitions in two different countries.

At the leisure centre

When I'm bored I go to the leisure centre. There are lots of fun activities to do there!

HOPFIELD LEISURE CENTRE

DAY	10–11AM	5–6PM	6–7PM	7–8PM
Monday		table tennis	trampolining	archery
Tuesday	archery	yoga	table tennis	fencing
Wednesday		fencing	archery	taekwondo
Thursday	table tennis	taekwondo	trampolining	fencing
Friday		archery	yoga	table tennis
Saturday	rollerblading	table tennis	trampolining	taekwondo

PLEASE NOTE
Taekwondo, trampolining and yoga: wear comfortable clothes
Fencing: masks and suits are provided
Archery: bows and arrows are provided
Table tennis: bats and balls are available for hire (£3 per hour)
Rollerblading: skates available for hire (£4 per hour)

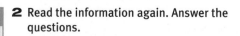
Step 1: Read

Exercise 1
yoga
taekwondo

1 Read the leisure centre timetable and the note. Which activities can you do without any special equipment?

SKILLS BUILDER

Understanding timetables
The following are sometimes used in timetables.
am = morning
pm = afternoon
per = for each

Exercise 2
1 Friday
2 yoga
3 three
4 fencing
5 table tennis, rollerblading

2 Read the information again. Answer the questions.

1 Lucy and Nina want to play table tennis once a week, but they aren't free until 7pm. What day can they play?
2 Chris wants to find an activity he can do on his own, but he is only free on Tuesday. Which activity can he do?
3 How many times a week can you do archery?
4 For which activity do people wear special clothes?
5 For which activities can you pay to hire equipment?

Step 2: Listen

3 🔊 3.17 Listen to four announcements at the leisure centre. Which day of the week is it?

Exercise 3
Friday

4 Listen again and answer the questions.

1 What time does the café close?
2 Which activity will not take place today?
3 Who can save money if they join the leisure centre?
4 When does the special offer end?
5 When will the leisure centre close?

Exercise 4
1 8pm
2 yoga
3 a family (two adults and two children)
4 at the end of this month
5 in fifteen minutes

Integrated skills
At the leisure centre

Warmer

Highlight Chris's speech bubble. Write *leisure centre* on the board. Ask students what sports they can *play* or *do* at their local leisure centre. Remind them that we use *go* with sports ending in *-ing*. Elicit examples from the class and write them in three columns on the board, eg *play table tennis, do yoga, go swimming*.

Step 1: Read

1
- Explain the task.
- Students read the leisure centre information and decide which activities do not require special equipment.
- They compare answers in pairs.
- Check answers as a class.

Skills builder

Understanding timetables

Focus attention on the Skills builder box and check students understand the use of the abbreviations *am* and *pm* and the meaning of the word *per*.

2
- Students read the questions carefully first.
- They look in the text and find the answers.
- They compare answers in pairs.
- Check answers as a class.

Step 2: Listen

3   3.17
- Explain the task. Students need to listen and decide which day of the week it is. Point out that they need to refer to the timetable while they listen.
- Play the CD.
- Students compare their answer in pairs.
- Check the answer as a class.

4
- Students read the five questions carefully first.
- Play the CD again. Students note down the answers.
- They compare answers in pairs.
- Check answers as a class.

3.17 Audioscript, exercise 3

Announcement 1
If you're feeling hungry after all that exercise, why not visit the Sports Zone café for a refreshing drink or a healthy snack? Enjoy an ice-cold fruit juice or a reviving tea or coffee. And you'll love our selection of fresh sandwiches and delicious cakes. We're open from 10am till 8pm, Monday to Saturday.

Announcement 2
This is an important announcement. Due to reasons beyond our control, today's yoga class at six o'clock has been cancelled. I repeat – there will be no yoga class today at 6pm. We would like to apologize for any inconvenience.

Announcement 3
If you and your family are frequent visitors to the leisure centre, a family pass could save you money. When two adults and two children join for a year, you don't pay anything for one child! This special offer is on for this month only. Don't join too late. Don't miss this special offer!

Announcement 4
We would like to inform you that the leisure centre will be closing in fifteen minutes. Please make sure you collect all your belongings from the changing rooms before you leave. Thank you. We look forward to seeing you again soon.

Integrated skills – continued
Making arrangements

5 🔘 3.18
- Students read the dialogue first.
- Play the CD. Students listen and follow the text in their books. They write answers 1–4 in their notebooks.
- They compare answers in pairs.
- Check answers as a class.

6
- Play the CD, pausing after each question or statement and each response for students to repeat as a class.
- Ask students to repeat the dialogue several times both chorally and individually with the correct stress and intonation.
- Note the falling intonation in the *wh-* questions *What do you want to do? What time does it start? Where shall we meet?* and the rising intonation in the *yes / no* question *Do you want a lift?*
- Students practise the dialogue in pairs. Then swap roles and practise the dialogue again.

Step 3: Write

7
- Students work individually. They copy the questions and phrase in bold into their notebooks.
- They look at the timetable on page 90 and choose a different activity from the activity Chris and Lucy chose to do.
- Students write answers to the questions and complete the phrase.

8
- Ask students to look at the Communication kit: Making arrangements. Encourage them to use these expressions when writing their dialogue.
- Students work individually and write their dialogue, using the dialogue in the book as a model.
- Monitor while they are writing and give help if necessary.

Step 4: Communicate

9
- Students practise their dialogues in pairs.
- For extra practice, they swap roles in both dialogues.

10
- Choose some pairs to act out their dialogue for the class.
- Students raise their hand if another pair has chosen the same activity as the activity they have chosen. This will encourage them to listen carefully to their classmates.

Integrated skills: Workbook page 118 〉〉

MAKING ARRANGEMENTS

Watch!

Do you have any plans this weekend? Shall we go to the leisure centre on (1) … ?	OK. **What do you want to do?**
Let's go (2) … .	Yeah, that sounds fun. **What time does it start?**
Ten.	Do you want a lift?
No, it's fine, thanks. I'll probably go on my (3) … .	OK. **Where shall we meet?**
(4) … the leisure centre at quarter to ten.	OK, great.
OK, I'll see you then!	Bye!

Exercise 5

1 Saturday
2 rollerblading
3 bike
4 Outside

5 🔊 3.18 Listen to Chris and Lucy planning a visit to Hopfield Leisure Centre. Complete 1–4 in your notebook.

6 Listen again and repeat. Practise your intonation.

Step 3: Write

7 Copy the questions and phrase in bold in your notebook. Then choose a different activity. Write your answers to the questions and complete the phrase.

8 Write a new dialogue about your activity. Write both parts. Use the dialogue in exercise 5 to help you.

Shall we go to the leisure centre on Tuesday?
OK. What do you want to do?

Step 4: Communicate

9 Work in pairs. Take turns to practise your dialogues.

💬 *Shall we go to the leisure centre on Saturday?*
💬 *OK. What …?*

10 Act your dialogue for the class.

COMMUNICATION KIT

Making arrangements

Shall we go to … ?
What do you want to do?
Let's go / do / play …
What time does it start?
What time shall we meet?
Where shall we meet?
Do you want a lift?
I'll see you outside / near / at …

Writing
An email

Hi Luke,   ✉ Send   ◁ Reply

What are you up to? I've just played a new video game with my brother. It's called 'Rollerblade heroes 3' and it's an adventure game. Have you played it? It's a game for two players and you have to skate around a city to collect special coins. It was great fun, 🙂 but I found it very difficult because you have to be very fast. We played it three times and I lost every time. 😣 I was really annoyed because my brother was really good! Anyway, I'm going to practise more so I can win. Next time, you could play with us if you want.

Hope you're enjoying your weekend!

Bye for now,

Natalie

Exercise 1
1 happy
2 unhappy

1 🔊 3.19 **Read and listen to Natalie's email. How did she feel when she …**

1 was playing the game?
2 lost the game?

Exercise 2
1 e annoyed
2 c happy
3 a unhappy
4 d laughing
5 b surprised

2 Match the emoticons with the meanings.

1   **a)** unhappy

2   **b)** surprised

3   **c)** happy

4   **d)** laughing

5   **e)** annoyed

3 Read the Writing focus. Do adjectives go before or after a noun in your language?

WRITING FOCUS
Using adjectives

We use adjectives to describe our feelings. In a sentence, adjectives can go before a noun or after the verbs *be* and *look*. In emails, we sometimes use emoticons to show what we feel or felt about something.

I'm having a nice weekend. 🙂
I was really embarrassed! 😞

4 Order the words to make sentences.

1 computer game / the / looks / fun / good .
2 was / the / difficult / very / computer game .
3 She's / a / team / captain / great .
4 were / in the stadium /some / happy / there / supporters .
5 unhappy / looked / after / the match / they .

Writing task

Write an email about a game you played recently.

Plan   Plan your email. Make notes about the game and what you liked or disliked about it. Include adjectives and emoticons to describe how you felt.

Write   Write the email. Use the email in exercise 1 to help you.

Check   Check your writing.

☑ *Hi* at the start, your name at the end
☑ adjectives and emoticons to describe your feelings
☑ verb tenses

Exercise 4
1 The computer game looks good fun.
2 The computer game was very difficult.
3 She's a great team captain.
4 There were some happy supporters in the stadium.
5 They looked unhappy after the match.

Writing
An email

Lesson objectives

In this lesson students will:
- read an email
- use a set of adjectives to describe feelings
- write an email

Warmer

Write the adjectives *happy, friendly, cold, loud, difficult, comfortable, expensive, interested, fast* on the board. Put students into pairs. They write the opposite adjectives (*sad, unfriendly, hot, quiet, easy, uncomfortable, cheap, bored, slow*). The first pair to write all nine correctly wins.

1 🔊 **3.19**
- Explain the task.
- Play the CD.
- Students listen and follow in their books.
- They compare answers in pairs.
- Check answers as a class.

2
- Students match the emoticons and the meanings.
- They compare answers in pairs.
- Check answers as a class.

3
- Students read the information in the Writing focus box. Highlight the position of adjectives before a noun or after the verbs *be* and *look* and the use of emoticons in emails to emphasize what people feel.
- They answer the question about the position of adjectives in their language.
- Listen to answers as a class.

4
- Make sure students understand the task.
- They complete the task individually and order the words to make sentences.
- They compare answers in pairs.
- Check answers as a class.

Writing task

The aim of this activity is for students to write a short email that includes adjectives and emoticons to describe feelings and the correct use of tenses. Ask the students to follow the stages in the Student's Book and to use *Hi* at the start of their email and their name at the end. At the Check stage, ask them to swap notebooks and check each other's writing.

> Writing reference and practice: Workbook page 134 ❯❯

Study guide
Grammar Vocabulary and Speaking

Tell the students the Study guide is an important page which provides a useful reference for the main language of the unit: the grammar, the vocabulary and the functional language from the Integrated skills pages. Explain that they should refer to this page when studying for a test or exam.

Grammar

- Tell the students to look at the example sentences of the present perfect + *for* and *since*. Make sure students understand the use of the tense with each word.
- Then tell students to look at the usage explanation of the present perfect and past simple. Ensure they understand the different uses.
- Refer students to the Grammar reference on pages 98–99 of the Workbook for further revision.

Vocabulary

- Tell students to look at the list of vocabulary and check understanding.
- Refer students to the Wordlist on page 151 of the Workbook where they can look up any words they can't remember.

Speaking

- Check that students understand the phrases to use for making arrangements.
- Tell students to act out a conversation between two friends making plans to meet and do an activity together next Sunday.

Additional material

Workbook

- Progress check page 70
- Self-evaluation page 71
- Grammar reference and practice pages 98–99
- Vocabulary extension page 109
- Integrated skills page 118
- Writing reference and task pages 134–135

Teacher's Resource File

- Basics section pages 47–52
- Vocabulary and grammar consolidation pages 31–34
- Translation and dictation pages 9, 19
- Evaluation rubrics pages 1–7
- Key competences worksheets pages 15–16
- Culture and CLIL worksheets pages 29–32
- Culture video worksheets pages 15–16
- Digital competence worksheets pages 15–16
- Macmillan Readers worksheets pages 5–6

Tests and Exams

- Unit 8 End-of-unit test: Basic, Standard and Extra
- CEFR Skills Exam Generator

Study guide

Grammar
Present perfect + *for* and *since*

present perfect + *for* and *since*
We use *for* and *since* with the present perfect to talk about a period of time up to the present. We use *for* when we are talking about the **length of time** up to the present. I've been a supporter **for two years**. We use *since* when we state the **starting point** of the period of time up to the present. I've been a supporter **since 2012**. I've been a supporter **since I was 13**.

Present perfect and past simple

present perfect and past simple
We use the present perfect to talk about: • actions that happened in the past, but we don't specify when they happened.   • actions that began in the past and continue now.   • recent actions.   We use the past simple to talk about: • completed actions in the past.   • states or repeated actions in the past.

Vocabulary
Sport and competitions

captain	match	team
champion	opponent	tournament
coach	race	winner
goal	stadium	
loser	supporter	

Verbs of movement (2)

break	drop	pick	spill
carry	meet	put	touch
cross	open	scratch	walk

Speaking
Making arrangements

Shall we go to ... ?
What do you want to do?
Let's go / do / play ...
What time does it start?
What time shall we meet?
Where shall we meet?
Do you want a lift?
I'll see you outside / near / at ...

 LEARNING TO LEARN

Organize new vocabulary in your notebook in topic groups. Make a page for sport and competitions. Then you can add extra words when you learn them.

UNIT 9 — TAKE CARE

Unit objectives and key competences

In this unit the student will learn ...

- understand, memorize and correctly use vocabulary related to personal issues and health **CLC SCC CMST**
- understand and correctly use *should / shouldn't* and *must / mustn't* and review present, past and future tenses **CLC L2L**
- about how to survive in the Australian outback and compare the Australian outback with a remote area in their country **CLC CMST CAE SCC**
- about Australia by watching a short video **CLC DC CMST CAE**

In this unit the student will learn how to ...

- identify specific information in an information leaflet about cyberbullying **CLC SCC DC**
- look online for information about social networking sites and share your notes with the class **CLC CAE DC SIE**
- identify specific information in two phone calls to a helpline **CLC SCC CAE**
- read about a first aid kit, listen to two friends talking about a mobile phone app and learn how to talk about health **CLC SCC DC CMST**
- write an instant message **CLC DC SIE L2L**
- prepare for and do a listening exam about correcting sentences **CLC SIE L2L**

Linguistic contents

Main vocabulary

- Personal issues: *exercise, stress, bullying,* etc
- Health: *stomach ache, eye strain, bee sting,* etc

Grammar

- *should / shouldn't* and *must / mustn't*
- Tense review: present, past and future
- Time expressions and which tense to use with them

Functional language

- Phrases for talking about health

Pronunciation

- Intonation: Expressing feelings

Skills

Reading

- Read an information leaflet about cyberbullying
- Read an Australian outback survival guide
- Read about a first aid kit
- Read an instant message

Writing: Interaction and production

- Write a personalized dialogue about talking about health
- Write an instant message in three steps: plan, write, check
- Learn how to use different tenses

Listening

- Listen to phone calls to a helpline
- Listen to friends talking about a mobile app

Spoken interaction

- Ask and answer questions about health and personal issues
- Ask for and give advice about a health problem

Spoken production

- Prepare and act out a dialogue about a health problem

Lifelong learning skills

Self-study and self-evaluation
- Study guide:
  Student's Book page 103
- Progress check and self-evaluation:
  Workbook pages 78–79
- Grammar reference and practice:
  Workbook pages 100–101
- Wordlist:
  Workbook pages 151–157

Learning strategies and thinking skills
- Answering questions giving as much useful information as possible

Cultural awareness
- The Australian outback – a survival guide
- Comparing the Australian outback with a remote area in students' own countries

Cross-curricular contents
- Personal, Social, Health and Economic Education (PSHE), the Australian outback
- Language and literature: reading and writing an instant message
- ICT: searching the internet for information

Key competences

CLC	Competence in linguistic communication
CMST	Competence in mathematics, science and technology
DC	Digital competence
SCC	Social and civic competences
SIE	Sense of initiative and entrepreneurship
L2L	Learning to learn
CAE	Cultural awareness and expression

Evaluation
- Unit 9 End-of-unit test: Basic, Standard and Extra
- CEFR Skills Exam Generator
- End-of-term test, Units 7–9: Basic, Standard and Extra
- End-of-year test: Basic, Standard and Extra

External exam trainer
- Listening: Correcting sentences

Digital material
Pulse Live! Digital Course including:
- Interactive grammar tables
- Audio visual speaking model: Talking about health
- Audio visual cultural material: Australia

Student's website

Digital competence
- Web quest: A social networking site
- Digital competence worksheet: Online quizzes

Reinforcement material
- Basic worksheets, Teacher's Resource File pages 53–58
- Vocabulary and Grammar: Consolidation worksheets, Teacher's Resource File pages 35–36

Extension material
- Fast-finisher activity: Student's Book page 95
- Extra activities: Teacher's Book pages T96, T102
- Vocabulary and Grammar: Extension worksheets, Teacher's Resource File pages 37–38

Teacher's Resource File
- Translation and dictation worksheets pages 10, 20
- Evaluation rubrics pages 1–7
- Key competences worksheets pages 17–18
- Culture and CLIL worksheets pages 33–36
- Culture video worksheets pages 17–18
- Digital competence worksheets pages 17–18
- Macmillan Readers worksheets pages 5–6

TAKE CARE

THINK ABOUT IT

What kind of problems do teenagers have? Which do you think are the most important?

Vocabulary and Speaking

Personal issues

1 🔊 3.20 Read the web page. Listen and repeat the words in blue.

2 Which words in blue are shown in the pictures?

3 Read the definitions and write words in blue from the web page.

1 the time you spend going out with friends
2 someone who doesn't eat meat
3 the food you eat every day
4 how you look
5 unkind behaviour

👆 EXPRESS YOURSELF

4 Think about these questions. Use the ideas in the box to help you.

> eat more fruit
> start a new sport / hobby
> talk to your parents / friends / teachers
> go for a walk   listen to music

1 Do you have a healthy diet?
2 Do you take one hour of exercise a day?
3 Are you happy with your social life?
4 Do you worry about school work?

5 Work in pairs. Ask and answer the questions from exercise 4. Offer advice.

> 🔴 *Do you have a healthy diet?*
> ⚪ *No, I don't.*
> 🔴 *Why don't you eat more fruit?*
> ⚪ *That's a good idea!*

Exercise 2

Possible answers
health
exercise
social life
diet
vegetarian
relationship
appearance

Exercise 3

1 social life
2 vegetarian
3 diet
4 appearance
5 bullying

Take care of yourself

If you're aged 13–18, read our guide to staying healthy – both mentally and physically!

❋ A great way to look after your **health** is to take regular **exercise**. Try to exercise for at least one hour every day. Try new sports such as skateboarding or Zumba, or exercise outside with your friends – sport can be good for your **social life** as well as your health! Remember, exercise can also help with **stress**, so if you're preparing for exams, it might be a good idea to try a relaxing activity such as yoga.

❋ It's also important to eat a healthy **diet**. Eat three balanced meals every day plus two healthy snacks. You should eat five portions of fruit and vegetables every day. If you're a **vegetarian**, make sure you eat enough protein to help you grow.

❋ Remember to look after your mental health too. If you have problems at school or home, find an adult you can talk to, such as a school counsellor. He or she can help with issues like **bullying** and **depression**. Every **relationship** has good and bad moments, so it's normal to have **arguments** with friends and family. Always try to discuss your worries calmly with people who can help.

❋ Try not to worry about your **appearance** – remember that your body changes a lot when you're a teenager! If you eat healthily and take exercise, you'll look great too.

Vocabulary and Speaking
Personal issues

Warmer

Write *healthy diet* and *not so healthy diet* on the board. Put students into pairs. Ask them to make a list of as many words as they can for different foods in English under these headings. Set a time limit of two minutes. Listen to their ideas as a class and make a list on the board, eg *healthy diet: salad, oranges; not healthy diet: burgers, sugar*.

Culture note

Many nutritionists agree that the healthiest foods to eat are lemons, broccoli, dark chocolate, salmon and, surprisingly, boiled or jacket potatoes. Unhealthy foods are those that contain a large amount of oil, fat, sugar and salt. These include items such as shop-bought pasta, white bread and potato crisps or chips (French fries). Fizzy drinks with a large amount of sugar are not good for your health if you regularly drink large quantities.

Think about it

Students read the questions. They discuss their answers in pairs. Listen to their ideas as a class. Be aware of anything students may have personal issues about throughout the unit.

1 **3.20**
- Students read the web page.
- Play the CD. Students listen and repeat the words in blue.
- Students repeat the words chorally and individually. Make sure they pronounce the words correctly with the correct stress, especially *diet* /ˈdaɪət/, *vegetarian* /veʤɪˈteərɪən/ and *bullying* /ˈbʊlɪjɪŋ/.

2
- Explain the task.
- Students work individually and note down their answer to the questions in their notebooks.
- They compare answers in pairs.
- Listen to their ideas as a class.

3
- Students read the definitions.
- They work individually and find the words in blue in the text that match the definitions.
- They compare answers in pairs.
- Check answers as a class.

4
- Check that students understand all the questions. Make sure they know the word *worry* (to feel nervous and upset because you keep thinking about a problem that you have).
- Students work individually and answer the questions, writing notes in their notebooks.
- Monitor while they are writing and give help if necessary.

5
- Nominate two students to read aloud the example questions and answers.
- Highlight the use of *Why don't you ...?* to give advice.
- Put students into pairs. They ask and answer the questions from exercise 4.
- Listen to some pairs as a class.

Vocabulary extension: Workbook page 110

Reading
Text type: An information leaflet

Lesson objectives

In this lesson students will:
- read a text about cyberbullying
- discuss the advantages and disadvantages of social networking sites

Recommended web links

www.nhs.uk/Livewell/Bullying/Pages/Cyberbullying.aspx

www.gov.uk/bullying-at-school/reporting-bullying

Warmer

Write *social networking sites* on the board. Check students understand the meaning of the phrase. Elicit examples of well-known social networking sites, eg *Facebook, Tuenti*. Ask students if they use social networking sites. If so, which ones do they use? If not, why not?

1
- Students read the questions.
- They look at the picture and note down their answers in their notebooks.
- Students compare answers in pairs.
- Listen to their ideas as a class.

2 🔘 **3.21**
- This exercise gives students practice in reading and listening for gist. Key words in each paragraph will quickly tell them what the topic of each paragraph is. This is an important skill for effective reading and listening, especially when reading or listening to longer pieces of authentic text.
- Students read the questions.
- Play the CD. Students listen and follow the text in their books.
- They write the answers to the questions in their notebooks.
- Students compare answers in pairs.
- Check answers as a class.

3
- Students read the questions carefully first.
- Students look in the text and find the information.
- Check answers as a class.

Word check

Make sure students understand the words. Ask them to translate them into their language. Note that *get through to* here means *make contact with* and *put up with* means *tolerate*. You could also check that students understand *deal with a problem* (take action to solve a problem) and can pronounce *nasty* /ˈnɑːstɪ/, *unkind* /ʌnˈkaɪnd/ and *hurtful* /ˈhɜːtfl/ correctly with the correct stress.

4
- Explain the task.
- Students work individually and write two more advantages and two more disadvantages of online social networking sites in their notebooks.
- They compare answers in pairs.
- Listen to their ideas as a class.

Finished?

Ask fast finishers to write answers to the two questions about the internet. Listen to their ideas as a class.

Web quest

Students choose a social networking site. Highlight the Web quest tip.

1
- Ask students to open an internet web browser such as Internet Explorer. Students open a search engine (eg Google) and type in the subject of their search.
- Students work individually. They find information about the social networking site and make notes about the history of the site and where it is popular.

2
- Students work in pairs and report on the information they have found out about their social networking site to their partner.

3
- They share their information with the class.

Reading
An information leaflet

CYBERBULLYING
AND HOW TO DEAL WITH IT

Someone is sending you nasty messages or posting rude comments about you on the internet. Should you ignore them or do something about it? Do you need advice about what to do? Read these five tips.

1 Don't reply. Bullies love it when they get a reaction, so don't let them know they're causing you stress.

2 Block the horrible messages. The best thing to do is to avoid all electronic communication so the bully can't get through to you. If you really can't live without using your phone or social networking sites, use filters to block the unkind messages. If someone bullies you in a chat room, don't get into an argument with them. You should report the messages to the chat room moderator.

3 Talk to someone. You mustn't try to deal with the problem on your own. Ask for help – from your parents, a teacher or another adult you can trust. Some victims of cyberbullying feel the problem is their fault and they delay getting help. You don't have to put up with the bullying, and the sooner the bully knows this, the better.

4 Save the evidence. If you have been the victim of online bullying, then you've probably got written proof of it. You can save the messages, print them out and show them to someone who'll take action to stop it. It might be your teacher or even the police.

5 Help the victims of cyberbullying. Don't encourage cyberbullies as this will make the problem worse. You shouldn't be afraid to report the bullies if they continue sending hurtful messages to someone you know.

Word check

ignore block get through to filter put up with victim proof

1 Look at the picture. How do you think the boy feels? Why is he feeling like this?

2 🔊 3.21 Read and listen. Which pieces of advice are for victims of bullying? Which piece of advice isn't for someone who is being bullied?

3 Read the advice leaflet again. Answer the questions.

1 What is cyberbullying?
2 Give two ways of stopping a bully communicating with you.
3 What is the best way to deal with bullying in a chat room?
4 Some people don't ask for help with this problem immediately. Why not?
5 If you receive messages from a cyberbully, who could you show them to?

4 What are the advantages and disadvantages of online social networking sites? Write two more for each heading in your notebook.

Advantages
1 You can communicate easily with your friends.
2 ...
3 ...

Disadvantages
4 People you don't know can find out information about you.
5 ...
6 ...

 FINISHED?

Does the internet improve life for teenagers or make it worse? How?

WEB QUEST

Choose a social networking site.

1 Make notes about:
• The history of the site   • Where it is popular
2 Work in pairs. Talk about your networking sites.
3 Share your notes with the class.

Web Quest tip!

Use different websites to check your facts.

Exercise 1

Possible answers
He feels sad and depressed.
He has a problem with bullying.

Exercise 2

Pieces of advice for victims of bullying: 1, 2, 3, 4
Pieces of advice not for someone who is being bullied: 5

Exercise 3

1 Sending nasty messages or posting rude comments about someone on the internet.
2 Don't reply. Block the horrible messages.
3 Don't get into an argument with the bully. Report the messages to the chat room moderator.
4 Because they feel the problem is their fault.
5 Your teacher or even the police.

Exercise 4

students' own answers

Grammar

should / shouldn't

affirmative
You **should tell** someone about the problem.

negative
You **shouldn't forward** nasty messages.

questions
Should you **reply**?

short answers
Yes, you **should**. / No, you **shouldn't**.

LOOK!

We use *should / shouldn't* to give advice or make recommendations.

1 Study the table. Which form of the main verb always follows *should*?

2 Complete the sentences with *should* or *shouldn't*.

1 You ... spend so long on the computer.
2 Rosie ... shout at her little sister.
3 I ... do Zumba. It sounds fun.
4 We ... be friendly to the new girl at school.

3 Write the questions using *should* to ask for advice.

I / get / a new phone? *Should I get a new phone?*

1 we / order / a pizza?
2 they / tell someone / about the problem?
3 Vicky / go to the cinema / with Matt?
4 you / paint / your bedroom black?

must / mustn't

affirmative
They **must stop** their behaviour.

negative
You **mustn't deal** with the problem alone.

questions
Must I **tell** my friends?

short answers
Yes, you **must**. / No, you **mustn't**.

LOOK!

We use *must / mustn't* to express obligation or prohibition.

4 Study the table. Look at the sign and write sentences with *must* or *mustn't*.

1 *You mustn't enter before 11am!*

Roxy's bedroom

1 Don't enter before 11am!
2 Knock before you open the door!
3 Take off your shoes!
4 Don't make the bed!
5 Don't move anything!

5 Study the sentences. Which sentence is an obligation? Which one is a piece of advice?

1 He should eat less fast food.
2 They must wear a school uniform.

6 Write sentences which mean the same as the five rules about social networking sites. Use *should*, *shouldn't*, *must* or *mustn't*.

1 *You mustn't post photos of people without their permission.*

SOCIAL NETWORKING SITES: 5 RULES

1 It's wrong to post photos of people without their permission.
2 It isn't a good idea to give your personal information to people you don't know.
3 It's better to write polite comments on other people's profiles.
4 It isn't a good idea to believe everything people write about themselves.
5 It's very important to remember that online friends aren't the same as real friends!

 3.22–3.23 Pronunciation lab: Intonation: expressing feelings, page 125

Exercise 1

the infinitive without *to*

Exercise 2

1 shouldn't
2 shouldn't
3 should
4 should

Exercise 3

1 Should we order a pizza?
2 Should they tell someone about the problem?
3 Should Vicky go to the cinema with Matt?
4 Should you paint your bedroom black?

Exercise 4

2 You must knock before you open the door!
3 You must take off your shoes!
4 You mustn't make the bed!
5 You mustn't move anything!

Exercise 5

1 a piece of advice
2 an obligation

Exercise 6

2 You shouldn't give your personal information to people you don't know.
3 You should write polite comments on other people's profiles.
4 You shouldn't believe everything people write about themselves.
5 You must remember that online friends aren't the same as real friends!

Grammar
should / shouldn't

Lesson objectives

In this lesson students will:
- learn / revise *should / shouldn't* and *must / mustn't*
- read a text about rules for social networking sites

Warmer

Write *Improve your English* on the board. Draw two columns with the headings *good advice* and *bad advice*. Elicit from the class some good advice, eg *always speak English in class, watch English films on TV, revise new words regularly, read magazine articles in English.* Then elicit some bad advice, eg *speak your language in class, only look at websites in your language on the internet, always ask for a translation of English words.*

1
- Students copy the table into their notebooks.
- Highlight the contraction in the negative short answer.
- Students answer the question.
- Check the answer as a class.

Look!

Ask student to read the rule in the Look! box carefully. Make sure they understand that *should / shouldn't* is used to give advice or make recommendations and that it does not indicate an obligation.

2
- Explain the task.
- Students work individually and complete the sentences using *should* or *shouldn't*.
- They compare answers in pairs.
- Check answers as a class.

3
- Read the example question aloud to the class.
- Point out that as *should* is a modal verb, we form the question by inverting the verb and the subject and we do not use *do / does* to make the question form.
- Students complete the exercise individually.
- They compare answers in pairs.
- Check answers as a class.

✚ Extra activity

Students work in pairs and decide what people *should* and *shouldn't* do to get fit or stay fit. Listen to their ideas as a class. Make two lists on the board, eg *should: walk to school; shouldn't: go everywhere by car.*

must / mustn't

Look!

Highlight the fact that *must* is much stronger than *should* because it expresses obligation or prohibition rather than advice or recommendation.

4
- Students copy the table into their notebooks.
- Point out that *must* is followed by the infinitive without *to* and highlight the contraction in the negative short answer.
- Introduce the exercise by drawing a no smoking sign on the board and eliciting the sentence *You mustn't smoke.*
- Highlight the example and show how the sentence *Don't enter before 11am!* is changed using *mustn't* to *You mustn't enter before 11am!*
- Students complete the exercise individually.
- They compare answers in pairs.
- Check answers as a class.

5
- Students read the two sentences.
- They answer the questions.
- They compare answers in pairs.
- Check answers as a class.

6
- Students read the five rules about social networking sites.
- Explain that they can use either *should / shouldn't* or *must / mustn't* to rewrite the rules but remind them that *should / shouldn't* is only advice whereas *must / mustn't* is an obligation.
- Students work individually and complete the exercise.
- Check answers as a class.

Pronunciation lab: Intonation: expressing feelings, page 125

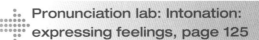

Digital course: Interactive grammar table

Study guide: page 103

T96

Vocabulary and Listening
Health

Warmer
Revise words for parts of the body. Write the letter *a* on the board. Elicit *arm*. Continue by writing the first letter of other words.

1 💿 3.24
- Students read the health advice.
- Play the CD. Students listen and repeat the health problems in blue.

Language note

We do not use the indefinite article with *earache, toothache* and *backache*, eg *I've got toothache*, but we do use it with *headache*, eg *She's got a headache*. With *stomach ache*, we can say *I've got a stomach ache* or *I've got stomach ache*. Both are correct.

2
- Students read the text again and note down in their notebooks which of the health problems in blue they have had and never had.
- They compare answers in pairs.
- Listen to their ideas as a class.

3
- Students match the pictures with the health problems.
- They compare answers in pairs.
- Listen to their ideas as a class.

👆 **EXPRESS YOURSELF**

4
- Put students into pairs. They state different health problems and ask for and give advice.
- Listen to some pairs as a class.

5 💿 3.25
- Play the CD. Students write the answer in their notebooks.
- They compare answers in pairs.
- Check the answer as a class.

6
- Students read the doctor's notes carefully first.
- Play the CD again. Students listen and complete the missing information.
- Check answers as a class.

💿 **3.25 Audioscript, exercise 5**

Dr Maggie: Hello. Teen helpline. This is Dr Maggie. How can I help you?
David: Well, er, I've got this problem and I don't know what to do about it.
Dr Maggie: That's what I'm here for. Can you tell me your name?
David: David.
Dr Maggie: OK, David. What's the problem?
David: I keep getting backache. I don't know why.
Dr Maggie: Is your school bag very heavy?
David: Yes, it is quite heavy. And I cycle to school with my bag on my back.
Dr Maggie: Do you carry it on both shoulders?
David: No, I don't. I carry it on one shoulder.
Dr Maggie: Well, that's the problem, David. You're carrying all the weight of the bag on one side of your body, which is very bad for your back. Why is your bag so heavy?
David: I have to take a lot of books to school.
Dr Maggie: Yes, but remember you don't need to carry all your books around with you all the time. Just take the books you need for that day.
David: OK, I will. Thank you for the advice.
Dr Maggie: No problem, David. I hope you start feeling better soon ... Hello. Teen helpline. This is Dr Maggie. How can I help you?
Molly: Er, hello. My name's Molly. Can I ask your advice about something, please?
Dr Maggie: Yes, of course, Molly. Go ahead.
Molly: Well, I've had lots of headaches recently and I'm not sleeping very well.
Dr Maggie: Is anything else worrying you?
Molly: No, not really.
Dr Maggie: How many hours a day do you spend on your computer?
Molly: About three – from six o'clock till nine o'clock every evening.
Dr Maggie: I think that's too long, Molly. I'm not surprised you're getting headaches. Do you play any sports or get any exercise?
Molly: No I don't. I hate sport! The only thing I love is playing computer games.
Dr Maggie: Well, my advice to you is find another hobby. Don't stop playing computer games completely, but an hour a day is enough. If you start taking more exercise, I think you'll feel much better.
Molly: Do you think my headaches will stop?
Dr Maggie: Yes, I do. I'm 99% sure the time you spend on your computer is the problem.
Molly: OK. Thank you.
Dr Maggie: Thank you for your call. Bye, Molly.

Vocabulary and Listening
Health

THE A-Z OF TEENAGE HEALTH

Dr Maggie gives you advice about some common teen health issues.

Anxiety
Do you lie awake worrying at night? Do you get a **stomach ache** before an important event like an exam? Exercise is a great way to deal with stress. Play football, dance or just go for a walk.

Computers
Staring at your computer screen for hours will give you a **headache**. To avoid **eye strain**, look away from the screen every five minutes.

Food
Eat lots of fruit and vegetables and you won't catch a **cold** and a **cough** in the winter. And don't eat too many sweets because they will give you **toothache**.

Greasy skin
Lots of teenagers have greasy skin and **spots** because of hormone changes as they grow. A healthy diet and some sun can help. (But not too much sun – see below.)

Holidays
Sunburn never looks good! Always use suncream and wear a hat in the sun. Avoid getting a **mosquito bite** by wearing clothes that cover your arms and legs in the evenings. And if you get a **bee sting,** put some ice on it to relieve the pain.

MP3 players
Do you really have to have the music so loud? You could get **earache** and also risk damaging your ears.

School
Carry your books in a rucksack and wear it on your shoulders in the correct way so you don't get **backache**.

Have you got a health problem and don't know what to do about it? Email Dr Maggie or call the Teen helpline on 0800 572301.

---

1 **3.24** Read the health advice. Listen and repeat the health problems in blue.

2 Which of the health problems in blue have you had? Which problems have you never had?

3 What do you think is the matter with the people in pictures a–c?

👆 EXPRESS YOURSELF

4 Work in pairs. Choose a health problem and ask for and give advice.

🔵 *I've got a cold.*
🔵 *You should have lots of hot drinks and stay at home.*

5 **3.25** Listen to two phone calls to the helpline. Who isn't very active?

6 Complete the doctor's notes.

Name: (1) …
Problem(s): backache
Likely cause: carrying his school bag on (2) …
Advice: carry school bag correctly, carry fewer (3) … in the bag
Name: Molly
Problem(s): (4) … , (5) …
Likely cause: spending too much time on her computer
Advice: spend less time playing computer games, do more (6) …

Exercise 3

Possible answers

a He's got a cold.

b She's got a headache.

c She's got sunburn / a mosquito bite / a bee sting.

Exercise 5

Molly

Exercise 6

1 David
2 one shoulder
3 books
4 headaches
5 not sleeping very well
6 exercise

Cultural awareness
The Australian Outback

Fact box

The Outback is a large, mainly desert area of Australia where very few people live. Temperatures can reach 50°C in summer!

 # THE OUTBACK SURVIVAL GUIDE

IF YOU'RE PLANNING A TRIP TO THE AUSTRALIAN OUTBACK, FOLLOW THIS ADVICE TO STAY SAFE.

DO ...

... take enough water with you. You can survive for many days without food, but not without water. Remember the heat makes you very thirsty, so you'll need to drink several litres of water a day.

... wear a hat and sun cream to avoid sunburn. The sun is one of the biggest dangers in Australia. It is at its hottest between 1pm and 5pm, so only hike in the mornings and evenings.

... plan your route carefully. Make sure you have a detailed, up-to-date map which shows places where you can find water. You should also have a GPS receiver to prevent getting lost.

... tell someone where you are going, what route you plan to take and when you expect to arrive.

DON'T ...

... worry too much about snakes. There are many different kinds of poisonous snake in Australia, but only two or three people a year are killed by snakebites. If you leave the snakes alone, they won't hurt you!

... rely on your mobile phone if you get lost. In many remote areas, there will be no signal, so you won't be able to use it.

... swim in deep, muddy water or where you see crocodile warning signs. Crocodiles are dangerous animals and attacks often happen in Australia!

... leave your vehicle if you break down in the middle of nowhere. If a plane is searching for you, it's much easier to spot a car than a person from the air.

DANGER CROCODILES NO SWIMMING

Word check

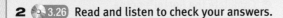 survive   hike   up-to-date   GPS   poisonous   remote   muddy

---

Exercise 1

heat
sunburn
getting lost
snakes
crocodiles

1 Look at the picture. What dangers does it show?

2 3.26 Read and listen to check your answers.

3 Read the text again and choose the correct answers.

1 What is it more important to have with you in the Australian Outback?
   a) food   **b)** water

2 When shouldn't you go walking?
   a) in the morning   **b)** in the afternoon

3 What is probably more useful?
   a) a GPS receiver   **b)** a mobile phone

4 Which animals are more dangerous?
   a) snakes   **b)** crocodiles

5 What should you do if your car breaks down?
   a) continue on foot   **b)** wait for help

Exercise 3

1 b
2 b
3 a
4 b
5 b

CULTURAL COMPARISON

4 Think of a remote area of your country. What advice would you give to visitors? Think about ...

1 clothes.
2 equipment.
3 transport.
4 wild animals.

You should wear warm clothes.

Culture video: Australia

Cultural awareness
The Australian Outback

4
- Explain the task.
- Students work individually and think about the advice they would give to visitors going to a remote area of their country. They make notes in their notebooks.
- They compare their ideas in pairs.
- Listen to their ideas as a class.

Culture video: Australia »

Lesson objectives

In this lesson students will:
- read about the Australian Outback
- give advice to visitors going to a remote area of their country

Warmer

Write *Australia* on the board. Elicit from the class what they know about the country, eg famous sights (*Uluru, Sydney Opera House*), things to do (*surfing at Bondi Beach, diving at the Great Barrier Reef*).

1
- Make sure students understand the task.
- Students look at the picture and note down the dangers.
- Listen to their ideas as a class.

2 🔘 3.26
- Play the CD. Students listen and follow the text in their books.
- They check their answers to exercise 1.
- Check answers as a class.
- Focus students on the Fact box. Check that they understand the word *desert* (a large area with no vegetation and lots of sand and rocks).

 ### Culture note

Point out that the Bush is another name for the Outback. Deserts cover 18% of Australia. Most are situated in the central or western parts of Australia and in total cover 1,371,000 square kilometres.

3
- Students read the questions and the different possible answers carefully.
- They read the text again and choose the correct answers.
- They compare answers in pairs.
- Check answers as a class.

Word check

Make sure students understand the words. Ask them to translate them into their language. Note the pronunciation and stress of *poisonous* /ˈpɔɪzənəs/.

 T98

Grammar

Tense review: present, past and future

Warmer

Write three incorrect sentences on the board: *She is never playing tennis. They have bought a new car yesterday. I will buy a new computer game next week.* Explain that in each sentence the tense is incorrect. Put students into pairs and ask them to rewrite each sentence with the correct tense. Invite students to come to the board and write the correct sentences: *She never plays tennis. They bought a new car yesterday. I'm going to buy a new computer game next week.*

1
- Students copy the table in their notebooks.
- They write the negative examples for each tense. Encourage them to use contracted forms.
- They compare answers in pairs.
- Check answers as a class.

2
- Students read the time expressions carefully.
- They work individually and add the time expressions to the last column of the table.
- They compare answers in pairs.
- Check answers as a class.

3
- Students work individually and choose the correct words.
- They compare answers in pairs.
- Check answers as a class.

4
- Do the first example with the whole class to demonstrate the activity. Write a true sentence about yourself on the board, eg *I watch TV every day*. Elicit that *watch* is the present simple because it is followed by *every day*.
- Students work individually and complete the sentences.
- Students compare answers in pairs.
- Listen to their answers as a class. Correct any errors in the tense or form of the verb.

CLIL Grammar in context: Personal, Social, Health and Economic Education (PHSE)

5
- Ask students to read each section of the quiz carefully before they choose the correct words.
- Students work individually to complete the exercise.
- They compare answers in pairs.

6
- Ask students to read the quiz again and choose the correct picture to answer the question *What should you do?* for situations 1–4.
- Students work individually and complete the task.
- Listen to their ideas as a class but do not correct them at this stage.

7 ⊙ 3.27
- Play the CD. Students listen and check their answers to exercises 5 and 6.

CLIL task

Students use the internet to find out what to do in two more first aid situations.

Digital course: Interactive grammar table ❯❯

Study guide: page 103 ❯❯

💿 3.27 Audioscript, exercise 7

Amy: In PSHE we are learning about first aid at the moment. When an accident happens you must act quickly and calmly. What should you do in these situations?
Question 1. Your little brother has burned himself on the cooker.
The correct answer is b). You should put cold water on the burn.
Question 2. A woman is lying on the ground and isn't moving.
The correct answer is a). You shouldn't try to move someone in this situation. Call an ambulance.
Question 3. Your nose hasn't stopped bleeding for five minutes.
The correct answer is a). You should lean forward and hold your nose tightly.
Question 4. You've banged your head and you think you're going to collapse.
The correct answer is b). You should sit down and put your head between your knees.

Grammar
Tense review: present, past and future

1 Copy the table in your notebook. Complete the negative examples in the table.

	affirmative	negative	time expressions
present simple	Crocodiles **attack** people.	(1) Crocodiles don't attack people.	never, usually, often, (8) …
present continuous	They**'re** travel**ling** around Australia.	(2) …	now, (9) …
past simple	Lucy **left** on Tuesday.	(3) …	yesterday, two months ago, (10) …
past continuous	Chris **was** watc**hing** a programme about snakes.	(4) …	while
present perfect	I**'ve seen** photos of the Australian Outback.	(5) …	(11) … , just
will	You**'ll need** to drink a lot of water.	(6) …	later, tomorrow, soon
be going to	We**'re going to** fly to Sydney.	(7) …	tomorrow, (12) …

2 Add the time expressions in the box to the table in your notebook.

> next week   at the moment   last weekend
> sometimes   never

3 Choose the correct words.

My trip to Australia
by Scott Winter

DAY 5

I (1) **had** / **'ve had** a scary experience yesterday. While I (2) **watched** / **was watching** TV in my room, I (3) **saw** / **'ve seen** a tarantula on the wall! Tarantulas (4) **be** / **are** very big, poisonous spiders which (5) **are living** / **live** in hot places. You shouldn't (6) **to touch** / **touch** them because they (7) **must** / **can** bite. Luckily this tarantula (8) **didn't bite** / **wasn't biting** me!

We (9) **stay** / **'re staying** in Alice Springs at the moment. Tomorrow we're going to (10) **climbing** / **climb** Uluru, a big rock in the desert. Maybe we (11) **'ll see** / **'re seeing** some kangaroos!

4 Complete the sentences so that they are true for you. Use verbs in the correct tense or form.

1 I … every day.

2 I'm … at the moment.

3 I … last week.

4 I was … at five o'clock this morning.

5 I've never … in my life!

6 I'm going to … on my birthday.

7 Maybe I'll … later.

CLIL Grammar in context:
Personal, Social, Health and Economic Education (PSHE)

5 Read the quiz and choose the correct words.

In PSHE we (1) **learn** / **do learn** / **are learning** about first aid at the moment. When an accident (2) **happen** / **happens** / **is happening** you must (3) **to act** / **act** / **acting** quickly and calmly. What (4) **you should do** / **should do you** / **should you do** in these situations?

1 Your little brother (5) **burned** / **was burning** / **has burned** himself on the cooker.

2 A woman (6) **lies** / **lying** / **is lying** on the ground and (7) **doesn't** / **isn't** / **aren't** moving.

3 Your nose hasn't stopped bleeding (8) **five minutes ago** / **since five minutes** / **for five minutes**.

4 You've banged your head and you think you (9) **'re going to** / **going to** / **go to** collapse.

6 Now do the quiz. Choose the correct picture for each situation 1–4.

7 🔊 3.27 Listen and check your answers.

CLIL TASK

Go online. Find out what to do in two more first aid situations.

All about holiday health

I got sunburnt on my last holiday. Have you ever had any health problems on holiday?

➕ Remember to take some **plasters** with you in case you get a blister on your foot from too much walking. Take some **antiseptic cream** too. Use it if you cut yourself by accident.

➕ Take a **bandage** if you are travelling to a country where there are snakes. If you get a snake bite on your arm or leg, wrap the bandage tightly around the bite.

➕ You should always put some **sun cream** on your skin before you go out in the sun so that you don't get sunburn.

➕ Do you always get mosquito bites in hot countries? Remember to take some **insect repellent** to spray over you when you go out at night.

➕ The heat can sometimes give you a headache. Put a box of **aspirins** in your suitcase and take one or two aspirins with a glass of water.

➕ Take some **mints** on holiday. Eat a mint if you feel sick when you are travelling.

Step 1: Read

1 Look at the first aid kit and the words in bold in the text. When you go on holiday, do you take a first aid kit with you? What first aid items do you take?

2 Read the advice and answer the questions.

1 What should you put on a blister?
2 What should you do if a snake bites you?
3 What should you always wear in the sun?
4 When should you use the insect repellent?
5 What should you do if you get a headache?
6 What should you do if you feel sick when you're travelling?

Exercise 2

1 a plaster
2 wrap a bandage tightly around the bite
3 sun cream
4 when you go out at night
5 take one or two aspirins with a glass of water
6 eat a mint

Step 2: Listen

3 🔊 3.28 Listen to two friends talking about a mobile app. What is the app called?

Exercise 3

Travel Doctor

> **LOOK!**
>
> An app is a kind of program for a mobile phone or tablet computer. The word *app* is short for *application*.

4 Listen again and choose the correct answer.

1 With this app, you can ...
   a) talk to a real doctor.
   b) learn what to do in an emergency.
2 You can ...
   a) hear some advice.
   b) watch and listen to someone giving advice.
3 The girl once had a ...
   a) bee sting.
   b) snake bite.
4 The app gives information about ...
   a) different kinds of medicine.
   b) local chemists.
5 The boy is planning to go ...
   a) camping.
   b) mountain climbing.

Exercise 4

1 b
2 b
3 a
4 b
5 a

Integrated skills
All about holiday health

Warmer

Highlight Nina's speech bubble. Write the question on the board. Put students into pairs. Students answer the question and tell each other about any holiday problems they have had. Listen to some pairs' problems as a class.

Step 1: Read

1
- Students look at the first aid kit and the words in bold in the text.
- Make sure students understand the words.
- Elicit answers to the questions as a class.

2
- Students read the questions carefully first.
- They look in the text and find the answers.
- They compare answers in pairs.
- Check answers as a class.

Step 2: Listen

3 ◉ 3.28
- Explain the task. Students only need to listen for the name of the app.
- Play the CD.
- Check progress. If necessary, play the CD again.
- Students compare their answer in pairs.
- Check the answer as a class.

Look!

Highlight the information in the Look! box.

4
- Students read the five questions and the different possible answers carefully first.
- Play the CD again. Students work individually and choose the correct answers.
- They compare answers in pairs.
- Check answers as a class.

◉ 3.28 Audioscript, exercise 3

Girl: What are you looking at?
Boy: I've got this new 'Travel Doctor' app for my phone. It's going to be great for the summer holidays.
Girl: Why? What does it do?
Boy: It's got lots of information about first aid. Like if a bee stings you and you don't know what to do, it tells you. Look!
App: Here's what to do if a bee stings you.
Girl: Hmm ... that happened to me once actually ...
Boy: And you can click here for a video showing you what you should do, step by step. This one shows you what to do if a snake bites you.
Girl: Ooh, I bet that really hurts ... Hmm, that's amazing! It's like having a doctor on your phone!
Boy: I know. There's advice for hundreds of different health problems. And it even tells you where the nearest chemist is if you need to buy medicine or something.
Girl: Wow!
Boy: I'm going camping in Wales in August, so it'll be really useful if I have an accident or anything.
Girl: But just a minute – if you're camping on a mountain, miles away from anywhere, it's not really going to be very useful, is it?
Boy: Why not?
Girl: Because you won't be able to use your phone!
Boy: Oh, I didn't think of that!

Integrated skills – continued
Talking about health

5 〔🔘 3.29〕
- Students read the dialogue first.
- Play the CD. Students listen and follow the text in their books. They write answers 1–4 in their notebooks.
- They compare answers in pairs.
- Check answers as a class.

6
- Play the CD, pausing after each question or statement and each response for students to repeat as a class.
- Ask students to repeat the dialogue several times both chorally and individually with the correct stress and intonation.
- Note the falling intonation in the *wh-* questions *What's the matter? When did that happen?* and *How do you feel?*
- Students practise the dialogue in pairs. Then swap roles and practise the dialogue again.

Step 3: Write

7
- Students work individually. They copy the questions in bold into their notebook.
- They choose a different health problem from the text on page 100.
- Students write answers to the questions.

8
- Ask students to look at the Communication kit: Talking about health. Encourage them to use these expressions when writing their dialogue.
- Students work individually and write their dialogue, using the dialogue in the book as a model.
- Monitor while they are writing and give help if necessary.

Skills builder

Speaking: Answering questions
Focus attention on the Skills builder box. Emphasize the importance of giving as much useful information as possible when answering questions.

Step 4: Communicate

9
- Students practise their dialogues in pairs.
- For extra practice, they swap roles in both dialogues.

10
- Choose some pairs to act out their dialogue for the class.
- Students raise their hand if another pair has chosen the same health problem as the health problem they have chosen. This will encourage them to listen carefully to their classmates.

Integrated skills: Workbook page 119 〉〉

TALKING ABOUT HEALTH

Watch!

Hi there. What's the matter?	I've got some (1) … on my legs.
Oh dear! **When did that happen?**	They (2) … me yesterday when I was in the park.
Oh no! **How do you feel?**	I feel OK, but they're quite painful.
Right. I think you should use this (3) … on the bites and make a doctor's appointment if they get worse.	Yes, I'll do that. How much is this?
It's 3.99.	OK. Here you go.
I hope you feel (4) … soon!	Thanks!

Exercise 5

1 mosquito bites
2 bit
3 cream
4 better

5 3.29 Listen to Nina telling the pharmacist about a health problem. Complete 1–4 in your notebook.

6 Listen again and repeat. Practise your intonation.

Step 3: Write

7 Copy the questions in bold into your notebook. Then choose a different health problem from page 100 and write your answers to the questions.

8 Write a new dialogue about a health problem. Write both parts. Use the dialogue in exercise 5 to help you.

Hi there. What's the matter?
I've got a headache.

SKILLS BUILDER

Speaking: Answering questions
When you answer a question try to give as much useful information as possible. If you are answering questions about your health, use adjectives to describe the problem clearly.

Step 4: Communicate

9 Work in pairs. Take turns to practise your dialogues.

🟢 *Hi there. What's the matter?*
🔵 *I've got …*

10 Act your dialogue for the class.

COMMUNICATION KIT

Talking about health

What's the matter?
What happened?
How do you feel?
It's / It isn't painful.
I think you should …
Why don't you … ?
Hope you feel better soon!

Writing
An instant message

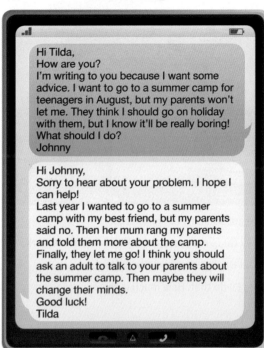

Hi Tilda,
How are you?
I'm writing to you because I want some advice. I want to go to a summer camp for teenagers in August, but my parents won't let me. They think I should go on holiday with them, but I know it'll be really boring! What should I do?
Johnny

Hi Johnny,
Sorry to hear about your problem. I hope I can help!
Last year I wanted to go to a summer camp with my best friend, but my parents said no. Then her mum rang my parents and told them more about the camp. Finally, they let me go! I think you should ask an adult to talk to your parents about the summer camp. Then maybe they will change their minds.
Good luck!
Tilda

1 **3.30** Read and listen to Johnny's instant message and Tilda's reply. What is Johnny's problem? Do you agree with Tilda's advice?

2 Look at the Writing focus. Then look at Johnny and Tilda's instant messages. Find four different tenses.

WRITING FOCUS
Using different tenses
When you finish writing, check the tenses you use carefully. Try to use different tenses to make your writing more interesting.
I like basketball.
I had a headache yesterday.
My parents will worry about me.
She's gone to the cinema.

3 Complete the sentences with the correct tense of the verb in brackets.

1 Last year I ... to buy a mobile phone. (want)
2 My parents ... their mobile phones. (not usually use)
3 I ... to the cinema since March. (not go)
4 I know it ... really exciting next term! (be)
5 I ... football every weekend. (play)
6 We ... here since 2011. (live)

Exercise 1
He wants to go to a summer camp for teenagers but his parents won't let him because they think he should go on holiday with them.

students' own answers

Exercise 2
present simple
are, want, think, know, hope

present continuous
'm writing

future with *will*
won't let, 'll be, will change

past simple
wanted, said, rang, told, let

Writing task
Write an instant message to a friend. Read Jenny's instant message below and write a reply to her.

Plan Make notes for the main paragraph of your instant message. Give an example of a similar situation and say what happened. Then advise Jenny what she should do.

Write Write your instant message. Use your notes and the instant message in exercise 1 to help you. Start your instant message like this:

Hi Jenny,
Sorry to hear about your problem.

Check Check your writing.

- ✔ verbs – spelling
- ✔ verbs – tense
- ✔ verbs – agreement with subject
- ✔ verbs – word order

Hi!
I hope you're well.
I'm writing to you because I want some advice. I want to buy a mobile phone, but my parents won't let me. What do you think I should do?
Jenny

Exercise 3
1 Last year I wanted to buy a mobile phone.
2 My parents don't usually use their mobile phones.
3 I haven't been to the cinema since March.
4 I know it'll be really exciting next term!
5 I play football every weekend.
6 We've lived here since 2011.

Writing
An instant message

Lesson objectives

In this lesson students will:
- read an instant message
- use different tenses
- write an instant message

Warmer

Write the word *holiday* on the board. Put students into pairs and ask them to discuss the best possible type of holiday and the worst possible type of holiday. Listen to their ideas as a class.

1 **3.30**
- Explain the task.
- Play the CD.
- Students listen and follow in their books. Elicit the answer to the question *What is Johnny's problem?* from the class (*He wants to go to a summer camp for teenagers but his parents won't let him because they think he should go on holiday with them.*).
- Students then work in pairs and discuss whether they agree with Tilda's advice.
- Listen to their ideas as a class.

2
- Students read the information in the Writing focus box.
- Elicit from the class the different tenses used in the four example sentences (*present simple, past simple, future with* will, *present perfect*).
- Students work individually and find four different tenses in the emails.
- They compare answers in pairs.
- Check answers as a class.

3
- Make sure students understand the task.
- Students work individually and complete the sentences with the correct tense of the verb in brackets.
- They compare answers in pairs.
- Check answers as a class.

Extra activity

Write some sentences with mistakes in them on the board for the students to correct: *1 I have this mobile phone for two years. 2 I often using my mobile phone to take photos. 3 I taked this picture yesterday.* Students correct the mistakes: *1 I have had this mobile phone for two years. 2 I often use my mobile phone to take photos. 3 I took this picture yesterday.*

Writing task

The aim of this activity is for students to write a short instant message giving advice to a friend that includes the correct use of verbs (spelling, tense, subject agreement and word order). Ask the students to follow the stages in the Student's Book. At the Check stage, ask them to swap notebooks and check each other's writing.

Writing reference and practice: Workbook page 136

Study guide
Grammar, Vocabulary and Speaking

Tell the students the Study guide is an important page which provides a useful reference for the main language of the unit: the grammar, the vocabulary and the functional language from the Integrated skills pages. Explain that they should refer to this page when studying for a test or exam.

Grammar

- Tell the students to look at the example sentences in the tense review: present, past and future.
- Then tell students to look at the example sentences to revise *should / shouldn't, must / mustn't*. Get students to translate into their own language if necessary.
- Refer students to the Grammar reference on pages 100–101 of the Workbook for further revision.

Vocabulary

- Tell students to look at the list of vocabulary and check understanding.
- Refer students to the Wordlist on page 151 of the Workbook where they can look up any words they can't remember.

Speaking

- Check that students understand the phrases to use for talking about health.
- Tell students to act out a conversation between two people talking about health issues and offering each other advice.

Additional material

Workbook

- Progress check page 78
- Self-evaluation page 79
- Grammar reference and practice pages 100–101
- Vocabulary extension page 110
- Integrated skills page 119
- Writing reference and task pages 136–137

Teacher's Resource File

- Basics section pages 53–58
- Vocabulary and grammar consolidation pages 35–38
- Translation and dictation pages 10, 20
- Key competences worksheets pages 17–18
- Culture and CLIL worksheets pages 33–36
- Culture video worksheets pages 17–18
- Digital competence worksheets pages 17–18
- Macmillan Readers worksheets pages 5–6

Tests and Exams

- Unit 9 End-of-unit test: Basic, Standard and Extra
- End-of-term test: Basic, Standard and Extra
- End-of-year test: Basic, Standard and Extra
- CEFR Skills Exam Generator

Study guide

Grammar
Tense review: present, past and future

	affirmative	negative	time expressions
present simple	Jon **does** exercise every day.	Jon **doesn't do** exercise every day.	never, usually, often, sometimes
present continuous	They**'re** watch**ing** a tennis match.	They **aren't** watch**ing** a tennis match.	now, at the moment
past simple	Nina **went** to London on Tuesday.	Lucy **didn't go** to London on Tuesday.	yesterday, two months ago, last weekend
past continuous	Jenny **was** drink**ing** water.	Jenny **wasn't** drink**ing** water.	while
present perfect	I**'ve been** to the zoo.	I**'ve** never **been** to the zoo.	never, just
will	You**'ll need** to buy a train ticket tomorrow.	You **won't need** to buy a train ticket tomorrow.	later, tomorrow, soon
be going to	I**'m going to** go to the party next week.	I**'m not going to** go to the party next week.	tomorrow, next week

should / shouldn't

affirmative
You **should go** to the doctor if you feel ill.

negative
You **shouldn't forget** to eat fruit and vegetables.

questions
Should you **tell** an adult?

short answers
Yes, you **should**. / No, you **shouldn't**.

must / mustn't

affirmative
He **must go** to the hospital if his condition gets serious.

negative
You **mustn't react** to bully's behaviour.

questions
Must I **tell** my teacher?

short answers
Yes, you **must**. / No, you **mustn't**.

Vocabulary
Personal issues

appearance	diet	social life
arguments	exercise	stress
bullying	health	vegetarian
depression	relationship	

Health

backache	earache	spots
bee sting	eye strain	stomach ache
cold	headache	sunburn
cough	mosquito bite	toothache

Speaking
Talking about health
What's the matter?
What happened?
How do you feel?
It's / It isn't painful.
I think you should ...
Why don't you ...?
Hope you feel better soon!

 LEARNING TO LEARN

Make a list of health vocabulary. Add new words to your list when you learn them.

Making a tourist information leaflet

TASK

Work in groups of four to create an advice leaflet about going on holiday in your area or country.

Step 1: Think

1 Look at the final draft of a leaflet. Find ...

1 information about local cuisine
2 information about the weather
3 helpful information about travelling

@ DIGITAL LITERACY

When you write a tourist leaflet, remember to:

- include different types of information – text, photos, links ...
- use different fonts and colours.
- look up words in an online dictionary.

2 Match the headings in the box with sections 1–6 of the leaflet.

> When to visit   And finally ...
> Things to do and not to do   Where to visit
> What to do   Other information

Exercise 2

1 Where to visit
2 What to do
3 When to visit
4 Things to do and not to do
5 Other information
6 And finally ...

helpful information about travelling

Andalucía

Are you are visiting this beautiful region of Spain for the first time? You will find useful information here to help you.

(1) …
You should definitely go to Sevilla, Córdoba and Granada. The white villages such as Ronda and Arcos are also worth visiting. You can then finish your trip with a few days on the beaches in Málaga or Almería – perfect!

(2) …
The *Mezquita* in Córdoba and the Alhambra Palace in Granada are two of the most famous buildings in the world – don't miss them! Enjoy walking round the old cities and eating out in the many bars and restaurants. Try some *tapas* such as prawn fritters (*tortillitas de camarones*) or fried small squid (*puntillitas*).

(3) …
Summer can be very hot, so April, May, June and September are good months to visit. If you come in April, you can also enjoy the Easter celebrations (*Semana Santa*) and the April Fair (*Feria*).

information about local cuisine

information about the weather

(4) …
✔ Be careful when swimming as jellyfish can be a problem. You should check with local people before swimming.
✔ Buy train tickets in advance for special offers. See: www. renfe.es
✔ Remember to use suncream as it can reach 45°C in Córdoba and Sevilla in July and August.
✘ Go shopping at midday – many shops are closed.
✘ Leave your bag on a table or the floor.

(5) …
• 112 is the number for emergency services.
• You should get a free European Health Insurance Card before you leave. If you have any serious health problems, the card gives you access to Spanish hospitals.

(6) …
We hope you have a wonderful time here and enjoy your stay!

Collaborative project 3

Making a tourist information leaflet

Lesson objectives

In this lesson students will:
- create a tourist information leaflet about holidaying in their area or country.
- read a leaflet and match headings with sections
- listen to a group planning a leaflet
- read and complete a conversation extract

Warmer

Write the heading on the board: *Top 10 tourist attractions in my country*. In pairs or groups, students make a list. Then they compare with another pair/group and make a new list by agreeing on ten places. Feedback with the class and make one list that all the class agrees on. Briefly discuss why tourists should visit these places.

TASK

Read the task with the class and check students understand.

Step 1: Think

1. • Briefly discuss information leaflets with the class. What types of information should you include? What types of advice can you give?
   • Read the list of items students have to identify and help with any vocabulary.
   • Ask students to read the final draft of a leaflet about Andalucía and to find the information listed.
   • Check answers as a class. Ask if there are any other items which could be included in the list.
   • Read the Digital literacy box with the class and check students understand. Discuss why it is important to include different types of information and to look up words in an online dictionary.
   • Point out that advice leaflets are more interesting when you use different fonts and colours.

2. • Read the first heading *When to visit* aloud to the class and elicit what type of information students would expect to find in this section. Continue with the other headings. Listen to students' ideas, but don't confirm or correct.
   • Ask students to read the leaflet and match the headings to the sections.
   • Check answers as a class.

3 3.31
  - Ask students to read the questions carefully.
  - Play the CD. Students listen and answer the questions.
  - Check answers as a class.

4
  - Students read the conversation extract and complete it in pairs.
  - Play the CD again. Students listen and check their answers.
  - Check answers as a class. Students practise the converstion in groups.

5
  - Read the Useful language box with the class and help with any vocabulary.
  - Practise as necessary. Elicit other examples of each phrase, eg *We've done our first draft. Is this sentence correct?*
  - Students work in groups of four and plan their leaflets. Ask one or two groups to report back to the class to explain their plans.

Step 3: Create

6
  - Read the three steps with the class to give students a clear idea of what they have to do.
  - Monitor while they are working and give help if necessary.

Share information
Students share their information. They decide what sections to include, what information to include in each section and write headings for each section. They discuss their first draft and how they can improve it. Then they write the second draft. They check each draft for grammar, spelling and punctuation mistakes. If possible, they exchange their second draft with another group and check each other's work for mistakes.

Create the leaflet
Each group creates their leaflet. Encourage them to be creative and try to make the leaflet as interesting as possible. Remind them to use their own words and to check for errors. Give help as necessary.

Show and tell
Each group shows their leaflet to the class. Allow time for the other students to ask questions. If you prefer, a few groups can show their leaflets over several different classes. If you like, the class can vote for their favourite leaflet.

7
  - Look at the evaluation grids with the class.
  - Read through the different options and help with any vocabulary as necessary.
  - Students complete their self-evaluation. Give help if necessary.

Extra activity

In pairs or groups, students write advice for new students at their school. They can include information about the school and good places to go at the weekend, what extra activities students can do, how to make friends, etc.

3.31 Audioscript, exercise 3

Sonia: OK, so we've done our second draft of the text for our leaflet and we've got all the pictures. Let's make the leaflet now.
Edu: I think we should revise our draft before we do that.
Mario: Why? The information is well organized.
Sonia: I agree with Mario, I think it's OK.
Edu: Well, I think there are some mistakes. We should check the grammar, spelling and punctuation. For example, how do you spell 'passport'? Is it one 's' or two?
Mario: We've put it with one 's'. That's right, isn't it?
Sonia: Let's check in a dictionary. Oh, OK. It's with two. P-A-S-S-P-O-R-T.
Edu: OK … and what about this sentence? Should it be 'makes' or 'gives'? Should it be 'The train company RENFE *gives* discounts' or 'The train company RENFE *makes* discounts'?
Mario: OK, let's check that. Ah, on this website it says 'give a discount'. Let's change that to 'RENFE gives a discount'.
Sonia: OK, but the sentence is about a general fact, so we should put it in the plural.
Mario: Right, OK. Hey, look at the first sentence in the introduction. It's a question, isn't it? But in English you only put the question mark at the end.
Sonia: Yes, that's right. OK … anything else? Do we need to add a comma here?
Mario: I don't think so. Shall we write our final draft now?
Edu: I think we should ask another group to read our second draft and check for mistakes first. We can check their draft.
Mario: Good idea. Then if we aren't sure about anything, we can ask the teacher.
Sonia: Great, let's do that. After we've checked it, we can make the leaflet.
Edu: OK.

Step 2: Listen and plan

3 (🔊 3.31) Listen to Sonia, Mario and Edu doing the task and answer the questions.

1 Do they make the leaflet after they've done their second draft?
2 How do they check the spelling of 'passport'?
3 Do they correct any punctuation mistakes?
4 What do they decide to do before writing another draft?

4 Complete the conversation extract with the words in the box. Listen again and check.

spell   mistakes   dictionary   grammar   revise

Sonia: OK, so we've done our second draft of the text for our leaflet and we've got all the pictures. Let's make the leaflet now.

Edu: I think we should (1) … our draft before we do that.

Mario: Why? The information is well organized.

Sonia: I agree with Mario. I think it's OK.

Edu: Well, I think there are some (2) … . We should check the (3) … , spelling and punctuation. For example, how do you (4) … 'passport'? Is it one 's' or two?

Mario: We've put it with one 's'. That's right, isn't it?

Sonia: Let's check in a (5) … . Oh, OK. It's with two. P–A–S–S–P–O–R–T.

5 Work in groups. Plan your leaflet.

• Choose whether you want to make your leaflet about your area or your country.
• Decide which places, suggestions, advice and information to include.
• Decide how to share the work.
• Decide when to meet again to share your information.

Step 3: Create

6 Follow the steps to create your leaflet.

Share information

Read or listen to each other's work. Discuss your work. Check these things:

• Have you got all the information you need?
• Is it in your own words?
• Can you use a wider variety of words?
• Is the spelling and punctuation correct?
• Is the grammar and vocabulary correct?

Create the leaflet

Decide what order the information should go in. Find photos and pictures and organize the layout. Make the leaflet. Then check grammar, vocabulary, spelling and punctuation.

Show and tell

• Show the rest of the class your leaflet.

Step 4: Evaluate

7 Now ask your teacher for the group and individual assessment grids. Then complete the grids.

USEFUL LANGUAGE

We've done our first draft.
We should (rewrite / reorganize / check) this draft.
I think we should check (the spelling / grammar / punctuation).
How do you spell ('discount')?
Is this (punctuation) correct?
Do we need to add a (comma / question mark / exclamation mark / full stop)?
I think there are some mistakes.
Let's ask (another group to check our work / the teacher for help).

UNIT 1 External exam trainer

Your exam preparation

Exercise 1

the student's friends

1 Read the example question. What topic is the examiner asking about?

> **Example question**
> Do all your friends go to your school?

Exercise 2

Antonio uses four sentences.

2 🔊 3.32 Read and listen to the questions and answers in the Model exam. How many sentences does Antonio use to describe his best friend?

> 📋 **EXAM TIP: Give as much information as possible**
>
> When the examiner asks you a question or for some information, make your answer longer than one sentence. Try to think of three things to say. This helps to make the exam into a conversation rather than an interview.

About the exam

A conversation

The examiner asks you questions about a familiar topic, such as your friends and family or interests. You must give as much information as possible. You must also ask the examiner a question. This tests your ability to have a conversation with someone.

3 Read the questions and answers again. How does Antonio make his answers interesting?

1
a) He gives extra information by telling the examiner how many friends he has got.
b) He gives extra information by telling the examiner how he knows his friends.

2
a) He uses adverbs of frequency to say how often they do the activities.
b) He describes the activities they do together.

3
a) He gives a short physical description and tells the examiner one of his best friend's hobbies.
b) He describes what his best friend is wearing today.

Exercise 3

1 b
2 a
3 a

1 We're going to talk about your friends. Do all your friends go to your school?

No, they don't. Some of my friends go to my school, but some of them are my neighbours.

2 That's nice. What activities do you do together?

We often play football and basketball. At the weekend, we sometimes go to the cinema or the youth club.

3 Tell me about your best friend.

My best friend's name is Javi. He's 13 years old and he goes to my school. He's tall and he's got brown hair. He loves playing football.

4 Thanks, Antonio. Do you want to ask me a question?

Yes, I do. Do all your friends live near you?

Lesson objectives

In this lesson students will:
- practise giving as much information as possible in answers to questions
- practise asking questions in order to have a conversation

Target exams

This section will prepare your students for the following external exams:
- PET / PET for Schools speaking part 1
- EOI speaking (A2)
- Trinity GESE Initial stage (grade 2-3)
- Trinity ISE speaking (level 0)

1
- Students look at the example question.
- They decide which topic the examiner is talking about.
- Check the answer as a class.

2 🔘 3.32
- Play the CD.
- Students read and listen to the questions and answers in the Model exam.
- Highlight how many sentences Antonio uses to describe his best friend.
- Check the answer as a class.

Exam tip

Point out that it is important for students to give more than one sentence when answering a question, eg *What's your favourite sport?* Possible answer: *My favourite sport is basketball. I play twice a week in a team. My best friend plays in the team.*

3
- Students read the questions and answers in the Model exam again.
- They work individually to complete the task.
- They compare answers in pairs.
- Check answers as a class.

🔘 **3.32 Audioscript, exercise 2**

Examiner: We're going to talk about your friends. Do all your friends go to your school?

Antonio: No, they don't. Some of my friends go to my school, but some of them are my neighbours.

Examiner: That's nice. What activities do you do together?

Antonio: We often play football and basketball. At the weekend, we sometimes go to the cinema or the youth club.

Examiner: Tell me about your best friend.

Antonio: My best friend's name is Javi. He's 13 years old and he goes to my school. He's tall and he's got brown hair. He loves playing football.

Examiner: Thanks Antonio. Do you want to ask me a question?

Antonio: Yes, I do. Do all your friends live near you?

Your exam practice

4 • Students read the questions in Your exam.
  • They make notes about their hobbies and prepare extra information to give in their answer to the instruction *Tell me about your favourite hobby.*
  • Check the answer as a class.

5 • Students think of a question to ask the examiner.
  • Encourage students to use the Model exam and the Exam kit to help them choose their question.
  • Check students' questions as a class.

Exam tip

Point out that at the end of an exam, students need to ask the examiner a question. This must be relevant to the topic of the conversation they have had with the examiner. Students should use question words such as *when, why, how* and the other question words listed in the Useful vocabulary box.

6 • Go through the Useful vocabulary box.
  • Students look at the questions in Your exam.
  • Students work with their partner to ask and answer the questions in Your exam.

Exercise 4

Possible answer: You can give information about how often you do / practise the hobby and why you like it.

Exercise 5

Possible answer: What is your favourite hobby?

Your exam practice

4 Read the questions in Your exam. Make notes about the topic to help you. What extra information can you give in your answer to the instruction *Tell me about ... ?*

5 Think of a question to ask the examiner and write it down. Use the Model exam on page 106 and the Exam kit to help you.

> **EXAM TIP: Ask appropriate questions**
>
> At the end of the exam, you need to ask your examiner a question. Always make sure it is relevant to the topic of your conversation. Use question words such as *when, why, how* etc.

6 Now ask and answer the questions in Your exam with your partner.

Exercise 6

students' own answers

Examiner's questions

We're going to talk about your hobbies.
- What are your hobbies?
- Who do you do these hobbies with?
- Tell me about your favourite hobby.
- Do you want to ask me a question?

EXAM KIT: Useful vocabulary

Friends and family	Hobbies	Adverbs of frequency
mum dad	going to the youth club	never sometimes
sister brother	playing football / basketball	often always
aunt uncle	skateboarding	
cousin (best) friend	doing judo / karate	**Question words**
neighbour	playing the guitar / piano	who what
	going to the cinema / watching films	where when
		why how

1 A conversation

2 Matching key information

4 Multiple-choice answers

5 Describing a photo

6 Completing a table or diagram

7 Talking about a prepared topic

8 Open questions

9 Correcting sentences

UNIT 2 — External exam trainer

Your exam preparation

About the exam

Matching key information

You listen to a conversation between two people who know each other. You match five people or things with five other things from a list. This tests your ability to identify important information in a conversation.

1 Read the instructions and answer questions 1 and 2.

  1 How many people will you hear talking?
  2 What will they talk about?

> Listen to Dan and Louise talking about a school project. What is each person's project about?

Exercise 1

1 Two people.
2 They will talk about a school project.

 EXAM TIP: Cross out options you have used

Put a line through the letters as you match them with the numbers, like this ~~M~~. This makes it easier to see what letters are left. Remember, the example helps you by giving you a letter that you won't need to use.

2 Read the rest of the instructions, the example answer and the two lists. Then answer the questions.

  1 Which letter **won't** you use?
  2 How many letters **will** you use from the list A–H?
  3 How many letters **won't** you use?

> Write a letter A–H next to each person. You will hear the conversation twice.
>
> Example:
>
>   **1** Dan C   **A** actor
>   **2** Louise   **B** musician
>   **3** Lisa   **C** ~~writer~~
>   **4** Poppy   **D** scientist
>   **5** Greg   **E** dancer
>   **6** Emily   **F** politician
>   **G** athlete
>   **H** painter

This is the order of the speakers.

Exercise 2

1 The letter C
2 Five letters
3 Two letters

3 🔊 3.33 Read and listen to the first part of the conversation between Louise and Dan.

  1 Which types of people from the list A–H do they mention?
  2 Who is Louise going to do her project on? Which type of person from the list A–H is he or she?

Exercise 3

1 They mention a writer, a scientist and an athlete.
2 Louise is going to do her project on an athlete.

MODEL ✓ EXAM

Who are you going to do your history project on?

That's easy. The writer Charlotte Brontë. She wrote one of my favourite books, *Jane Eyre*. Are you still going to do yours about a scientist?

No, I wanted to, but Lisa's doing hers about Albert Einstein, so I'm going to do mine on an athlete.

UNIT 2 — Your exam preparation

Lesson objective

In this lesson students will:
- practise identifying important information in a conversation

Target exams

This section will prepare your students for the following external exams:
- KET / KET for Schools listening part 2
- EOI listening (A2)

1
- Ask the students to read the instructions carefully.
- Ask how many people they will hear talking and what they will talk about.
- Check answers as a class.

2
- Ask the students to read the rest of the instructions, the example answer and the two lists.
- Ask students what type of person Dan is talking about.
- Remind students that examples 1–6 are the order in which they will hear the speakers in the conversation.
- Students answer questions 1–3.
- Check answers as a class.

Exam tip

Point out that it is important for students to put a line through the letters as they match them with the numbers. By doing this, it is clear which letters they still have to choose from. Highlight that the example helps students by giving them a letter they do not need to use.

3 3.33
- Play the CD.
- Students read and listen to the first part of the conversation between Louise and Dan.
- They work individually to answer the questions.
- They compare answers in pairs.
- Check answers as a class.

3.33 Audioscript, exercise 3

Louise: Who are you going to do your history project on?
Dan: That's easy. The writer Charlotte Brontë. She wrote one of my favourite books, Jane Eyre. Are you still going to do yours about a scientist?
Louise: No, I wanted to, but Lisa's doing hers about Albert Einstein, so I'm going to do mine on an athlete.

Your exam practice

Step 1:

4 • Explain the task.
• Students work individually to identify the key words. They then work in pairs to compare their answers.
• Check answers as a class.

Step 2:

5 • Students read the words in the list A–H and check they understand them.
• Students answer the question.
• Check the answer as a class.
• Go through the list A–H and ask students for an example of each kind of film.

Exam tip

Point out that students do not need to understand the meaning of all the words in the list A–H to find the correct answers.

Steps 3 and 4:

6 3.34
• Explain the task. Students then read the instructions carefully so that they are clear what is required.
• Play the CD. Students write a letter next to each day and also put a line through the letter and word on the right.
• Play the CD again for students to check their answers.
• Check answers as a class.

3.34 Audioscript, exercise 6

Claire: I've got this week's programme for the film club.
Steve: Oh, right. Is there anything good on?
Claire: Let me see. On Sunday, that's today, there's a horror film. Oh no, I hate horror films! Then on Monday, there's a James Bond film … You like adventure films, don't you?
Steve: Yeah, but I can't go out on Monday night. I've got a science test on Tuesday, so I've got to stay in and study.
Claire: Well there's something on Tuesday that looks good – *Snow White*.
Steve: Isn't that a cartoon for young kids?
Claire: No, it's a thriller. You have to be 15 or over to see it. I've heard it's quite scary.
Steve: Well, I'm not interested in seeing a fairy tale. What else is there?
Claire: On Wednesday, they're showing *One Day*. It's a love story.
Steve: Bor-ing!
Claire: Well, my mum says it's good, but she likes romances.
Steve: What about Thursday?
Claire: Oh, there's a Sherlock Holmes film! I love detective films. Shall we go to that?
Steve: OK, if you like. Friday's looks better, though.
Claire: Let me see. Mmm, it's a comedy with Ben Stiller.
Steve: He's brilliant. He always makes me laugh.
Claire: Let's go to that, then. At least we don't have to get up early for school the next day.
Steve: Yeah!

Listening: Matching key information

Your exam practice

Step 1: Read the instructions carefully.

4 Identify the key words. What are the key words in the instructions in the listening test below?

ercise 4

e key words
When,
d of film
d day.

Step 2: Read the list of words A–H.

5 Read the words in the list A–H in the test and check you understand them. What are they all different kinds of?

ercise 5

ey are all
erent kinds
ilms.

EXAM TIP: Find the answers in the list

Don't worry if you don't understand all the words in the list A–H. You don't need to know the meanings of them all to find the correct answers.

Step 3: Listen carefully to exercise 6 and choose the correct answers.

Step 4: Listen again and check your answers.

ercise 6

G
D
A
F
B

6 3.34 Listen to Claire and Steve talking about a film club. When is each kind of film on? Write a letter A–H next to each day. You will hear the conversation twice.

Example:
1 Sunday C
2 Monday
3 Tuesday
4 Wednesday
5 Thursday
6 Friday

A romance
B comedy
C horror
D thriller
E science fiction
F detective
G adventure
H cartoon

2 Matching key information
3 Discussing a topic
4 Multiple-choice answers
5 Describing a photo
6 Completing a table or diagram
7 Talking about a prepared topic
8 Open questions
9 Correcting sentences

Your exam preparation

About the exam

Discussing a topic
The examiner chooses a topic for discussion. He or she asks you some general questions about the topic and then some more specific questions.

Exercise 1

holidays: hotel, beach, airport, campsite

hobbies and sports: chess, football, cinema, dancing

weather: storm, icy, snow, wet

1 Match the words in the box with the topics shown in the pictures.

> storm hotel chess icy football beach snow cinema airport wet campsite dancing

holidays

hobbies and sports

weather

EXAM TIP: Prepare for all the topics

You will only talk about one topic, but before the exam prepare vocabulary on all the topics that you've studied this year.

2 🔊 3.35 Read and listen to the first part of a conversation between an examiner and a candidate. Which topic from exercise 1 are they discussing?

Examiner: What's the weather like here in winter, Sabina?
Sabina: It's cold.
Examiner: Does it snow?
Sabina: Yes, sometimes.
Examiner: And what do you do when it snows?
Sabina: I go for a walk sometimes.
Examiner: Do you like winter?
Sabina: Yes.

Exercise 2

They are discussing the weather.

3 🔊 3.36 Now read and listen to another candidate answering the same questions in the Model exam. Whose answers are better? Why?

Exercise 3

Carlos' answers are better because he gives more information.

What's the weather like here in winter, Carlos?

It's cold and wet. It rains a lot!

Does it snow?

Not very often … but it snowed last year!

And what do you do when it snows?

I play snowballs with my friends and we sometimes go snowboarding.

Do you like winter?

It's OK, but my favourite season is summer!

Your exam preparation

Lesson objectives

In this lesson students will:
- answer some general questions on a topic chosen by the examiner
- answer some more specific questions on the same topic

Target exam

This section will prepare your students for the following external exam
- EOI speaking (A2)
- Trinity GESE Initial stage (grade 3)

1
- Student read the instructions.
- They work individually to match the words in the box with the pictures.
- They compare answers in pairs.
- Check answers as a class.

Exam tip

Point out that students will only need to talk about one topic in the exam, but it is a good idea to prepare vocabulary on all the topics that they have studied during the year.

2 3.35
- Students read the instructions.
- Play the CD.
- Students read and listen to the first part of the conversation.
- Check the answer as a class.

3 3.36
- Make sure students understand the task.
- Play the CD.
- Students read and listen to the conversation in the Model exam. They identify whether Sabina's answers in exercise 2 or Carlos' answers in exercise 3 are better and why.
- Check answers as a class.

3.35 Audioscript, exercise 2

Examiner: What's the weather like here in winter, Sabina?
Sabina: It's cold.
Examiner: Does it snow?
Sabina: Yes, sometimes.
Examiner: And what do you do when it snows?
Sabina: I go for a walk sometimes.
Examiner: Do you like winter?
Sabina: Yes.

3.36 Audioscript, exercise 3

Examiner: What's the weather like here in winter, Carlos?
Carlos: It's cold and wet. It rains a lot!
Examiner: Does it snow?
Carlos: Not very often … but it snowed last year!
Examiner: And what do you do when it snows?
Carlos: I play snowballs with my friends and we sometimes go snowboarding.
Examiner: Do you like winter?
Carlos: It's OK, but my favourite season is summer!

Your exam practice

4 • Students read the examiner's questions in Your exam. Check students understand the questions.
- They copy the answer beginnings into their notebooks.

5 🔘 3.37
- Before students listen, refer them to the Useful vocabulary and Useful expressions boxes for any extra words or phrases they could use in their answers.
- Play the CD.
- Students listen to the examiner's questions. They complete the answers in their notebooks so that they are true for them.

6 • Students work in pairs.
- They take turns to ask and answer their questions from exercise 5. Remind students to close their books when it is their turn to answer.
- Ask some pairs to demonstrate one of their questions and answers to the class.

Exam tip

Point out that it is important for students to give extra details to support their answers and not to just answer *yes* or *no*.

🔘 **3.37 Audioscript, exercise 5**

1 What was the weather like here last summer?
2 What kind of things do you like doing in summer?
3 Where do you go when it's very hot?
4 What's your favourite season?
5 Why do you like it?

Speaking: Discussing a topic

Your exam practice

4 Read the examiner's questions 1–5. Then copy the answer beginnings into your notebook.

5 Listen to the examiner's questions and complete the answers. Make them true for you.

6 Work in pairs. Take turns to ask and answer the questions. When it's your turn to answer, shut your book!

EXAM TIP: Give detailed answers

Don't just answer *yes* or *no*. Give extra details to support your answers.

Exercise 5

Students' own answers

Examiner's questions

1 What was the weather like here last summer?
2 What kind of things do you like doing in summer?
3 Where do you go when it's very hot?
4 What's your favourite season?
5 Why do you like it?

1 *It …*
2 *I like …*
3 *I go …*
4 *My favourite season is …*
5 *I like it because …*

EXAM KIT: Useful vocabulary

go skiing
go snowboarding
go ice-skating
go for a walk
play snowballs
drink hot chocolate
wear a hat and scarf
wear gloves / a coat / boots

EXAM KIT: Useful expressions

My favourite season is …
It rains / snows a lot.
It's / It was hot / sunny / cold / windy / icy.
I like / love …ing.
I wear …

3 Discussing a topic

4 Multiple-choice answers

5 Describing a photo

6 Completing a table or diagram

7 Talking about a prepared topic

8 Open questions

9 Correcting sentences

UNIT 4 — External exam trainer

Your exam preparation

Exercise 1

1 He is going to talk about bees.
2 There are three possible answers.
3 The key word is *help*.

1 Read the example question. Then answer questions 1–3.

  1 What is the expert going to talk about?
  2 How many possible answers are there to the example question?
  3 What is the key word you should focus on in the example question?

> **Example question**
>
> Listen to an expert talking about bees.
> For each question, choose a, b or c.
>
> Bees help us because they …
> **a)** are amazing insects.
> **b)** like honey.
> **c)** do many useful things.

> 📋 **EXAM TIP: Identify key words**
>
> Before listening, read the questions and identify the key word or words. Focus on these words when you listen.

About the exam

Multiple-choice answers
You listen to someone talking about a subject. You read some questions, or sentences with a gap, and three possible answers. You choose the correct word or phrase to complete the questions or sentences.

2 **3.38** Read and listen to the Model exam. Answer the example question in exercise 1.

> 📋 **EXAM TIP: Listen for words that mean the same**
>
> The two wrong answers often contain words that you hear in the talk. The correct answer often uses different words to express the ideas you hear.

3 Find the words and phrases in the Model exam which give you the answer to the example question in exercise 1.

Exercise 2

c
Bees help us because they do many useful things.

Exercise 3

help us
many different ways

Bees are amazing insects, and they help us in many different ways. For one thing, they make honey, which we eat, but that's not all. Bees also do another job, which is very important for the environment.

Lesson objective

In this lesson students will:
- practise listening for key words in a listening in order to answer multiple-choice questions

Target exams

This section will prepare your students for the following external exams:
- KET / KET for Schools listening part 3
- PET / PET for Schools listening part 2
- EOI listening (A2)

1
- Students read the example question carefully.
- They then answer questions 1–3.
- Check answers as a class.

Exam tip

Point out that with listening exercises like this it is very important for students to identify the key word or words they need to listen out for before they listen. If they identify key words in advance, this will make the listening task easier.

2 🔊 3.38
- Play the CD.
- Students read and listen to the Model exam.
- Check students understand all the words in the Model exam.
- Students answer the question in the example question in exercise 1.
- Check the answer as a class.

Exam tip

Point out that the two wrong answers in a multiple-choice question often contain words that students will hear in the talk. The correct answer to the multiple-choice question often uses different words to express the ideas students hear.

3
- Students work individually to find words and phrases in the Model exam that give them the answer to the example question in exercise 1.
- Students compare their answers in pairs.
- Check answers as a class.

🔊 3.38 Audioscript, exercise 2

Man: Bees are amazing insects, and they help us in many different ways. For one thing, they make honey, which we eat, but that's not all. Bees also do another job, which is very important for the environment.

Your exam practice

Step 1:

4
- Students read the instructions and questions 1–5.
- They work in pairs to answer the question.
- Check the answer as a class.

Step 2:

5
- Students work individually to identify at least one key word in each question.
- Check answers as a class.

Steps 3 and 4:

6 3.39
- Students listen to the expert and choose the correct answer (a, b or c) for each question.
- Play the CD again for students to check their answers.
- Check answers as a class.

Exam tip

Point out to students once more the importance of focusing on the key words that they have identified. Advise students to listen carefully for these words and for words with a similar meaning before they answer the questions.

3.39 Audioscript, exercise 6

Bees are amazing insects, and they help us in many different ways. For one thing, they make honey, which we eat, but that's not all. Bees also do another job, which is very important for the environment. When they take nectar from plants to make into honey, they take pollen from them too. Then as they move from plant to plant, they leave the pollen on different plants. This helps new flowers, fruit and vegetables to grow.

All over the world, however, bees are disappearing. In Britain, for example, 30 years ago there were 50% more bees than there are now. In the past, some scientists believed that the chemicals used by farmers were the problem, but now there is a new explanation. Some of them think that mobile phones may be the cause.

Scientists have noticed that signals from mobile phones can disturb bees. When people use mobile phones near bees, the bees start behaving differently. They don't seem to know which way to go and so they get lost. Mobile phones have been part of our lives for about 30 years – and that's the same time in which the number of bees has been falling. If we continue using mobile phones, who knows if these insects will survive?

Listening: Multiple-choice answers

Your exam practice

Step 1: Read the instructions carefully.

4 Read the instructions and questions 1–5. What kind of information about bees do you think you will hear?

- Is the talk going to be about how bees make honey?
- Is it going to be about something else – possibly something to do with the environment?

Step 2: Identify key words.

5 Identify at least one key word in each question.

Step 3: Listen carefully and choose the answers.

 EXAM TIP: Listen to key words

As you listen, try to focus on the key word or words you identified. Listen for these words and for words with a similar meaning and think before you choose your answer.

Step 4: Listen again and check your answers.

6 3.39 Listen to an expert talking about bees. For each question choose the correct answer (a, b or c). You will hear the information twice.

1 What do bees take to plants to help them to grow?
   a) honey   b) pollen   c) nectar

2 The number of bees in Britain has
   a) got smaller.   b) got bigger.   c) stayed the same.

3 Scientists think mobile phones
   a) are bad for farmers.   b) stop chemicals being a problem.   c) affect bees' behaviour.

4 When bees are close to mobile phones, they
   a) fly towards them.   b) go in the wrong direction.   c) disturb the phone signal.

5 The number of bees in Britain began to decrease … people started using mobile phones.
   a) before   b) after   c) at the same time as

113

Side tabs

4 Multiple-choice answers

5 Describing a photo

6 Completing a table or diagram

7 Talking about a prepared topic

8 Open questions

9 Correcting sentences

Left margin notes

Exercise 4
...e talk is ...ing to ...e about ...mething to ...o with the ...vironment.

Exercise 5
...estion 1: ...es, plants, ...ow
...estion 2: ...mber, bees, ...tain
...estion 3: ...ientists, ...obile phones
...estion 4: ...es, close, ...obile phones
...estion 5: ...mber, bees, ...crease, ...arted, mobile ...ones

Exercise 6
...b
...a
...c
...b
...c

External exam trainer

Your exam preparation

About the exam

Describing a photo

The examiner gives you and the other candidate one photo each. You each talk about your photo for about a minute. You talk about what is happening in your photo – who you can see, where the people are and what they are doing.

✓ **EXAM TIP: Use *might* and *maybe***

Use *might* and *maybe* to make guesses about what's happening in the photo.

💬 *Maybe it's a science lesson.*

💬 *The teacher might be explaining an experiment.*

Exercise 1

1 a
2 a

1 **3.40 Listen to an examiner explaining what the first candidate has to do. Choose the correct answers.**

  1 The two photos are about …
    a) the same subject.
    b) different subjects.
  2 The girl must talk about …
    a) one photo.
    b) both photos.

2 **3.41 Read and listen to Juan talking about a photo. Which photo is he describing?**

Exercise 2

Juan is describing photo A.

A

B

The photo shows a lesson. Maybe it's a science lesson because I can see science equipment on the table. The teacher is explaining something and the pupils are listening. I think the lesson is fun because they look very interested in it. One pupil is looking at the teacher. The teacher might have an answer to her question.

Your exam preparation

Lesson objective

In this lesson students will:
* practise describing a photo
* use *might* and *maybe* to make guesses about what is happening in the photo

Target exams

This section will prepare your students for the following external exams:
* PET / PET for Schools speaking part 3
* EOI speaking (A2)
* Trinity GESE Initial stage (grade 3)
* Trinity ISE speaking (level 0)

1 🔘 3.40
* Students read the instructions explaining what they need to do.
* Play the CD.
* Students listen and choose the correct answers to questions 1 and 2.
* Check answers as a class.

Exam tip

Point out that students should use *might* and *maybe* to make guesses about what is happening in a photo.

2 🔘 3.41
* Play the CD.
* Students read and listen to Juan talking about one of the photos.
* They identify which photo he is describing.
* Check answers as a class.

3.40 Audioscript, exercise 1

Examiner: Now I'm going to give each of you a photograph of people learning in different ways. Maria, here is your photograph.
Maria: Thanks.
Examiner: Would you show it to Mark and talk about it please?
Maria: OK.
Examiner: Would you start now please?
Maria: Yes.

3.41 Audioscript, exercise 2

Boy: The photo shows a lesson. Maybe it's a science lesson because I can see science equipment on the table. The teacher is explaining something and the pupils are listening. I think the lesson is fun because they look very interested in it. One pupil is looking at the teacher. The teacher might have an answer to her question.

Your exam practice

3 • Students read the examiner's instructions carefully and look at the photos.

> **Exam tip**
>
> Point out to students that if they can't think of anything to say about the photo, they don't need to worry. The examiner will ask them a question to help them start talking about the photo.

4 • Students work in pairs.
 • They look at the Useful expressions and Useful vocabulary boxes to help them complete their sentences.
 • Student A completes the sentences about photo A.
 • Student B completes the sentences about photo B.

5 • Student A talks about photo A to Student B for one minute.
 • Student B talks about photo B to Student A for one minute.
 • Remind students to use their sentences from exercise 4 and the Useful expressions and Useful vocabulary boxes to help them.
 • Also remind students to ask their partner a question to help them if they can't think of anything to say.
 • For additional practice students could work in pairs and describe photo B on page 114.

Speaking: Describing a photo

Your exam practice

3 Read the examiner's instructions and look at the photos.

Examiner's instructions

Now I'm going to give each of you a photo. The photo shows people doing different jobs. Here is your photo. Show it to your partner and discuss the photo.

EXAM TIP: Help in the exam

If you can't think of anything else to say about the photo, don't worry. The examiner will ask a question to help you.

A

B

5 Describing a photo

6 Con tab

Exercise 5
students' own answers

7 Talking about a prepared topic

8 Open questions

9 Correcting sentences

Exercise 4

students' own answers

4 Work in pairs. Student A complete the sentences about photo A. Student B: complete the sentences about photo B.

1 The photo shows ...
2 She's in ...
3 She looks ...
4 She's probably ...
5 Maybe ...

5 Talk about your photo for about a minute. Then listen to your partner talking about the other photo.

- **When you're talking**, use your sentences from exercise 4 and the Exam kit to help you.
- **When you're listening**, if your partner stops talking, ask him or her a question about the photo.

EXAM KIT: Useful expressions

Describing
The photo shows ...
In the photo there is / are ...
In the background there is / are ...

Guessing
Maybe it's a ...
He / She may / might be ...
She / He's probably ...

Expressing your opinion
I (don't) think ...
He / She looks ...
I'm not sure if ...

EXAM KIT: Useful vocabulary

classroom   lesson   science
space   boring   exciting
interested (in)   relaxed   happy

External exam trainer

Your exam preparation

Exercise 1

Job
Name of
company
Number of
hours per
week
Salary

1 Look at the example question and the table. Which things do you need to listen for?

Example question
You are going to hear a woman enquiring about a job. Complete the table with the relevant information.

1) Job:	
2) Name of company:	
3) Number of hours per week:	
4) Salary:	

 EXAM TIP: Read the questions first

Before you listen, read the questions carefully. This will help you to know what information to listen for.

About the exam

Completing a table
You hear a conversation. You are given a table to complete. You complete it using the information you hear.

2 Look at the example question again. What type of information do you need to complete 1–3 in the table? You might need to use the same answer more than once.

> a number   a job title   a name

3 3.42 Read and listen to the Model exam. Is the information that Kirsty has completed correct?

4 Listen to the Model exam again. Complete the missing information.

Exercis

1 a job 1
2 a nam
3 a num
4 a num

Exercis

Yes, it is

Exercis

Number
hours pe
week: 1
hours
Salary: §
per hou

You are going to hear Kirsty making a phone call to ask for information about a job advertisement she has seen in the newspaper. Listen and complete the information in the table.

Job title:	Dog walker
Name of company:	Happy pets
Location:	Birmingham
Number of days per week:	2
Number of hours per week:	
Salary:	

UNIT 6 Your exam preparation

Lesson objective

In this lesson students will:
- listen to conversations about job advertisements and complete tables with missing information

Target exams

This section will prepare your students for the following external exams:
- KET / KET for Schools listening part 4
- PET / PET for Schools listening part 3
- EOI listening (A2)

1
- Ask students to read the example question and the table.
- They identify which things they need to listen for.
- Check answers as a class.

Exam tip

Tell students to read the questions very carefully before they listen as this will help them to know what information to listen for.

2
- Students look at the example question again.
- They decide which type of information they need to complete 1–4 in the table in exercise 1. Highlight that they might need to use the same answer more than once.
- Check answers as a class.

3 3.42
- Ask students to read the instructions in the Model exam. Remind students that they only need to check whether the information already completed is correct.
- Play the CD.
- Students listen to the Model exam.
- Check the answer as a class.

4
- Play the CD again.
- Students listen carefully to complete the two missing pieces of information.
- Check answers as a class.

3.42 Audioscript, exercise 3

Man: Hello, Happy Pets, how can I help you?
Kirsty: Oh hi, I'm calling to ask for more information about the dog walker job at Happy Pets. I saw it advertised in the newspaper.
Man: Great, thanks for calling. Well, the job is based in Birmingham. We need someone to work part-time – that's two days a week. I assume you like animals?
Kirsty: Yes, I love them! I've got two cats at home. Two days a week sounds fine. How many hours would I have to work each day?
Man: Five hours a day – so that's ten hours per week in total. Oh, and we pay £5 per hour.
Kirsty: That sounds great! How do I apply?

Your exam practice

Step 1:

5 • Students read the instructions in Your exam
and identify who they are going to hear.
• Check the answer as a class.

Step 2:

6 • Students read the table in Your exam.
• They decide what type of information they
need to complete 1–6.
• Point out to students that they might need to
use the same answer more than once.
• Check answers as a class.

Steps 3 and 4:

7 🔘 3.43
• Students read the instructions carefully.
• Ask students to quickly look again at their
answers from exercise 6 so they are prepared
for the type of information they are listening
for.
• Play the CD.
• Students listen and complete questions 1–6.
• Check answers as a class.

Exam tip

Point out to students that when they read
questions where they have to complete
information they should always think about
what type of information is required: is it a
name, a date, a number or a place?

🔘 3.43 Audioscript, exercise 7

Paul: Hi, I saw an advert for a sports coach
here at Sports Solutions on the noticeboard at
my college. Please can you give me some more
information about the job?
Woman: Yes, of course. We need a sports coach
to work at our children's camp this summer. We
need someone to work Wednesday to Friday.
Paul: So I would need to work Wednesday,
Thursday and Friday?
Woman: Yes, that's right. The camp starts at
9am and finishes at 4pm.
Paul: And what would I have to do?
Woman: You would need to teach children how
to play football, tennis and basketball. Are you
good at sports?
Paul: Yes, I love sports, especially football!
Woman: Great! Well, we pay £6 an hour. Would
you like to come for an interview tomorrow?
Paul: Yes, that sounds great. Will the interview
be here, at the office?
Woman: No, it's at the sports camp – it's at 23
Queen Street. See you tomorrow at 4 o'clock!

Listening: Completing a table

Your exam practice

5 Read the instructions in Your exam. Who are you going to hear?

Step 2: Read the questions.

6 Now read the table in Your exam. What type of information do you need to complete 1–6? You might need to use the same answer more than once.

> responsibilities a day   a number   an address
> a job title

Step 3: Listen carefully and write the answers.

Step 4: Listen again and check your answers.

> ✓ **EXAM TIP:** Knowing what information you need
>
> When you read the questions, think about what information you need to complete them. For example, do you need a name, a date, a number or a place?

7 (3.43) You are going to hear Paul enquiring about a job advertisement he has seen on a noticeboard. Listen and complete questions 1–6.

ENQUIRING ABOUT A JOB	
1 Job:	
2 Days they need to work:	
3 Start time:	
4 Duties:	
5 Salary:	
6 Address of company:	

Side panel (left):

Exercise 5
...ul enquiring
...but a job
...vertisement

Exercise 6
...b: a job title
...ys they
...ed to work:
...day
...art time: a
...mber
...ties:
...sponsibilities
...lary: a
...mber
...dress of
...mpany: an
...dress

Side panel (right):

Exercise 7

1 Job: sports coach
2 Days they need to work: Wednesday to Friday
3 Start time: 9am
4 Duties: teach children how to play football, tennis and basketball
5 Salary: £6 an hour
6 Address of company: 23 Queen Street

Your exam preparation

About the exam

Talking about a prepared topic
Before the exam, you prepare to talk about a topic that interests you. In the exam, you complete a form about your topic and give it to the examiner. You have a conversation with the examiner about your topic.

Exercise 1

Possible answer
My favourite way to travel

1 Look at the mind map about Javier's chosen topic. Can you think of one more main point about the topic that he could discuss?

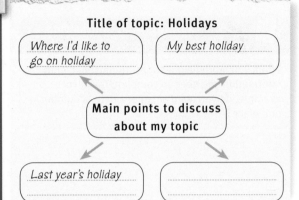

Title of topic: Holidays

- Where I'd like to go on holiday
- My best holiday

Main points to discuss about my topic

- Last year's holiday
- ....

EXAM TIP: Choose an interesting topic

Choose a subject that really interests you and that you know a lot about. Try not to choose the same subject as the other students in your English class.

2 🔊 3.44 Read and listen to the first part of the discussion between the examiner and Javier. Which points from his topic form did the examiner ask him about?

Exercise 2

Last year's holiday

Where I'd like to go on holiday

So you're going to talk to me about holidays. Where did you go on holiday last year?

I went to the island of Mallorca.

What did you do there?

I went to the beach every day and swam in the sea. And in the evening, I went out with my family to different restaurants.

So you had a good time?

Yes, it was great.

Are there any other places you'd really like to visit? Why?

Yes. I'd love to go to Paris! I've heard it's a very beautiful city.

What would you like to do there?

I'd like to walk around, see the sights and go to the Louvre. I love art and Paris has got some great art galleries!

Your exam preparation

Lesson objective

In this lesson students will:
- prepare a form about a topic they are going to talk about
- have a conversation with a partner about their prepared topic

Target exams

This section will prepare your students for the following external exams:
- EOI speaking (A2)
- Trinity GESE Elementary stage (grade 4)
- Trinity ISE speaking (level 0)

1
- Check that students understand what a mind map is and what it helps them to do by looking at Javier's mind map.
- Point out that Javier has put the title of the topic he is going to talk about at the top of the mind map and has put *Main points to discuss about my holiday* in a circle in the middle. From here he has drawn four more circles. In three of these he has written a main point to discuss. Visually this is a very helpful way for students to organize their thoughts and prepare their topic.
- Students work in pairs and think of one more main point that Javier could discuss.
- Check answers as a class.

Exam tip

Point out that it is a very good idea for students to choose a subject that they are interested in and know a lot about. By doing this, they will have lots of ideas in the preparation stage. Suggest that students try to choose a different subject from the subjects the other students in their class have chosen.

2 🔊 3.44
- Make sure students understand the task.
- Play the CD.
- Check answers as a class.

🔊 3.44 Audioscript, exercise 2

Examiner: So you're going to talk to me about holidays. Where did you go on holiday last year?

Javier: I went to the island of Mallorca.

Examiner: What did you do there?

Javier: I went to the beach every day and swam in the sea. And in the evening, I went out with my family to different restaurants.

Examiner: So you had a good time?

Javier: Yes, it was great.

Examiner: Are there any other places you'd really like to visit? Why?

Javier: Yes. I'd love to go to Paris! I've heard it's a very beautiful city.

Examiner: What would you like to do there?

Javier: I'd like to walk around, see the sights and go to the Louvre. I love art and Paris has got some great art galleries!

Your exam practice

3
- Students choose one of the three topics.
- Check that students understand the task. They choose a topic which will be the title of the topic in the mind map. They then think of four main points that they are going to talk about. They write one main point in each of the four circles in the mind map.
- Students copy and complete the mind map.

> ### Exam tip
>
> Point out to students that it is important that they do not learn a speech for their topic. Instead advise students to have a clear idea of their four main points for discussion and to think about the kind of questions the examiner might ask them about each main point.

4
- Students work in pairs.
- They look at each other's mind maps and write four questions that they could ask about their partner's topic.
- Check students' questions as a class feedback activity so that students can add more questions to their list of four questions.

5
- Students work in the same pairs.
- Before they start, ask students to look at the Useful vocabulary and Useful expressions boxes for any language they can use.
- Students take turns to ask and answer questions about their topics.

Speaking: Talking about a prepared topic

Your exam practice

3 Choose one of the topics. Copy and complete the mind map in Your exam for your topic.

- Foreign travel
- My country
- My favourite kind of transport

> 📝 **Exam tip: Don't learn a speech!**
>
> Don't prepare a speech about your topic. Instead, think about the kind of questions the examiner might ask you. Then think about how you could answer the questions.

4 Work in pairs. Look at each other's mind map and write four questions that you could ask about your partner's topic.

5 Work in the same pairs. Take turns to ask and answer questions about your topics.

Exercise 4

Possible questions for the topic 'My country': How many people live there? What is the food like in your country? What is the weather like in your country? Can you name some places for a tourist to visit in your country?

Exercise 5

students' own answers

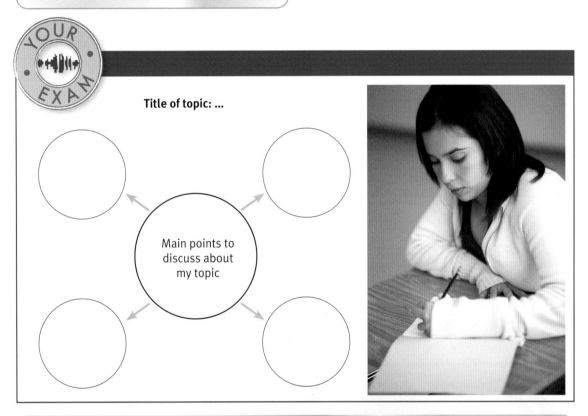

Title of topic: ...

Main points to discuss about my topic

Exam kit: Useful vocabulary

go to the beach
swim
play volleyball
go to cafés / restaurants
see the sights
go shopping

Exam kit: Useful expressions

Talking about likes/dislikes
I (don't) like doing / seeing / going to ...
My favourite ... is ...
The best / worst thing about ... is ...

Talking about wishes/ambitions
I'd like / love to do / see / go to ...

Talking about past experiences
I had a (really) good time.
It was great / amazing / awful / boring.

7 Talking about a prepared topic

8 Open questions

9 Correcting sentences

119

Your exam preparation

1 Look at the instructions and questions 1–3 from a listening test. Match the questions with the type of information you need to answer them.

Example question

Listen to a talk about snowboarding. Read the questions before listening. Then listen and answer the questions.
1 When did people first start snowboarding?
2 What equipment do you need to go snowboarding?
3 How many styles of snowboarding are there?

Type of information
a) a number
b) names of things
c) a date

 EXAM TIP: Read the questions first

Before you listen, read the questions and try to predict the type of information you need to answer them. Focus on question words like *who* and *where*.

About the exam

Open questions
You will hear someone talking about a topic. You are given some questions to answer about the topic. You listen and write the answers.

2 3.45 Read and listen to the first part of the talk in the Model exam. Are there any words you don't understand? Can you guess their meaning?

3 Write the answers to questions 1–3 of the listening test in exercise 1.

 EXAM TIP: Don't worry about words you don't know

When listening, don't worry if you hear some words that you don't understand. You don't need to understand every word to find the correct answers.

Snowboarding is a popular extreme sport. It started in the USA in the 1960s. Other sports inspired snowboarding, such as skateboarding and sledging. Now, snowboarding is popular all around the world, and there are many snowboarding competitions.
To try snowboarding, you need a snowboard and some special boots. You also need a warm jacket – it's cold in the snow!
There are around 10 types of snowboarding. In each type, snowboarders do different tricks.

Your exam preparation

Target exam

This section will prepare your students for the following external exam:
- EOI listening (A2)

1
- Students read the instructions and questions carefully.
- They match the questions with the type of information needed to answer the questions.

Exam tip

Point out how important it is to read the questions carefully before listening to someone talking about a topic. Advise students to predict the type of information they need to answer each question so that they know what to listen out for. Highlight the importance of question words, for example *who* or *where* indicate that students need to listen for a person or a place.

2 🔵 3.45
- Explain to students that they are going to read and listen to the first part of the Model exam. They are going to identify any words they don't understand, and also try to guess the meaning of these words.
- Play the CD.
- Students work in pairs to compare the words they identified and guess their meaning.
- Check that all new words have been correctly defined as a class.

3
- Students read the questions again from exercise 1.
- They write the answers to the questions.
- Check answers as a class.

Exam tip

Remind students that if they don't understand every word when they listen, they don't need to worry.

They don't need to understand every word to find the correct answers.

🔵 3.45 Audioscript, exercise 2

Man: Snowboarding is a popular extreme sport. It started in the USA in the 1960s. Other sports inspired snowboarding, such as skateboarding and sledging. Now, snowboarding is popular all around the world, and there are many snowboarding competitions.

To try snowboarding, you need a snowboard and some special boots. You also need a warm jacket – it's cold in the snow!

There are around 10 types of snowboarding. In each type, snowboarders do different tricks.

Your exam practice

Step 1:

4
- Students work in pairs.
- They read the questions in Your exam and check they understand them. They then identify the question word(s) in each question.
- They compare answers in pairs.
- Check answers as a class.

Step 2:

5
- Students look at questions 1–5 again in Your exam.
- They match the questions with the kinds of information the answer will be.
- Point out to students that they will need to use the same answer more than once.
- Check answers as a class.

Steps 3 and 4:

6 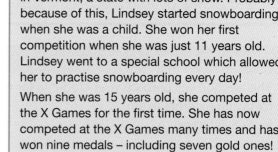 3.46

- Play the CD.
- Students listen to the talk and answer the questions.
- Check answers as a class.

Exam tip

Point out to students that they don't need to write full sentences. What is important is that the answer gives the correct information, which can be just words or phrases.

3.46 Audioscript, exercise 6

Lindsey Jacobellis is a famous American snowboarder. She's from the town of Stratton in Vermont, a state with lots of snow. Probably because of this, Lindsey started snowboarding when she was a child. She won her first competition when she was just 11 years old. Lindsey went to a special school which allowed her to practise snowboarding every day!

When she was 15 years old, she competed at the X Games for the first time. She has now competed at the X Games many times and has won nine medals – including seven gold ones! She has also competed in the Winter Olympics twice.

In her free time, Lindsey enjoys watching films. She also likes fashion, and has got a big collection of shoes!

Listening: Open questions

Your exam practice

xercise 4

Where
How old
How many
How many
What

Step 1: Read the instructions carefully.

4 Read questions 1–5 in Your exam and check you understand them. Find the question word(s) in each one.

Step 2: Think about the answers.

xercise 5

b
a
d
d
c

5 Look again at questions 1–5. Match the questions with the kinds of information the answer will be. You will need to use the same answer more than once.

Kind of information
a) someone's age
b) the name of a place
c) a hobby
d) a number

Step 3: Listen carefully and write the answers.

Step 4: Listen again and check.

> **EXAM TIP: Answers that might be correct**
>
> Think about the kind of answers that might fit. Remember you don't always need to write full sentences – your answers can be words or phrases.

6 🔊 3.46 Listen to a talk about Lindsey Jacobellis. Read the questions before listening. Then listen and answer the questions.

1 Where is Lindsey from?
2 How old was she when she won her first competition?
3 How many X-Games gold medals has she got?
4 How many times has Lindsey competed in the Winter Olympics?
5 What does Lindsey do in her free time?

Exercise 6

1 Stratton in Vermont
2 11
3 7
4 twice
5 watches films and collects shoes

8 Open questions

9 Correcting sentences

121

Your exam preparation

1 Look at the instructions for the example question.
Then answer the questions.

   1 Which word in sentence 1 is wrong?
   2 What is the correct word?

Example question

You will hear a news report twice. Read the
sentences and find the incorrect word or short
phrase in each sentence. Write the correct
information in your notebook. Sentence 1 has
been corrected as an example.
   1 Lessons in dealing with stress will begin in UK
secondary schools next ~~month~~. *year*

About the exam

Correcting sentences

You will hear several extracts from the news.
You are given some sentences to read about
what you hear. There is a mistake in each of
the sentences. Find the mistakes and write the
correct sentences.

 **EXAM TIP: Look for incorrect words and
incorrect phrases**

The incorrect information could be a word or it
could be more than one word. In some sentences,
you may need to correct a short phrase.

2 🔊 3.47 Read and listen to the first news item in
the Model exam. Identify the part of the item that
contains the answer to the Example question in
exercise 1.

3 🔊 3.48 Read and listen to the second news item
in the Model exam. Identify the incorrect phrase
in the sentence below.

   Police are warning people not to use mobile
phones while they're driving their car.

Students in secondary schools will soon
have lessons to help them deal with stress.
The lessons, for 13–18 year olds, will
start in schools all over the UK next year.
They will teach students how to deal with
stress, especially the stress of exams and
relationships.

Talking on your mobile phone can be
dangerous – and not just when you're driving
your car. Police in London say that more road
accidents are happening now because of
people who talk or send messages on their
phones while they're crossing the road. Last
year, in London, 52 people were injured and
three were killed while they were walking
across busy roads. More than half of them
were using mobile phones at the time.

Your exam preparation

Target exams

This section will prepare your students for the following external exams:
- EOI listening (A2)

1
- Students read the example question and answer the questions.
- Check the answer as a class.

Exam tip

Point out that the incorrect information in a sentence could be a word or it could be a short phrase.

2 🔘 3.47
- Play the CD.
- Students read and listen to the first news item in the Model exam.
- They identify the part of the news item that contains the answer to the example question in exercise 1.
- Check the answer as a class.

3 🔘 3.48
- Explain to students that they are going to read and listen to the second news item and identify the incorrect phrase in the sentence below.
- Play the CD.
- Check the answer as a class.

🔘 3.47 Audioscript, exercise 2

Newsreader: Students in secondary schools will soon have lessons to help them deal with stress. The lessons, for 13–18-year-olds, will start in schools all over the UK next year. They will teach students how to deal with stress, especially the stress of exams and relationships.

🔘 3.48 Audioscript, exercise 3

Newsreader: Talking on your mobile phone can be dangerous – and not just when you're driving your car. Police in London say that more road accidents are happening now because of people who talk or send messages on their phones while they're crossing the road. Last year, in London, 52 people were injured and three were killed while they were walking across busy roads. More than half of them were using mobile phones at the time.

Your exam practice

4
- Students work in pairs.
- Students look at sentences 1–5 in Your exam and identify what they think are the key words.
- Check answers as a class.

Exam tip

Point out that if students identify key words and phrases in sentences before they listen, such as dates, numbers, places and actions, they can then focus on those key words and listen to information that matches them.

5 ⊙ 3.49
- Play the CD.
- Students listen to the five items in the news report and look at sentences 1–5.
- Students try to find the incorrect information in sentences 1–5.

6
- Students write the correct sentences in their notebooks.

7
- Play the CD again.
- Students listen again carefully to check their answers. Highlight the Exam tip box below. Ask students to check their corrections and to make sure that their corrections are the same type of words as the incorrect words.
- Check answers as a class.

Exam tip

Point out to students that their correction should be the same kind of word as the incorrect word. If the incorrect word is a verb, then the correct word should also be a verb. Remind students to make sure their corrections are written correctly.

⊙ 3.49 Audioscript, exercise 7

1
Newsreader 1: A recent report shows that people's diets are getting worse. Scientists at Reading University have found that people spend less time cooking now than they did ten years ago. They believe that longer working hours are the reason.

2
Newsreader 2: The singer Miley Beck has cancelled her concert in London on Wednesday because of a mystery illness. The singer's doctor says she is suffering from headaches and stomach pains, but nobody knows why. Beck, whose song *Girl* reached number one in the USA last week, is in the middle of a European tour.

3
Newsreader 1: A 16-year-old boy in Canada had a lucky escape yesterday when a bear nearly attacked him. Mark Owen was listening to music on his MP3 player on his way home from school when a bear suddenly appeared in front of him. The teenager turned the music up loud, and the bear became frightened and ran away.

4
Newsreader 2: The Sutton Summer Bazaar will take place at Sutton School on Saturday morning. Second-hand clothes, books and toys will be on sale, and all money will go to the local children's hospital. Anyone who can help should contact Sue Brooks on 344872.

5
Newsreader 1: And the weather tomorrow will be hot and sunny, with temperatures reaching 32 degrees Celsius in some parts of the country. So if you're going to be outdoors, remember to wear a hat and some suncream!

Listening: Correcting sentences

Your exam practice

| **Step 1:** | Read the sentences. |

4 Look at sentences 1–5 in Your exam and identify the key words. Find at least one key word in each sentence.

| **Step 2:** | Listen and focus on the key words in each sentence. |

5 Listen to the five items in the news report and look at the sentences. Find what you think is the incorrect information in each sentence.

| **Step 3:** | Write the correct sentence. |

6 Write the correct sentences in your notebook.

 EXAM TIP: Focus on key words and phrases

Read the sentences first, before you listen, and find the key words or phrases in them – for example, dates, numbers, places and actions. Then when you listen, focus on the key words and phrases and listen carefully for information that matches them.

| **Step 4:** | Listen again and check your answers. |

| **Step 5:** | Check your corrections. |

EXAM TIP: Check your corrections

Make sure your correction is the same kind of word as the wrong word. For example, if the wrong word is a verb, make sure your correction is also a verb and that you have written it correctly.

Exercise 4

less,
cooking, 10
years ago

concert,
New York,
won't take
place

dog,
attacked,
teenager,
yesterday

Sue
Brooks,
344873,
help, school

cold,
cloudy,
tomorrow

7 (● 3.49) **You will hear a news report twice. Read sentences 1–5 and find the incorrect word or short phrase in each sentence.**

1 People spent less time cooking 10 years ago.
2 Miley Beck's concert in New York won't take place.
3 A dog attacked a teenager yesterday.
4 Please contact Sue Brooks on 344873 to help at the school.
5 It will be cold and cloudy tomorrow.

Exercise 7

1 People spent ~~less~~ time cooking 10 years ago. *more*

2 Miley Beck's concert in ~~New York~~ won't take place. *London*

3 A ~~dog~~ attacked a teenager yesterday. *bear*

4 Please contact Sue Brooks on 344873 to help at the school 2

5 It will be ~~cold and cloudy~~ tomorrow. *hot and sunny*

123

PRONUNCIATION LAB

UNIT 1
» Third person verb endings

1 🔊 1.10 Listen and repeat the verbs. Can you hear the different sounds?

/s/	paints	cooks	works
/z/	tells	sings	wears
/ɪz/	practises	wishes	matches

2 🔊 1.11 Copy and complete the table with the verbs in the box. Then listen and check.

watches chats dances listens bakes
finishes rides acts draws

/s/	/z/	/ɪz/
chats		

» Intonation in questions

1 🔊 1.17 Listen and repeat the sentences. Do the speakers use rising or falling intonation?

1 Is she enjoying the trip?
2 Where are they skateboarding?
3 What are you baking?
4 Is he playing the guitar?
5 Are we swimming with sharks?
6 Why isn't he studying?

UNIT 2
» Past simple endings

1 🔊 1.24 Copy the words into your notebook. Listen and repeat the past simple verbs. Write the ending /ɪ/, /d/ or /ɪd/ next to each verb.

1 enjoyed   4 played   7 chatted
2 painted   5 listened 8 washed
3 finished   6 watched   9 invented

2 🔊 1.25 Choose the past simple verb that sounds different. Then listen and check.

1 posted   finished   expected
2 liked   tidied   loved
3 danced   wished   downloaded
4 asked   disagreed appeared
5 started   performed wanted

» /ə/

1 🔊 1.31 Listen to the words. Pay attention to the /ə/ sound. Listen again and repeat.

invent – invent**or**   teach – teach**er**
dance – danc**er**   explore – explor**er**

2 🔊 1.32 Listen and write the words you hear in your notebook.

1 paint / painter   4 invent / inventor
2 explore / explorer   5 read / reader
3 write / writer   6 dance / dancer

UNIT 3
» Weak forms: *was* /wəz/ and *were* /wɜ:/

1 🔊 1.38 Listen and repeat.

1 Was he swimming?
2 No, he wasn't. / Yes, he was.
3 I wasn't lying on my bed.
4 They were talking to him.

2 Listen again. Which two are weak forms?

a) yes / no questions   c) short answers
b) negative sentences   d) affirmative sentences

3 🔊 1.39 Listen and repeat. Pay attention to the weak and strong forms of *was* and *were*.

1 Were you skiing? No, I wasn't.
2 We weren't listening to her.
3 She was ice-skating.
4 They were riding their bikes.

UNIT 4
» /ə/ in comparatives and superlatives

1 🔊 1.51 Listen and repeat the words. Which syllables have the /ə/ sound?

1 colder   the coldest
2 safer   the safest
3 healthy   the healthiest

2 Complete the rule.

We only use the /ə/ sound in **stressed** / **unstressed** syllables.

3 🔊 1.52 Listen and write the sentences in your notebook. Underline the syllables that have the /ə/ sound. Listen and repeat.

Exercise 2
/s / chats, bakes, acts
/z / listens, rides, draws
/ɪz/ watches, dances, finishes

Exercise 1
1 rising
2 falling
3 falling
4 rising
5 rising
6 falling

Exercise 1
1 /d/
2 /ɪd/
3 /d/
4 /d/
5 /d/
6 /t/
7 /ɪd/
8 /d/
9 /ɪd/

Exercise 2
1 finished
2 liked
3 downloaded
4 asked
5 performed

Exercise 2
1 painter
2 explorer
3 write
4 inventor
5 read
6 dancer

Exercise 2
a
d

Exercise 1
1 colder, the coldest
2 safer, the safest
3 healthy, the healthiest

Exercise 2
unstressed

Exercise 3
1 Jane is better at maths.
2 Wales is wetter than Spain.
3 Sam is the quietest in class.
4 Dave is the friendliest man I know.

Pronunciation lab

UNIT 1

»Third person verb endings

1 `1.10` Play the CD, pausing at the end of each set of verbs. Students repeat the verbs chorally.
- Play the CD again. Students repeat the verbs chorally and then individually.

2 `1.11` Students copy and complete the table by putting the verbs in the box into the correct column.
- Play the CD. Students listen and check their answers.
- Check answers as a class.

»Intonation in questions

1 `1.17` Play the CD. Students listen and repeat the questions.
- Play the CD again. Students identify either rising or falling intonation in each question.
- Check answers as a class.

UNIT 2

»Past simple endings

1 `1.24` Students copy the words into their notebooks.
- Play the CD, pausing after each word. Students repeat the words chorally.
- Play the CD again. Students write /t/, /d/ or /ɪd/ next to each word.
- Check answers as a class.

2 `1.25` Students choose the past simple ending in each group of three words that sounds different.
- Play the CD. Students listen and check their answers.
- Check answers as a class.

»/ə/

1 `1.31` Play the CD. Students listen to the words, paying attention to the /ə/ sound.
- Play the CD again, pausing after each word. Students repeat the words chorally.

2 `1.32` Play the CD. Students listen and write the words they hear in their notebooks.
- Check answers as a class.

UNIT 3

»Weak forms: *was* /wəz/ and *were* /wɜː/

1 `1.38` Play the CD, pausing after each sentence. Students repeat the sentences chorally.
- Play the CD again. Students repeat the words individually.

2 • Play the CD again. Students identify which sentences have weak forms of *was* and *were*.
- Check answers as a class.

3 `1.39` Play the CD, pausing after each sentence. Students repeat the sentences chorally.
- Play the CD again. Students repeat the sentences individually, paying attention to the weak and strong forms of *was* and *were*.

UNIT 4

» /ə/ in comparatives and superlatives

1 `1.51` Play the CD, pausing after each word. Students repeat the words chorally.
- Play the CD again. Students decide which words have the /ə/ sound.
- Check answers as a class.
- Write *healthy,* ____, *the healthiest* on the board. Elicit the comparative *healthier* and underline the schwa.

2 • Students complete the rule.
- Check answers as a class.

3 `1.52` Play the CD, pausing after each sentence. Students write each sentence in their notebooks.
- Students underline the syllables with the /ə/ sound.
- Play the CD again for students to check their answers.
- Check answers as a class. Point out that the superlative ending *-est* can be pronounced with or without the /ə/ sound.
- Play the CD again, pausing after each sentence for students to repeat the sentence chorally.

»Difficult sounds: /g/ and /dʒ/

1 ⊙ 2.07 Play the CD, pausing for students to listen and repeat the words chorally.
• Play the CD again. Students repeat the words individually.

2 ⊙ 2.08 Students copy and complete the table with the words in the box.
• Play the CD. Students listen and check their answers.
• Check answers as a class.

UNIT 5
»Short form of *will*: *'ll*

1 ⊙ 2.14 Play the CD, pausing at the end of each sentence for students to assess what they have heard.
• Check answers as a class.

2 ⊙ 2.15 Play the CD, pausing for students to repeat the sentences chorally and individually.
• Play the CD again. Students choose the option they hear.
• Check answers as a class.

UNIT 6
»Difficult sounds: /w/

1 ⊙ 2.27 Play the CD, pausing at the end of each sentence for students to repeat it.
• Play the CD again so that students can repeat the sentences individually. Check that students pronounce the /w/ sound correctly.

2 ⊙ 2.28 Students work in pairs and practise saying the sentences to each other. Monitor to check they pronounce the /w/ sound correctly.
• Play the CD, pausing after each sentence for students to check their pronunciation.

»Difficult sounds: /s/ at the beginning of words

1 ⊙ 2.34 Play the CD, pausing after each word for students to repeat chorally and then individually. If you like, get them practise the pronunciation of words beginning with an *s* + a consonant: *spend, scan, Spain,* etc.

2 ⊙ 2.35 Students practise saying the sentences.
• Play the CD for them to check their pronunciation; at the end of each sentence they say it individually.

UNIT 7
Difficult sounds: /ɪ/ and /iː/

1 ⊙ 2.44 Play the CD, pausing after each set of words for students to repeat the words chorally.
• Play the CD again, pausing as before for students to repeat the words individually.
• Point out that for the longer /iː/ sound the lips are more spread, almost in a smile.

2 ⊙ 2.45 Play the CD, pausing after each set of words for students to write the word they hear in their notebooks.
• Check answers as a class.

UNIT 8
»Linking words: final consonant + vowel sound

1 ⊙ 3.10 Play the CD, pausing for students to listen and repeat each sentence chorally.
• Play the CD again, pausing as before for students to repeat the sentences individually.
• Check that students are sure about the linking sound between the final consonant and vowel sound in each sentence.

2 ⊙ 3.11 Students copy the sentences into their notebooks.
• Play the CD, pausing after each sentence for students to write the linking lines.
• Play the CD again for students to check their answers.
• Check answers as a class.

UNIT 9
»Intonation: expressing feelings

1 ⊙ 3.22 Play the CD, pausing for students to repeat each sentence, A and B.
• Play the CD again. Students repeat the sentences again, emphasizing the rising and falling intonation in B's responses.

2 ⊙ 3.23 Play the CD, pausing for students to repeat each sentence, A and B.
• Students work in pairs and take turns to be Student A and Student B. They practise saying the sentences and responses. Remind students that falling intonation is used to express feelings about bad news, whereas rising intonation is used to express feelings about good news or for a question response, eg *Really?*

» Difficult sounds: /g/ and /dʒ/

1 🔊 2.07 Listen and repeat the words.

/dʒ/ giant Egypt energy jellyfish
/g/ goldfish dog global pig

2 🔊 2.08 Copy and complete the table with the words in the box. Then listen and check.

gerbil gorilla tiger giant jungle begin egg giraffe

/g/	/dʒ/
gorilla	

Exercise 2

/g/ gorilla, tiger, begin, egg
/dʒ/ gerbil, giant, jungle, giraffe

UNIT 5

» Short form of *will*: *'ll*

1 🔊 2.14 Listen to the sentences. Can you hear the difference?

1 a) Scientists will find a cure.
  b) Scientists'll find a cure.
2 a) People will live on other planets.
  b) People'll live on other planets.

2 🔊 2.15 Listen and repeat. Then listen again. Which option do you hear?

1 Sweets will have / 'll have vitamins.
2 Computers will be / 'll be smaller.
3 People will feel / 'll feel happier.
4 Cars will drive / 'll drive themselves.

Exercise 2

1 Sweets'll have vitamins.
2 Computers will be smaller.
3 People'll feel happier.
4 Cars'll drive themselves.

UNIT 6

» Difficult sounds: /w/

1 🔊 2.27 Listen and repeat the sentences. Pay attention to the /w/ sound.

1 Would you like to go shopping on Wednesday?
2 Would you mind taking the dog for a walk?
3 What are you watching?
4 Which one do you want?

2 🔊 2.28 Practise saying the sentences. Then listen and check.

1 Why are you working?
2 What are doing next weekend?
3 I wouldn't like to walk there.
4 Would you mind washing the car?

» Difficult sounds: /s/ at the beginning of words

1 🔊 2.34 Listen and repeat the words.

/s/ say sell see second summer

2 🔊 2.35 Practise saying the sentences. Then listen and check.

1 Let's go to the sales on Saturday.
2 You can save money at swap shops.
3 Don't spend your money, save it!
4 My watch is seven seconds fast.

UNIT 7

» Difficult sounds: /ɪ/ and /i:/

1 🔊 2.44 Listen and repeat the words.

/ɪ/ live will ship
/i:/ leave wheel team

2 🔊 2.45 Listen and write the words you hear in your notebook.

1 live / leaf   4 grin / green
2 sit / seat   5 hill / heel
3 chip / cheap

Exercise 2

1 live
2 seat
3 cheap
4 green
5 hill

UNIT 8

» Linking words: final consonant + vowel sound

1 🔊 3.10 Listen and repeat. Pay attention to the linking ‿ between the final consonant and the following vowel sound.

1 What‿are you doing?
2 How‿are you today?
3 When‿is the football match?
4 How's‿it going?

2 🔊 3.11 Copy the sentences into your notebook. Listen and draw the linking ‿ where you hear it.

1 What is he reading?
2 Who's in the school basketball team?
3 How old is she?
4 Why are you tired?

Exercise 2

1 What‿is he reading?
2 Who's‿in the school basketball team?
3 How‿old is she?
4 Why‿are you tired?

UNIT 9

» Intonation: expressing feelings

1 🔊 3.22 Listen and repeat.

1 **A:** I've got a headache.   **B:** Oh dear!
2 **A:** I've got a part-time job.   **B:** That's great!
3 **A:** She teaches Zumba classes. **B:** Really?
4 **A:** A snake bit me!   **B:** Oh no!

2 🔊 3.23 Listen and repeat.

1 **A:** I'm going to Australia.   **B:** Wow! That's great!
2 **A:** I've lost my mobile phone. **B:** Oh no!
3 **A:** I've never been skiing.   **B:** Really?
4 **A:** I've got toothache.   **B:** Oh dear!

WORKBOOK ANSWER KEY

STARTER UNIT

Vocabulary

1
1 Easter
2 Christmas
3 birthday
4 Valentine's Day

2
1 New Year's Day
2 carnival
3 Halloween
4 April Fool's Day
5 Christmas Eve

Grammar

3
1 New Year's Eve is on the 31st of December.
2 Three Kings' Day is on the 6th of January.
3 Valentine's Day is on the 14th of February.
4 The next public holiday is on the …

4
1 What do you do on Christmas Day?
2 When do you give presents?
3 Which day of the week do you like best?
4 How do you celebrate your birthday?

5 Students' own answers

Vocabulary

1

body	legs	feet
dress	jeans	boots
jacket		sandals
jumper		trainers
scarf		
T-shirt		

2
1 dress
2 scarf
3 jacket
4 boots
5 trainers

Grammar

3
1 its   4 your
2 his   5 our
3 their

4
1 Snowball's   4 parents'
2 Sam's   5 father's
3 girls'

Vocabulary

5
1 Spanish   6 German
2 French   7 Russian
3 Italian   8 Dutch
4 Chinese   9 Polish
5 Japanese

Grammar

1
1 Animals can't talk.
2 Sharks can bite.
3 Children can't drive cars.
4 I can speak English.

2
1 He hates doing homework.
2 He likes eating pizza.
3 He loves listening to music.
4 He doesn't like waiting for the bus.

3
1 is/isn't   4 are
2 aren't   5 Is
3 'm not

4
1 Are you a teenager?
2 Is your school bag red?
3 Are your parents English?
4 Is Facebook your favourite website?
Short answers: students' own answers

5
1 There are
2 There aren't
3 There isn't
4 There are
5 There isn't

Integrated skills

1
1 school bag   5 notebook
2 pencil case   6 board
3 rubber   7 pen
4 poster   8 pencil

2 Students' own answers

3
1 What does 'rubber' mean?
2 Can you write it on the board?
3 How do you say 'estuche' in English?
4 How do you spell 'school bag'?

4
1 (It means) 'goma'.
2 Yes, of course.
3 (It's) 'pencil case'.
4 (It's spelled) s-c-h-o-o-l b-a-g.

5 Students' own answers

UNIT 1

Vocabulary 1

1
1 go to the gym
2 go to a concert
3 play volleyball
4 hang out with your friends
5 surf the internet
6 go shopping
7 go for a run

2
2 c   5 b
3 a   6 d
4 f

3
1 go   4 hang
2 do   5 go for
3 listen to

4
1 sporty   4 shy
2 sociable   5 lazy
3 friendly

5 Students' own answers

Grammar 1

1
1 comes   5 worries
2 does   6 passes
3 has   7 watches
4 buys

2
1 Amelia doesn't take her phone to school.
2 My parents don't like heavy metal music.

T126

3 I don't go swimming every morning.

4 We don't have lessons on Saturdays.

3 **1** Do your mum and dad watch DVDs?

2 Does your best friend have a smartphone?

3 Do your grandparents use the internet?

4 Does your English teacher wear jeans?

4 **1** having   **5** sitting
2 eating   **6** making
3 putting   **7** chatting
4 saying

5 **1** The boy isn't reading a book. He's writing an essay.

2 The girls aren't dancing. They're watching a DVD.

3 The woman isn't eating a sandwich. She's drinking a cup of coffee.

4 The dogs aren't sleeping. They're running around.

6 **1** Are you doing your homework?

2 Is the sun shining?

3 Are your parents working?

4 Is your phone ringing?

Short answers: students' own answers

Vocabulary 2

1

J	H	C	O	O	K	O	S
D	A	I	M	S	I	O	I
R	D	A	N	C	E	B	N
A	R	W	U	X	T	L	G
W	I	P	T	P	M	A	E
E	C	E	R	A	C	T	E
U	T	S	S	D	K	M	I
B	O	P	A	I	N	T	O

2 **1** drive   **5** do
2 tell   **6** play
3 ride   **7** write
4 bake

3 **1** speak   **6** doing
2 play   **7** tell
3 sing   **8** dance
4 act   **9** bake
5 ride

4 Students' own answers

Grammar 2

1 **1** 's playing
2 don't like
3 's driving
4 Are you listening
5 start

2 present simple: always, never, often, once a week, sometimes, usually
present continuous: at the moment, now, today

3 **1** isn't working
2 takes
3 's starting
4 're going
5 don't meet

4 **1** Is Paul playing football at the moment? No, he isn't.
2 Do Tom and Jenny often use their phones? Yes, they do.
3 Is Tessa acting in a play now? Yes, she is.
4 Does David always win chess games? No, he doesn't.

5 Students' own answers

Reading

1 Because she hates being bored.

2 **a** pottery
b t'ai chi
c a skydive

3 **1** fears   **4** skills
2 heights   **5** subway
3 deal with

4 **1** week   **3** isn't
2 few   **4** strangers

5 **1** She's a writer from Pennsylvania, USA.
2 She usually watches DVDs and plays computer games.
3 She wants to try parkour, pottery and t'ai chi.
4 She's learning new skills, and how to deal with some of her biggest fears.

Listening

 **Audioscript, exercises 1, 2 and 3**

Matt: Hello and welcome to Nineteen, the programme that's all about young people. My name's Matt and today I'm in Manchester to find out what you do with your free time. Er … excuse me? Have you got a moment?

Jenny: Hi, sure.

Matt: What's your name?

Jenny: Jenny.

Matt: Do you do any interesting activities, Jenny? And I don't mean surfing the internet …

Jenny: Er … yeah! I like dancing.

Matt: What kind of dancing?

Jenny: I'm learning salsa at the moment. I'm a beginner, but I enjoy it – and it keeps me fit!

Matt: Great, thanks Jenny! Now, here's someone carrying a musical instrument. Excuse me?

Theo: Yes?

Matt: What are you carrying in that bag?

Theo: It's a guitar.

Matt: Right! Do you play?

Theo: No, it's my brother's. It's broken, so I'm just taking it to a shop so they can fix it for him.

Matt: What about you? Do you play anything?

Theo: Well, not music. I play football in the park sometimes!

Matt: Right. OK, thanks for talking to us, er …

Theo: Theo.

Matt: Thanks, Theo. Now let's ask this person … Hi there, we're interviewing people about their activities. Have you got a favourite activity?

Seb: Yes. Food!

Matt: What, eating?

Seb: And cooking!

Matt: What do you like cooking?

Seb: Italian food! I'm Italian, you see. I make amazing pizzas!

Matt: Mmmm! What's your name?

Seb: Seb.

Matt: Thanks Seb. Now back to the studio – and I'm going to hang out a bit more with everyone in Manchester.

1
1 c   3 a
2 b

2
1 a   4 a
2 b   5 b
3 c

3
1 T   4 T
2 S   5 J
3 J

Speaking

4
1 What's your name?
2 What's your date of birth?
3 What's your address?
4 What's your phone number?
5 Have you got an email address?

Writing

5
1 so
2 because
3 because
4 so
5 because
6 so

Progress check

1
1 text messages
2 concert
3 computer game
4 friends
5 DVD
6 run
7 music
8 internet

2
1 bake   4 tells
2 play   5 do
3 rides

3
1 Eleanor doesn't go out every Saturday night.
2 My sister paints beautiful pictures.
3 How many languages do you speak?
4 Colin doesn't like heavy metal music.
5 Do your parents play a musical instrument?

4
1 Are … playing
2 'm watching
3 are doing
4 Is … riding
5 's dancing
6 are … leaving

5
1 spends
2 don't like
3 loves
4 finds
5 gets
6 's looking
7 's coming
8 doesn't know
9 's doing
10 thinks
11 's studying

Extension
1 are you reading
2 never buy
3 think
4 have
5 isn't
6 her
7 is
8 don't
9 goes
10 are going
11 can't
12 always go out
13 are you doing
14 'm reading

UNIT 2

Vocabulary 1

1
1 cookery book
2 detective novel
3 travel guide
4 science fiction novel
5 fairy tale

2
1 adventure story
2 biography
3 comic novel
4 thriller
5 romantic novel
6 historical novel

3
1 book
2 science fiction
3 detective
4 travel guide
5 fairy

4
1 historical novel
2 thriller
3 comic novel
4 adventure story
5 biography

5 Students' own answers

Grammar 1

1
1 said   6 slept
2 started   7 finished
3 came   8 knew
4 did   9 thought
5 carried

2
1 played   3 slept
2 know   4 road

3
1 My dad bought that book one/a week ago.
2 Charlotte wrote a poem two days ago.
3 My sister celebrated her birthday one/a month ago.
4 I read that book two years ago.

4
2 started   8 met
3 didn't have   9 taught
4 lived   10 looked
5 didn't like   11 found
6 didn't have   12 came
7 ran   13 went

5
1 Did Oliver have parents? No, he didn't.
2 Did Oliver like the workhouse? No, he didn't.
3 Did Oliver go to London? Yes, he did.
4 Did Nancy look after Oliver? Yes, she did.

Vocabulary 2

1

C	I	N	V	E	N	T	O	R	P
E	X	P	L	O	R	E	R	E	O
D	N	H	W	M	P	W	D	C	L
A	A	G	T	I	L	X	W	U	I
N	W	R	I	T	E	R	H	E	T
C	L	O	K	N	U	O	T	S	I
E	N	E	Z	R	E	U	O	R	C
R	I	Y	Q	S	P	E	O	V	I
S	Y	M	B	G	S	P	R	F	A
C	O	M	E	D	I	A	N	R	N

2
1. pilot
2. athlete
3. astronaut
4. painter
5. scientist

3
1. writer
2. musician
3. astronaut
4. explorer
5. inventor
6. athlete
7. scientist

4
1. inventor
2. writer
3. comedian
4. politician
5. Students' own answers

Grammar 2

1
1. was
2. was
3. were
4. was
5. Were

2
1. Were Ponce de León and Columbus explorers? Yes, they were.
2. Was the island in the Atlantic Ocean? No, it wasn't.
3. Was the island beautiful? Yes, it was.
4. Were the people unfriendly? No, they weren't.
5. Was Puerto Rico the island's real name? No, it wasn't.

3
1. There was brilliant film on TV last night.
2. There were some dinosaur bones in the museum.
3. There was a Picasso painting for sale on the internet.
4. There were some strange fashions in the past.

4
1. Could … hear
2. could walk
3. Could … send
4. could play
5. couldn't swim

5 Students' own answers

Reading

1 four

2
2. d
3. a
4. g
5. f
6. e
7. c

3
1. a
2. e
3. c
4. b
5. d

4
1. The main character was a young boy called Eragon.
2. He helps his people and saves them from en evil king.
3. People compared him with J.R.R. Tolkien.
4. It had great characters and an exciting plot.
5. He writes for several hours every day, even at the weekend.
6. To get ideas for his books.

Listening

1
2. She studied physics and English.
3. She started to learn how to be an astronaut.
4. She taught physics.
5. She wrote books for children.

2
1. b
2. b
3. b
4. a

3
1. She saw the advert in a student newspaper.
2. She was 32 years old.
3. She taught at Stanford University and the University of California.
4. They were about space and science.

Speaking

4
1. have
2. interesting
3. did you do
4. most
5. glad
6. pity

Writing

5 **1** John Travolta is a famous actor, but he's also a pilot.
2 I often play *CityVille* and I love *Angry Birds* too.
3 I read *Diary of a Wimpy Kid* and my mum also read it.
4 *Twilight* is a novel, but there's a film of it too.
5 I like detective novels and I also like historical novels.

Progress check

1 **1** romantic novel
2 cookery book
3 comic novel
4 travel guide
5 detective novel

2 **1** musician
2 comedian
3 dancer
4 pilot
5 explorer

3 **1** became
2 didn't paint
3 sang
4 didn't go
5 appeared

4 **1** Did Henry Ford invent the car? No, he didn't.
2 Did Galileo discover Jupiter's moons? Yes, he did.
3 Did Leonardo da Vinci come from Spain? No, he didn't.
4 Did Sally Ride die in a space shuttle accident? No, she didn't.

5 **1** James Dean was an actor.
2 My grandparents were fans of the Rolling Stones.
3 I wasn't angry!
4 Were you at the concert?

6 **1** I couldn't walk when I was six months old.
2 Mozart could write music when he was four.
3 Serena and Venus Williams could play tennis when they were six.

4 We couldn't go to the film because there were no tickets left.

Extension

1 didn't like
2 met
3 could design
4 were
5 Jobs'
6 say
7 wasn't
8 his
9 isn't
10 are buying
11 remember
12 could

UNIT 3

Vocabulary 1

1 hailstones
thunder
blizzard
heatwave
warm
damp
dry
cloudy

2 Across: 3 wet 5 rainy
7 windy 8 snowy
Down: 1 foggy 2 stormy
4 sunny 6 icy

3 **1** warm
2 thunder
3 dry
4 sunny
5 hailstones
6 damp
7 blizzard
8 rainy

4 Students' own answers

Grammar 1

1 **1** cooking
2 helping
3 coming
4 getting
5 lying
6 carrying
7 walking
8 enjoying
9 talking

2 **2** were walking
3 was working
4 weren't carrying
5 were getting
6 weren't talking
7 was cooking
8 wasn't helping
9 were lying
10 weren't helping

3 **1** Was Tom wearing warm clothes? Yes, he was.
2 Were Tom and his family staying in a hotel? Yes, they were.
3 Was Tom swimming in the pool? No, he wasn't.
4 Were Tom and his brother watching DVDs? Yes, they were.

4 **1** carefully
2 correct
3 heavily
4 well
5 correct

Vocabulary 2

1 **1** tornado
2 avalanche
3 flood
4 earthquake
5 volcano

2 **1** flood
2 tornado
3 earthquake
4 volcano
5 avalanche

3 **1** famine
2 drought
3 hurricane
4 wildfire
5 landslide

4 **2** volcano
3 earthquake
4 drought
5 landslide
6 Students' own answers

Grammar 2

1 **1** were talking
2 started
3 met
4 was sending
5 flew

2 **1** noticed, were driving
2 were watching, felt
3 began, were skiing
4 heard, was listening
5 was getting, started

3
1 Were you sleeping when the tornado started?
2 Where were you going?
3 What did you do when you saw the tornado?
4 What were other people doing?
5 How long did the tornado last?

4
1 No, I wasn't. I was taking the dog for a walk.
2 I was going to the park.
3 I held on to a tree.
4 They were running away and shouting.
5 It lasted for about 10 minutes.

5 Students' own answers

Reading

1 volcano surfing

2
1	d	4	e
2	a	5	c
3	b		

3
1	VS	4	VS
2	IS	5	IS
3	VS	6	VS

4
1 They climb to the top of the volcano.
2 You can stand or sit on a board.
3 They can travel at 80 km an hour.
4 Ice swimming is common in Russia.
5 He / She went swimming with the Swimming Club.
6 He / She swam for about five minutes.

Listening

07 Audioscript, exercises 1, 2 and 3

Cerys: My name's Cerys and this is my brother Jamie. We're from St Asaph in Wales.
Jamie: Last November, there was some really stormy weather. It was raining hard for days, and the River Elwy got really high. There are two rivers in St Asaph – the River Elwy and the River Clywd. Our street is next to the Elwy.

Cerys: Anyway, one night, at about half past 12, while we were sleeping, a man knocked on our door.
Jamie: Dad answered it. The man said the River Elwy was flooding. But dad didn't think it was too serious, so he didn't wake us up.
Cerys: Big mistake! Jamie Yeah!
Cerys: At about 5am I woke up because I heard a strange sound. I looked downstairs. Water was coming in underneath the front door and the hall was filling up with water.
Jamie: Cerys shouted to mum and dad, and for about an hour, we were all running around in our pyjamas, carrying all the furniture from downstairs up to the bedrooms. Then we waited upstairs. We couldn't get out, because by now the water was about two metres high. At about midday, we were sitting in mum and dad's bedroom, when I saw an orange lifeboat coming up our street.
Cerys: Because our street wasn't a street anymore, it was a river!
Jamie They were firefighters, looking for people trapped inside their houses.
Cerys: We waved, and they helped us climb through the window into the boat. And that's how we got rescued!

1 downstairs, flooding, high, knocked, lifeboat, river, trapped

2
1	c	4	c
2	b	5	a
3	a		

3
1 Their street is next to the River Elwy.
2 The flood happened because there was a lot of rain and the River Elwy flooded.
3 They carried the furniture upstairs to stop it from getting wet.
4 Firefighters helped them climb through the bedroom window and into a lifeboat.

Speaking

4
1	What	4	Why
2	No way	5	When
3	exciting	6	Good luck

Writing

5
1 One day my friend and I decided to go for a bike ride in the countryside.
2 We left early, and soon we were cycling past green fields and forests.
3 Later we stopped and had a picnic by a river. It was beautiful!
4 Then we heard the sound of thunder and saw lightning in the sky.
5 We got back on our bikes quickly, but by then it was starting to rain.
6 We cycled home as fast as we could, but in the end we got very wet.

Progress check

1
1	blizzard	4	foggy
2	hailstones	5	warm
3	lightning		

2
1	volcano	4	landslide
2	wildfire	5	drought
3	flood		

3
1	quietly	4	well
2	safely	5	heavily
3	happily		

4
1 were taking the dog for a walk.
2 was cleaning her bedroom.
3 was studying for a history test.
4 met Lucy.
5 were walking to Adrian's party.

5
1 While we were driving home, we saw a strange light in the sky.
2 When my mum met my dad, she was living in Paris.
3 While I was getting ready for bed, I heard the noise.
4 When the phone rang, Tessa was watching the weather forecast.

Extension

1. do
2. 're doing
3. happens
4. did it happen
5. Were you living
6. were
7. thick
8. was walking
9. couldn't
10. brightly
11. Did the smog last
12. died

UNIT 4

Vocabulary 1

1
1. cave
2. beach
3. ocean
4. waterfalls
5. lake

2 Across: 3 canyon, 5 island,
6 reef, 7 coast, 8 rivers
Down: 1 valley, 2 mountain,
3 cliffs, 4 desert

3
2. Oceans
3. desert
4. beaches
5. reef
6. river
7. Australia

4 Students' own answers

Grammar 1

1

adjective	comparative	superlative
small	smaller	smallest
long	longer	longest
wet	wetter	wettest
easy	easier	easiest
old	older	oldest
expensive	more expensive	most expensive
big	bigger	biggest
good	better	best
bad	worse	worst

2
1. wetter
2. hotter
3. easier
4. bigger
5. more expensive

3
1. … isn't as old as Madonna.
2. … isn't as tiring as running.
3. … isn't as short as the River Thames.
4. … aren't as dangerous as big cities.
5. … aren't as cold as mountains.

4
2. biggest
3. longest
4. most expensive
5. hottest
6. oldest

5
1. Tokyo is hotter than London / colder than Madrid. Tokyo is the most expensive city.
2. Madrid is cheaper / hotter than Tokyo / London. Madrid is the hottest / cheapest city.

Vocabulary 2

1 polar bear, butterfly, rhinoceros, owl, penguin, gorilla

2
1. snake
2. tiger
3. giraffe
4. turtle
5. bee
6. whale
7. crocodile

3
1. penguin
2. gorilla
3. bee
4. snake
5. whale

4 Students' own answers

Grammar 2

1 Singular countable nouns: beach, bird, city, house, person, tree
Plural countable nouns: beaches, birds, cities, houses, people, trees
Uncountable nouns: air, pollution, sand, traffic, water, wildlife

2
1. a
2. a
3. a
4. any
5. a
6. any
7. some
8. any
9. any
10. some
11. an
12. a

3
1. many
2. a lot of
3. much
4. a lot of

4
1. many
2. much
3. many
4. much
Students' own answers

5 Students' own answers

Reading

1 Because he wanted to save the animals in Baghdad Zoo.

2
1. f
2. b
3. a
4. g
5. e
6. c
7. d

3
1. T
2. F
3. T
4. F
5. F
6. F

4
1. Many
2. is
3. they didn't have much food
4. is
5. a lot of the
6. with other people

Listening

Presenter: Hello and welcome to *The world we live in*. Today my guest is Martin Jenkins from Liverpool. Now Martin, you ran in a race last year in the coldest place on Earth. Can you tell me about it?
Martin: Well, it's called the Ice Marathon and it happens every year in Antarctica. It's a normal marathon, so it's about 42 km long. The only difference is that you run on snow and ice!
Presenter: It sounds extremely difficult! How did you prepare for running in the freezing cold?
Martin: Well, I wore two pairs of gloves and three pairs of socks! But the cold isn't the biggest problem. You get warm when you're running, even when the temperature is below zero.
Presenter: So what was the biggest problem?
Martin: The wind. Antarctica is one of the windiest places on Earth. The wind can blow at 300 km an hour! When you're running against wind like that, it really slows you down.
Presenter: I can imagine! Where did the race start?
Martin: It started near the Ellsworth Mountains, several hundred kilometres from the South Pole.

Presenter: Some people probably think you're crazy, running a marathon in the snow and ice in freezing temperatures. Why did you do it?

Martin: I like a challenge! It was also a chance to go to a place that's different from anywhere else on Earth.

Presenter: And did you finish the marathon?

Martin: Yes, I did, but I didn't win!

Presenter: Well, maybe next time …

1 No, he didn't.

2
1. the Ice Marathon
2. Antarctica
3. (about) 42 km
4. snow, ice, very windy
5. the wind

3
1. He ran in the Ice Marathon last year.
2. It happens every year.
3. He wore two pairs of gloves and three pairs of socks.
4. Because you get warm when you're running, even when the temperature is below zero.
5. It started near the Ellsworth Mountains, several hundred kilometres from the South Pole.
6. Because he likes a challenge, and he wanted to go to a place that's different from anywhere else on Earth.

Speaking

4
1. like to
2. a nice idea
3. a better idea
4. 'd rather
5. sounds more fun than

Writing

5
1. That is a very high mountain.
2. The beaches in Greece are white and sandy.
3. We visited an ancient stone castle yesterday.
4. They saw some big lions in the zoo.
5. The forest is dark and scary.

Progress check

1
1	Beach	4	waterfall
2	river	5	Islands
3	mountains		

2
1	Owls	4	polar
2	turtle		bears
3	snake	5	Whales

3
1. healthiest
2. better
3. hottest
4. bigger
5. more dangerous

4
1. water
2. food
3. people
4. information
5. traffic
6. Butterflies
7. beaches

5
1	a	5	some
2	an	6	A lot of
3	some	7	any
4	many	8	much

Extension

1	c	8	c
2	a	9	c
3	c	10	b
4	b	11	a
5	a	12	c
6	b	13	c
7	b	14	b

UNIT 5

Vocabulary 1

1 battery, cure, vaccine, clone, disease, satellite, DNA
The other letters spell: planet

2
1	battery	4	cure
2	satellite	5	clone
3	panels		

3
1	c	3	d
2	b	4	a

You write 'spacecraft' as one word.

4
1. cure
2. clone
3. genetically modified crops
4. spacecraft
5. disease

5 Students' own answers

Grammar 1

1
1. You won't miss the bus.
2. They'll do the washing-up.
3. Mum and Dad won't be angry.
4. I'll tell you a secret.
5. He won't finish his homework.

2
1. He'll travel around the world.
2. He won't work in an office.
3. He won't have a dog.
4. He won't drive a car.
5. He'll fall in love.

3
1. Will everyone speak the same language? No, they won't/Yes, they will.
2. Will people eat meat? Yes, they will.
3. Will machines make life easier? Yes, they will.
4. Will dinosaurs exist? No, they won't.
5. Will people travel around the world? Yes, they will.

4
1. Will you lend me €10? No, I won't.
2. Will Tim have a birthday party? No, he won't.
3. Will we win the game? Yes, we will.
4. Will I like that film? Yes, you will.

5 Students' own answers

Vocabulary 2

1
1	gravity	4	air
2	acid	5	temperature
3	pressure		

2
1 air
2 temperature
3 chemical reaction
4 pressure
5 acid

3
2 liquid
3 gas
4 explosion
5 jug
6 test tube
7 bubbles
8 thermometer

4
1 temperature
2 gravity
3 thermometer
4 bubbles, gas, explosion
5 laboratory
6 acid

5
1 thermometer
2 temperature
3 chemical reaction
4 bubbles
5 test tube
6 acid

Grammar 2

1
1 'll save   4 'll break
2 grow   5 mix
3 'll be

2
1 'll pass
2 heat
3 doesn't rain
4 won't happen
5 hits

3
1 If you switch off your computer, you'll save energy.
2 The teacher will be angry if you don't do your homework.
3 If he eats a lot of chocolate, he won't lose weight.
4 If she doesn't study computer science, she won't get a good job.
5 My mum will save money if she walks to work.

4
1 What will you do if you pass your exams?
2 Will we have fun if we go on holiday?
3 If Jane learns to drive, will she be more independent?
4 If he doesn't have a map, will he find the café?
5 Who will you go with if you go to Jessica's party?

5 Students' own answers

Reading

1 Students' own answers

2 There are at least 20 Castilian Spanish cognates in the text: opinion, planets, habitable, conditions, extreme extremely, rare, atmosphere, exist, million, variable, factors, science, fiction, ocean, Saturn, astronauts, decade, different, oxygen.

3
1 GB   4 GB
2 MR   5 GB
3 MR   6 MR

Listening

11 Audioscript, exercises 1, 2 and 3

Rachel: Wow, this museum is amazing! Look at that spacecraft over there!
Sam: What do you want to do first, Rachel?
Rachel: How about we take the Astronaut Test?
Sam: The Astronaut Test? What's that?
Rachel: It's a test, Sam. To see if you've got the ability to be an astronaut. If we pass, they'll give us a prize!
Sam What prize?
Rachel: Er ... it says here ... a DVD about the Apollo missions to the Moon.
Sam: Oh. What's this here ... The Human Spaceflight Experience.
Rachel: Oh yeah! It's like going on a journey into space. Apparently you really feel like you're flying a spacecraft!
Sam: Cool! Look, it's just over there. If we do the Human

Spaceflight Experience first, we'll have time to do the Astronaut Test after.
Rachel: OK! And after that we'll go to the Space Kitchen.
Sam: The Space Kitchen?
Rachel: Yeah, it sounds fun – you'll love it. They show you how they make the food for astronauts, and you can even taste some!
Sam: Yuck! No thanks! Astronauts only eat dried food out of packets, don't they?
Rachel: No. Now the meals are much better. They can eat spaghetti – and cake! Apparently if we taste all the food, they'll give us a recipe for Space Station cake.
Sam: Space Station cake?
Rachel: It's what the astronauts on the International Space Station eat.
Sam: I bet that will taste delicious.
Rachel: Come on, Sam, how do you know you won't like it if you don't try it?
Sam: OK, OK. Come on then. Let's go!

1 The boy, Sam

2
1 Human Spaceflight Experience
2 Astronaut Test
3 Space Kitchen

3
1 DVD
2 simulated spacecraft flight
3 eat
4 spaghetti and cake
5 instructions for making a Space Station cake

Speaking

4
1 don't   4 How about
2 then   5 could
3 shall   6 let's

Writing

5
1 one   4 In
2 other   5 In
3 Maybe

Progress check

1
1 solar
2 turbines
3 batteries
4 cure
5 diseases
6 planets

2
1. air
2. laboratory
3. explosion
4. liquid
5. test tube
6. thermometer
7. gravity
8. acid

3
1. They won't pass the maths test.
2. What time will you call me tonight?
3. We'll be hungry after the film.
4. Tom won't finish his homework tonight.
5. Will Helen win the game?

4
1. Will computers get smaller?
2. Will Chinese be an international language?
3. Will wars stop?
4. Will the European Union exist?

Short answers: students' own answers

5
1. play, won't pass
2. do, 'll have
3. 're, 'll order
4. won't enjoy, rains
5. loses, won't be

Extension
1. quickly
2. were
3. worst
4. are you
5. were sharing
6. began
7. their
8. Some
9. don't usually tell
10. will talk
11. won't
12. find
13. best
14. will talk
15. many

UNIT 6

Vocabulary 1

1
2. f
3. a
4. e
5. d
6. b

2
1. lay the table
2. do the ironing
3. deliver newspapers
4. clean the windows
5. make the beds

3
1. make
2. washing-up
3. lay
4. pet sit
5. tidying

4
1. washing-up
2. tidy
3. gardening
4. pet sit
5. wash

5 Students' own answers

Grammar 1

1
2. They aren't going to have a drink. They're going to have an ice cream.
3. I'm not going to spend my pocket money. I'm going to save it.
4. We aren't going to phone Tim. We're going to send him a text message.
5. He isn't going to go to bed. He's going to watch a film.

2
2. Is the shop going to close soon? f
3. Are the boys going to miss the bus? c
4. Is Lucy going to go to the party? b
5. Are we going to arrive soon? d
6. Are you going to phone me later? a

3
2. 's going to help
3. 'm going to give
4. Are they going to go
5. 're going to take
6. Are you going to put
7. 's going to be

4
1. 'll
2. 'll
3. 'll
4. is going to
5. 'm going to
6. 'll

5 Vocabulary 2

1

M	G	A	C	O	S	T	O	I	C
E	I	N	X	A	B	R	E	V	O
F	B	O	R	R	O	W	Q	I	L
J	O	E	T	K	O	M	P	O	L
P	C	L	X	R	L	A	S	N	E
U	W	V	L	O	S	E	A	I	C
P	Y	A	U	V	T	C	V	W	T
L	E	N	D	X	B	W	E	I	K
N	A	X	H	O	Y	I	C	O	W
H	L	C	R	M	E	N	U	T	I

2
1. pay
2. buy
3. swap
4. earn
5. spend

3
1. spend
2. buy
3. earn
4. pay
5. swap

4
1. earn
2. borrow
3. save
4. win
5. lend
6. cost
7. collect
8. lose

5 Students' own answers

Grammar 2

1 tomorrow, next week, one day, this summer, soon

2
1. We'll, we
2. I'm, I'll
3. We'll, you
4. saves, he'll
5. I'll, I

3
2. 'll live
3. visit
4. won't cook
5. 'll order
6. won't get
7. doesn't need
8. visit
9. 'll clean

4
1. wouldn't like to eat
2. would like to meet
3. wouldn't like to do
4. would like to visit
5. would like to earn

5
1. Would Matt like to eat sushi? No, he wouldn't.
2. Would Rebecca like to meet me tomorrow? Yes, she would.
3. Would you like to do chores all the time? No, I wouldn't.

4 Would you like to visit us this summer? Yes, we would.

5 Would they like to earn a lot of money one day? Yes, they would.

6 Students' own answers

Reading

1 his mother's

2
1	e	4	c
2	a	5	d
3	f	6	b

3
1	c	4	c
2	b	5	a
3	b	6	b

Listening

 13 Audioscript, exercises 1 and 2

John: Hello and welcome to *Money Matters*, the programme that tells you everything you need to know about money. Now the problem with going shopping is that we usually come home with less money than we started with! But believe it or not, there is actually a way to earn money while you shop! Karen, can you tell us more?

Karen: Yes, John. It sounds too good to be true, doesn't it? But mystery shopping, as it's called, is very popular in the USA and in the UK, and we think it will be a success in Europe too.

John: So what exactly does a mystery shopper have to do?

Karen: Well he or she – for some reason it's usually a she – visits shops, buys something, and gets information about the shops.

John: What kind of information?

Karen: How polite the shop assistants are, if they help you with any problems or questions, that kind of thing.

John: So you pretend to be a customer?

Karen: Yes. The people who work in the shop don't know that you're there to report on them. That's why it's called mystery shopping.

John: So you just go to a shop and buy something?

Karen: Yes, and then you answer some questions about the experience afterwards.

John: I see. And how much do you earn as a mystery shopper?

Karen: Well it's only a part-time job, but you get between 10 and 20 pounds for every shop you report on. You also get money to pay for the product you buy – and you can keep it, too! You can also visit restaurants to report on them.

John: You mean earn money by writing a review of the restaurant?

Karen: Yes. You get a free meal too, of course!

John: And do you need any special qualifications for this kind of work?

Karen: Well, there's a lot of talking involved so you have to be able to communicate well. It's also important to be good at writing.

John: Why's that?

Karen: Because you have to complete a long questionnaire after each visit.

John: I see. Well, for any of our listeners interested in becoming mystery shoppers – or diners – you can get more information online. Now it's time for our next song...

1 the USA and the UK

2
2 £20
3 restaurants
4 meal
5 questionnaire
6 writing

3
1	T	3	F
2	F	4	T

Speaking

4
1	go	3	giving
2	can I	4	buy

Writing

5
1	He	6	his
2	It	7	They
3	him	8	it
4	he	9	him
5	her	10	them

Progress check

1
1 walks
2 make
3 washing-up
4 lay
5 windows
6 gardening
7 tidy
8 ironing
9 wash
10 newspapers

2
1	swap	4	lend
2	cost	5	save
3	pay for	6	earn

3
1 're going to go
2 are you going to spend
3 's going to buy
4 isn't going to wash
5 'm not going to pass
6 Is … going to get

4
1 'll
2 'll
3 Are...going to
4 'll

5
1 We'll go to the supermarket when we finish lunch.
2 Will you take the dog for a walk when you get home?
3 When the neighbours go on holiday, Billy will pet sit for their cat.
4 Mum and Dad won't be happy when they see the broken window!

6
1 Mum and Dad would like to go to an expensive restaurant.
2 My English teacher wouldn't like to teach maths.
3 I'd like to get more pocket money.
4 Adam wouldn't like to have a pet dog.
5 Would you like to be famous?

Extension

1	aren't	6	to collect
2	're collecting	7	took
3	are going to	8	Their
4	largest	9	will do
5	collect	10	some
		11	isn't going
		12	easy

UNIT 7

Vocabulary 1

1
1. horse and carriage
2. ship
3. the Underground
4. coach
5. hot-air balloon
6. caravan

2 Across: 3 helicopter, 6 bicycle, 7 ferry
Down: 1 plane, 2 motorbike, 4 lorry, 5 yacht

3
1. caravan
2. yacht
3. tram
4. Helicopters
5. by ship
6. bicycles

4 land: horse and carriage, the underground coach, caravan, bicycle, motorbike, lorry
sea: ship, ferry, yacht air: hot-air balloon, helicopter, plane

5 Students' own answers

Grammar 1

1

verb	past participle
travel	travelled
ride	ridden
go	gone
crash	crashed
win	won
fly	flown
break	broken
buy	bought

2
1. has
2. haven't
3. have
4. has
5. hasn't
6. haven't

3
1. 've ridden
2. 's won
3. has crashed
4. 've flown
5. 's broken

4
1. I haven't ridden a motorbike.
2. He hasn't won the Tour de France.
3. A plane hasn't crashed in Russia.
4. They haven't flown in a hot-air balloon.
5. She hasn't broken a world record.

5
1. been
2. gone
3. gone
4. gone
5. been

6 Students' own answers

Vocabulary 2

1 crash, arrive, take off, land, follow, push, carry
The other letters spell: fall

2
1. climb
2. cross
3. pull
4. fly
5. sail

3
1. land
2. crash
3. arrive
4. takes off
5. Follow

4
1. follow
2. flew, took off
3. crossed
4. sailed
5. arrives

5 Students' own answers

Grammar 2

1
2. Have
3. Has
4. Have
5. Has
6. Has

2
a. 5
b. 4
c. 1
d. 2
e. 6
f. 3

3
2. Have you put up
3. Have you eaten
4. Has Gary phoned
5. Have they phoned
6. Has he remembered

4
1. Has a friend ever told you a secret?
2. Have your parents ever lived abroad?
3. Has a film ever made you cry?
4. Have your friends ever bought you a present?
5. Have you ever ridden a camel?
6. Has your teacher ever given you a really difficult test?

Short answers: students' own answers

5 Students' own answers

Reading

1 c

2
1. b
2. c
3. d
4. a

3
1. F
2. F
3. T
4. F
5. F

4
1. Rolf and Magnus are Danish soldiers. They patrol the coast of Greenland.
2. There's a lot of ice and snow and it's very cold, −31°C.
3. Because dogs don't break down in the cold. If your vehicle stops, you'll die!
4. They make a special noise to warn them if a polar bear is near.
5. He fell off the sledge and cut his leg badly.
6. It's when a bit of your skin freezes and dies.

Listening

15 Audioscript, exercises 1, 2 and 3

David: Hi, can I sit here?

Emily: Sure, go ahead. Are you travelling on your own?

David: No, my family's sitting over there. We're going on holiday to Paris.

Emily: Oh, cool. I'm going to stay with my aunt in Nantes. So … have you travelled on the Eurostar before?

David: No, I've never been to France! I guess you've been on it a lot.

Emily: Yes, I come here every summer.

David: It's brilliant isn't it? It's so fast!

Emily: I know! It goes about 200 kilometres an hour. Much faster than the ferry!

David: Wow! I've never crossed the Channel, but I've been on the ferry to Ireland. I got seasick! Going on a train is much nicer.

Emily: I always get seasick when I sail across the Channel! I've flown to France a lot too, but I prefer the Eurostar.

David: I know what you mean. Going through airports takes a long time. This is great – we got on the train at St Pancras station at quarter to twelve, we left at twelve o' clock, and we're in the tunnel already!

Emily: So have you flown to many countries?

David: A few. We've been to Mallorca and Italy by plane, and … one year we went to Germany too.

Emily: And … here we are – we're out of the tunnel. Hello France!

David: Wow! That was quick. How long were we in the tunnel?

Emily: Just 20 minutes, I think.

David: Next stop, Paris – Gare du Nord! What time does the train arrive?

Emily: Er … at 2.15.

David: Oh yeah, it's one o' clock already. Do you want to get some lunch from the buffet car? I'm really hungry.

Emily: Me too, I haven't eaten all morning. Let's go! I'm Emily, by the way.

David: And my name's David!

1 airports, buffet car, ferry, plane, seasick, station, stop, tunnel

2
1 two hours and 15 minutes
2 200
3 St Pancras
4 Paris
5 20

3
1 a   3 b
2 c   4 b

Speaking

4
1 Could   4 time
2 change   5 get
3 much

Writing

5
1 Coach journeys are a bit uncomfortable.
2 That girl is really pretty.
3 This map is a bit old.
4 New York is a really big city.
5 It's really warm today.

Progress check

1
1 bicycle   4 caravan
2 carriage   5 Underground
3 ship   6 yacht

2
1 fly   5 arrive
2 take off   6 carry
3 land   7 pull
4 drive

3
1 've taken
2 hasn't sent
3 has run
4 haven't been

4
1 Have Mum and Dad taken the dog for a walk? Yes, they have.
2 Has Anna ridden a horse? No, she hasn't.
3 Has Max fallen off his bicycle? Yes, he has.
4 Have you slept in a tent? No, I haven't.

5
1 We've never been to Scotland.
2 Have you ever seen a shark?
3 Katie has never met a famous person.
4 Has Grandma ever played a computer game?

Extension
1 are travelling
2 drive
3 better
4 left
5 Did you know
6 going to
7 were walking
8 ever seen
9 noisy
10 'll tell
11 'm not
12 Have

UNIT 8

Vocabulary 1

1

A	T	C	C	O	A	C	H	L	I
W	O	T	U	K	M	A	T	C	H
L	U	Z	N	C	D	P	F	P	X
R	R	S	T	A	D	I	U	M	O
B	N	X	R	E	Q	D	O	B	G
Y	A	Z	A	N	L	Y	Q	A	O
O	M	E	R	V	R	W	O	M	A
V	E	W	A	L	E	I	J	C	L
Q	N	R	C	I	N	O	R	U	B
I	T	T	E	H	T	E	A	M	R

2
1 loser   4 opponents
2 supporter   5 winner
3 champion   6 stadium

3
1 play   5 go
2 do   6 do
3 go   7 play
4 play

4
1 team   4 loser
2 captain   5 stadium
3 supporter

5
1 tournament
2 match
3 coach
4 race
5 opponent

Grammar 1

1

since	for
last week	a few days
Christmas	a long time
2013	many years
	three weeks

2
1 for   4 for
2 since   5 since
3 since

3
1 We've lived here for many years.
2 Jack hasn't seen his uncle since 2013.
3 I haven't eaten chocolate for three weeks.
4 Isabel has been at this school since Christmas.
5 My parents have been married for a long time.

T138

4
  1 since her birthday
  2 for two hours
  3 since 1966
  4 for a long time
  5 since January

5
  1 How long has he been a professional cyclist?
  2 How long have his friends called him 'Wiggo'?
  3 How long has he supported Liverpool Football Club?
  4 How long have he and his family lived near Manchester?

Vocabulary 2

1 put, touch, walk, meet, drop, cross

2
1	spill	4	carry
2	scratch	5	break
3	open		

3
1	touch	4	scratch
2	drop	5	put
3	spill	6	open

4
1	cross	4	drop
2	put	5	pick
3	touch		

5 Students' own answers

Grammar 2

1

infinitive	past simple	past participle
get	got	got
make	made	made
be	was / were	been
go	went	gone
say	said	said
win	won	won
want	wanted	wanted

2
1	gone	4	been
2	won	5	break
3	get		

3
  1 Have you seen
  2 broke
  3 Did Isaac win
  4 've wanted
  5 've lived
  6 got

4
  2 've had
  3 happened
  4 broke
  5 has gone
  6 died
  7 lost
  8 stole
  9 Did you leave
 10 've just found

5 Students' own answers

Reading 1

1 They wear leather sandals.

2
1	c	5	g
2	e	6	f
3	d	7	b
4	a		

3
  1 F 'They're from Mexico …'
  2 T '… running is part of their everyday lives.'
  3 F '… they don't often get injuries!'
  4 T 'For them, a normal marathon of 42 km is too short!'
  5 F '… the Leadville Run, a 160 km race …'
  6 T '… a medicine man gives the runners a special drink to make them stronger …'

4
  1 The Tarahumara live without electricity and running water.
  2 Because they live in an area with a lot of mountains, so running is the quickest way to travel.
  3 They don't eat high-energy food, and they don't wear expensive trainers.
  4 They drink a special drink from a medicine man.

Listening

 **Audioscript, exercises 1, 2 and 3**

Presenter: Welcome to *Sports World*. This is Sal Brewley. She's only 14, but she's a British junior golfer and she's just won the under-16 Girls' Tournament. Hi, Sal!

Sal: Hi!

Presenter: A lot of people think golf is a sport for older men. Is that true?

Sal: No, things have changed! Now there are a lot of young women players.

Presenter: Why did you start playing? Did your parents play it?

Sal: No, my parents don't play. But when I was young we lived next to a golf course. I saw other people playing, so I asked my parents for lessons.

Presenter: How old were you when you started playing?

Sal: Eight. And I've loved it since then!

Presenter: What do your parents think of your success?

Sal: They're happy that I've found a sport that I love, but they don't let me play golf all day - I have to do my school work too!

Presenter: Do you go to a normal school?

Sal: Yes. Some junior golfers don't go to school, they have tutors to teach them at home. But I'd hate that.

Presenter: Why?

Sal: Because I love seeing my friends every day!

Presenter: Is golf good exercise?

Sal: Definitely. Golf courses are very big and I usually walk about ten kilometers during a game.

Presenter: Wow! What are your ambitions, Sal?

Sal: My dream is to be on the British women's golf team in the 2016 Olympics. Golf hasn't been an Olympic sport since 1904, so I'm really happy it's going to be in the 2016 games!

1
1   1 c   3 b
     2 a

2
1   1 T   4 T
     2 F   5 F
     3 T

3
1 Sal is from the UK.
2 She does her school work.
3 She loves seeing her friends there.
4 It's good exercise because golf courses are very big and Sal usually walks about 10 km during a game.
5 Her dream is to be on the British women's golf team in the 2016 Olympic Games.

Speaking

4
1 What do you want to do tomorrow?
2 I'm not sure. Shall we go to the cinema?
3 OK … but I don't think there are any good films at the moment.
4 So let's go swimming then.
5 Yeah, that sounds fun. What time shall we meet?
6 Twelve o'clock?
7 OK, twelve o'clock is fine. Where shall we meet?
8 Do you want a lift? My mum can take us in the car.
9 No, it's fine thanks. I'll probably walk.
10 OK. I'll see you outside the swimming pool.
11 Great. See you tomorrow!

Writing

5
1 surprised
2 annoyed
3 disappointed
4 bored
5 embarrassed
6 happy

Progress check

1
1 supporter   4 winner
2 stadium   5 loser
3 coach   6 captain

2
1 scratch   4 open
2 touch   5 drop
3 spill   6 carry

3
1 I've spoken English for four years.
2 It hasn't rained since Tuesday.
3 I've had my dog for eight years.
4 She hasn't played a computer game since January.
5 My football team hasn't won a match for a month.
6 We haven't been to London since 2010.

4
1 How long have you had that coat?
    I've just bought it.
2 How long has James spoken English?
    He's just started to learn.
3 How long have you lived in Santander?
    We've just moved here.
4 How long has Marta played chess?
    She's just finished her first game!
5 How long have you been here?
    I've just arrived!

5
1 's wanted
2 started
3 hasn't stopped
4 's won
5 took
6 became
7 's spent

Extension

1 've lost
2 was walking
3 bought
4 've had
5 always wear
6 'm going to
7 don't
8 'll lose
9 any
10 luckiest
11 haven't lost
12 'll win

UNIT 9

Vocabulary 1

1 Across: 4 health, 5 depression
Down: 1 social life, 2 diet, 3 vegetarian

2
1 stress
2 arguments
3 relationship
4 Bullying
5 appearance

3
1 depression
2 vegetarian
3 stress
4 health
5 arguments

4 Students' own answers

Grammar 1

1
1 should
2 shouldn't
3 should
4 shouldn't
5 shouldn't

2
1 Should they eat lots of chocolate?
    No, they shouldn't.
2 Should I lend Jim some money?
    No, you shouldn't.
3 Should we have a party?
    Yes, you / we should.
4 Should Isabel lie to her mum?
    No, she shouldn't.
5 Should I eat more fruit?
    Yes, you should.

3
1 mustn't
2 mustn't
3 mustn't
4 must
5 mustn't

4
1 mustn't walk
2 must put
3 mustn't drink
4 must wear
5 mustn't use

5 Students' own answers

Vocabulary 2

1 1 toothache   4 cough
   2 backache   5 cold
   3 headache

2 2 bee sting
   3 eye strain
   4 sunburn
   5 mosquito bite
   6 stomach ache
You write 'earache' and 'sunburn' as one word.

3 1 sunburn   4 cold
   2 backache   5 toothache
   3 eye strain

4 Students' own answers

Grammar 2

1 1 'm doing   3 happened
   2 doesn't go   4 were sitting

2 1 'll have
   2 'm going to go
   3 will find
   4 won't get

3 1 taken   3 I've
   2 broke   4 ~~has~~ discovered

4 2 Will you call me later?
   3 Do they always go to the beach in the summer?
   4 How long has Miriam had toothache?
   5 What were you doing at eight o'clock yesterday?
   6 What are you going to study at university?
   7 How did Sam break his leg?

5 a 3   e 4
   b 1   f 6
   c 7   g 2
   d 5

6 2 Yes, I will.
   3 No, they don't.
   4 She's had toothache for three days.
   5 I was doing my homework.
   6 I'm going to study medicine.
   7 He fell off his bike.

Reading

1 b

2 1 b   4 a
   2 e   5 c
   3 d

3 1 a   3 b
   2 b   4 a

4 1 Strong wine, fresh fruit and vegetables are part of the traditional Ikarian diet.
   2 They walk everywhere (Ikaria has a lot of mountains), and they do a lot of gardening.
   3 It probably made lifestyle and diet more modern, e.g. people had more stress, ate less healthily, used cars more, got up earlier, didn't have an afternoon nap, etc.
   4 One piece of advice is about diet (4), and four pieces of advice are about lifestyle (1, 2, 3, 5).

Listening

1 2 painful
   3 online
   4 symptoms
   5 click
   6 swelling redness
   8 horsefly

2 1 11.30pm
   2 the park
   3 Oscar's
   4 big
   5 put some cream on the bites

3 1 F   4 F
   2 F   5 T
   3 T

Speaking

4 1 matter   4 should
   2 do   5 don't
   3 painful   6 feel

Writing

5 2 We're having
   3 We're staying
   4 I went
   5 was freezing
   6 I'm getting
   7 we are going
   8 doesn't think

Progress check

1
1 relationship
2 exercise
3 diet
4 depression
5 social life
6 stress

2
1 sunburn
2 sting
3 strain
4 cough
5 toothache
6 cold
7 backache

3
1 Should she go on a sailing holiday?
No, she shouldn't.
2 Should he tell his parents?
Yes, he should.
3 Should they eat ice cream every day?
No, they shouldn't.
4 Should we drink some water?
Yes, you should.

4
1 must come
2 must do
3 mustn't go
4 must wear
5 mustn't use

5
1 had
2 were eating
3 'll give
4 known
5 is

Extension
1 'm going to go
2 haven't had
3 ever been
4 was
5 was climbing
6 mustn't
7 was
8 better
9 healthily
10 eat
11 a
12 win

GRAMMAR EXERCISES

STARTER UNIT

1
1 How often
2 Why
3 When
4 Who
5 What
6 How

2
1 his
2 their
3 its
4 her
5 my

3
1 Jack's hair is brown
2 Charles' parents are from London.
3 My teachers' names are Ms Bow and Mr Jones.
4 My friend's eyes are unusual. She's got one blue eye and one brown one.

4
1 I can do this exercise, it's easy.
2 They can't speak Russian. It's difficult!
3 We can't swim ten kilometres. It's too far!
4 Her sisters can bake cakes. They are delicious.
5 She can go to the cinema. Her mum says yes.

5
1 Can Lucy dance? Yes, she can.
2 Can Mark and Paula speak French? Yes, they can.
3 Can Lucy speak French? No, she can't.
4 Can Simon dance? Yes, he can.
5 Can Mark and Paula swim? Yes, they can.

6
1 They aren't old, they're young.
2 He's in Bath, he isn't here.
3 I'm happy, I'm not sad.
4 You're from Spain, you aren't from England.

UNIT 1

1
1 doesn't wear
2 don't go
3 listen
4 don't belong
5 works

2
1 Does your sister chat online? Yes, she does.
2 Do your friends play computer games? Yes, they do.
3 Does your uncle go to concerts? No, he doesn't.
4 Do you ever buy DVDs? Yes, I do.
5 Do your classmates watch a lot of films? No, they don't.

3
1 They aren't doing urban sports. They're playing games.
2 I'm making a lot of friends. I'm having a great time.
3 She is studying photography. She's taking lots of photos.
4 We're speaking English. We aren't speaking French.
5 I'm not chatting online at the moment.

4
1 Are you going to the gym now? Yes, I am.
2 Are you feeling well? No, I'm not.
3 Is your sister doing her homework? Yes, she is.
4 Are your classmates having a party? No, they aren't.
5 Am I wearing trainers? No, I'm not.
6 Is your friend riding a motorbike? Yes, he / she is.

5
1 often go
2 have
3 is playing
4 sends
5 are feeling

6
1 visit
2 are telling
3 am painting
4 bakes
5 are doing

7
1 They don't often go to the cinema.
2 My best friend plays tennis every week.
3 They are sending text messages now.
4 My dad never sings in the shower.

UNIT 2

1
1 read
2 had
3 found
4 arrived
5 bought

2
1 My classmate didn't write a book last year.
2 My teacher didn't invent a new computer.
3 We didn't send an email a few minutes ago.
4 I didn't become famous last year.

3
1 When did Picasso paint *Guernica?*
2 Who did you see at the concert?
3 What did Mark Zuckerberg invent?
4 How often did they play football last year?

4
1 last week
2 two weeks ago
3 yesterday
4 last month
5 last summer

5
1 was   4 wasn't
2 weren't   5 weren't
3 were   6 was

6
1 Was it hot yesterday?
2 Where was Shakespeare from?
3 Was he at school last week?
4 Were you tired last night?
5 Why were your friends happy?

7
1 could speak
2 couldn't swim
3 could ride
4 couldn't make
5 couldn't perform

UNIT 3

1
1 were playing
2 was watching
3 was walking
4 were listening
5 were having

2
1 We weren't winning the match.
2 I wasn't feeling well.
3 My friends weren't staying at a campsite.
4 You weren't walking very fast.

5 My teacher wasn't smiling.
6 Andy wasn't sitting next to Jay.

3
1 Was Sophie watching TV at 5pm?
2 Were you studying yesterday morning?
3 Was he sleeping at 6am?
4 Were John and Andrew playing tennis at 4 o'clock yesterday?
5 Was it raining heavily an hour ago?

4

regular (-ly)	regular (-ily)	irregular
brightly	easily	well
warmly	heavily	

5
1 fell   4 were
2 was   doing
  working   5 woke
3 had

6
1 while   4 when
2 While   5 while
3 When

7
1 Lisa was studying in her bedroom.
2 We weren't feeling tired.
3 What were you doing yesterday at 6pm?
4 Were you watching TV when I phoned you?
5 You weren't dancing in the disco at 2am.

UNIT 4

1
1 heavy, heavier, the heaviest
2 rich, richer, the richest
3 busy, busier, the busiest
4 big, bigger, the biggest
5 dangerous, more dangerous, the most dangerous
6 intelligent, more intelligent, the most intelligent
7 difficult, more difficult, the most difficult

8 good, better, the best
9 bad, worse, the worst
10 far, further, the furthest

2
1 faster
2 more intelligent
3 busier
4 heavier
5 bigger
6 worse

3
1 Humans aren't as fast as ostriches.
2 Crocodiles aren't as intelligent as monkeys.
3 The train station isn't as busy as the bus station.
4 Snakes aren't as heavy as whales.
5 A penguin isn't as big as an elephant.
6 Water isn't as bad for you as cola.

4
1 London is the biggest city in the UK.
2 We are the best students in our school.
3 The Grand Canyon is the most beautiful place in the USA.
4 What is the most expensive city in the world?
5 My cousin is the worst singer in our family.
6 Kate is the most interesting person I know.

5
1 any   5 How much
2 How many   6 a
3 some   7 a lot of
4 any

6
1 a lot of   4 a lot of
2 isn't much   5 isn't much
3 not many

UNIT 5

1
1 will leave   4 will play
2 will get   5 will eat
3 will feel   6 will study

2
1 will work   4 won't fail
2 won't go   5 will like
3 will travel   6 will be

3
1 Will Tom work as a police officer?   Yes, he will.
2 Will Jess become an engineer?   Yes, she will.
3 Will Fred and Julia ride a scooter?   No, they won't. They will ride a bicycle.
4 Will Tom live in Hollywood? No, he won't. He will live in London.
5 Will Fred and Julia live in Paris?   No, they won't. They will live in Hollywood.

4
1 Our teacher will not be happy if we don't do our homework.
2 If the sun shines, we'll go to the beach.
3 If he doesn't come home soon, I'll be worried.
4 We'll take a plane if we go to New York.
5 I won't have a good time if my friends aren't at the party.

5
1 Mum will be angry if my brother doesn't phone her.
2 If Louise arrives late, she'll miss the start of the film.
3 If we sell our house, we'll move to a bigger one.
4 I'll stay at home tomorrow if it rains.
5 If they don't buy tickets, they won't be able to go to the concert.

UNIT 6

1
1 'm going to design
2 's going to live
3 're going to be
4 are going to have
5 's going to finish

2
1 We aren't going to meet outside the cinema. / We're not going to meet outside the cinema.
2 Lizzie isn't going to phone me later. / Lizzie's not going to phone me later.
3 My friends aren't going to study Chinese.
4 You aren't going to be late. / You're not going to be late.
5 I'm not going to babysit for my cousins tomorrow.

3
1 Is your brother going to play the piano in the concert?
2 Are you going to miss school tomorrow?
3 Is Maria going to do the washing-up?
4 Are your parents going to buy a new car?
5 Are we going to earn money this summer?
6 Am I going to tidy my room?

4
1 will help   4 will
2 will, will   5 am not
3 am going to   going to

5
1 b   4 a
2 a   5 b
3 c

6
1 would like to travel
2 wouldn't like to be
3 would like to work
4 wouldn't like to ride
5 wouldn't like to play
6 would like to buy

UNIT 7

1
1 stop, stopped R
2 play, played R
3 fly, flown I
4 open, opened R
5 have, had I
6 choose, chosen I
7 read, read I
8 travel, travelled R

2
1 My sister has promised to take me to the concert.
2 My uncle and aunt have flown a hot-air balloon.
3 I have met several famous people.
4 We have had fish for lunch.
5 They have played this computer game before.

3
1 My uncle hasn't sailed around the world alone.
2 I haven't finished this exercise.
3 My friend Dan hasn't bought a new phone.
4 We haven't been to a big city before.
5 My neighbours haven't moved to London.
6 We haven't visited a museum today.
7 Linda hasn't done very well in her exam.

4
1 Has your mum ever tried fly fishing?   No she hasn't. / Yes, she has.
2 Have you ever visited Paris?   Yes, I have. / No, I haven't.
3 Has your dad ever played video games?   Yes, he has. / No, he hasn't.
4 Have your parents ever driven a horse and carriage?   Yes, they have. / No, they haven't.
5 Have I ever met your cousin?   Yes, you have. / No, you haven't.
6 Have your friends ever stayed in New York?   Yes, they have. / No, they haven't.

5
1 ever   4 never
2 never   5 ever
3 ever

6
1 I have eaten all the biscuits.
2 Have you ever swum in the sea?
3 She hasn't finished her dinner.
4 Have you ever visited Paris?

UNIT 8

1

for	since
three years	2005
a few minutes	last week
hours	6pm
a long time	January
nine months	

2
1 for 4 for
2 since 5 for
3 since

3
1 How long has Dan had a headache? He's had a headache for an hour.
2 How long have you had your dog? We've had our dog since August.
3 How long have people believed in fairies? People have believed in fairies for a long time.
4 How long have Spaniards kept their traditions? They have kept their traditions for many years.
5 How long have you been the captain of the team? I've been the captain of the team since last year.
6 How long have Sue's parents been married? They've been married for twenty years.

4
1 have tried 4 was
2 have been 5 had
3 saw 6 have been

5
1 rained 5 haven't
2 gave tried
3 have taken 6 was
4 didn't come

6
2 have visited
3 did (you) go
4 went
5 have (your aunt and uncle) lived
6 Did (you) have
7 have (never) had

UNIT 9

1
1 shouldn't 4 shouldn't
2 should 5 shouldn't
3 should

2
1 mustn't 4 mustn't
2 must 5 must
3 must

3
1 My teacher uses a CD in class twice a week.
2 Sam is listening to music at the moment.
3 We aren't working today.
4 My dad doesn't work on Monday mornings.
5 Millions of people visit London every year.

4
1 was sitting
2 studied
3 rang
4 were walking
5 have studied, started
6 visited

5
1 a 4 b
2 b
3 c

6
1 is riding
2 was sitting
3 are getting
4 has been
5 were making
6 will be

VOCABULARY EXTENSION

UNIT 1

2
1 charts
2 solo artist
3 album
4 tribute band

3
1 lyrics
2 singles
3 singer-songwriter
4 number one
5 rhythm
6 hit
7 tune

UNIT 2

2
1 scene 4 lighting
2 special 5 stage
effects 6 character
3 sound

3
1 stage 5 scene
2 narrator 6 sequel
3 ending 7 plot
4 synopsis 8 trilogy

4
2 sequel 6 special
3 narrator effects
4 character 7 ending
5 plot

UNIT 3

2
1 deforestation
2 genetic engineering
3 forest fire
4 toxic emissions
5 oil spill
6 traffic jam

3
2 Global warming
3 Climate change
4 endangered animals
5 forest fire
6 overpopulation
7 deforestation
8 traffic jams
9 toxic emissions

UNIT 4

2
1 pyramid 5 temple
2 cathedral 6 art gallery
3 market 7 palace
4 national 8 ruin
park

3
1 palace 4 cathedral
2 pyramids 5 tomb
3 museums 6 market

4
2 temples 4 tomb
3 market 5 ruins

UNIT 5

2
1 the solar system
2 star
3 asteroid
4 comet
5 black hole
6 alien

7 satellite
8 spacesuit
9 spaceship
10 space station
(extra words: galaxy,
astronomer)

3 1 solar   5 astronomer
    system   6 star
    2 satellites   7 comet
    3 asteroids   8 black hole
    4 galaxy

4 1 spaceship   4 galaxy
    2 alien   5 space
    3 satellite   station

UNIT 6

2 1 wallet
    2 receipt
    3 note
    4 coin
    5 cash machine
    6 credit card
    7 PIN
    8 online shopping
    9 window shopping
    10 sales
    11 purse
    12 change

3 1 PIN, cash machine
    2 change
    3 coins, notes, wallet
    4 sales
    5 window shopping

4 1 receipt   6 PIN
    2 change   7 sales
    3 online   8 purse
      shopping   9 window
    4 credit card   shopping
    5 cash
      machine

UNIT 7

2 1 check in
    2 relax on the beach
    3 wear sun cream
    4 pack / unpack a case
    5 buy souvenirs
    6 exchange currency

3 1 go sightseeing
    2 check in
    3 catch a flight
    4 try local food
    5 unpack a case
    6 book a holiday

4 2 go sightseeing
    3 take a day trip
    4 book a holiday
    5 pack (a case)
    6 check in
    7 exchange currency
    8 souvenirs
    9 Send postcards
    10 try local food
    11 wear sun cream

UNIT 8

2 1 support
    2 get a trophy
    3 win a medal
    4 be in a team
    5 win, compete in a
      championship, break a record
    6 score a goal

3 1 beat
    2 compete in a championship
    3 got a trophy
    4 are in the semi-final
    5 scored a goal
    6 drew
    7 broke a record

4 2 beat   4 supported
    3 medals   5 won

UNIT 9

2 b split up
    c get married
    d hang out together
    e fall in love
    f fall out with

3

romantic relationships	friendships and romantic relationships
go on a date	get to know someone
ask someone out	
get together	fall out with
fall in love	hang out together
split up	get on with someone
go out with	
get married	share interests

4 2 fallen out   5 asked
    3 get on   6 date
    4 share ...   7 out with
      interests   8 in love

INTEGRATED SKILLS

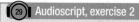

UNIT 1

1 1 F   2 T   3 T   4 F   5 F

🔊 29 Audioscript, exercise 2

Ellen: Hi Mark, how's it going?

Mark: Fine. What's new?

Ellen: Listen, I've just seen a great website – they've got an interesting course.

Mark: Oh yeah? What's it for?

Ellen: It's for teenagers who love music. It's this summer.

Mark: Summer? I don't want to study in summer!

Ellen: But you love music! Anyway, it's not about studying, it's just your kind of thing.

Mark: So what kind of thing is it?

Ellen: You learn about writing songs and about studios.

Mark: Really? That sounds great!

Ellen: Yeah, and you learn all about using different apps connected to music.

Mark: Apps for music? Brilliant! I don't know much about music apps.

Ellen: Yeah, and not only that. I'm looking at the website and one of their tutors is a famous musician.

Mark: Oh wow! Tell me the website and I'll have a look now!

2 1 Mark doesn't want to study in summer.
    2 On the course you learn about writing songs.
    3 Mark doesn't know much about music apps.
    4 One of the tutors on the course is a famous musician.

3 2 your name
    3 do you live
    4 It's 27th April 2000.
    5 spell that for me
    6 It's 07789 563402.
    7 You're welcome.

UNIT 2

1
1 Two
2 The Viking army attacked York in 866.
3 Huge rats
4 Teenagers and adults
5 By booking online

31 Audioscript, exercise 2

Sylvia: How was Edinburgh? Did you have a good time?
Jake: Yeah, I did. We went to Edinburgh Castle and we went on a ghost tour. It was fun.
Sylvia: Yeah? Why was it fun?
Jake: Well, the ghost tour wasn't really scary, but the actors were very funny.
Sylvia: So what did you like best?
Jake: I really liked the Castle … but I enjoyed the Camera Obscura most. It's a kind of big camera and you can see images of the city. It's a great way to learn, see the city and learn about its history. The guide there was brilliant. He told lots of really good stories about Edinburgh.
Sylvia: It sounds interesting. I'm glad you enjoyed it!

2
1 wasn't
2 the Camera Obscura
3 the city
4 told lots of good stories

3
2 went to the Creepy Caves
3 was it so much fun
4 were actors
5 enjoy most
6 were the best
7 quite scary

UNIT 3

1
1 They had to spend one night at sea.
2 Because there was a storm.
3 Because the boat was moving a lot.
4 They didn't have anything to eat.

33 Audioscript, exercise 2

Danny: Hi, Sophie?
Sophie: Yes, it's me … how are you Danny?
Danny: I'm OK, but …
Sophie: You don't sound OK. What happened?
Danny: Well, my dad was in a car accident.
Sophie: Oh no! That's terrible news! Is he OK?
Danny: Luckily he's fine. He had to go to hospital because he hurt his arm, but he's coming home this afternoon.
Sophie: I'm really pleased to hear he's OK. When did it happen?
Danny: Yesterday evening.
Sophie: Where?
Danny: He was driving on the M62 motorway … There was a blizzard and a car in front of him crashed. My dad's car hit his. Luckily, my dad was going very slowly.
Sophie: I can't believe it, it's awful, but I'm really glad your dad is OK.
Danny: Yes, me too. Are you busy tomorrow?
Sophie: No, let's meet at the café.
Danny: OK, see you there at 11 o'clock.

2
1 arm   3 blizzard
2 evening 4 café

3
2 What happened
3 When was that
4 can't believe
5 really pleased
6 Definitely

UNIT 4

1
1 Next month
2 Pick up litter, plant trees and give out information
3 They should enjoy working as part of a team
4 between 14-20 years old

35 Audioscript, exercise 2

Man: Hello. How can I help you?
Jim: Hi. I'd like to sign up for volunteering during the summer holidays.
Man: Great! Do you want to help young children learn to read?
Jim: Well, it's a nice idea, but I'd like to work with other teenagers. I don't know much about young children!
Man: OK. How about giving teenagers help with maths? We've got lots of young people who have problems understanding maths.
Jim: Maths? I don't like maths … I don't mind helping teenagers with problems but I don't really want to give classes. Could I help with organizing the trips? I know a lot about the local area.
Man: Sure, maybe that's a better idea for you. You can help to organize the trip to a theme park and there's a trip to the local sports centre too.
Jim: Thanks! That sounds more fun.
Man: And the volunteers go on all the trips too.
Jim: Oh fantastic!
Man: Now, if you could just fill in this form for me …
Jim: OK.

2
1 F 2 F 3 T 4 F 5 F

3
2 I'd rather
3 How about
4 I don't mind
5 a better idea
6 sounds more interesting

UNIT 5

1
1 environmental
2 four
3 Anyone
4 end

Ben: So, we've got to think of ideas for the science fair project. Which project area shall we choose?

Katie: What about a new development in technology?

Ben: OK, good idea. Why don't we think of a new app? It's quite easy to design apps.

Katie: That's a brilliant idea! Maybe we could design an app about places where you can eat that are cool for young people.

Ben: Yeah, or places to visit.

Katie: I know! Why don't we design an app for young people in this area? It could have general information about places to eat, places to go, places to do sports, places for shopping …

Ben: Yeah! And people will be able to add their comments about the places. Then you can read everyone's opinions. And people could add their suggestions.

Katie: Great. What shall we do first? Shall we make a list of places?

Ben: Yeah, OK. Then we'll find out about app design.

Katie: OK.

2
1 app
2 brilliant
3 eat
4 information
5 list

3
2 How about
3 Yes, you're right
4 That's a good idea
5 Why don't we
6 Maybe we could

UNIT 6

1 1 T 2 T 3 F 4 F 5 T

Charlie: Hi Grandma. Can I ask you a favour?

Grandma: Of course, Charlie. What is it?

Charlie: Well, I want to buy a present for Emma's birthday. It's next week.

Grandma: Yes?

Charlie: There's a bag she really wants, but I haven't got enough money. Could I borrow some money?

Grandma: How much do you need?

Charlie: Well, it's 15 pounds and I've only got 11 pounds … so can I borrow four pounds?

Grandma: I've got a better idea. How about earning some money instead?

Charlie: How?

Grandma: I'll pay you four pounds if you take the dogs for a walk every day this week.

Charlie: Fantastic! It's a deal, Gran.

Grandma: Would you mind helping me to clean the windows now?

Charlie: Of course not! I'll move the table and then we can start.

2
1 Emma's birthday is next week.
2 Emma wants a bag for her birthday.
3 Charlie wants to borrow £4.
4 Charlie agrees to take the dogs for a walk every day this week.

3
2 Would you mind
3 How much does it cost
4 Why don't you
5 I'll pay you
6 OK, it's a deal

UNIT 7

1
1 At Pelaw.
2 It's £3.10.
3 No, you can't. You have to change at Pelaw.
4 Yes, you can.

Dave: Hello?

Emma: Hi Dave, it's Emma here. How are you?

Dave: Great thanks!

Emma: Listen, we're coming to Newcastle next weekend to visit my cousins.

Dave: Oh, let's meet up!

Emma: Yes, definitely. How about Friday night?

Dave: OK, why don't you come for dinner? Where are you staying?

Emma: Dinner sounds great.

We're staying out near the airport, but my parents don't want to drive into the centre.

Dave: OK, why don't your parents drive to Kingston Park? There's a big car park there, so they can leave the car there.

Emma: OK. Can you tell me how to get to your house?

Dave: Sure … you take the green line and then you change onto the yellow line.

Emma: Where do I change?

Dave: At South Gosforth. Then you go on the yellow line to Hadrian Road. It's eleven stops. I'll meet you at the metro station.

Emma: Great, thanks. So, how much is it?

Dave: It's two zones, so £2.50 for your parents but you're under 16, so it's only 80p.

Emma: OK, thanks. What time shall we meet at the metro station?

Dave: At 7.30?

Emma: OK, see you on Friday!

2 1 F 2 T 3 F 4 T 5 F

3
2 Yes, please
3 Where do I
4 How much is
5 Yes, I am
6 Here you are

UNIT 8

1 1 T 2 T 3 F 4 T

Sam: Hi Jess … Listen, there's an activity fair at the sports centre this weekend. Shall we go?

Jess: What time does it start?

Sam: It starts at 10am, but it's on all day.

Jess: I'm busy in the morning, but I could go in the afternoon.

Sam: Great! What do you want to see? There's… fencing, a taekwondo tournament and rollerblading with coaches. I think there's an archery competition too.

Jess: Um … Let's go to see the fencing and then go rollerblading. That sounds fun!

Sam: OK.

Jess: What time does it start?

Sam: It starts at one o'clock.

Jess: OK, where shall we meet?

Sam: Do you want a lift?

Jess: No, thanks. I'll be at my grandma's house in the morning, so my mum will probably bring me.

Sam: OK, I'll see you outside the sports centre at quarter to one. I'll get the tickets. They're only two pounds each.

Jess: Great. See you then!

Sam: See you then! Bye!

2 1 ten 2 morning 3 fencing 4 mum 5 two

3 2 Let's go to watch
3 What time
4 want a lift
5 Where shall we
6 see you then

UNIT 9

1 1 Get Fit 2 My meditation 3 Good taste 4 Help!

(45) Audioscript, exercise 2

Lisa: Hi Dave. How are you?

Dave: I'm not very well.

Lisa: Oh dear, what's the matter?

Dave: I've got a bee sting, and …

Lisa: Really? What happened?

Dave: I was running in the park and a bee stung me!

Lisa: Do you feel OK?

Dave: Well, it's a bit painful, but that's not the problem.

Lisa: So what's the problem?

Dave: Well, when I got the sting, I fell over. Now I've got backache too!

Lisa: Oh no! Poor you! Why don't you lie down?

Dave: I am! I'm lying on my bed at the moment.

Lisa: Well, I hope you feel better soon. I'll call you tomorrow.

Dave: OK, thanks. Bye.

Lisa: Bye.

2 1 park 3 backache
2 a bit 4 lie down

3 2 screen 5 painkiller
3 feel 6 better
4 painful

WRITING REFERENCE

UNIT 1

1 1 Paragraphs 2 and 3
2 Paragraph 1
3 Paragraphs 2 and 3
4 Paragraph 1
5 Paragraph 1

2 1 I love music so I buy a lot of songs online.
2 I like skateboarding because it's fun.
3 I'm into swimming because it's a good way to exercise.
4 I like finding information so I often surf the internet.
5 I don't chat online because it's boring.
6 I enjoy reading books so I sometimes go to the library.

3 1 because 5 because
2 because 6 so
3 so 7 because
4 so

UNIT 2

1 1 It had over 5,000 sea creatures.
2 They were about sea life.
3 You could see a variety of fish and other sea creatures, you could watch shows and see the keepers giving food to the sharks.
4 He liked the Ocean Tunnel most.
5 There were a lot of people so it was hard to see sometimes.

2 1 You could buy presents too.
2 There were also a lot of people.
3 I also liked the sea horses.
4 I enjoyed it too.
5 You could also touch the crabs.

3 1 People also go up at night.
2 You could see the River Thames too.
3 We also had to wait a long time.

UNIT 3

1 1 c 6 h
2 e 7 b
3 a 8 g
4 i 9 d
5 f 10 j

2 1 b 2 c 3 a

3 1 One day 4 By then
2 soon 5 in the end
3 Then

UNIT 4

1 1 In the north. (Paragraph 3)
2 It's -6–3°C. (Paragraph 2)
3 Almost 40 million. (Paragraph 1)
4 The beach town of Gdynia. (Paragraph 4)

2 1 Paragraph 4 (places)
2 Paragraph 1 (introduction)
3 Paragraph 2 (climate)
4 Paragraph 3 (landscape)

3 1 Correct
2 There is a short sandy beach near the town.
3 You can explore the big ancient wood buildings.
4 Correct
5 The restaurant has delicious Indian food.
6 Correct

UNIT 5

1 Arguments in favour of the glasses: you can easily do many things without having to look at a separate screen. The glasses are light and comfortable.

Arguments against the glasses: The glasses will be very expensive and many people won't be able to pay for them.

2 The writer thinks that people will wear computer glasses in the future but that they won't wear them all the time, just for short periods of time.

3 1 a 2 b 3 a 4 b

UNIT 6

1 1 She bought her an MP3 player.
2 She's going to upload her favourite songs.
3 They're having a party on Saturday.
4 They're going to decorate the community centre.
5 The party will start at 7pm.
6 They're going to eat pizza and dance / a DJ is going to come.

2 1 She　　4 We
2 them　　5 they
3 me　　6 him

3 1 It　　5 they
2 we　　6 them / it
3 I　　7 He
4 They

UNIT 7

1 1 No, he hasn't.
2 He went to the old town.
3 Yes, he's already been there.
4 He's going to go to the Franz Kafka Museum.
5 No, he hasn't.
6 The Astronomical Clock.

2 1 The flight was a bit boring.
2 The people have been really friendly.
3 The weather has been a bit colder today.

4 The square was really busy yesterday. / Yesterday the square was really busy.
5 I was a bit frightened at the top of the tower. / At the top of the tower I was a bit frightened.

3 1 It was really hot yesterday.
2 It was a bit cold yesterday.
3 The restaurant was really expensive.
4 The museum was a bit small.
5 The train was really late.

UNIT 8

1 1 No, he hasn't.
2 He didn't do very well.
3 Because he couldn't hit the ball over the net.
4 He thinks he would really like it.
5 He's going to practise.

2 1 annoyed
2 bored
3 disappointed
4 happy
5 embarrassed
6 surprised

3 1 See you tomorrow! (E)
2 What are you up to? (B)
3 Hope you're enjoying your trip! (E)
4 How is it going? (B)
5 Hope you're having a good time! (E)

UNIT 9

1 1 He wants to go to a concert with his friends.
2 Because he'll have to come back on the train late at night.
3 Yes, they did.
4 Jake's dad drove them home.
5 He thinks Ed and his friends should talk to their parents.

2 1 asked
2 didn't think
3 hasn't seen
4 will go / 'll go
5 have lived
6 don't remember

3 1 'm writing / am writing
2 has invited
3 are going
4 won't let
5 visited
6 do

EXTERNAL EXAM TRAINER

EXAM 1

2 1 a 2 b

3 1 b 2 c 3 a

4 1 c 2 b 3 b

EXAM 2

1 1 c 2 a 3 b

2 a 1 c 2 b 3

3 1 c 2 b 3 c

4 1 c 2 a 3 b 4 c

EXAM 3

1 2 a number
3 a name of a sport
4 a day of the week

2 1 a number
2 a name of a street
3 a number
4 a number
5 a topic

3 1 b 2 a 3 c 4 d 5 e

4 1 14 years old.
2 11 Green Road, Manchester M20 6PJ
3 07654321
4 one week
5 renewable energy

5 1 Jackie
2 fifteen years old
3 do the gardening
4 take dogs for walks
5 £7 an hour
6 08536 884535

EXAM 4

1 Example task: The best option for Jorge is option b.

2 The best option is B.
Option C is not a good option because although you can do a water sport there are no restaurants or places to go out.
Option A is not a good option because she likes water activities and this is a place without water activities.

3 The best option for Sunil is C.

4 Joanne: B   Steve: C

EXAM 5

1 The writer should include:
a description of the party, a description of clothes and information about other activities on Saturday and Sunday (The writer doesn't have to include information about where the party was.

2 In the reply Ben doesn't say what clothes he wore to the party.

3 Possible answers
Yes, it is a good reply because he gives a lot of information, uses adjectives and informal language. / He doesn't answer all of Gloria's questions.

4 Students' own answers